THE CAMBRIDGE (
TO THE POSTCOLO

C000129584

The Cambridge Companion to the Postco
account of the postcolonial novel, fron
Chimamanda Ngozi Adichie, and others. Reflecting the development of postcolonial literary studies into a significant and intellectually vibrant field, this *Companion* explores genres and theoretical movements such as magical realism, crime fiction, ecocriticism, and gender and sexuality. Written by a host of leading scholars in the field, this book offers insight into the representative movements, cultural settings, and critical reception that define the postcolonial novel. Covering subjects from disability and diaspora to the sublime and the city, this *Companion* reveals the myriad traditions that have shaped the postcolonial literary landscape, and will serve as a valuable resource to students and established scholars alike.

Ato Quayson is Professor of English and Director of the Centre for Diaspora and Transnational Studies at the University of Toronto. He is Fellow of both the Ghana Academy of Arts and Sciences and of the Royal Society of Canada. His books include *Postcolonialism: Theory, Practice or Process*; *Calibrations: Reading for the Social*; and *Aesthetic Nervousness: Disability and the Crisis of Representation*.

THE CAMBRIDGE
COMPANION TO
THE POSTCOLONIAL NOVEL

ATO QUAYSON
University of Toronto

CAMBRIDGE
UNIVERSITY PRESS

CAMBRIDGE
UNIVERSITY PRESS

32 Avenue of the Americas, New York, NY 10013-2473, USA

Cambridge University Press is part of the University of Cambridge.

It furthers the University's mission by disseminating knowledge in the pursuit of
education, learning, and research at the highest international levels of excellence.

www.cambridge.org
Information on this title: www.cambridge.org/9781107588059

© Cambridge University Press 2016

First published 2016

A catalog record for this publication is available from the British Library.

Library of Congress Cataloging-in-Publication Data
The Cambridge companion to the postcolonial novel / [edited by] Ato Quayson, University of
Toronto.
pages   cm. – (Cambridge companions to literature)
Includes bibliographical references and index.
ISBN 978-1-107-13281-8 (Hardback)
1. Postcolonialism in literature.   2. Fiction–20th century–History and criticism.   3. Fiction–
21st century–History and criticism.   I. Quayson, Ato, editor.
PN56.P555C36 2016
809′.93358–dc23   2015033499

ISBN 978-1-107-13281-8 Hardback
ISBN 978-1-107-58805-9 Paperback

CONTENTS

CONTENTS

CONTRIBUTORS

ATO QUAYSON is Professor of English and inaugural Director of the Centre for Diaspora Studies at the University of Toronto. He is the author of *Strategic Transformations in Nigerian Writing* (1997), *Postcolonialism: Theory, Practice, or Process?* (2000), *Calibrations: Reading for the Social* (2003), *Aesthetic Nervousness: Disability and the Crisis of Representation* (2007), and *Oxford Street: City Life and the Itineraries of Transnationalism* (2014); co-editor of *African Literature: An Anthology of Criticism and Theory* (with Tejumola Olaniyan; 2007) and *Companion to Diaspora and Transnationalism* (with Girish Daswani; 2013); and also editor of the two-volume *Cambridge History of Postcolonial Literature* (2012).

TIM WATSON is Associate Professor in the Department of English at the University of Miami. He is the author of *Caribbean Culture and British Fiction, 1780–1870* (2008) and editor, with Candace Ward, of a new edition of the 1827 novel, *Hamel, the Obea Man* by Cynric R. Williams (2010).

DEBJANI GANGULY is Associate Professor at the Australian National University, where she was Director of the Humanities Research Centre from 2007 to 1015. She has published *Caste and Dalit Lifeworlds: Postcolonial Perspectives* (2008), *Rethinking Gandhi and Nonviolent Relationality: Global Perspectives* (ed. with John Docker; 2007), *Edward Said: The Legacy of a Public Intellectual* (ed. with Ned Curthoys; 2007), and *This Thing Called the World: The Novel in Our Time* (2015).

ZOE NORRIDGE is Lecturer in English and Comparative Literature at King's College, London and author of *Perceiving Pain in African Literature* (2012).

ANTHONY CARRIGAN is Lecturer in Postcolonial Literatures and Cultures at the University of Leeds. He is the author of *Postcolonial Tourism: Literature, Culture, and Environment* (2011) and co-editor with Elizabeth DeLoughrey and Jill Didur, *Global Ecologies and the Environmental Humanities: Postcolonial Approaches* (2015).

CLARE BARKER is Lecturer in English Literature at the University of Leeds and is the author of *Postcolonial Fiction and Disability* (2012).

EVAN MWANGI is Associate Professor in English at Northwestern University, he is the author of *Africa Writes Back to Self: Metafiction, Gender, Sexuality* (2009) and co-editor, with Simon Gikandi, of *The Columbia Guide to East African Literature in English since 1945*.

YOON SUN LEE is Mildred Lane Kemper Professor of English at Wellesley College. Her works include *Nationalism and Irony* (2004) and *Modern Minority: Asian American Literature and Everyday Life* (2012).

PHILIP DICKINSON obtained his PhD from the University of Toronto in 2014 and has published in *Mosaic* and *Postcolonial Text*. He is an SSHRC Post-Doctoral Research Fellow at Columbia University.

STEPHEN KNIGHT has had distinguished stints at the University of Sydney, De Montfort University, and the University of Wales, Cardiff. He is Fellow of the Australian Academy of the Humanities and is currently at the University of Melbourne. His publications include *Form and Ideology in Crime Fiction* (1980), *Arthurian Literature and Society* (1983), *Geoffrey Chaucer* (1987), *Robin Hood: A Complete Study* (1994), *Continent of Mystery: A Thematic History of Australian Crime Fiction* (1997), *Merlin: Knowledge and Power* (2009), and *The Mysteries of the Cities* (2012).

RASHMI VARMA is Associate Professor in English at the University of Warwick and the author of *The Postcolonial City and its Subject: London, Nairobi, Bombay* (2011; paperback 2014).

ROBERT ZACHARIAS is Banting Postdoctoral Research Fellow at the University of Waterloo. He is the author of *Rewriting the Break Event: Mennonites and Migration in Canadian Literature* (2013) and is the co-editor, with Smaro Kamboureli, of *Shifting the Ground of Canadian Literary Studies* (2012).

ACKNOWLEDGMENTS

I want to thank my contributors for their patience in bringing this volume to fruition and the University of Toronto for financial support in completing the manuscript. Nia Barbarossa was a very helpful work-study assistant as was Kamran Bozorgmehr, who stepped in to rescue a file without which the entire project might well have collapsed into complete disorder.

Ray Ryan remains, as always, a demanding editor. His persistence in asking the right questions at the wrong times helped to bring work on the volume to a timely conclusion.

CHRONOLOGY OF POLITICAL AND LITERARY EVENTS

This chronology starts from 1854, the year of the establishment of the reconstituted Colonial Office. The primary inspiration for the list of political and literary events laid out here is the one provided in Neil Lazarus's *Cambridge Companion to Postcolonial Literary Studies*. As he notes, highlighting world historical events from the perspective of the formerly colonized world means giving special place to acts of resistance and opposition to colonial and imperial rule, which may not have necessarily had an impact beyond the places from which they were launched yet were very meaningful for the local actors. It also means providing a slightly different inflection to certain significant dates in world history. The year 1945 is a good example of this. This date immediately invokes the end of World War II and it is also a date during which many significant changes were taking place in the formerly colonized world, not all of which had a bearing on war at all. And so, in the same year, we find the following events:

- In Algeria, French repression of nationalists, triggering major uprising; thousands killed.
- Revolution in Vietnam brings Ho Chi Minh's Viet Minh to power; French forces attempt to recapture colonial power; war ensues (1945–1954).
- Philippines liberated from Japanese occupation.
- Syria and Lebanon gain independence.
- Fifth Pan-African Congress held in Manchester, England; proclaims "right of all colonial peoples to control their own destiny."

The shifts in relations between colonizer and colonized, the alteration of the global political economy, and the rise of different social agents all over the world are best discerned when the chronology is read in comparative terms. At the same time, the correlation of political to literary events is not always self-evident, especially because there is often a lengthy time lag between the occurrence of a major historical event and its representation in literature. Some events have the effect of instituting a sense of immediacy that gets translated into the literary-aesthetic domain in a short time. That, we might argue, has been the effect of September 11, 2001, which just over a decade after the event has spawned an entire cultural industry of representations. For an event such as the Biafra secessionist bid in Nigeria (1967–1971), the almost immediate profusion of literary representations gave way to a lengthy period of quiet until the publication of Chimamanda Ngozi Adichie's *Half of a Yellow Sun* (2007), which revisits the events from the perspective of someone who grew up well after those events had occurred and yet had her consciousness shaped by the stories that persistently circulated about them. Such a revisiting also represents a reinterpretation of the historical event from a different generational perspective, thus inviting us to return to the event and see its potential world-historical significance in a completely new light. We come to note, for example, the population dispersal that came out of that war and that now creates the diasporic imaginary of an entirely new brand of Igbo and Nigerians. This is but one example of the dialectical relationship between what appears at inception to be a purely local event and its more world-historical dimensions that come to the foreground only with the passage of time.

Despite the fact that the *Companion* has as its central interest the postcolonial novel in English, it would have been impossible to exclusively list only events and literary texts that occurred or were published within the Anglophone-speaking world. The Cuban Revolution, the Algerian liberation struggle, and the Vietnam War have had such an impact on the imagination of postcolonials everywhere as to merit inclusion. Similarly, Ralph Elison's *Invisible Man* and Toni Morrison's Nobel Prize are significant literary landmarks for all of the postcolonial world. A justification can also be made for critical texts considered to be have had a significant impact on the field, such as Vladimir Lenin's *Imperialism: The Highest Stage of Capitalism*, Eric Williams' *Capitalism and Slavery*, and Immanuel Wallerstein's *The Modern World System* (Vols. 1 and 2).

The literary chronology is built on three broad principles of inclusion. The first has been to list texts from as wide a variety of postcolonial literary traditions as possible. This has also meant establishing a balance between texts from the former settler colonies of Canada and Australia and those from the colored majority countries such as Nigeria, India, and South Africa. Even though the inclusion of Ireland under the rubric of postcolonialism is still considered somewhat controversial by some, there has been enough comparative work relating Ireland to the rest of the postcolonial world to justify the inclusion here of at least W.B. Yeats, James Joyce, and Samuel Beckett, all three of whom have wielded a significant influence on postcolonial writing across the world.

When Nobel Prize winners are listed more than once, their dates of birth and death (where applicable) have been entered against their names in the year in which they won the prize. Other writers are listed according to their countries of origin, except in cases where they are considered canonical in the field do not have their dates of birth and death listed. The dates of the founding of significant literary journals in the field from various regions have been provided, along with those for the important literary prizes.

Political Events	*Literary Events*
1854 -Reconstituted Colonial Office established	
1855 -Britain annexes Oudh, India, and establishes Natal as Crown Colony	
1857 -Indian mutiny over British rule; siege of Delhi begins; Delhi captured; British enter Cawnpore	
1861 -American Civil War (until 1865)	
1867 -British North America Act establishes Dominion of Canada	
1873 -Republic proclaimed in Spain -Abolition of slave market and exports in Zanzibar	
1873 -Britain annexes Fiji islands	1852 -Harriet Beecher Stowe, *Uncle Tom's Cabin*
1875 -Britain buys 176,602 Suez Canal shares from Khedive of Egypt	
1879 -British Zulu War: Zulus massacre British soldiers in Isandhlwana, British capture Cetewayo -French Panama Canal Company organized under Ferdinand de Lesseps	
1880 -France annexes Tahiti -Transvaal declares itself independent of Britain; Boers led by Kruger declare a republic	
1883 -British decide to evacuate Sudan	
1884 -Berlin Conference of 14 European nations on African affairs	

1885 -The Congo becomes a personal
possession of King Leopold II of
Belgium
-Germany annexes Tanganyika and
Zanzibar
-Great Britain establishes protector-
ate over North Bechuanaland, the
Niger river region, and south New
Guinea; occupies Port Hamilton,
Korea

1886 -First Indian National Congress
meets

1887 -First Colonial Conference opens in
London

1888 -Suez Canal convention

1890 -Britain exchanges Helgoland with
Germany for Zanzibar and Pemba

1893 -Natal granted self-governance
-Swaziland annexed by Transvaal
-France acquires protectorate over
Laos

1894 -Uganda becomes a British
protectorate

1895 -British South Africa Company territory south of Zambezi becomes
Rhodesia
-Cuba fights Spain for its
independence

1896 -France annexes Madagascar

1898 -Russia obtains lease of Port Arthur,
China; Britain, the lease of Kowloon
-United States declares war on Spain
over Cuba; Americans destroy
Spanish fleet at Manila; Treaty of
Paris between United States and
Spain; Spain cedes Cuba, Puerto
Rico, Guam, and the Philippines for
$20 million

1882 -James Joyce, Irish
novelist, born (died
1941)

1883 -Oliver Schreiner
(South Africa), *The
Story of an African
Farm*

1899 -Philippines demand independence
from United States
1900 -Commonwealth of Australia
created
1901 -Edmund Barton inaugurated as first
Prime Minister of Commonwealth
of Australia
-The Boers begin organized guerilla
warfare
-Cuba Convention makes country a
U.S. protectorate
1902 -Colonial Conference meets in
London
-First meeting of Committee of
Imperial Defense
1903 -British complete conquest of
Northern Nigeria
-King Edward VII visits Paris;
French President Loubet visits
London, the "Entente Cordiale"
established

1894 -Rudyard Kipling,
The Jungle Book

1904 -Hereros and Hottentots revolt in
German South-West Africa until
1908

1897 -Joseph Conrad,
*The Nigger of the
Narcissus*

1905 -Sinn Fein Party founded
-Alberta and Saskatchewan become
provinces of Canada
1906 -South Africa Bambatha (Zulu
uprising), begins as protest against
poll tax
-Algeciras Conference gives France
and Spain control of Morocco
-Self-government granted to the
Transvaal and Orange River
colonies
-U.S. troops occupy Cuba (until
1909) after reconciliation following
Liberal revolt fails
1907 -New Zealand becomes a dominion
within the British Empire

1899 -Joseph Conrad,
Heart of Darkness

Britain grants dominion status to its self-governing (white) colonies

-Rudyard Kipling, *The White Man's Burden*

1908 -Leopold II transfers the Congo (his private possession since 1885) to Belgium
-Union of South Africa established
-Dutch establish rule in Bali

1900 -Joseph Conrad, *Lord Jim*
-Solomon T. Plaatje (South Africa), *Boer War Diary*
-José Enrique Rodó (Uruguay), *Ariel*

1909 -Anglo–German discussions on control of Baghdad Railroad
-India: Morely–Minto reforms
-U.S. troops occupy Nicaragua (until 1925)

1901 -Rudyard Kipling, *Kim*
-Nobel Prize for Literature established

1902 -J.A. Hobson, *Imperialism*

1903 -E.D. Morel, *The Congo Slave State*

1910 -Egyptian Premier Boutros Ghali assassinated
-Union of South Africa becomes a dominion within the British Empire with Louis Botha as premier
-W.E.B. Du Bois founds National Association for the Advancement of Colored People (NAACP) in United States
-Start of the Mexican revolution
-Korea: annexation by Japan (colonial rule until 1945)

1911 -China: Revolution ends imperial regime, establishes provisional republic

1904 -Joseph Conrad, *Nostromo*

1907 -Rudyard Kipling, Nobel Prize for Literature (20 Dec. 1865–18 Jan. 1936),

1913 -Mahatma Gandhi, leader of Indian Passive Resistance Movement, arrested
-South Africa: Native Land Act

1914 -Northern and Southern Nigeria united

1908 -Rabindranath Tagore (India),

-General Zamon becomes President of Haiti
-Start of World War I
-Gandhi returns to India and supports government

Home and the World
1909 -Mohandas K. Gandhi (India), *Hind Swaraj*

1915 -Ceylon: Sinhala anti-Muslim riot; colonial government declares martial law
-U.S. troops occupy Haiti

1916 -T.E. Lawrence ("Lawrence of Arabia") appointed British political and liaison officer to Emir Faisal's army

1917 -United States purchases Dutch West Indies
-Bolshevik Revolution first erupts in St. Petersburg
-Balfour Declaration promises a "national home" for Jews in Palestine and protection of civil and religious rights of non-Jews in the territory

1918 -British government abandons Home Rule for Ireland
-Armistice treaty signed, brings First World War to an end Declaration of the Irish Republic

1911 -Iliya Abu Madi (Lebanon), *The Memorial of the Past*
-J.E. Casely-Hayford (Gold Coast), *Ethiopia Unbound*
-Muhammad Iqbal (India), *Complaint*

1919 -Peace Conference opens in Versailles
-German colonies in Africa to Britain, France, and Belgium as Mandates
-India: Montagu–Chelmsford reforms permitting limited self-government; Rowlatt Act gives police wide powers to investigate and

1912 -Léon Damas born (died 1978)
1913 -Rabindranath Tagore (India), Nobel Prize for Literature (7 May 1861–7 Aug. 1941)
1914 -E.R. Burroughs: *Tarzan of the Apes*

CHRONOLOGY OF POLITICAL AND LITERARY EVENTS

prosecute opposition; Gandhi calls
for all-India mass protest move-
ment; massacre of civilians at Jal-
lianwallah Bagh in Amritsar
-President Wilson presides over first
League of Nations meeting in Paris
-War between British, Indian, and
Afghan forces
-Edward Carson demands repeal of
Home Rule in Ireland
-U.S. House of Representatives
moves to curtail immigration
-Third British–Afghan War
-First Palestinian National Congress
rejects Balfour Declaration, calls for
Arab independence
1920 -In Paris, League of Nations comes
into being
-Government of Ireland Act passed
by British Parliament Northern and
Southern Ireland each to have own
Parliament
-India: Gandhi launches Non-
Cooperation Movement
-Indonesia: Communist Party (PKI)
formed
1921 -First Indian Parliament meets
-Winston Churchill becomes Colo-
nial Secretary
-Britain and Ireland sign peace treaty
-Lord Reading appointed Viceroy of
India, succeeding Lord Chelmsford
-Ireland: outbreak of civil war (until
1921)
1922 -Gandhi sentenced to six years
imprisonment for civil disobedience
-League of Nations approves man-
dates for Egypt and Palestine
-Declaration of Irish Free State
-Arab Congress at Nablus rejects
British mandate for Palestine

-Gabriela Mistral
(Chile), *Sonnets of
Death*
1915 -Nikolai Bukharin,
*Imperialism and
World Economy*
-Mariano Azuela
(Mexico), *The
Underdogs*
1916 -Rabindranath
Tagore (India),
Nationalism
-Yi Kwang-su
(Korea),
Heartlessness
1917 -Vladimir Lenin,
*Imperialism: The
Highest Stage of
Capitalism*
1918 -U.S. Post Office
burns installments
of James Joyce's
Ulysses published
in *Little Review*
1919 -Chu Yo-han
(Korea), *Fireworks*
1920 -Albert Memmi
born (15 Dec.)

-Mustafa Kemal proclaims Turkey a
republic
-Irish Free State officially proclaimed
1924 -India: communalist violence
between Hindus and Muslims;
Gandhi begins hunger strike as a
"penance and a prayer"
1925 -Cyprus becomes a British Crown
Colony
-British Dominions office established
1927 -International Conference Against
Imperialism and Colonial Oppression, Brussels
1928 -Italy signs 20-year treaty of friendship with Ethiopia

1921 -Frederick Lugard,
*The Dual Mandate
in British Tropical
Africa*

1929 -Inter-Americas Treaty of Arbitra-
tion signed in Washington
-Nigeria: Aba women's riots
-Geneva Convention signed, regu-
lating treatment of prisoners of war

1922 -Herman Hesse,
Siddartha
-Frederick Lugard,
*The Dual Mandte
in British Tropical
Africa*
-M.N. Roy (India),
India in Transition
-René Maran (Mar-
tinique), *Batouala*

1930 -India: Gandhi launches Civil Disobedience Movement
-Vietnam: peasant uprising, coincides with formation of Communist
Party

1923 -William Butler
Yeats (Ireland),
Nobel Prize for Lit-
erature (13 June
1865–28 Jan. 1939)
-Albert Sarraut, *The
Economic Devel-
opment of the
French Colonies*

1931 -British Commonwealth of Nations
created

1924 -EM Forester, *A
Passage to India*
-Pablo Neruda
(Chile), *20 Love*

Poems and a Song of Despair

1932 -Indian Congress declared illegal;
      Gandhi arrested

1933 -U.S. congress votes independence
      for Philippines

1934 -Gandhi suspends civil disobedience
      campaign in India

1935 -Mussolini's forces invade and
      occupy Ethiopia
      -Passage of Government of India Act

1936 -Eruption of Spanish Civil War
      -Palestine: Arab revolt (1939), pro-
      testing British rule and disposses-
      sions cause by Zionist settlement;

1925 -Thomas Mofolo
      (Lesotho), *Chaka*

1926 -Hô Chí Minh
      (Vietnam), *Colon-
      ization of Trial*
      -Ricardo Güiraldes
      (Argentina), *Don
      Segundo Sombra*
      -Martin Luis Guz-
      mán (Mexico), *The
      Eagle and the
      Serpent*
      -Thomas Mofolo
      (South Africa),
      Chaka

1927 -André Gide,
      *Voyage to the
      Congo*
      -Taha Husain
      (Egypt), *The Days*
      (Vol. 2, 1939)
      -José Vasconcelos,
      Calderon (Mexico),
      The Cosmic Race

1928 -Édouard Glissant
      born
      -Mario de Andrade
      (Brazil), *Macunaima*
      -José Carlos Mariá-
      tegui, *Seven Essays
      towards an Inter-
      pretation of Peru-
      vian Reality*

1929 -Taha Hussein, *The
      Days* (3 vols.,
      1929–1967)

xix

crushed by British, with more than
1,000 Palestinian deaths

1937 -Jamaica: riots against British rule
(until 1938)
-Trinidad: nationalist riots

1930 -Chinua Achebe
born (died 2013)
-Mao Tse-tung
(China), "A Single
Spark Can Start a
Prairie Fire"
-Launch of Negri-
tude movement in
Paris by Franco-
phone intellectuals
including Léopold
Sédar Senghor,
Aimé Césaire, and
Léon Damas
-Nicolás Guillén
(Cuba), *Son
Montifs*
-Solomon T. Plaatje
(South Africa),
Mhudi

1938 -U.S. Supreme Court rules the University of Missouri Law School
must admit black students because
of lack of other facilities in the area
-President Roosevelt recalls American ambassador to Germany; Germany recalls ambassador to the
United States

1932 -Evelyn Waugh,
Black Mischief
-Gregorio López y
Fuentes (Mexico),
The Land
-Ahmad Shawqi
(Egypt), *Diwan*

1939 -Start of World War II

1933 -Mulk Raj Anand
(India),
Untouchable
-Tewfiq al-Hakim
(Egypt), *People of
the Cave*
-Claude McKay
(Jamaica), *Banana
Bottom*
-Mao Tun (China),
Midnight

-Gilberto Freyre,
*The Master and the
Slaves*

1941 -Ethiopia: Allies capture Addis
Ababa, allowing Haile Selassie to
return after a five-year absence

1942 -India: Gandhi launches Quit India
Movement
-Japanese forces capture Singapore,
Java, Burma, and the Philippines
and attack Solomon Islands and
Papua New Guinea

1934 -George Orwell,
Burmese Days
-Jorge Icaza (Ecua-
dor), *Huasipungo*
-Alfred Mendes
(Trinidad), *Pitch
Lake*

1935 -Jorge Luis Borges
(Argentina), *A Uni-
versal History of
Infamy*
-Mulk Raj Anand
(India),
Untouchable

1943 -India: armed struggle under leadership of Subhas Chandra Bose
launched against British forces in
the northeast; devastating famine in
Bengal (until 1944) kills estimated 4
million people

1936 -Mao Tse-tung,
*Problems of Strat-
egy in China's
Revolutionary War*
-Jayaprakash Nara-
yan (India), *Why
Socialism*
-Jawarharlal Nehru,
An Autobiography
-Manik Bandopad-
hyay (India), *The
History of Puppets*
-C.L.R. James
(Trinidad), *Minty
Alley*
-Lao She (China),
Camel Hsiang-tzu
-Premchand (India),
The Gift of a Cow

1944 -Vietnam: major famine kills 2 million people

-United States: Bretton Woods con-
ference; foundation of International
Monetary Fund (IMF) and World
Bank

1945 -End of World War II
-United States drops nuclear bombs
on Hiroshima and Nagasaki in
Japan, leading to surrender of
Japan
-Algeria: French repression of
nationalists, triggering major upris-
ing; thousands killed
-Revolution in Vietnam brings Ho
Chi Minh's Viet Minh to power;
French forces attempt to recapture
colonial power; war ensues (until
1954)
-Philippines liberated from Japanese
occupation
-Syria, Lebanon gain independence
-Fifth Pan-African Congress held in
Manchester, England, proclaims
"right of all colonial peoples to
control their own destiny"

1937 -Karen Blixen (Den-
mark), *Out of Africa*
-Hafiz Ibrahim
(Egypt), *Diwan*
-R.K. Narayan
(India), *The Bach-
elor of Arts*
-Siburapha (Thai-
land), *Behind the
Painting*

1938 -C.L.R. James, *The
Black Jacobins*
-Jomo Kenyatta
(Kenya), *Facing
Mount Kenya*
-D.O. Fagunwa
(Nigeria), *The
Forest of a Thou-
sand Daemons*
-Raja Rao (India)
Kanthapura

1939 -James Joyce, *Finni-
gan's Wake*
-Margaret Atwood
born
-Joyce Cary, *Mr
Johnson*
-Aimé Césaire (Mar-
tinique), "Note-
book of a Return to
the Native Land"

1940 -Australian journal
Meanjin established
-Fernando Ortiz
(Cuba), *Cuban
Counterpoint:
Tobacco and Sugar*

1946 -United Nations convenes for the
first time
-Thailand: military overthrows
nationalist leader Pridi
Phanomyong
-Philippines gains independence

1947 -India is proclaimed independent
and partitioned into India and
Pakistan; hundreds of thousands die
in intercommunal violence; estimated 8.5 million refugees cross
border in both directions
-Palestine: UN announces plans for
partition, granting bulk of land to
Jewish population
-Burma: U Aung San, hero of the
independence movement is
assassinated

1948 -Gandhi assassinated
-State of Israel comes into existence
-Indo-Pakistan war over disputed
Kashmir
-British Citizenship Act grants Brit-
ish passports to all Commonwealth
citizens
-Burma, Sri Lanka (Ceylon) gain
independence
-South Africa: Afrikaner Nationalist
Party comes to power, implements
policy of *apartheid*
-UN adopts Declaration of Human
Rights

1941 -H.I.E Dhlomo
(South Africa),
*Valley of a Thou-
sand Hills*
-Edgar Mittelholzer
(Guyana), *Corten-
tyne Thunder*
-Ibrahim Tuqan
(Palestine), *Diwan*

1942 -Albert Camus, *The
Outside*

1943 -Ishaq Musa al-
Husaini (Palestine),
*A Chicken's
Memoirs*

1944 -José Maria Argue-
das (Peru), *Every-
one's Blood*
-Ismat Chughtai
(India), *The Quilt
and Other Stories*
-Jacques Roumain
(Haiti), *Masters of
the Dew*
-Eric Williams, *Cap-
italism and Slavery*

1945 -Gabriela Mistral
(Chile), Nobel Prize
for Literature (7
April 1889–10 Jan.
1957)
-Gopinath Mohanty
(India), *Paraja*

1949 -India adopts constitution as federal
republic
-Holland transfers sovereignty to
Indonesia; France to Vietnam
-The Commonwealth of Nations is
formerly constituted comprising
mostly former territories of the
British Empire.

1950 -Outbreak of U.S.–Korea war (until   1946 -Jawaharlal Nehru
1953); casualties top 1 million   (India), *The Dis-*
-China invades Tibet, assumes   *covery of India*
control   -Peter Abrahams
-Indonesia gains independence   (South Africa),
under Sukarno   *Mine Boy*
-Jordan annexes West Bank,
absorbing 600,000 Palestinians

1951 -Libya gains independence   1947 -Salman Rushdie
-Egypt launches guerilla war against   born
British forces in the Suez Canal   -Jawaharlal Nehru
Zone   delivers "Tryst with
-Iran nationalizes its oil industry   Destiny" speech
                                         -Babani Bhatta-
                                         charya (India), *So
                                         Many Hungers!*
                                         -Birago Diop (Sene-
                                         gal), *Tales of
                                         Amadou Koumba*
                                         -Suryakant Tripathi
                                         "Nirala" (India),
                                         *The Earthly
                                         Knowledge*
                                         -Badr Shakir al-
                                         Sayyab (Iraq),
                                         Withered Fingers

1952 -Honolulu Conference of three-   1948 -Graham Greene,
power Pacific Council (Australia, the   *The Heart of the
United States, and New Zealand)   Matter*
-South Africa: African National   -Alan Paton (South
Congress launches Defiance   Africa), *Cry, the
Campaign   Beloved Country*

-Kenya: State of Emergency declared as anticolonial insurrection ("Mau Mau") intensifies
-Vietnam: France launches massive offensive against Viet Minh forces

-G. V Desani (India), All About H Hatterr
-Saadat Hasan Manto (Pakistan), "Toba Tek Singh"
-Jean-Paul Sartre, "Black Orpheus"

1953 -London Conference of Commonwealth prime ministers
-Cuba: Fidel Castro leads abortive assault on Moncada Baracks in Santiago de Cuba; many of the militants are killed, others, including Castro, are captured
-British Guiana: uprising, led by People's Progressive Party, against colonialism; put down by military force; constitution suspended

1949 -Miguel Angel Asturias (Guatemala), Men of Maize
-Alejo Carpentier (Cuba), The Kingdom of This World
-Khalil Mutran (Lebanon), Diwan
-V.S. Reid (Jamaica), New Day

1950 -Pablo Neruda (Chile), Canto général
-Octavio Paz, Labyrinth of Solitude
-Doris Lessing, The Grass Is Singing
-Aimé Césaire, Discourse on Colonialism

1954 -Start of Algerian War of Independence (until 1962)
-Vietnamese army led by Ho Chi Minh defeats French colonial forces; France sues for peace; Viet Minh take Hanoi take Hanoi
-Egypt: Gamel Abdel Nasser takes power
-Algeria: war of independence begins (until 1962)

1951 -Nirad C. Chaudhuri (India), The Autobiography of an Unknown India

1955 -Bandung Conference of independent Asian and African states;

1952 -Samuel Beckett, Waiting for Godot

xxv

declaration upholds principles of
national sovereignty, human rights,
and equality among states
-South Africa: Freedom Charter
adopted at Congress of the People

-Frantz Fanon,
*Black Skin, White
Masks*
-Ralph Ellison,
Invisible Man
-Ralph de Boissière
(Trinidad), *Crown
Jewel*
-Andrée Chedid
(Egypt), *From Sleep
Unbound*
-Mochtar Lubis
(Indonesia), *A
Road with No End*
-Amos Tutuola
(Nigeria), *The
Palm-Wine
Drinkard*

1956 -Sudan proclaimed independent
democratic republic
-Nasser nationalizes Suez Canal;
Egypt invaded by Israel, with British and French support
-Fidel Castro lands in Cuba with
intent to overthrow dictator Ful-
gencio Batista
-Morocco, Tunisia gain
independence
-Yemen: anti-British strikes in Aden;
clashes between British and Yemeni
troops
-Hungary: anti-Stalinist uprising
crushed by Soviet troops
-China: Mao introduces "Hundred
Flowers" campaign ("Let a hundred flowers bloom, let a hundred
schools of thought")

1953 -Fidel Castro
(Cuba), "History
will absolve me"
-Alejo Carpentier
(Cuba), *The Lost
Steps*
-George Lamming
(Barbados), *In the
Castle of My Skin*
-Camara Laye
(Guinea), *The Afri-
can Child*
-Roger Mais
(Jamaica), *The
Hills Were All
Joyful Together*

1957 -Gold Coast gains independence,
changing its name to Ghana
-Peninsular Malaya becomes
Malaysia in 1963 with

1954 -Sahitya Akademi
Award established

incorporation of Sarawak, Sabah
and Singapore)
-Indonesia: Sukarno declares martial
law; revoked in 1963
-Algeria: Battle of Algiers

1958   -Pakistan: military coup brings
Mohammed Ayub Khan to power
-Guinea gains independence
-Cameroun: Rueben Um Nyobé,
UPC leader, killed
-All-African People's Conference
held in Accra, Ghana
-Sri Lanka: Riots erupt, as Sinhala
militants attack Tamils; hundreds
killed; state of emergency eventually
declared

1959   -Cuba: overthrow of Batista regime;
Fidel Castro assumes power
-China: devastating famine (1961)
kills as many as 40 million
-Zambia: Kenneth Kaunda
imprisoned by British colonial government; leads civil disobedience
campaign when released
-Tibet: rebellion crushed by Chinese
forces; Dalai Lama flees into exile

-Samira 'Azzam
(Palestine), *Little
Things*
-Martin Carter
(Guyana), *Poems
of Resistance*
-Driss Chraibi
(Morocco), *The
Simple Past*
-Kamala Markan-
daya (India),
Nectar in a Sieve
-Nicanor Parra
(Chile), *Poems and
Antipoems*
-Abd al-Rahman
Shasrawi (Egypt),
The Earth

1955   -Aimé Césaire
(Martinique), *Dis-
course on
Colonialism*
-Amrita Pritam
(India), *Messages*
-Juan Rulfo
(Mexico), *Pedro
Paramo*
-Saadi Youssef
(Iraq), *Songs Not
for Others*

1956   -Octavio Mannoni,
Pamela Powesland,
*Prospero and Cali-
ban: The Psych-
ology of
Colonization*
-First international
conference of black
writers and artists
(Paris)

-George Padmore (Trinidad), *Pan Africanism or Communism?*
-Carlos Bulosan (Philippines), *America is in the Heart*
-Mongo Beti (Cameroon), *The Poor Christ of Bomba*
-David Diop (Senegal), *Hammer Blows*
-Faiz Ahmed Faiz (Pakistan), *Prison Thoughts*
-Nagiub Mahfouz (Egypt), *Cairo Trilogy* (finished 1957)
-Samuel Selvon (Trinidad), *The Lonely Londoners*
-Octavio Paz (Mexico), *Sunstone*

1957 -Albert Memmi, *The Colonizer and the Colonized*
-Kwame Nkrumah (Ghana), *Ghana: Autobiography*

1958 -Chinua Achebe (Nigeria), *Things Fall Apart*
-Édouard Glissant (Martinique), *The Ripening*
-NVM Gonzalez (Phillipines), *Bread of Salt*

1960 -Belgian Congo granted full independence
-Harold Macmillan's "winds of change" speech
-South Africa: Sharpville massacre, as police open fire on unarmed gathering – 67 killed; ANC and Pan-African Congress banned
-Benin, Burkina Faso, Central African Republic, Chad, Congo, Gabon, Ivory Coast, Madagascar, Mali, Mauritania, Niger, Nigeria, Senegal, Somalia, and Togo gain independence
-Congo: attempted secession of Katanga province; martial law declared by ne President Patrice Lumumba;

military seizes power, supported by United States and Belgium; Lumumba arrested

1961 -UN General Assembly condemns apartheid
-U.S.-sponsored Bay of Pigs invasion of Cuba thwarted
-Cameroon, Sierra Leone, Tanzania attain independence
-Lumumba murdered while in custody
-Angola: armed struggle begins
-South Africa: Albert Luthuli, President of the ANC, awarded Nobel Peace Prize
-First Conference of Non-Aligned Nations, Belgrade

1962 -Algeria, Burundi, Jamaica, Rwanda, Trinidad and Tobago, Uganda gain independence
-Border war between India and China
-Cuban missile crisis: U.S. President Kennedy authorizes blockade of Cuba in bid to prevent deployment of Soviet nuclear weapons

1963 -Kenya becomes independent
-Formation of the Organization of African Unity

1964 -Zanzibar declared a republic and unites with Tanganyika to form Tanzania
-Malawi, Zambia, Malaya gain independence
-Mozambique: FRELIMO launches armed struggle
-Guyana: Cheddi Jagan's government is overthrown
-South Africa: ANC leaders Nelson Mandela and Walter Sisulu sentenced to life imprisonment for

-Ludu U. Hla (Burma), *The Caged Ones*

1959 -Qurratulain Hyder (India), *River of Fire*
-Es'kia Mphahlele (South Africa), *Down Second Avenue*

1960 -Wilson Harris (Guyana), *Palace of the Peacock*
-Ousmane Sembene (Senegal), *God's Bits of Wood*
-George Lamming, *The Pleasures of Exile*

1961 -Frantz Fanon, *The Wretched of the Earth*
-Rajat Neogy (Uganda) founds *Transition Magazine: An International Review*
-Nnamdi Azikiwe (Nigeria), *Zik: Selected Speeches*

treason – incarcerated on Robben
Island
-Martin Luther King, Jr., Nobel
Peace Prize (15 Jan. 1929–4 April
1968)

-Ernesto "Che"
Guevara (Argen-
tina/Cuba), *Guer-
rilla Warfare*
-Adonis (Syria),
*Songs of Muhyar
the Damascene*
-Cyrpian Ekwensi
(Nigeria), *Jagua
Nana*
-Attia Hossain
(India), *Sunlight on
a Broken Column*
-Cheikh Hamidou
Kane (Senegal),
*Ambiguous
Adventure*
-VS Naipaul (Trini-
dad), *A House for
Mr. Biswas*

1965 -Gambia becomes independent
replacing 1921 law based on
nationality
-Rhodesian Unilateral Declaration
of Independence, Britain imposes
oil embargo on Rhodesia
-Central African Republic: Jean
Bedel Bokassa takes power in coup;
has himself crowned *Emperor*;
dictatorship until 1979
-Congo (Zaire): Mobuto Sese Sekou
takes power in coup; dictatorship
until 1997
-Indonesia: Suharto takes power in
coup; initiates pogrom (until 1966)
against the left: half a million
people are murdered; hundreds of
thousands more imprisoned in
brutal conditions
-Thailand: rural insurgency, led by
Communist Party (until 1978)

1962 -Alan Hill at Heine-
mann initiates its
African Writers
Series (AWS)
-Mehdi Ben Barka
(Algeria), "Resolv-
ing the Ambiguities
of National
Sovereignty"
-Kenneth Kaunda
(Zambia), *Zambia
Shall Be Free*
-Patrice Lumumba
(Congo), *Congo
My Country*
-Albert Luthuli
(South Africa), *Let
My People Go*
-Carlos Fuentes
(Mexico), *The*

-Singapore breaks from Malaysia and becomes separate state under Lee Kwan-yew
-Mozambique: FRELIMO leader, Eduardo Mondlane, assassinated

Death of Artemio Cruz
-Alex La Guma (South Africa), *A Walk in the Night*
-Carlos Martinez Moreno (Uruguay), *The Wall*
-Mario Vargas Llosa (Peru), *The Time of the Hero*

1963 -Julio Cortázar (Argentina) *Hopscotch*
-Ghassan Kanafani (Palestine), *Men in the Sun*
-Severo Sarduy (Cuba), *Gestures*
-C.L.R. James, *Beyond a Boundary*
-Govan Mbeki (South Africa), *South Africa: The Peasants' Revolt*
-Forugh Farrokhzad (Iran), *Another Birth*

1964 -First conference on Commonwealth Literature, University of Leeds
-*Journal of Commonwealth Literature founded*
-Govan Mbeki (South Africa), *The Peasant's Revolt*

1966 -Mrs. Indira Gandhi, Nehru's daughter, becomes Prime Minister of India

1965 -Paul Scott, *The Raj Quartet* (finished 1975)

-British Guyana becomes the inde-
pendent nation of Guyana
-Barbados, Botswana, Guyana,
Lesotho gain independence
-Zimbabwe: armed struggle against
British colonialism launched
-Namibia: armed struggle launched
-Ghana: Kwame Nkrumah ousted in
coup
-First Tricontinental Conference,
Havana
-China: Mao inaugurates "Cultural
Revolution" (until 1976), empha-
sizing permanent revolution and
class struggle; widespread persecu-
tion of intellectuals one conse-
quence of the movement's radical
antiurban and antibourgeois
ideology

-Albert Memmi,
*The Colonizer and
the Colonized*
-Nelson Mandela
(South Africa), *No
Easy Walk to
Freedom*
-Kwame Nkrumah
(Ghana), *Neo-
Colonialism: the
Last Stage of
Imperialism*
-Michael Anthony
(Trinidad), *The
Year in San
Fernando*
-Guillermo Cabrera
Infante (Cuba),
*Three Trapped
Tigers*
-Kamala Das (India),
Summer in Calcutta
-Shahnon Ahmad
(Malaysia), *Rope
of Ash*
-Wole Soyinka
(Nigeria), *The
Road*

1967 -Nigeria: civil war erupts as federal
government attempts to prevent
secession of Biafra (until 1970)
-Six-day Arab–Israeli war; victory
for Israel, which proceeds to seize
Sinai and Gaza from Egypt, West
Bank from Jordan; Israeli annex-
ation of Old City of Jerusalem
-Bolivia: capture and execution of
Ernesto "Che" Guevera by Bolivian
Rangers in collaboration with CIA
operatives

1966 -Paul Scott, *The
Jewel in the Crown*
-U.R. Anantha-
murthy (India),
Funeral Rites
-Louise Bennett
(Jamaica), *Jamaica
Labrish*
-Jose Lezama Lima
(Cuba), *Paradiso*
-Flora Nwapa
(Nigeria), *Efuru*

-Jean Rhys (Dominican) *Wide Sargasso Sea*
-Marta Traba (Argentina/Colombia) *Rites of Summer*
-Mario Vargas Llosa (Peru), *The Green House*
-Mahmoud Darwish (Palestine), *Lover from Palestine*

1968 -British colony of Mauritius becomes independent state within Commonwealth
-British government restricts immigration from India, Pakistan, and the West Indies
-Martin Luther King, Jr. assassinated
-Student-led uprising in France, Mexico, and the United States

1969 -Britain sends troops to Northern Island to quell rioting

1967 -Miguel Ángel Asturias (Guatemala), Nobel Prize for Literature (19 Oct. 1899–9 June 1974)
-Oginga Odinga (Kenya), *Not Yet Uhuru*
-Gabriel García Márquez (Colombia), *One Hundred Years of Solitude*
-V.S. Naipaul (Trinidad), *The Mimic Man*
-Nguigi wa Thiong'o (Kenya), *A Grain of Wheat*

			-Wole Soyinka (Nigeria), *Idanre, and Other Poems* -Andre Gunder Frank, *Capitalism and Underdevelopment in Latin America* -Wilson Harris, *Tradition, the Writer and Society*
1970	-Biafra capitulates to federal Nigerian government; end of civil war which began 2.5 years previously -Gambia proclaimed a republic within British Commonwealth -Fiji, Tonga gain independence -Chile: Socialist Salvador Allende elected President	1968	-Man Booker Prize for Literature established -Julius K. Nyerere (Tanzania), *Ujamaa: Essays on Socialism* -Ayi Kwei Armah (Ghana), *The Beautyful Ones Are Not Yet Born* -Dennis Brutus (South Africa), *Letters to Martha* -Ahmadou Kourouma (Ivory Coast),*The Suns of Independence* -Nizar Qabbani (Iraq), "Comments on the Notebook of Decadence" -Andrew Salkey (Jamaica), *The Late Emacipation of Jerry Stoker* -Paulo Freire, *Pedagogy of the Oppressed*

1971 -Civil war breaks out in East Pakistan, following declaration of independent state of Bangladesh; subsequent war between India and Pakistan ends with defeat of Pakistan; Zulfikar Ali Bhutto elected Prime Minister, ending 13 years of military rule
-Uganda: Idi Amin seizes power in coup; brutal dictatorship until 1979
-Bahrain gains independence

1972 -Bangladesh (East Pakistan) established as sovereign state
-Philippines: Ferdinand Marcos declares martial law; rebellion by Filipino Muslims in the south; met with extreme state violence
-Northern Island: "Bloody Sunday," British paratroops kill 13 marchers in Derry; IRA retaliates; direct rule imposed

1969 -Neustadt International Prize for Literature established
-Samuel Beckett (Ireland), Nobel Prize for Literature (13 April 1906–22 Dec. 1989)
-Eduardo Mondlane (Mozambique), *The Struggle for Mozambique*
-Elena Poniatowska (Mexico), *Until We Meet Again*
-Tayeb Salih (Sudan), *Season of Migration from the North*
-Fadwa Tuqan (Palestine) *Horseman and the Night*

1970 -*ARIEL: A Review of International English Literature*
-*Research in African Literature* journal established
-Sala 'Abd al-Sabur (Egypt), *Journey at Night*
-Ama Ata Aidoo (Ghana), *No Sweetness Here*
-Merle Hodge (Trinidad), *Crick Crack Monkey*
-Jabra Ibrahim Jabra (Palestine), *The Ship*

1973 -Bahamas granted independence
after 3 centuries of colonial rule
-Oil crisis as Organization of Petrol-
eum Exporting Countries (OPEC)
raises prices and cuts back on
production
-Collapse of Bretton Woods polit-
ical-economic system; United States
comes off gold standard; paves way
for globalization of capital and neoliberal economic policies
-Egypt and Syria launch joint attack
on Israel; Israel victorious after
fierce exchange

1974 -Ethiopia: Haile Selassie deposed
after general strike
-Guinea-Bissau gains independence
after armed struggle

-Neustadt Prize
established

1971 -Pablo Neruda
(Chile), Nobel Prize
for Literature (12
July 1904–23 Sept.
1973)
-V.S. Naipaul
(Trinidad), Booker
Prize for *In a Free
State*
-Mahmoud Darwish
(Palestine) *Lover
from Palestine*
-Christopher
Okigbo (Nigeria),
Labryinths
-Roberto Fernandez
Retamar, "Caliban"

1972 -Steve Biko (South
Africa), *I Write
What I Like*
-Dhoomil (India)
*From the Parlia-
ment to the Street*
-Athol Fugard
(South Africa),
Sizwe Banzi Is Dead
-Manohar Malgon-
kar (India) *The
Devil's Wind*
-Simone Schwarz-
Bart (Guadaloupe),
*The Bridge of
Beyond*
-Paulo Freire
(Brazil) *Pedagogy
of the Oppressed*
-Walter Rodney
(Guyana) *How*

Europe Under-
developed Africa

1975 -Vietnam War ends with defeat of the United States and capture of Saigon by People's Army of Vietnam
-Angola, Mozambique, Cape Verde gain independence after armed struggles
-Indonesia invades and occupies East Timor
-Lebanon: outbreak of civil war

1973 -Patrick White (Australia), Nobel Prize for Literature (28 May 1912–30 Sept. 1990)
-Amilcar Cabral (Guinea-Bissau), *Return of the Source*
-Mahsweta Devi (India), *Mother of 1084*
-Eduardo Galeano, *The Open Veins of Latin America*
-J.G. Farrell, Booker Prize for *The Siege of Krishnapur*

1976 -Spain relinquishes colonial control of the Spanish Sahara; Morocco and Mauritania divide the territory, ignoring the Sahara nationalists' proclamation of independence
-Commonwealth Conference reaches Lancaster House agreement on future of Rhodesia as the independent state of Zimbabwe
-South Africa: student uprising begins in Soweto township, spreads to other parts of the country; hundreds killed

1974 -Nadine Gordimer (South Africa), Booker Prize for *The Conservationist*
-M. Gopalkirshna Adiga (India), *Song of the Earth and Other Poems*
-Nadine Gordimer (South Africa) *The Conservationist*
-Emile Habiby (Palestine), *The Secret Life of Saeed, the Ill-Fated Pessoptimist*
-Bessie Head (South Africa/Botswana), *A Question of Power*
-Mahasweta Devi (India), *Mother of 1084*

-Immanuel Waller-
stein, *The Modern
World System:
Capitalist Agricul-
ture and the
Origins of the
European World-
Economy in the
Sixteenth Century*

1977 -South Africa: Steve Biko dies in
police custody
-Pakistan: Bhutto ousted in military
coup lead by General Zia-ul-Huq

1978 -Iran: mass demonstrations against
Shah
-Egypt and Israel Camp David
Accords; Israel agrees to withdraw
from Sinai; "self-rule" pledged in
occupied territories

1975 -Bharati Mukherjee
(India/United
States), *Wife*
-Indira Sant (India),
*The Snake-skin and
Other Poems*
-Ruth Prawer Jhab-
vala (India),
Booker Prize for
Heat and Dust
-Nawal el-Saadawi
(Egypt), *Woman at
Point Zero*

1979 -Soviet invasion of Afghanistan
-Nicaragua: popular uprising over-
throws Somoza dictatorship, brings
Sandinista National Liberation
Front (FSLN) to power; United
States moves to destabilize the San-
dinista regime; 30,000 killed in
ensuing violence

1976 -Alex Haley, *Roots*
-*Callaloo* journal
established
-Jaranta Mahpatra
(India), *A Pain of
Rites*
-Manuel Puig
(Argentina), *The Kiss
of the Spider Woman*
-Antonio Torres
(Brazil), *The Land*
-Wole Soyinka,
*Myth, Literature
and the African
World*

1977 -Bessie Head (South Africa/Botswana), *The Collector of Treasures*
-Elias Khoury (Lebanon), *Little Mountain*
-Clarice Lispector (Brazil), *The Hour of the Star*
-Ngugi wa Thiong'o (Kenya), *Petals of Blood*
-Sergio Ramirez (Nicaragua), *To Bury Our Fathers*
-Manuel Rui (Angola), *Yes Comrade!*
-Samir Amin, *Imperialism and Unequal Development*

1980 -President Carter restricts grain sales to USSR in protest against the Soviet invasion of Afghanistan
-Indira Gandhi voted back into power
-Zimbabwe, formerly Rhodesia, gains independence
-Outbreak of Iran–Iraq War (until 1988)

1978 -Edward Said, *Orientalism*
-Noma Award for Publishing in Africa established
-Isaac Bashevis Singer, Nobel Prize for Literature (21 Nov. 1902–24 July 1991)
-Dambudzo Mare-chera (Zimbabwe), *The House of Hunger*
-O.V. Vijayan (India), *Short Stories*

1981 -Belize gains independence
      -Egypt: President Sadat assassinated

1979 -*Kunapipi* journal
      established
      -Mariama Bâ (Sene-
      gal), *So Long a
      Letter*
      -Buchi Emecheta
      (Nigeria), *The Joys
      of Motherhood*
      -Nuruddin Farah
      (Somalia), *Sweet
      and Sour Milk*
      -Nadine Gordimer
      (South Africa),
      Burger's Daughter
      -Roy Heath
      (Guyana), *The
      Armstrong Trilogy
      (1918)*
      -Earl Lovelace
      (Trinidad), *The
      Dragon Can't
      Dance*
      -Pramoedya Ananta
      Toer (Indonesia),
      Buru Quartet
      (finished 1988)
      -

1982 -Canada's Constitution Act comes
      into force, severing the nation's last
      legal ties to the United Kingdom
      -South Africa adopts a new consti-
      tution giving limited political rights
      to "Colored" and "Asian" but not
      "Black" South Africans
      -Falklands/Malvinas war between
      the United Kingdom and Argentina
      -Mexico: moratorium on loan
      repayment triggers international
      debt crisis

1980 -J.M. Coetzee
      (South Africa),
      *Waiting for the
      Barbarians*
      -Anita Desai (India),
      Clear Light of Day
      -Pepetela (Angola),
      Mayombe
      -Salman Rushdie
      (India), *Midnight's
      Children*

-Michael Thelwell
(Jamaica), *The
Harder They Come*
-Albert Wendt
(Samoa), *Leaves of
the Banyan Tree*
-Immanuel Waller-
stein, *The Modern
World System, Vol.
2: Mercantilism and
the Consolidation
of the European
World Economy,
1600–1750*

1983 -Philippines: Assassination of
opposition leader Beningo S.
Aquino, Jr., as he returns to country
to fight election against Marcos
-Grenada: following murder of
Prime Minister Maurice Bishop,
U.S. forces intervene to topple New
Jewel Movement

1981 -Salman Rushdie,
Booker Prize for
Midnight's Children
-Ariel Dorfman
(Chile), *Widows*
-Mongane Wally
Serote (South
Africa), *To Every
Birth Its Blood*
-Aminata Sow Fall
(Senegal), *The
Beggar's Strike*
-Malek Alloula, *The
Colonial Harem*
-Benedict Anderson,
*Imagined Commu-
nities: Reflections
on the Origins and
Spread of
Nationalism*
-Edouard Glissant,
*Caribbean
Discourse*

1984 -India: Indira Gandhi assassinated
-Ethiopia: devastating famine kills
500,000

1982 -Gabriel García
Márquez (Colum-
bia), Nobel Prize

for Literature (b. 6
March 1927)
-Thomas Keneally
(Australia), Booker
Prize for *Schind-
ler's Ark*
-Inaugural Issue of
the series *Subaltern
Studies*, edited by
Ranajit Guha
-Isabel Allende
(Chile), *The House
of the Spirits*
-Reinaldo Arenas
(Cuba), *Farewell to
the Sea*
-Edward Kamau
Brathwaite (Barba-
doas), *The Arrivants*

1986 -Haitian President Jean-Claude
Duvalier flees to France after
nationwide demonstrations against
his rule

1983 -J.M. Coetzee
(South Africa),
Booker Prize for
*Life and Times of
Michael K*
-Jamaica Kincaid
(Antigua), *Annie
John*
-Njabulo Ndebele
(South Africa),
*Fools and Other
Stories*
-Grace Nichols
(Guayana), *i is a
long-memoried
woman*
-Sony Labou Tansi
(Zaire), *The
Antipeople*
-Luisa Valenzuela
(Argentina), *The
Lizard's Tail*

-Nirmal Verma
(India), *The Crows
of Deliverance*
-Johannes Fabian,
Time and the Other
-Abdelkebir Khatibi
Maghreb pluriel
1984 -*Wasafiri* journal
established
-Rigoberta Menchú
(Guatemala), *I,
Rigoberta Manchu:
An Indian Woman
in Guatemala*
-Miguel Bonasso
(Argentina),
Memory of Death
-Maryse Condé
(Guadeloupe), *Segu*
-Abdelrahman
Munif (Saudi
Arabia), *City of Salt*
-Cristina Peri Rossi
(Uruguay), *The
Ship of Fools*
-Edward Kamau
Brathwaite, *History of the Voice*

1987 -Portugal and China agree on the   1985 -Keri Hulme (New
return to China in 1999 of Macao, a   Zealand), Booker
Portuguese colony since the six-   Prize for *The Bone
teenth century   People*
-Israel: insurrection (intifada) breaks   -Tahar Ben Jelloun
out as Palestinians protest continu-   (Morocco), *The
ing Israeli oppression (until 1990);   Sand Child*
several hundred killed   -Assia Djebar
                                            (Algeria), *Fantasia,
                                            An Algerian
                                            Cavalcade*
                                            -Gabriel Garcia
                                            Marquez

(Colombia), *Love in
the Time of Cholera*
-Nayantara Sahgal
(India), *Rich Like
Us*
-Ken Saro-Wiwa
(Nigeria), *Sozaboy*
-Sidney Mintz,
*Sweetness and
Power*
1986 -Wole Soyinka
(Nigeria), Nobel
Prize for Literature
(born 13 July 1934)
-Nuruddin Farah
(Somalia), *Maps*
-Waleed Khazindar
(Palestine), *Present
Verbs*
-Hanif Kureishi
(United Kingdom),
*My Beautiful
Laundrette*
-Álvaro Mutis
(Colombia), *The
Snow of the
Admiral*
-Carly Phillips (St.
Kitts), *A State of
Independence*
-Anton Shammas
(Israel), *Arbasques*
-Derek Walcott (St.
Luica), *Collected
Poems*
-Partha Chatterjee,
*Nationalist
Thought and the
Colonial World: A
Derivative
Discourse*

-Peter Hulme, *Colonial Encounters: Europe and the Native Caribbean, 1492–1797*
-Nguigi wa Thiong'o, *Decolonising the Mind: the Politics of Language in African Literature*
-Frederic Jameson, "Third World Literature in the Era of Multinational China"

1989 -Pakistan: Benazir Bhutto, daughter of Zulfikar Ali Bhutto, elected Prime Minister as country returns again to civilian rule
-Afghanistan: uncompromising resistance from guerillas forces withdrawal of Soviet troops; Civil War ensues as rival factions bid for power

1987 -Commonwealth Writers' Prize established
-Agha Shahid Ali (India), *The Half-Inch Himalayas*
-Jesus Diaz (Cuba), *The Initials of the Earth*
-Daniel Maximin (Guadeloupe), *Soufrieres*
-Horacio Vazquez Rial (Argentina), *Triste's History*
-Shrikant Verma (India), *Magadh*

1989 -Khomeini announces Fatwa on Salman Rushdie after release of Satanic Verses
-Pakistan rejoins commonwealth after leaving in 1972

1988 -Naguib Mahfouz (Egypt), Nobel Prize for Literature (11 Dec. 1911–30 Aug. 2006)
-Peter Carey (Australia), Booker Prize for *Oscar and Lucinda*

-Upamayu Chatter-
jee (India), *English,
August*
-Amit Chaudhuri
(India), *Afternnon
Raag*
-Michelle Cliff
(Jamaica/United
States), *No Tele-
phone to Heaven*
-Tsitsi Dangarembga
(Zimbabwe), *Ner-
vous Conditions*
-Amitav Ghosh
(India), *The
Shadow Lines*
-Suong Thu Huong
(Vietnam), *Para-
dise of the Blind*
-Chenjerai Hove
(Zimbabwe), *Bones*
-Tomás Eloy Martí-
nez (Argentina),
The Peron Novel
-Salman Rushdie
(India), *Satanic Verses*
-Bapsi Sidhwa
(Pakistan),
Cracking India
-Héctor Tizón
(Argentina), *The
Man Who Came to
a Village*
-Chandra Talpade
Mohanty, "Under
Western Eyes: Femi-
nist Scholarship and
Colonial Discourse"
-V.Y. Mudimbe,
*The Invention of
Africa: Gnosis,*

*Philosophy, and
the Order of
Knowledge*

1990 -Nambia becomes independent state
-Nelson Mandela (South Africa) is
released from jail after 27 years in
prison
-Jean-Bertrand Aristide becomes first
democratically elected President of
Haiti
-German reunification, 3 Oct.

1991 -End of twenty-year Ethiopian Civil
War
-Start of Somali Civil War

1989 -Kazuo Ishiguro
(Japan/United
Kingdom) Booker
Prize for *The
Remains of the Day*
-Bill Ashcroft,
Gareth Griffiths,
Helen Tiffin, *The
Empire Writes Back*
-Nissim Ezekiel
(India), *Collected
Poems*
-Kazou Ishiguro
(Japan/United
Kingdom), *The
Remains of the Day*
-Nugui Ka Thiong'o
(Kenya), *Matigari*
-MG Vassanji
(Kenya/Canada),
The Gunny Sack
-Jean Bernabe, Pat-
rick Camouiseau,
and Raphael Con-
fiant, *In Praise of
Creoleness*

1993 -Israel and the PLO sign peace
accord

1990 -Octavio Paz
(Mexico), Nobel
Prize for Literature

(31 March 1941–
19 April 1998)
-Gayatri Spivak,
The Postcolonial Critic
-Robert Young,
White Mythologies
-Mia Couto
(Mozambique),
Every Man Is a Race
-Abd al-Wahhab
Bayati (Iraq), *Love Death and Exile*
-Terry Eagleton,
Fredric Jameson,
Edward Said,
Nationalism, Colonialism and Literature

1994 -The Rwandan Genocide (6 April–
mid-July)
-Start of the Zapatista indigenous
movement in Mexico
-South Africa holds first post-apartheid elections, returning the African
National Congress (ANC) to
power; Nelson Mandela elected
President

1991 -Nadine Gordimer
(South Africa),
Nobel Prize for Lit-
erature (b. 20 Nov.
1923)
-Ben Okri (Nigeria),
Booker Prize for
The Famished Road
-Khalil Hawi (Leba-
non), *From the Vineyards of Lebanon*
-Timothy Mo
(United Kingdom),
The Redundancy of Courage
-Ben Okri (Nigeria),
Booker Prize for
The Famished Road
-Derek Walcott (St.
Luica), *Omeros*

1995 -Rwanda: long-simmering civil war
degenerates into massive interethnic
massacres; death toll tops 1 million
-Nigeria: military regime executes
Ogoni leader and writer Ken Saro-
Wiwa

1996 -The Taliban seize control of
Afghanistan

1997 -Zaire renamed Democratic Republic
of Congo after the overthrow of long-
time dictator Mobuto Sese Seko
-Britain hands over sovereignty of
Hong Kong back to China

-Salman Rushdie,
*Imaginary Home-
lands: Essays and
Criticism 1981–
1991*

1992 -Derek Walcott (St
Kitts), Nobel Prize
for Literature (b. 23
Jan. 1930)
-Michael Ondaatje
(Canada), Booker
Prize for *The Eng-
lish Patient*
-Ambai (C.S.
Lakshmi) (India),
The Purple Sea
-Patrick Chamoi-
seau (Martinique),
Texaco
-Michael Ondaatje
(Sri Lanka/Canada)
The English Patient
-Aijaz Ahmad, *In
Theory: Class,
Nations,
Literatures*
-Marie Louise Pratt,
*Imperial Eyes:
Travel Writing and
Transculturation*
-Arturo Uslar Pietri,
*The Creation of the
New World*

1993 -Toni Morrison
(United States),
Nobel Prize for Lit-
erature (b. 18 Feb.
1931)

-Roddy Doyle (Ireland), Booker Prize for *Paddy Clarke Ha Ha Ha*
-Salman Rushdie (India), Booker of Bookers for *Midnight's Children*
-Edward Said, *Culture and Imperialism*
-Amin Maalouf (Lebanon), *The Rock of Tanios*
-Vikram Seth (India), *A Suitable Boy*
-Ivan Vladislavic (South Africa), *The Folly*

1998 -Peace Agreement signed for Northern Ireland
-Indonesia: Suharto dictatorship overturned after 32 years

2000 -Israeli–Palestinian summit fails; second *intifada* breaks out
-Reformists win control in Iran

1994 -Muhammad al-Maghut (Syria), *Joy Is Not My Profession*
-Shyam Selvadurai (Sri Lanka/Canada), *Funny Boy*
-Homi K Bhabha, *The Location of Culture*

1995 -Seamus Heaney (Ireland), Nobel Prize for Literature (b. 13 April 1939)
-Subcommandante Marcos (Mexico), *Shadows of Tender Fury*

l

2001 -Islamist suicide bombers hijack
planes, fly them into World Trade
Center towers and Pentagon building in the United States; casualties
exceed 3,000; United States declares
"War on Terrorism," invades
Afghanistan in pursuit of Osama
bin Laden, alleged mastermind of
hijackings and attacks; ruling Taliban overthrown by U.S. forces
-Five militants attack New Delhi
Parliament

-Keki Daruwalla
(India), *A Summer
of Tigers*
-Declan Kiberd,
*Inventing Ireland:
The Literature of
the Modern Nation*
1996 -Rohinton Mistry
(India/Canada),
*Love and Longing
in Bombay*
-Nizar Qabbani
(Syria), *On
Entering the Sea*
-Ivan Vladislavic
(South Africa),
*Propaganda by
Monuments and
Other Stories*
1997 -Arundhati Roy
(India), Booker
Prize for *The God
of Small Things*
-*Jouvert: Journal of
Postcolonial Stud-
ies* (until 2003)
-Vikram Chandra
(India), *Love and
Longing in
Bombay*
-Arundhati Roy
(India), *The God of
Small Things*
-A Sivanandan (Sri
Lanka), *When
Memory Dies*
1999 -J.M. Coetzee
(South Africa),
Booker Prize for
Disgrace

2003 -U.S. invasion of Iraq by international coalition dominated by
U.S. forces

2000 -Margaret Atwood
(Canada), Booker
Prize for *The Blind
Assassin*
-Caine Prize for
African Writing:
Short Story
established
-Naiyer Masud
(India), *Essence of
Camphor*
-Zadie Smith
(United Kingdom),
White Teeth
-J.M. Coetzee
(South Africa),
Commonwealth
Writers' Prize: Best
Book
-Funso Aiyejina
(Nigeria), Regional
Commonwealth
Writers' Prize: Best
First Book
-Jhumpa Lahiri
(India/United King-
dom), Pulitzer Prize
for Fiction
-Leila Aboulela
(Sudan), Caine Prize
for African Writing
-Michael Ondaatje
(Sri Lanka/Canada),
Giller Prize.

2004 -Madrid train bombings, Al Qaeda
claims responsibility
-Palestinian leader Yasser Arafat
dies

2001 -V.S. Naipaul
(Trinidad), Nobel
Prize for Literature
(b. 17 Aug. 1932)
-Peter Carey (Aus-
tralia) Booker Prize

for *True History of the Kelly Gang*
-Binod Bihari Verma (India), *Adim Purkha*
-Helon Habila (Nigeria), Caine Prize for African Writing
-K. Sello Duiker (South Africa), Regional Commonwealth Writers' Prize: Best First Book
-V.S. Naipaul (Trinidad), Nobel Prize for Literature.
-Zakes Mda (South Africa), Regional Commonwealth Writers' Prize: Best Book
-Peter Carey, *True History of the Kelly Gang*

2005 -Four terrorist attacks on the London public transit system
-Lebanon Former Prime Minister Rafik Hariri is assassinated

2002 -Yann Martel (Canada), Booker Prize for *Life of Pi*
-Alaa Al Aswany (Egyptian), *The Yacoubian Building*
-Alvaro Mutis (Colombia), Nuestadt International Prize for Literature
-Austin Clarke (Barbados), Giller Prize
-Binyavanga Wainaina (Kenya),

Caine Prize for
African Writing
-Manu Herbstein
(South Africa),
Commonwealth
Writers' Prize: Best
First Book
-Nadine Gordimer
(South Africa),
Regional Common-
wealth Writers' Best
Book Prize

2006 -Ethiopian troops invade Somilia,
causing conflict
-Iraqi President Saddam Hussein
executed

2003 -J. M. Coetzee (South
Africa), Nobel Prize
for Literature (b. 9
Feb. 1940)
-The Iraq National
Library and Arch-
ive is burnt down in
battle of Baghdad
(14 April)
-Andre Brink (South
Africa), Regional
Commonwealth
Writers' Prize: Best
Book
-Azar Nafisi (Iran),
*Reading Lolita in
Tehran*
-Chimamanda
Ngozi Adichie
(Nigeria), *Purple
Hibiscus*
-Helon Habila
(Nigeria), Regional
Commonwealth
Writers' Prize: Best
First Book
-J.M. Coetzee
(South Africa),
Nobel Prize for

			Literature (b. 9 Feb. 1940) -Khaled Hosseini (Afghanistan), *The Kite Runner* -Jhumpa Lahiri (India), *The Namesake* -M.G. Vassanji (Kenya), Giller Prize -Yvonne Adhiambo Owuor (Kenya), Caine Prize for African Writing -D.B.C. Pierre, Booker Prize for *Vernon God Little*
2007	-UN Climate Change Conference held in Bali, Indonesia -Pakistan: Benazir Bhutto assassinated	2004	-*Postcolonial Text* established -Afua Cooper, *The Hanging of Angelique* -Bharati Mukherjee (India), *The Tree Bride* -Bryan Chikwava (Zimbabwe), Caine Prize for African Writing -Damon Galgut (South Africa), Regional Commonwealth Writers' Prize: Best Book -Helon Hebila (Nigeria), *Waiting on an Angel*
2008	-Afghanistan Presidential elections held -India plants flag on moon for first time	2005	-John Banville (Ireland), Booker Prize for *The Sea*

lv

-Man Booker International Prize established
-Chimamanda Ngozi Adichie (Nigeria), Commonwealth Writers' Prize: Best Book
-Diane Awerbuck (South Africa) wins Regional Commonwealth Writers' Prize: Best First Book
-Ismail Kadare (Albania), Man Booker Prize
-Lindsey Collen (South Africa), Regional Commonwealth Writers' Best Book Prize
-Rupa Bajwa (India) wins Regional Commonwealth Writers' Prize: Best First Book
-S.A. Afolabi (Nigeria), Caine Prize for African Writing
-Uzodinma Iweala (Nigeria), *Beasts of No Nation*

2009 -Rio de Janeiro wins bid for 2016 summer Olympic Games
2010 -Earthquake in Haiti
      -Clashes between Muslims and Christians cause Nigerian Jos riots

2006 -Orhan Parmuk (Turkey), Nobel Prize for Literature (b. 7 June 1952)
      -Kiran Desai (India), Booker Prize for

The Inhertiance of Loss
-Benjamin Kwakye (Ghana), Regional Commonwealth Writers' Prize: Best Book
-Caribel Alegria (Nicaragua), Nuestadt International Prize for Literature
-Chimamanda Ngozi Adichie, *Half a Yellow Sun*
-Doreen Baingana (Uganda), Regional Commonwealth Writers' Prize: Best First Book
-Kiran Desai (India), Nation Books Critics Article Award
-Marc McWatt (Guyana), Commonwealth Writers' Prize: Best First Book
-Mary Watson (South Africa), Caine Prize for African Writing

2011 -Libyan civil war begins
2012 -U.S. military formally ends mission in Iraq
      -North Korea Leader Kim Jong Il Dies
2013 -Pope Benedict XVI resigns
      -South African anti-apartheid revolutionary, politician, and first post-apartheid President Nelson Mandela dies

2007 -Doris Lessing (Zimbabwe/United Kingdom), Nobel Prize for Literature

-Kenya: attack on Westgate Mall by Islamic militants; an estimated 67 people were killed and another 175 were injured

(22 Oct. 1919–17 Nov. 2013)
-Anne Enright (Ireland), Booker Prize for *The Gathering*
-Chinua Achebe (Nigeria), Man Booker International Prize
-Junot Diaz, *The Brief Wonderous Life of Oscar Wao*
-M.G. Vassanji (Kenya), *The Assassin's Song*
-Monica Arac de Nyeko (Uganda), Caine Prize for African Writing
-

2008 -Aravind Adiga (India), Booker Prize for *The White Tiger*
-Harrietta Rose-Innes (South Africa), Caine Prize for African Writing.
-Junot Diaz (Dominican Republic), Pulitzer Prize for Fiction
-Roberto Bolaño (Chile), Nation Books Critics Article Award
-Uwem Akpan (Nigeria), *Say You're One of Them*

-Mohamed Hanif, *A Case of Exploding Mangoes*

2009 -Alice Munro (Canada), the Man Booker International Prize
-Penguin African Writing Prize launched
-United Nations Educational, Scientific and Cultural Organization launch the world digital library
-E.C. Osondu (Nigeria), Caine Prize for African Writing

2010 -Daniyal Mueenuddin (Pakistan), Pulitzer Prize for Fiction
-Olufemi Terry (Sierra Leone), Caine Prize for African Writing

2011 -Ahmet Hamdi Tanpinar Literature Museum Library opens in Istanbul, Turkey
-Aminatta Forna (Sierra Leone), Commonwealth Writers' Best Book Prize
-Esi Edugyan (Ghana), Giller Prize
-Noviolet Bulawayo (Zimbabwe), Caine

Prize for African
Writing

2012 -Babatunde Rotimi
(Nigeria), Caine
Prize for African
Writing

2013 -Chimamanda
Ngozi Adichie
(Nigeria), Nation
Books Critics Art-
icle Award
-Tope Folarin
(Nigeria), Caine
Prize for African
Writing
-Windham Camp-
bell Literary
awards established
-Etisalat Prize for
African Literature
established
-Eleanor Catton
(New Zealand),
Booker Prize for
The Luminaries

2014 --Mia Couto
(Mozambique),
Nuestadt Inter-
national Prize for
Literature
-Okwiri Oduor
(Kenya), Caine
Prize for African
Writing
-Richard Flanagan
(Australia), Booker
Prize for *The
Narrow Road to
the Deep North*

I

ATO QUAYSON
University of Toronto

Introduction

Changing Contexts of the Postcolonial Novel

The postcolonial novel, to echo Dorothy Hale in another context, "is a rich problematic rather than a monolithic idea."[1] This insight is fundamental in attempting to set out the literary history of the form. Provisionally, the historical background to the postcolonial novel in the English-speaking world may be broken into four overlapping period clusters: (1) the phase of formal colonialism stretching from the establishment of the reconstituted Colonial Office in 1854 to the end of World War II in 1945; (2) the period of decolonization and postcolonial nation-state formation in Africa, India, Southeast Asia, and the Caribbean, roughly from 1945 to 1965; (3) post-independence until the end of the Cold War, roughly from 1966 to 1989; and (4) the period of intensified globalization, transnationalism, and the attendant reconfiguration of the nation-state in both the formerly colonized world and their counterpart metropolitan colonial centers, from 1966 to the present time. These four periods are subject to finer internal differentiations to take account of regional variations and also to subperiod themes that fall within the individual phases. These historical periods were in turn shaped by global population flows and multistriated forms of information technology and communications systems that continually evolved and came to be sedimented in the social media platforms of Facebook, Twitter, Instagram, and the like. As Debjani Ganguly shows in Chapter 3, the post-1989 period has proved especially significant in bringing together a confluence of factors that have influenced the representational protocols of the postcolonial novel. She outlines the changing political and demographic landscapes and new modes of media representation that have gained prominence since the end of the Cold War. We should also note the significance of the period after September 11, 2001, which she also attends to. September 11 has not only engendered variant forms of aggrieved nationalisms but also given birth to new inflections of proselytizing monotheisms. Proselytizing monotheisms such as Christianity and Islam have historically always adduced to themselves the privileged authority for determining the contours of teleological imagination. What is different in today's post-September 11 world is that the teleological imagination and its consequent actions have been harnessed to forms of delirious sovereignty, as well as to the desperate attempts at either exiting the state or otherwise transcending it. The second form of harnessing is what we see in globalized evangelical Christianity and in ISIS (the Islamic State of Iraq and al-Sham, alternatively known as ISIL: the Islamic State of Iraq and the Levant), raising the question of what our current historical configuration contributes to the "sense of an ending," to appropriate Frank Kermode's concept for thinking about the teleological imagination.[2] All these have an impact on and have been reflected in the postcolonial novel since September 11.

From a purely historicizing postcolonial perspective, however, we are obliged to pursue the literary history of the postcolonial novel by first accounting for the variegated character of its precursor, the colonial novel. This is a somewhat false beginning, first because postcolonialism as a set of theoretical dispositions and not a period marker is not conventionally considered necessarily to be exclusive to the period after colonialism. What came to coalesce around the colonial novel may also strictly speaking be traceable to the relentless stream of letters, reports, chronicles, and travel narratives by Europeans from the earliest period of contact with people outside of Europe.[3] The term "colonial novel" is somewhat problematic as it may be taken to cover anticolonial works (as in critical of empire and colonialism) as well as colonial works (as in providing subtle-and-not-so-subtle justifications for it). As we see in Chapter 2, for this volume the term is thus deployed to designate at least two orientations. Along with Shakespeare's *The Tempest, Othello,* and *Merchant of Venice,* the novels of Conrad, Kipling, Forster, and Orwell have inspired some of the most fascinating responses of the postcolonial novel to the Western canon.[4] From Achebe's directly stated intent of responding to Conrad in *Things Fall Apart,* to Rushdie's subtle reprisal of the character of Forster's Dr. Aziz in *Midnight's Children,* the colonial novel has produced a rich payout of characters, symbols, metaphors, and contexts for reimagining the colonial encounter within the postcolonial novel. However, the colonial novel was far from monolithic in either content or form, as Watson proceeds to show. It is thus possible to trace its genealogy to representations of the colonial encounter enshrined in the masculine adventure stories popularized during the course of the nineteenth century. The stories for boys by G. M. Ballantyre, R. L. Stevenson, and H. Rider Haggard provided the initial templates for the colonial novel that were subsequently to be rendered into more sophisticated representations by Conrad, Kipling, Forster, Orwell, and others. Switching to the colonized world itself, the novels of authors such as Sol Plaatje, Olive Schreiner, Mulk Raj Anand, and Joseph Casely-Hayford provided significant reorientations to the representations of colonial encounters and of empire in general. Finally, and in sharp contrast to the masculine adventure narratives of R. L. Stevenson and others, the colonial novel is further complicated with representations of colonial discomfiture to be found in the works of Graham Greene, Evelyn Waugh, E. M. Forster (again), and various others. Typically the Europeans in such works are shown to suffer the loss of epic certitude evident in their novelistic adventuring forebears such that the sense of malaise and loss they express paves the way for a new expression of the European's place in the (post)colonial world.

With the term "postcolonial," understood not as limited to the implicit temporal marking of the "post-," but as the sign of a critical orientation, postcolonial literature in general is thus taken to designate the representation of experiences of various kinds that subtend yet transcend the colonial encounter, including those of slavery, oppression and resistance, migration, race, gender, and colonial space-making, as well as the responses to the discourses of a reconstituted imperial Europe in modern times. As noted earlier, it is conventionally assumed that postcolonial literature is as much a reflection of conditions under imperialism and colonialism proper as it is of conditions coming after the historical end of empires.[5] Despite the many genres that have contributed to the field it is the novel that has provided the main testing ground for central concepts and ideas in postcolonial studies. Furthermore, the rise of interdisciplinarity in the human sciences, especially in the emphasis on the "readerly" nature of cognate disciplines such as history and anthropology and the progressive significance of literary texts and literary methodologies for organizing and thinking about such disciplines, has also helped to give further salience to the postcolonial novel.

If, following Edward Said, Franco Moretti, Mario J. Valdés, and other literary historians who have had an impact on debates in the field, we take as central to the exploration of the postcolonial novel the problems of constituting historical and rhetorical series, of defining the elements proper to each series, and of describing the specific relations between the two, we find that in the literary history of the postcolonial novel the emphasis has always been to combine the explication of historical and political contexts with explorations of the rhetorical dimensions of the novels in question.[6] Since much of the literatures of formerly colonized societies were first introduced to Western audiences whose reading tastes had been deeply influenced by colonial histories of conquest, the early scholars of Commonwealth literature were obliged to educate their readers on cultural context. This was far from straightforward, as any number of anthologies and the pages of the *Journal of Commonwealth Literature* (founded in 1965) amply show. With the consolidation of postcolonial studies from the late 1980s to the mid-1990s onward context was to undergo a number of changes and transpositions, further becoming much more elusive. The early concern with the explication of local cultural context common under the model of Commonwealth literary studies was given a more theoretical inflection by Edward Said, then further complicated by Gayatri Spivak, Homi Bhabha, Robert Young, Abdul JanMohamed, Neil Lazarus, and Frederic Jameson, among various others.[7] The analytical models of colonial discourse analysis elaborated by Said and others were joined to the interdisciplinary offerings put forward by nonliterary scholars such as Arjun Appadurai and Mary Louise Pratt (anthropology), Anne Laura Stoler and Dipesh Chakrabarty (history), and Achille Mbembe (political theory) to offer a heady theoretical and cultural mix that inspired intense debates in the field.[8] The collocation of colonial discourse analysis with the interdisciplinary infusions from outside literary studies had the net effect of shifting emphasis in the field away from the examination of literary and aesthetic products as such and toward the exploration of their discursive contexts and conditions of production. Thus the study of rhetorical devices in the postcolonial novel made way for the analysis of discursive ensembles, yet such discursive ensembles were not necessarily couched in historical terms. The postcolonial novel did not so much respond directly to these shifts as provide more complex materials for framing the central questions of context.

Important in understanding the postcolonial novel and its contexts are also the two orientations Biodun Jeyifo designates as the postcoloniality of "normativity and proleptic designation" and "interstitial or liminal" postcoloniality.[9] The first category embraces that in which the writer or critic speaks to, for, or in the name of the postindependence nation-state, the regional or continental community, the panethnic, racial, or cultural agglomeration of homelands and diasporas. In Jeyifo's account the normativity in this conception of post-coloniality often entails a return to cultural sources, the projection of a futurist agenda, and the celebration of authenticity. This dimension of postcoloniality is often saturated with what could be described as an ethical will-to-identity, an expression of which is that of Chinua Achebe's regularly cited assertion in "The Novelist as Teacher," that he wrote *Things Fall Apart* as an object lesson to his readers to prove that indigenous Africa had a viable culture before the white man came.[10] That this normativity depends ultimately on a perception of literature as part of the contest against colonial hegemony it is impossible to deny, and the implication of "writing back" to the center that was first suggested by Bill Ashcroft, Gareth Griffiths, and Helen Tiffin in *The Empire Writes Back* is taken by many commentators to be very much in evidence in the postcolonial novel.[11] However, as Ato Quayson shows in his chapter in the *Companion*, the question of writing back is complicated by the nature of postcolonial adaptations of classical texts and the character of intertextuality implied in them. This is especially pertinent to discussions of the relationship between tragedy and the postcolonial novels. Thus in Alain Mabanckou's *Broken Glass*, Tayeb Salih's *Season of Migration to the North*, Salman Rushdie's *Midnight's Children* and *The Moor's Last Sigh*, Dambudzo Marechera's *The House of Hunger*, Jean Rhys's *Wide Sargasso Sea*, and Mohsin Hamid's *The Reluctant Fundamentalist*, classical models are combined with intertexual references to import a tragic gravitational pull on the matters being represented. We shall have more to say on this point a little bit later in our introduction.

For Jeyifo whatever politics is derived from the standpoint of proleptic designation normally intersects with another type of politics, again fed by an ethical imperative, but this time not aligned solely to racial or cultural identity. This is the dimension of internal political and social critique that writers and critics feel themselves obliged to undertake on behalf of their people. Neil Lazarus, elaborating a Fanonian perspective on African literature, identifies this impulse as partly due to an unacknowledged messianism that draws on the heady dynamics of decolonization struggles and the disillusionment with internal political conditions that were their aftermath.[12] African writers, and indeed postcolonial writers, feel themselves to be part of a larger social struggle in the quest for absent or vanishing agents of democratic social change. In many respects this dimension of their literary practice defines postcolonial writers as effectively taking on the role traditionally assigned to the press. The same intensity of focus on pursuing social goals that marks the quest of the vigilant press everywhere in the world also informs the work and lives of such postcolonial writers. And so politically committed writers join the press to become the fourth estate of the postcolony.

Jeyifo's second category, that of "interstitial or liminal" postcoloniality, embraces what is normally perceived as a hybrid cosmopolitan sensibility. He notes that

> the interstice or liminality here defines an ambivalent mode of self-fashioning of the writer or critic which is neither First World nor Third World, neither securely and smugly metropolitan, nor assertively and combatively Third-Worldist. The very terms which express the orientation of this school of post-colonial self-representation are revealing: diasporic, exilic, hybrid, in-between, cosmopolitan.[13]

He goes on to name Salman Rushdie as the paradigmatic figure of this mode of postcoloniality, along with Derek Walcott, J. M. Coetzee, and Dambudzo

Marechera. One would have to add to this provisional list the names of Gabríel García Márquez, Junot Díaz, and Zadie Smith as other supreme examples of interstitial postcoloniality. The two forms of postcoloniality – proleptic designation and interstitial/liminal – are often expressed within the same postcolonial text such that it is preferable to speak of the two poles as a dialectical continuum, rather than as polarized and mutually exclusive entities. This is certainly the case with postcolonial novelists who, though defining a subject matter critical of the colonial heritage, simultaneously critique their own nation-states that to them reproduce oppressive frames of reference on the excuse of nationalist sentiment. This duality can be seen, for example, in Alain Mabanckou's *Broken Glass* and NoViolet Bulawayo's *We Need New Names*, both novels published since 2010. The eponymously named narrator of *Broken Glass* sits in a bar called Credit Gone West in the Congo to write down a compendium of stories told to him by customers of the bar.[14] The narrative set up rivals the omnibus narrative format of Chaucer's *The Canterbury Tale* and the *Arabian Nights*. Originally in French, the novel has the distinction of being written from beginning to end without a single full stop. Instead commas provide natural pauses and unnumbered chapter breaks institute demarcations for turning points in the narrative. At the same time, the hilarious stories that Broken Glass writes down as related to him by the people that come to the bar are given an inflection of seriousness via the wide range of intertextual references that are also to be found in the text. At a rough count there are at least seventy-five references to literary titles and segments of literary texts incorporating everything from the Greeks, Shakespeare, Albert Camus, Gabríel Garcia Márquez, Mario Vargas Llosa, Mongo Beti, Chinua Achebe, Ben Okri, and Conrad, among numerous others. Holden Caulfield from J. D. Salinger's *Catcher in the Rye* makes an appearance toward the end of the novel and repeats the question: "can you tell me what happens to the poor little ducks in cold countries during winter, do they get put in a the zoo, or do they migrate to other countries or do the poor little ducks get stuck in the snow, I want to know what you think," to which Broken Glass's response is an ill-tempered: "I don't want to listen to you, I don't want to listen to anyone in this bar anymore, I've had enough, I don't give a shit about the ducks, I don't give a shit if they put them in cages, or if they die in the snow, or migrate to other countries" (151–152). The introduction of Holden Caulfield from Salinger's novel is a major modulation to the narrative. It represents an uncanny postmodernist device reminiscent of historiographic metafiction, except that here it is not a real historical personage who is incorporated into the fictional account (say in the manner of the film *Forrest Gump*), but a real fictional personage from another literary text who is inserted into a completely different text and context. It is the repetition of Holden's signature question from *Catcher in the Rye* that serves to distinguish him from every other fictional character in literary history.[15] Though *Broken Glass* is firmly set in the context of the Congo, the novel's lack of punctuation and its effervescent intertextuality place it at an interface with the universe of world literature, also making it liminal in key dimensions of its narrative structure. What we might take for hybridity or cosmopolitanism should also be tempered by the fact that the stories Broken Glass tells us are mired in a palpable sense of malaise and scatological decay; references to urine (there is a hilarious pissing competition on display in the text), feces (Broken Glass is at one point forced to pick up his own excrement), and sex (several times) situate the text as a carnivalesque novel quite different from the cosmopolitan offerings of a Rushdie, a Márquez, or a Coetzee.

NoViolet Bulawayo's novel is, on the other hand, divided into two sections, with the first being set in the ironically named slum district of Paradise in Zimbabwe and the second in Kalamazoo, "Destroyedmichygen," in the United States.[16] The novel is narrated entirely from the childhood perspective of Darling, who as a 10-year-old plays with her friends in the slum Paradise before moving as a 14-year-old to the United States. The first part of the novel, a celebration of childhood innocence, provides us with an inventory of maledictions produced either directly or indirectly by the heartless political regime of her native Zimbabwe: childhood pregnancy, rabid political violence, unscrupulous religious leaders, AIDS, insensitive camera-wielding NGOs, and hunger. Plenty of it. And yet we also find that Darling's sojourn in the United States brings only ambiguous relief, for it is a country where the anxieties of illegal migration means that the life of migrants from all over the world is conducted through fugitive identities and furtive nostalgias. The chapter titled "How They Lived" is an elegiac detailing of the diasporic life cycle of migrants, filled with inexorable loss, bewilderment, and lamentation. Like Mabanckou, Bulawayo's novel is not easily reducible to either pole of Jeyifo's nomenclature but has to be seen as incorporating both in a heady new arrangement.

Implicit also to Jeyifo's propositions is the relationship between national and post-national allegories. This is not entirely accidental, since it is the nation-state that provides the readiest template for understanding the postcolonial novel, even in its diasporic and transnational iterations. The sometimes violent birth of nations following colonialism (we think here of India and Pakistan, Algeria and Angola) and the general euphoria produced from the initial feeling of being freed from the shackles of colonialism served to install an idea of the nation-state as being epochal, guaranteeing that it provided the preferred horizon for elaborating social, political, and cultural history that the postcolonial novel then refracted. It is in part this epochality that leads to Jeyifo's proleptic postcolonialism. However this was in no small part because the epochality of the nation took shape under the aegis of a decolonization process that then succeeded in elevating the struggles and sacrifices of political elites against colonialism to the level of an ontological necessity and thereby projected them as the privileged subjects of representation. As Anthony Kwame Appiah points out in the context of African literature, the early novels after decolonization came to reflect the recapitulation of "the classic gestures of nation-formation in the domain of culture."[17] And even with the sharp critiques of postcolonial nation-states that were later to be found in the works of Ngugi wa Thiongo, Ben Okri, Junot Díaz, Kiran Desai, Aravind Adiga, and others, the critiques served only as variations on the themes of nation and narration that were well grounded in postcolonial literary history. This is not to say that other themes were not present in the literature, but that somehow what Frederic Jameson came to call the national allegory has remained a central pivot of the postcolonial novel.[18] Even with Salman Rushdie, whom Jeyifo places firmly within the interstitial category of postcoloniality, there is a sense from his work that the nation-state performs the function of a performative epochality and that it is the oscillation between its repeated affirmations and its dissolution by way of heightened narrative experimentations that makes him appear as an exemplary *griot* of the Indian condition, even if he is in fact writing from its disenchanted postcolonial diaspora.[19] In elaborating a complex diasporic and transnational aesthetic in the course of his career, Rushdie has maintained a long-standing interest in moments of epochality as a creative inspiration for his best writing, whether this was the birth of India in *Midnight's Children*, of Pakistan in *Shame*, or of Islam in *The Satanic Verses*. However, after the infamous fatwa of 1989 Rushdie turned decisively away from the trope of the epochal, nation-state-inflected or otherwise. He deploys a somewhat attenuated form of it in *The Moor's Last Sigh* and by *The Ground Beneath Her Feet* has abandoned the trope altogether. *Fury*, *Shalimar the Clown*, and *The Enchantress of Florence* have nothing epochal in them, but his latest, *Luka and the Fire of Life*, reprises the terrific storytelling for young adults he showed himself a master of twenty years earlier in *Haroun and the Sea of Stories*.

As Yoon Sun Lee points out in Chapter 8, novels of diaspora help to put another inflection on the epochality of the nation-state. Postcolonial novels of diaspora insist on seeing the nation-state as only one vector for understanding societies and the cultures that they produce. Rather, the emphasis is on the multifaceted character of identities that are stretched over transnational borderlands, and the concomitant opportunities and pitfalls that they produce for understanding such identities in the first place. Making central the rubric of diaspora, Lee's chapter discusses some common themes that constitute a singular genre out of which characters in the novels are linked to disparate literary, linguistic, and political histories across the once-imperial world.

From a completely different perspective, it can also be shown that the decolonization project and the postcolonial nation-states that were its direct products also harboured implicitly privileged values of able-bodiedness and certain sexual and gender hierarchies. The able-bodied character was assumed as the focal point of narration, while those with impairments or disabilities were considered either anomalous or otherwise peripheral. In Chapter 6, Clare Barker inverts this template by arguing for the centrality of disabled characters to the postcolonial national allegory in the first place. Through readings of Salman Rushdie's *Shame,* in which the brain-damaged Sufiya Zinobia Shakil embodies the "shame" of Pakistan's violent origins, and Kate Grenville's *Lilian's Story,* in which the protagonist's journey through the mental health system is chronicled in tandem with Australia's twentieth-century history, she shows among other things how the interaction between normate and disabled embodiments come to define the essentially unstable and problematic nature of the postcolonial nation-state.[20] Barker also explores the ways in which disabled characters telescope material narratives of violence, corruption and impoverishment in contexts of decolonization and resistance, with a range of examples from Ngũgĩ's *A Grain of Wheat* and *Petals of Blood,* V. S. Naipaul's *Guerrillas,* and J. M. Coetzee's *Foe* being used to show how the postcolonial novel mobilizes disability to address questions of voice, self-representation, and agency that are so fundamental to many such novels. In Chapter 7, on the other hand, Eve Kosofsky Sedgwick's *Between Men* is invoked by Evan Mwangi to read sexuality as an important signifier of power relations that interacts with other variable power asymmetries to define historically situated modes of representation of both sexuality and gender within the postcolonial novel. In both chapters the novelistic representations of the postcolonial nation-state are no longer interpreted as just emblematic of national allegories but rather the crucibles within which social hierarchies are situated, critiqued, and reimagined.

Following the global popularity of magical realist novels from the boom period of Latin American writing in the 1960s, the genre was taken as the signature genre of the global south. That this genre drew liberally from traditions of folklore, myth, and fantasy to infuse its brand of literary representation and pose a challenge to existing Western hegemonic forms of realism was generally celebrated. Zoe Norridge shows in Chapter 4, however, that this celebration ignored a major dimension of the representational protocols of magical realism, namely the fact that the so-called "real" itself has always been mediated in the postcolonial novel. She argues that while the postcolonial novel is interested in a corresponding referent in reality – *real* societies, geographies, political regimes, and histories – it is also wary of taking for granted any possibility that such a relationship might be established without being framed through individual and group subjectivities, colored with prejudice, prevailing ideologies, and also alternative means of representation. Thus she suggests a dialectical relationship between enchantment and realism in both the realist and magical realist novels that she discusses.

If realism has been the source of extensive experimentation, then so has also been the representation of the natural environment. This last point has not been prominent in commentaries on the postcolonial novel until the rise of ecocritical theories in the last decade or so. Chapter 5 provides a corrective to this lacuna by a rich ecocritical account of representations of nature and the environment in the postcolonial novel. Anthony Carrigan explores how texts produced in relation to diverse cultural and geographical locations in the period following World War II refract pressing environmental issues such as the relationship between development and urbanization, land and sea rights, and the dynamic links between nonhuman animals, disaster, waste, and ecological imperialism. At the heart of his chapter is a focus on the ways in which postcolonial novels depict power relations as environmentally embedded while at the same time presenting alternative narratives of space and place that dramatize the tensions associated with decolonizing nature in an era of rampant globalization.

The transition from traditional societies depicted in famous works by Chinua Achebe and Raja Rao has come alongside a more general depiction of postcolonial societies as harnessed to the fate of urbanization and modernity. As Rashmi Varma shows in Chapter 11, a central question in the postcolonial novel concerns the city's emergence as a powerful signifier of relations of colonial rule, and of urbanism as key to the colonial project, such that the metropolitan city of the colonial world became the exemplary model of modernist urbanity everywhere. At the same time, she argues, such a modular view ran counter to the real ways in which notions of center and periphery were scattered, twisted, and reconstituted by contestations with, and transformations of, the imperial project, and the centrality of the city within it, leading to literary representations of alternative modernities in which the city served as crucible, hub, and switchboard for the reconstitution of identities. Undergirding representations of the city in postcolonial novels has also been latent ideas of space and space-making. For Robert

Zacharias (Chapter 12), this has been due to the fact that linguistic, cultural, and geographical displacements that characterized the colonial experience and its aftermath have served to focalize the postcolonial novel on the constitution and contestation of space as a primary vector of interest. Hence Zacharias's series of questions that end with perhaps the most important one: How might a consideration of postcolonialism's inherent spatiality help us to better understand novels of the postcolonial condition?

With chapters on itineraries of the sublime and crime fiction, the *Companion* also incorporates themes that have rarely attracted sustained attention in discussions of the postcolonial novel. To Philip Dickinson (Chapter 9) the attempts of the postcolonial novel to articulate visions of nation, place, landscape, and even time have been irreducibly bound up with the sublime as an aesthetic discourse. This irreducible relation can most obviously be seen in the early postcolonial novels of Chinua Achebe and Ngũgĩ wa Thiong'o, in which we see a rejection of the sublime representation of a generalized African continent associated with the work of Joseph Conrad. But he also shows how the sublime has also been a resource for the postcolonial novel, particularly as a way of articulating ideas of historical time and memory, sovereignty and community, serving to expose a diversity of representational politics in writers as different as David Malouf, J. M. Coetzee, and Jamaica Kincaid, among others. That we might relate to questions of the sublime the general issue of epistemology is to be seen if we read Dickinson's chapter alongside the one by Stephen Knight, Chapter 10. As Knight adroitly shows, as a genre crime fiction developed when older narratives showing rural crimes identified by local knowledge or sometimes Christian guilt were felt out of date, and a professional investigator was required to trace credibly the deceptive threats to property and life among the teeming masses of the modern city. This also launches new models of veridical procedures that also come to challenge established ways of understanding the relationship between the obvious and the concealed. Implicit in Knight's argument is that the entire apparatus of verification exposed in postcolonial crime fiction foregrounds entangled questions about process and epistemology, but in ways that link firmly with some of the fraught concerns of representation that remain central to the postcolonial sublime, magical realism, representations of nature, and the other fraught dimensions of the postcolonial novel demonstrated in this volume.

Note on Citations and Dates of Publication

As a general rule, the dates for the publication of literary texts have not been provided against their titles except in instances where they were the direct subjects of sustained discussion. In such instances the citations to the relevant texts are provided in the endnotes to the individual chapter. There are two exceptions to this rule, however. The first exception has to do with reference to texts published before 1900, where the dates provide a significant historical dimension to the argument contained within the relevant chapter. This is the case with Chapter 2, on the colonial novel, where the dates Tim Watson provides for pre-1900 colonial novels establish an important historical template for the later parts of his discussion. Chapter 10, on postcolonial crime fiction, is also excluded from this general rule. In his case the rationale for exclusion is the fact that unlike in the other chapters, which tend to share a common and thus repeated corpus of literary references, the crime novels Stephen Knight discusses are rarely cited in discussions of postcolonial literature. His corpus of novels is completely distinct within the field and requires a different kind of treatment.

Notes

1 Dorothy Hale, *The Novel: An Anthology of Criticism and Theory 1900–2000* (New York: Blackwell, 2006), p. 2.
2 Frank Kermode, *The Sense of an Ending: Studies in the Theory of Fiction*, 2nd ed. (Oxford: Oxford University Press, 2003).
3 See, for example, Ramón Grosfoguel, "World-System Analysis and Postcolonial Studies: A Call for a Dialogue from the "Coloniality of Power" Approach," eds. Revanthi Krishnaswamy and John C. Hawley, *The Post-Colonial and the Global*, (Durham, NC: Duke University Press, 2007), pp. 94–104; Anibal Quijano and Immanuel Wallerstein, "Americanity as a Concept, or The Americas in the Modern World-System," *International Journal of Social Sciences* (1992), pp. 134–58; Walter Mignolo, *Local Histories/Global Designs: Essays on the Coloniality of Power, Subaltern Knowledges, and Border Thinking*, (Princeton, NJ: Princeton University, 2000), Gareth Griffiths, "Postcolonialism and Travel Writing," and Elisabeth Mudimbe-Boyi, "Missionary Writing and Postcolonialism," both in ed. Ato Quayson, *The Cambridge History of Postcolonial Literature*, Vol. 1, (Cambridge: Cambridge University Press, 2012), pp. 58–80 and 81–107, respectively.
4 On postcolonial responses to the Western canon, see Ankhi Mukherjee's fine recent book *What is a Classic?* (Stanford, CA: Stanford University Press, 2013).
5 On current definitions of postcolonialism that take account of the complex history of the term, see Neil Lazarus, "Introducing Postcolonial Studies," *The Cambridge Companion to Postcolonial Literary Studies*, ed. Neil Lazarus (Cambridge: Cambridge University Press, 2004), pp. 1–18, Ato Quayson, "Introduction: Postcolonial Literature in a Changing Historical Frame," ed. Ato Quayson, *The Cambridge History of Postcolonial Literature*, Vol. 1 (Cambridge: Cambridge University Press, 2012), pp. 3–29, and Graham Huggan, "Introduction: Postcolonialism and Revolution," in ed. Graham Huggan, *The Oxford Handbook of Postcolonial Studies* (Oxford: Oxford University Press, 2013), pp. 1–28.

6 See especially Moretti, "Conjectures on World Literature," *New Left Review* 1 (2002), pp. 54–68 and also *Distant Reading* (London: Verso, 2013), Mario J. Valdes, "Re-thinking the History of Literary History," in *Rethinking Literary History: A Dialogue on Theory* (Oxford: Oxford University Press, 2002), pp. 63–115, and the many works of Edward Said.

7 For a broader account of these new postcolonial theoretical inflections on the question of context, see Ato Quayson, "The Sighs of History: Postcolonial Debris and the Question of (Literary) History," *New Literary History* 43.2 (2012), pp. 359–370.

8 See Arjun Appadurai, *Modernity at Large* (Minneapolis: Minnesota University Press, 1996); Dipesh Chakrabarty, *Provincializing Europe: Postcolonial Thought and Historical Difference* (Princeton, NJ: Princeton University Press, 2000); Ann Laura Stoler, *Race and the Education of Desire: Foucault's History of Sexuality and the Colonial Order of Things* (Durham, NC: Duke University Press, 1995); Mary Louise Pratt, *Imperial Eyes: Travel Writing and Transculturation* (London: Routledge, 1992); and Achille Mbembe, *On the Postcolony* (Berkeley: California University Press, 2000). We should also not forget the landmark effect on the human sciences of James Clifford and George Marcus's *Writing Culture: The Poetics and Politics of Ethnography* (Berkeley: University of California Press, 1986). This edited collection, coinciding as it did with the rise of postcolonial studies, was to alter the terms by which other cultures were represented in anthropology, further leading to a new interest in how such others represented themselves and thus lending a new salience to postcolonial literature in humanities curricula all over the world.

9 Biodun Jeyifo, "For Chinua Achebe: The Resilience of Obierika," in eds. Kirsten Holst Petersen and Anna Rutherford, *Chinua Achebe: A Celebration* (Oxford: Heinemann), pp. 51–70.

10 Chinua Achebe, "The Novelist as Teacher," eds. Tejumola Olaniyan and Ato Quayson, *African Literary Criticism and Theory: An Anthology of Exploration* (New York: Blackwell, 2007), pp. 103–6.

11 Bill Ashcroft, Gareth Griffiths, and Helen Tiffin, *The Empire Writes Back: Theory and Practice in Post-Colonial Literatures* (London: Routledge, 1989).

12 Neil Lazarus, *Resistance in Postcolonial African Fiction* (New Haven, CT: Yale University Press, 1990).

13 Biodun Jeyifo, "For Chinua Achebe," pp. 53–4

14 Alain Mabanckou, *Broken Glass*, trans. Helen Stevenson (New York: Soft Skull Press, 2010).

15 Linda Hutcheon, "Historiographic Metafiction: Parody and the Intertexts of History," in eds. P. O'Donnell and Robert Con Davis, *Intertextuality and Contemporary American Fiction* (Baltimore, MD: Johns Hopkins University Press, 1989), pp. 3–32.

16 NoViolet Bulawayo, *We Need New Names* (New York: Back Bay Books, 2014).

17 Anthony K. Appiah, *In My Father's House: Africa in the Philosophy of Culture* (London: Methuen, 1992), p. 98.

18 For Frederic Jameson's highly insightful yet controversial take on this question, see his "Third World Literature in the Era of Multinational Capitalism," *Social Text* 15 (1986), pp. 65–88. The debates on this essay are still ongoing, but perhaps the most trenchant is the response of Aijaz Ahmad's "Jameson's Rhetoric

of Otherness and the 'National Allegory,'" in *In Theory: Classes, Nations, Literatures* (London: Verso, 1992), pp. 95–122.

19 On the differences between the old and new Indian diasporas from a literary-historical perspective, see Vijay Mishra, "The Diasporic Imaginary: Theorizing the Indian Diaspora," *Textual Practice* 10.3 (2008), pp. 421–47.

20 The term "normate" is a key concept in disability studies first put forward by Rosemarie Garland Thomson in *Extraordinary Bodies: Figuring Disability in American Literature and Culture* (New York: Columbia University Press, 1997).

2

TIM WATSON
University of Miami

The Colonial Novel

It could be argued that the novel in English, from its very beginnings, has been "colonial" through and through. It is not mere temporal coincidence that the novel form, whether we trace its origins in English to Bunyan's *Pilgrim's Progress* (1678), Behn's *Oroonoko* (1688), or Defoe's *Robinson Crusoe* (1719), developed, spread, and flourished in conjunction with the rise of the British Empire from the seventeenth-century onward. The historical shifts that enabled the novel to grow and attract readers were the same ones that allowed England, and subsequently Britain, to conquer and settle large portions of the world: an emphasis on the individual as a source of value and initiative; the growth of long-distance commerce and a shift away from feudal relations; on-the-spot observation, data collection, and empiricism; and a marked and sustained rise in social and geographical mobility, coupled with new forms of political domination such as chattel slavery. As Edward Said says in the introduction to *Culture and Imperialism*, the novel was "immensely important in the formation of imperial attitudes, references, and experiences ... [it was] *the* aesthetic object whose connection to the expanding societies of Britain and France is particularly interesting to study."[1] The ever-expanding corpus of scholarship illuminating the colonial facets of what appears on the surface to be the most resolutely English fictions can be taken as evidence of the truth of Said's claim. We would be hard pressed to find a significant eighteenth- or nineteenth-century novel in English that has not at this point been subjected to a postcolonial reading and thereby transformed into a colonial novel. Moreover, numerous scholars have demonstrated the extent to which literary education, including the study of the novel, functioned effectively throughout the empire as a form of social control, inculcating the values of the colonizer via a tendentious version of its literary history: in this respect, too, novels in English were all potentially colonial novels.[2]

However, despite the plausible proposition that "the novel" and "the colonial novel" are in the final analysis synonymous terms, for the purposes

15

of this chapter I will retain a more restricted sense of the latter term. In a volume devoted to the postcolonial novel in English – and in keeping with the revisionary impulse behind the analyses of pre-1900 fiction carried out by postcolonial scholars – it makes sense to define the phrase "colonial novel" proleptically: novels that, directly or indirectly, postcolonial fiction in English has made use of, whether through negation, imitation, negotiation, or appropriation. At one extreme, this would include canonical novels that have been explicitly rewritten or complemented by postcolonial writers, as Coetzee's *Foe* reworks Defoe's *Robinson Crusoe*, Rhys's *Wide Sargasso Sea* functions as a kind of prequel to Brontë's *Jane Eyre*, or Achebe's *Things Fall Apart* acts as a riposte to Conrad's *Heart of Darkness*. At the other end of the spectrum, this idea of the colonial novel would include a host of novels, from the mid-eighteenth century to the mid-twentieth century, that set out to describe, define, or display colonial people and places in relation to – and in contrast to – English ones. This is the colonial novel that is defined in opposition to the English novel, of which it nevertheless remains a part. Often these novels are less well known today, suffering from what E. P. Thompson famously called (referring to ordinary people who did not easily fit into the grand historical narrative of progress) the "enormous condescension of posterity."[3] I want to argue in this chapter, however, that these national tales, historical novels, gothic melodramas, and the like left their lasting imprint not only on the development of the English novel during the age of empire, but on the postcolonial novel that followed in its wake. In the first half of the chapter I will trace the development of this line of fiction in the period before the zenith of the British Empire in the late nineteenth century, focusing in particular on the category of the "creole" that turns out to be crucial for so many of these novels. In the second half of the chapter, I turn to some of the key late nineteenth- and early twentieth-century colonial novels, by Schreiner, Conrad, Forster, Rhys, Greene, and others, that have had a more visible impact on postcolonial fiction in English.

Creole Fictions

In her influential book *Bardic Nationalism*, Katie Trumpener made a powerful and convincing case for the importance of novels produced in and about Britain's internal colonies, Wales, Scotland, and Ireland, for the development of the English novel more generally. In her literary history of the novel in English, folk and popular customs that were in danger of disappearing in the British peripheries in the eighteenth century were salvaged in Welsh, Irish, and Scottish literary antiquarianism in the 1770s and 1780s, and then were reformulated and revived once again in the new national tales and historical novels in the first decades of the nineteenth century; from there, they were "transported out ... into the colonies of the new British Empire, where they form the primary models for early colonial fiction ... [in] Canada, Australia, and British India."[4] These novels – gothic tales of terror, romantic narratives of primitive but intriguing colonial subjects, and national surveys of colonial social relations – were relegated to the margins of the critical consensus of the history of the English novel, which had, since Ian Watt's *The Rise of the Novel*, emphasized realism and the representation of English social facts.[5] Trumpener put them back at the heart of Anglophone literary history, and in the process demonstrated the influence of the colonial novel on the English novel, from the periphery to the center.

As she says, the late eighteenth- and early nineteenth-century novel in English was "obsessed with the formal problem of how to represent the differences between European and non-European cultures (the mental, geographical, and political distances that separate them, their incommensurability and simultaneity) and the political problem of how to use the vantage point and perspective of the colonies to reassess and criticize British society."[6] One figure in particular embodies this paradox that European and non-European places and people were both incommensurable and simultaneous, totally different and yet uncannily linked: the figure of the creole. Ironically, however, this figure is all but absent from Trumpener's critical history, which mostly bypasses the West Indies and the American colonies before U.S. independence, in favor of a model of diffusion that begins in the British peripheries around the time of the end of the so-called First British Empire and travels outward from there to the future Dominions and to India in the nineteenth century; it is a model, in other words, that takes its framework from the historical endpoint of the empire and projects it back in time. Despite the immensely useful conceptual and retrieval work carried out by Trumpener, I want to supplement her model with one that brings the early conquests and settlements of the Americas back into the early history of the colonial novel. I argue here no figure better embodies the ambiguities of the early novel form than the American creole.

To begin with, at least, the creole in the English novel is a Briton born in the Americas, or raised there from childhood – although the flexibility and malleability of the category are indicated by the fact that we could call Robinson Crusoe, one of the earliest creole figures in fiction, who does not arrive in the New World until he is an adult, and whose transformation there is a kind of symbolic rebirth rather than a biological one. The American environment – its physical geography and its social formation, or lack thereof – has a powerful shaping effect: creoles are *different*. But if creoles are figures of social and geographical mobility and change, they are also signs of the slipperiness of the very classification schemes of which they are a part: every Briton is potentially a creole, and confusion about how long a residence in the Americas is necessary for creolization to occur is a common feature of fiction in English of this period. How many Caribbean voyages and adventures does Tom Cringle have to take before he is a creole? For that matter, how many years residence in the West Indies are required for Michael Scott, the author of *Tom Cringle's Log*, one of the most popular of all nineteenth-century novels in English, to be classified as a creole novelist? Underlying the confusion is the question: how can you tell the difference between a Briton and a creole? And lying behind that question – and making this discussion more immediately relevant to the status of the postcolonial novel – is the recognition that the novel in the age of commercial empire must deal with a broader range of characters and peoples than Englishmen and-women. If the novel is the privileged space for working out "the formal problem of how to represent the differences between European and non-European cultures," as Trumpener argues, then the question of difference between Briton and creole is at the same time a question of the difference – or potential sameness – of Briton and "Coromantee" (Akan), Briton and Cherokee, and so forth. The definition of the word "creole" in English almost from the beginning allowed it to be applied to nonwhite people – "creole slaves" or "creole Negroes" were relatively common terms. As the nineteenth century went on, the increasingly common ascription of racial ambiguity or miscegenation to the category of the creole (as in the figure of Bertha imprisoned in the attic in *Jane Eyre*) is an indication of the ambiguity of the term itself when it came to social and racial inclusiveness.[7] As I will argue, elements of that ambiguity surface in earlier creole fictions as well, and make them intriguing, albeit distant, forebears of the postcolonial novels that must similarly grapple with questions of ethnic and racial difference in the forging of new societies in the wake of colonial rule.

In his groundbreaking book *Imagined Communities*, as is well known by now, Benedict Anderson tied one specific form of modern commerce, what he called "print capitalism," to the emergence of nationalism and concepts of a national community; it was only when readers of newspapers and novels could imagine themselves as part of a community of other readers similarly engaged that the modern form of nationalism came into existence, he argued.[8] It is less well remembered, however, that Anderson identified this process as beginning not in Europe but in the eighteenth-century Americas, where those he termed "creole pioneers" were printing and reading newspapers, chafing at the restrictions imposed on them from the imperial centers in Madrid, London, and Paris, and beginning to turn colonial administrative units into potential nation-states – a process that led ultimately to the wars of independence in the western hemisphere of the late eighteenth and early nineteenth centuries. Interestingly, in this chapter of his book Anderson barely mentions fiction, but an argument could be made that creole novels are the missing piece of the puzzle to supplement both Trumpener's and Anderson's influential accounts of the rise of the novel. Beginning with Aphra Behn's *Oroonoko*, written after the author's extended stay in Surinam, a colony newly captured by the English from the Dutch, a steady stream of novels portrayed the New World as a place of European reinvention, of tropical danger, of slavery and freedom, and of new forms of social organization. In what follows I will be discussing collectively novels that are ordinarily classified separately, as "American" or "British," whereas I think the category of the creole enables us to think about a body of fiction that addresses similar questions across colonial and national borders. "American" novelists, most obviously after independence, rejected the category of the creole as they sought to create a noncolonial culture; as critic Sean Goudie and others have convincingly argued, however, it makes good sense for historical and critical reasons to use the term "creole" to describe the cultural configuration of the early U.S. republic, and it reminds us of the profound links between the mainland American colonies and the West Indies, links that were altered but by no means broken by the American Revolution at the end of the eighteenth century.[9]

Novels, then, like Edward Bancroft's *The History of Charles Wentworth* (1765), Susanna Rowson's *Charlotte Temple* (1791), St. John de Crèvecoeur's *Letters from an American Farmer* (1782), and Charles Brockden Brown's *Wieland* (1798) work to create and describe new colonial spaces by tinkering with the existing forms of the novel: the gothic (Brown), the sentimental (Rowson), the picaresque (Bancroft), the epistolary (Crèvecoeur), and so forth. Of course, these novels do not represent American colonies in uniform ways. In some, the New World is a venue for commercial success and personal advancement (Bancroft), while in others it is a place of violence and death (Rowson); in some the emphasis is on the creation of new, pastoral settlements (Crèvecoeur), while in others an apparently recognizable English-style estate is in fact a place of instability and fear (Brown). Likewise, novels of the Americas are diverse in their modes of address, from the informational/didactic (Bancroft, Crèvecoeur) to the sentimental/affective (Rowson, Brown). In their heterogeneity and expansiveness, they help to unsettle and rework the English novel more generally, as evidenced perhaps most clearly by the recurring, destabilizing figure in metropolitan fiction of the West Indian (white) Creole who is caricatured as a foolish provincial or an immoral *nouveau riche*: Vincent, the irresponsible suitor of the

eponymous heroine in Maria Edgeworth's *Belinda* (1801), for example, or
Rhoda Swartz in William Thackeray's *Vanity Fair* (1848).

Sometimes, though, peregrinations within the novel form make it hard to
decide where the dividing line between settler and native, British and Creole
ought to be drawn. In John Galt's *Bogle Corbet; or, The Emigrants* (1831),
for example, the eponymous protagonist is born in Jamaica (therefore a
creole), is orphaned at a very young age and sent to Scotland, where he
receives his education and apprenticeship (therefore British, although, significantly, not English), before he travels as an adult to the West Indies, back
to Scotland, and finally to Canada. In his author's preface, Galt downplays
the comic and entertainment aspects of the novel in order to highlight its
informational and didactic qualities: "The object of this work has been to
give expression to the probable feelings of a character upon whom the
commercial circumstances of the age have had their natural effects, and to
show what a person of ordinarily genteel habits has really to expect in
emigrating to Canada."[10] The composite creole (by birth) and Briton (by
education) becomes an unmarked "character," simultaneously ordinary and
genteel; the novel suggests that neither birth (Jamaica) nor teenage apprenticeship (Glasgow) nor adult experiences (Jamaica and Canada) is sufficient
by itself to create a "character." The fact that the category of the creole
seems to embody both the effects of birthplace (roots) and the effects of
travel to a new environment (routes) serves to make it a potential synonym
for "character," the sine qua non of the novel (as opposed to the allegorical
or typical figure of the epic). The creole is the face of the modern world, then,
the best representative of the "commercial circumstances of the age."

This dynamic, which we might call the tension between settlement and
unsettlement, is of course present in many early novels in English, whether
they are set in the Americas, other colonial spaces, or England itself. (A quick
analysis of any year of the useful database *British Fiction, 1800–1829* will
show that the bulk of early nineteenth-century fiction published in Britain
was not set in a contemporary England, but rather in the colonies or British
peripheries; in the rest of Europe, especially Italy, France, and Spain; or in
medieval or early modern England.)[11] Georg Lukács, in *The Theory of the
Novel*, suggests that the dynamic energy, heterogeneity, and mobility of the
novel has to be kept in check to forestall it spinning off into what he calls,
following Hegel, "bad infinity": a potentially endless and formless chain of
cause-and-effect links.[12] One way to ward off this possibility is to tie the
novel to the plot of biography, hence the *Bildungsroman*, which has typically
linked, via analogy, metonymy, or allegory, the development of the individual character to the progress of the community, the region, or the nation.
The early, unsettled, but energetic stage of the (usually male) character's life

is reined in eventually in a domestic settlement that validates family and property and brings stability to the community: hence, the ubiquitous marriage plot.

Creole novels of the Americas, however, present a particular challenge to this model. Whereas the antiquarian novels of the British peripheries documented and ambivalently celebrated folk life, and novels of English life (such as those of Jane Austen) could be set in the context of more or less stable communities facing new challenges, the creole novel of the Americas perpetrated the fiction that communities were being created out of nothing: the enslaved Africans and their descendants, and the indigenous Native populations, could not easily be presented as the source of quaint folk customs or of an ancient civilization. (In this respect, novels of the New World tended to be quite different from the "Oriental tales" that characterized the initial literary representations of British incursions into India and the Indian Ocean territories, which evinced genuine, if condescending, interest in the cultures and customs of the people they encountered and were forced to negotiate with there.) And yet while white creoles in the Caribbean and North America, dependent for their livelihood on the violent expropriation of native land and the brutal exploitation of enslaved Africans, tended to be thoroughgoing racists, committed to ideas of white superiority, the fiction that they wrote, or that was written by visitors or long-term residents with extensive first-hand knowledge of the region, could not so easily dismiss the world the enslaved made, or the world of the indigenous Americans that was being pushed aside by Anglophone settlement. In novels such as James Fenimore Cooper's *The Pioneers* (1823), Cynric Williams's *Hamel, the Obeah Man* (1827), and E. L. Joseph's *Warner Arundell* (1838), the category of the creole expands to include, however ambivalently and hesitantly, non-European colonial residents.

While the history of British settlement and conquest in the Caribbean and North America is obviously somewhat different from that of the Spanish to the south, Benedict Anderson's question in his chapter on the "creole pioneers" in *Imagined Communities* is pertinent here: "Why was it precisely *creole* communities that developed so early conceptions of their nationness – *well before most of Europe*? Why did such colonial provinces, usually containing large, oppressed, non-Spanish-speaking populations, produce creoles who consciously redefined these populations as fellow-nationals?"[13] To put the question this way is of course to privilege creole elites in the formation of national identity, but when it comes to the role that fiction played in that formation this is hardly surprising, since such novels were written by, and largely read by, exactly this group. What is surprising, rather, is the appearance of a black creole protagonist such as Hamel, who leads the large-scale slave revolt that dominates the second half of the novel that bears his name.

The novel is patently, sometimes ludicrously, on the side of the slave-owners, but the pressure to represent Jamaica as a place under threat from English outsiders (in this case Roland, an evil Methodist missionary), and to validate the status of the white creole elite, leads the novel to include its black and brown characters in ways that cannot be reduced to paternalist condescension. In rejecting the methods and customs of what the white creole planter Guthrie calls the "old stupid world," the novel ends up, despite its intentions, at least partially validating the experiences and even some of the grievances of the enslaved Jamaicans.[14] Likewise, the complicated transatlantic and intra-Caribbean travels of the eponymous hero of *Warner Arundell* are matched by the complex, heterogeneous Caribbean communities he passes through and eventually, in Trinidad, settles in as a doctor: racial mixing and a degree of social fluidity are accepted as normal in the novel. In *The Pioneers*, as in all the Leatherstocking tales, Cooper follows Walter Scott's model in *Waverley* and celebrates the ways of the all but vanished local people (for Scott, the Highlanders, for Cooper, the Mohegan). While Natty Bumppo embodies the utopian wish fulfillment of the American who wants to symbolically align him- or herself with indigeneity and with the land, Chingachgook, the last of the Mohegan, represents a more accurate record of cultural hybridity, even if Cooper's language follows the customary hierarchies of the whites: "from his long association with the white men," Chingachgook possesses "habits" that are "a mixture of the civilized and savage states."[15] Just as Anderson's creole pioneers have to include nonelite, nonwhite, non-Spanish-speaking residents in their creation of new nations in the southern half of the hemisphere, much of the Anglophone fiction that we can call "creole novels" from the Caribbean and North America before the middle of the nineteenth century is forced – often against the grain – to include the enslaved and indigenous populations who in the political, legal, and military world were being systematically excluded and worse.

Such novels certainly do not offer the kind of wide-ranging critique of imperial rule and methods that Siraj Ahmed, for instance, sees in the eighteenth- and early nineteenth-century novels in English that focus on India.[16] But it is my argument here that these creole novels of the Americas, while politically unpalatable from the perspective of twentieth-century antiracism and anticolonialism, in fact help to lay the groundwork for the flourishing of the anticolonial and postcolonial novels from the 1950s onward. Because they tried – but, albeit in interesting ways, failed – to imagine and represent the settlement and creation of a new colonial/national society that would be a radical break from the past, they were formally analogous to the first wave of anticolonial and postcolonial fiction that sought to shed its links to the British political, educational, and cultural system. Likewise, in a comparison that might seem an odd one to make, the British-educated writers who chose the novel in English as the venue for their creative and political thinking were in a structurally similar position to the Caribbean and North American creole writers in the age of revolutions, attached to Britain linguistically and culturally and yet determined to create new literary and political forms in the Americas.

Of course, as an analogy, this holds only up to a certain point. The United States, for instance, was "postcolonial" in the 1780s and 1790s in very different ways than India, say, or Kenya, or Jamaica were in the 1950s and 1960s. Obviously there were enormous structural and political differences between the preemancipation, pre-American Revolution conservative slave-owning creole elites of the late eighteenth/early nineteenth centuries and the anticolonial, mostly leftist nationalist leaders of the twentieth century. Granting these distinctions, however, need not stop us from seeing similarities when it comes to the place of the *novel* in particular (as opposed to other political and cultural forms).

The creole is the ambiguous figure for the process of becoming national, which involves imagining egalitarian, horizontal links connecting diverse groups of people while at the same time creating a classification system and hierarchy that enables one figure (male, white, virtuous) to speak in the name of the others. The novel is an important part of this process, and yet its inability to tie down loose ends, its openness to the contradictory possibilities of new social and psychological forms, ensures that in practice it expands the categories of the creole and the nation beyond the narrow limits it seeks to establish. While hierarchies of race, gender, linguistic group, and social class are asserted and ultimately enforced, the creole novel – and indeed the novel in general – must spend some of its time exploring the horizontal, more egalitarian, metonymic links between people that create the illusion of social density in fiction and to some extent overturn or call into question typical social hierarchies.

In *Hamel, the Obeah Man*, for instance, the white creole hero, Fairfax, is eventually restored to his property and marries his childhood sweetheart, and yet he ends the novel gazing in admiration and disappointment at the receding figure of the real creole hero, Hamel, who has chosen exile over a planter-dominated Jamaica.[17] In the twentieth century, these intersecting horizontal and vertical axes of the novel recur. The writer–intellectual, so often the ambivalent protagonist at the center of the anticolonial/postcolonial novel, at least for the first generation of writers in the 1950s and 1960s, often functions as a link to "the people," a symbol of national awakening and popular consciousness, while at the same time he (the figure is almost always male) represents superior insight and values that go unrecognized, or even punished, by the colonial power and the emerging postcolonial elite. An example would be Obi Okonkwo in Chinua Achebe's *No Longer at Ease*, struggling to overcome the legacies of caste and ethnicity in a new Nigeria but eventually caught up in the corruption that is both a legacy of colonial rule and a harbinger of postcolonial misrule. G., in George Lamming's *In the Castle of My Skin*, is another example: his childhood friendships represent a fraternal Barbados in the making, but his ability to rise through the social hierarchy by his success in the colonial school system eventually forces him into exile in Trinidad, and perhaps subsequently into the same category as the cohort of migrants who make up the travelers to London in Lamming's next novel, *The Emigrants*.

Just as the creole was the ambiguous embodiment of the native-national crossed with the potentially mobile/migrant outsider, the postcolonial intellectual is similarly positioned between a new national belonging and an awareness that this form of social organization, in the context of the novel form, is a colonial legacy that will leave its representative an outsider to the very social relationships it claims to encompass. When postcolonial writers declared their debts to the English novel – or announced their revolutionary difference from it – they did so in terms of the literary giants of the later nineteenth and, especially, the twentieth centuries; however, I want to argue here, their novels quite often end up repeating tropes, figures, and problems first worked through by these late eighteenth- and early nineteenth-century novelists of the Americas. If Anderson's "creole pioneers" of Spanish America are the unacknowledged precursors of nineteenth-century European nationalism, then the creole novels I have been discussing are the unacknowledged forebears of twentieth-century postcolonial fiction. For all the differences of setting, style, and character between the colonial and the postcolonial novel, the dialectic of settlement and unsettlement forms a concrete, albeit deeply buried, link between them. In the second half of this chapter, I turn to a set of novels that are far more explicitly connected to their postcolonial counterparts.

Colonial Modernist Fictions

To focus on the scrappy, critically devalued fictions of the late eighteenth and early nineteenth century and then move directly to the widely acknowledged twentieth-century highlights of the colonial novel might seem a puzzling critical trajectory. What of the great Victorian novels in which "the colonies" figure prominently, whether as places in which personal transformations can occur (for Heathcliff, probably, in *Wuthering Heights*, for example, or for Magwitch and Pip, certainly, in *Great Expectations*), or as sources of objects and people that can transform England, and English-men and-women, as occurs in *Jane Eyre* and *The Moonstone*? What of the steady stream, swelling to a flood toward the end of the nineteenth century, of juvenile fiction, adventure stories, and historical romances set in the colonies, especially southern Africa after the British incursions there, of which H. Rider Haggard's novels (*King Solomon's Mines*, *She*, and so forth) could be considered the epitome? In part, the answer is that many other critics have already magnificently discussed the importance of the colonies and imperialism in nineteenth-century British fiction: Patrick Brantlinger's recent *Victorian Literature and Postcolonial Studies* is a useful recent survey of the major critical developments in the field, in which the key figures are Edward Said, Gauri Viswanathan, Deirdre David, and Brantlinger himself.[18] But the main reason I bypass much of this fiction is that it generally touches only lightly on the complexity of social, cultural, and psychological relations in particular colonies and colonial spaces. While the critical scholarship on colonial references and subtexts in Victorian fiction undermines J. R. Seeley's notorious claim that the British "have conquered and peopled half the world in a fit of absence of mind," it is certainly true that British novelists in the nineteenth century rarely gave their full attention to the specificities of colonial spaces.[19] How much would it have mattered if Pip had achieved his commercial success and moral rehabilitation in Singapore rather than Cairo? Is the "India" to which St. John Rivers tries to persuade Jane Eyre to travel as his wife and helpmeet anything more than a vague idea of non-Christian heat and misogyny? Doesn't the well-known map in *King Solomon's Mines* schematically and allegorically depict a naked woman, waiting to be conquered, rather than a geographical account of any actual place in southern Africa? For more complex representations of and from Britain's colonial dependencies we need to turn to some of the more highly wrought texts of the modernist period, where, ironically, we encounter some of the same thematic questions and formal problems that were widespread in the creole novels I discussed in the first half of this chapter – although of course the answers to these questions and resolutions to these problems were different for the late nineteenth- and early twentieth-century writers.

Jed Esty, for example, in his study of the colonial *Bildungsroman*, suggests that the form survives into the high period of empire but requires significant adaptation; as in the earlier period of commercial/imperial expansion, the biographical form works to mediate and manage the networks linking metropolitan center and provincial-colonial periphery, but now that these networks are at least potentially global rather than intra-British or transatlantic, they test the limits of the form almost to breaking point.[20] Esty points to several key modernist novels in which the psychological and social development of the protagonist is blocked and/or repetitive, leading to hybrid adult-child figures such as Lord Jim (in Joseph Conrad's novel of the same name), Stephen Daedalus (in *Ulysses* and *Portrait of the Artist as a Young Man*), Rachel Vinrace (in Virginia Woolf's early novel *The Voyage Out*), and the eponymous hero in Kipling's *Kim*. But if the customary forms of the novel – like the empire itself – were in crisis, they were still recognizably linked to earlier incarnations and questions. What relationship do colonial characters have to lands and environments of which their ownership or settlement is not well established, or morally suspect, or both? How will colonial society organize itself amongst its diverse peoples and in relation to neighboring regions and to the distant imperial center? Some later colonial novels are explicit about the connections to questions of creolization entailed in such questions.

Olive Schreiner's *The Story of an African Farm* (1883), for example, begins with an epigraph from Alexis de Tocqueville's *Democracy in America* that explicitly connects the "growth of nations" to the development of a child, suggesting, though, that the adult character is molded in infancy: "The entire man is, so to speak, to be seen in the cradle of the child."[21] Tocqueville's passage comes from a chapter on the "origin of the Anglo-Americans," and explains the creation of a unique creole society; Schreiner nods further to this story of the making of Americans by giving her questioning, philosophical character the name Waldo, as a token of the importance of Emerson's writing on her thought. But, as in the Caribbean creole and early American novels that were unable to maintain the myth of a white society created in *terra nullius*, Schreiner begins her novel by placing her characters in the shadow of the ancient rock paintings carried out by the indigenous San ("Bushmen") in the Karoo.

However, where the creole novels of the turn of the nineteenth century were preoccupied with establishing the legitimacy of white settlers as national representatives, the colonial novels of the turn of the twentieth century had more or less accepted the *illegitimacy* of settler elites and colonial rule; the drama lay in how domestic, personal, and social relations would play out in light of that injustice and the simultaneous recognition that the conquerors and settlers had transformed colonial societies in ways that could not be undone. Schreiner's novel is full of white creoles, if we stretch that term beyond its roots in the Americas: ex-Europeans whose genealogical roots are obscured but whose ties to South African land are legally and symbolically tenuous. The marriage plot – with its promise of

26

legally sanctioned, property-owning future generations on the land – is treated either as absurd (Tant' Sannie's union with Piet Vander Walt, or Bonaparte Blenkins' pursuit of Trana) or as oppressive (Lyndall's refusal to marry her lover, which is what makes Schreiner's novel a landmark in feminist fiction). The most thoughtful and sympathetic characters, Lyndall and Waldo, have symbolic rather than sexual or biological kinship with each other, and both are dead by the end of the novel. Yet, if the drama of the illegitimacy of white settlement is the novel's central concern, it nevertheless renders its contemporary black Africans all but invisible; instead, in a formally inventive and disruptive move, Schreiner bestows consciousness on nonhuman animals, Hans the ostrich and Doss the dog, and gives the final narrative point of view to the chickens perching on Waldo's corpse. In some ways, *Story of an African Farm*, if it represents an advance in terms of formal experimentation and feminist politics, actually works less hard than earlier creole novels to solder the various multinational and multiracial segments of society together in an imagined community.

If Schreiner herself, the child of a British mother and a German father, was a creole South African, the best known twentieth-century novels written from the point of view of the imperialists also work through the problems of colonial guilt and violence by sidelining or mythologizing those on the receiving end of British settlement and conquest – although there is often at least one hybrid, Anglicized colonial figure who can serve as a symbolic switch point and potential link to what Frantz Fanon called "the zone of occult instability where the people dwell."[22] In Joseph Conrad's *Lord Jim* (1900), the eponymous hero is the symbol both of the failure of imperial protection (when he abandons the Muslim pilgrims on board the *Patna*) and of the lure and limits of imperial conquest, when he installs himself as de facto ruler of Patusan and finds himself paradoxically "imprisoned within the very freedom of his power."[23] Although Conrad's narrator Marlow claims that Jim becomes part of "the innermost life of the people" (195), the novel as a whole is far more ambivalent about Jim's legacy. He is linked sexually and romantically to the local woman Jewel, but her name reveals the excess of symbolism involved in a relationship that the novel cannot really take seriously. Ultimately – and perhaps this is intended as a hopeful sign – Jim's mark on the land will be a light one after his death. While he offers himself up as a sacrificial victim, in a sense his killing redeems the ineffectual local leader, Doramin, by investing him with the righteous anger of the grieving father, enraged at Jim's role in Doramin's son's death. It is not exactly postcolonial independence that Patusan achieves, but at least the European interlopers, whether well intentioned (Jim) or malign (Brown), are eventually cast out. In the text that marks Marlow's most famous appearance, *Heart of Darkness* (1899), the idea of European settlement is all but abandoned. To explore the rapacity of empire requires the narrative to depict all whites as temporary visitors, clinging to the edge of the African continent in "huts," "offices," and "stations" whose names suggest the idea of commercial transit rather than residence. The only exception is the monstrous Kurtz, who is a modernist reimagining of the figure of the mad creole, turned insane by too intense a connection with the land and people of the colony.

The title of E. M. Forster's *A Passage to India* also suggests imperialism in transit. Although the British have been living in the subcontinent for hundreds of years, they live in completely separate enclaves and fail utterly to understand the Indians with whom they work and, very occasionally, socialize. Forster venerates the idea of friendship between respectable Indians and Britons, but works hard to show its impossibility, mostly neglecting to notice that what makes it untenable is his unacknowledged commitment to a respectability that is itself a product of colonial rule. So Fielding, the British character who scandalizes his bigoted compatriots through his belief in an "interchange" of ideas, thinks that men can "reach one another" in the world through "good will plus culture and intelligence."[24] As in Schreiner's novel, there is a vague sense that Indian life is teeming beyond the purview of the main characters – and perhaps beyond the purview of narrative fiction in English itself. The English-educated Indian, Dr. Aziz, dreams of writing a national poem that will unite Hindus and Muslims, but "the poem ... never got written" (298). Instead, the idea of India gets reduced to a quasi-geological symbol, the Marabar Caves, scene of Adela's fantasy of Aziz's sexual assault, the source of the mystical echo that drives Mrs. Moore to her death. Characters continually announce that India cannot be defined, understood, encompassed, or described; at the same time they are forever summing it up in a word ("a muddle," "a mystery") or even a sound ("Boum"). In the end, the British will be defeated by the land itself, "prehistoric," "far older" even than its ancient cultures (135), a place that produces the caves that, unlike the painted rock walls of Schreiner's Karoo, actively repel human contact: "Some sadhus did once settle in a cave, but they were smoked out" (136), just as the modern characters are all undone by the outing to the caves organized by Aziz.

Twenty years later, at the very end of empire, the colonial policeman Scobie in Graham Greene's *The Heart of the Matter* is a figurative descendant of Fielding, trying in vain to be an ethical person in an unethical environment. Scobie is staying on in the novel's unnamed West African country (modeled on Sierra Leone, where Greene was a spy for the British secret service during World War II), trying to gain "these people's trust and affection."[25] What saves the novel, however, from being just another tale in which the colony and the colonized function only as the setting for the white man's psychological (and in this case spiritual) drama is the way in which it indicates some of the complexity of colonial societies transformed by internal and external migrations and the imposition of British laws. Syrians and Indians are becoming creolized Africans, and the Krio community – called "Creoles" by the British characters in the novel – are long established as a professional-managerial elite who "rule the coast. Clerks in the stores, city council, magistrates, lawyers" (5–6). Although the Krio community remains marginal to the novel, they are in fact a direct link between decolonizing West Africa and the late eighteenth-century rebellions against colonial rule in the Americas, and thus between the creole novels of the Americas I discussed in the first half of the chapter – with their likewise marginal-yet-central non-European figures – and this twentieth-century colonial novel of West Africa. The Krios are the modern descendants of the black "loyalists," enslaved African Americans who were offered freedom by the British to fight on the side of the colonial power during the American Revolution, subsequently transported by the defeated British to Nova Scotia, then to London, and finally to Sierra Leone, where they were established as a model colonial settlement meant to bring "civilization" and Christianity to West Africa. Subsequent settlers who mixed with this group in Sierra Leone included deported Jamaican Maroons and freed Africans taken from slaving ships intercepted by the British navy enforcing the abolition of the transatlantic slave trade after 1807.

Tracking the way in which residential geography maps onto social and political power, the narrator shows how Scobie has been "relegated" from the "main European quarter" to a house "built originally for a Syrian trader," from the windows of which Scobie "looked directly out to sea over a line of Creole houses" (14–15). As the novel goes on, however, its focus progressively narrows, with Scobie's declaration that he "loved" his murdered servant Ali (277) working as a kind of second killing, since Ali's corpse becomes almost literally the vehicle for colonial projection, as Scobie sees "the image of God" (277) in the body, and all the African characters disappear from the remainder of the novel. The intensity of Scobie's spiritual crisis, although presented very differently from that of Kurtz at the end of *Heart of Darkness*, seems to require the erasure of the very people who produced it in the first place.

One colonial novel, however, appears to offer a very different perspective: Rudyard Kipling's *Kim* revels in the heterogeneity and expanse of Indian life, as experienced through the perspective of a thoroughly creolized protagonist, born and raised in the subcontinent, fluent in its languages and customs, "burned black as any native," and yet indubitably white: "Kim was English ... Kim was white."[26] (In fact, however, by birth Kim is Irish, making the narratives of race, nation, creolization, and empire that much more interesting and complicated.) The world of compounds and clubs, the de facto and de jure segregation of Briton and Indian depicted in *Passage to India*, may make the term "creole" an unlikely one to describe an inhabitant of the subcontinent, but Kipling's eponymous child hero comes as close as any character in twentieth-century fiction to reincarnating the hybrid proto-national figures of the turn of the nineteenth century I discussed in the first half of this chapter. A peripatetic orphan adventurer, like Bogle Corbet, Kim "borrowed right- and left-handedly from all the customs of the country he knew and loved" (121). Whereas in Forster, Conrad, and Greene the popular life of India and West Africa hovers off-stage, glimpsed and powerful but disavowed, in Kipling's tale the boy is in the thick of it whenever possible, "thrill[ing] with delight ... [to the] bustling and shouting, the buckling of belts, and beating of bullocks and creaking of wheels, lighting of fires and cooking of food, and new sights at every turn of the approving eye" (121). In the end, however, the description of the dazzling whirligig of a sumptuous, chaotic India functions in the interests of empire. The trains and maps and spy networks of the modern Indian empire are perfectly constructed to make use of Kim's native knowledge and turn it into administrative efficiency, obliterating the supposedly ancient divisions of caste and religion, even incorporating the spiritual wisdom of the Tibetan Buddhist lama, Kim's guide and fellow traveler, into the Great Game. While *Kim* works hard to give the illusion of representing "all India spread out to left and right" (111) from the point of view of the creole insider, in the end it subordinates the "native" elements of its title character to the quasi-aristocratic idea that blood and birth transmit some kind of immutable essence: "Once a Sahib is always a Sahib" (136). The creolized Arabic-Urdu-Hindi-English honorific, however, gives just a hint that this romantic logic of bloodlines cannot be sustained within the world of the novel.

If Kipling's novel is in part a nostalgic homage on the part of the white writer born in the colonies, it has an unlikely, distant cousin in the much grimmer, spare vision of Jean Rhys's *Voyage in the Dark*, first published in 1934 but largely written in the 1920s. For Anna Morgan, born in Dominica in the Caribbean but brought to England by her stepmother Hester after her father's death, London is a bleak, oppressive place where the chill of the weather is exceeded only by the coldness of calculation in what passes for human relationships, especially between men and women. The imperial center is a desperate place for a woman without wealth, where "a girl's clothes cost more than the girl inside them," according to Anna's only real friend, the working-class Englishwoman Maudie.[27] But Anna's nostalgia for the "very beautiful" (52) Caribbean of her childhood is tempered by her recognition that it is the English point of view that really counts – "on the other hand, if England is beautiful, it [the estate of her mother's family]'s not beautiful. It's some other world" (52) – and by the reality of race and class relations in the West Indies, which produces both Anna's primitivist investment in the authenticity of the Caribbean majority – "I wanted to be black, I always wanted to be black" (31) – and its flipside, her casual racism: "the narrow street smelt of niggers and woodsmoke and salt fishcakes fried in lard" (7). Nevertheless, the Caribbean colony is at least potentially a multiracial community, in which Anna has many nonwhite "cousins" (64) and in which her English father after thirty years had become the kind of creole who "didn't see any harm" (64) in Anna giving presents at Christmas to her maternal uncle Bo's children of all races. Moreover, the straightforward equation of English gentility with thoroughgoing racism is explicitly present in the figure of Hester, whose concern to save Anna from cross-racial contamination – "that awful sing-song voice you had! Exactly like a nigger you talked – and still do" (65) – blinds her to the dangers of London life for a single woman and produces the tragedy of the colonial migrant swallowed up by the modern imperial center.

Rhys's fiction, despite the later success of *Wide Sargasso Sea* (her reworking of the Bertha Mason story in *Jane Eyre*), is still rarely acknowledged as an influence on the postcolonial novel, but Anna has many literary analogues in the figures of migrant artists and intellectuals, both women and men, in exile from their homelands in the period during and after decolonization, figures such as Collis in George Lamming's *The Emigrants* or Adah in Buchi Emecheta's *In the Ditch* and *Second-Class Citizen*. Anna is also literary kin to Bita Plant in Claude McKay's novel *Banana Bottom,* in which Bita is likewise the victim of sexual exploitation and is moved to England, supposedly for her own good. In McKay's novel, however, Bita is able to resist the alienation that an English missionary education provides by returning to her eponymous Jamaican village home and finding redemption as an enlightened member of the peasantry in which she was raised. McKay's imaginative solution to the problem of cultural crossing may sometimes be too neat, as his reliance on the marriage plot as a device to link Bita to her home and her people suggests. But the novel's careful, almost sociological attentiveness to the songs, dances, and other daily customs of rural folk links it both to other contemporary modernist writers' investment in everyday life and to the postcolonial fiction of the 1950s and 1960s that sought to convey the structures of feeling of communities that were longstanding but at the same time undergoing rapid change. The novel manages even to redeem the figure of the white creole, in the character of the eccentric Squire Gensir, who serves as the best man at Bita and Jubban's wedding, and is mourned by the people when he reluctantly leaves for England where – as a sign of his creolization – he does not survive his first winter. Bita's marriage to Jubban implausibly but effectively links imperial culture in the form of education to the agricultural labor of the people on the land, and in so doing links McKay's novel back to the creole romance novels of the Americas over a century earlier: "Her music, her reading, her thinking were the flowers of her intelligence and he [Jubban] the root in the earth upon which she was grafted, both nourished by the same soil."[28]

Conclusion

The far-flung settings of McKay's novels – his first, *Home to Harlem*, in the United States, the second, *Banjo*, in Marseilles – and his socialist politics and focus on the black diaspora show that sometimes the term "colonial novel" could be a limiting rather than an illuminating one to apply to a writer; nevertheless, the literary return to McKay's Jamaican homeland in *Banana Bottom* links him to the creole fictions and creole novelists discussed in the first half of this chapter and to the questions they raised and tried to resolve in fictional form: Who are "the people" in a colonial setting? What are the connections and differences among them? How are they to be represented? These same questions – supplemented, adapted, and modified as circumstances required – are the ones at the heart of many of the first generation of postcolonial novels in English.

However, I should end this chapter with a warning about the hegemony of the term "postcolonial" as it has come to be institutionalized in English and cultural studies programs around the Anglophone world. A survey of the "colonial novel" like this chapter can lead to a simple observation of historical fact: many of the novels that we now routinely call postcolonial were of course written and published before the end of colonial rule. Are they too "colonial novels"? Chinua Achebe's *Things Fall Apart* and *No Longer at Ease*, Sam Selvon's *The Lonely Londoners*, V. S. Naipaul's *A House for Mr. Biswas*, Wilson Harris's *Palace of the Peacock*, and many other "postcolonial" classics were in fact novels of the period of decolonization: perhaps we mislabel them because of the extent to which they predict, sometimes with uncanny accuracy, the preoccupations and problems of postcolonial states and cultures. If in this chapter I have highlighted the persistence of the concept of creolization in colonial fiction in English, I would like to end by suggesting – following a remark of Simon Gikandi in a recent interview – that what comes after the colonial novel, with its unfinished process of creolization, is not the postcolonial novel, with its implication of a break with the past, but rather the novel of the unfinished process of decolonization.[29]

Notes

1 Edward W. Said, *Culture and Imperialism* (New York: Knopf, 1993), p. xii, emphasis in original.

2 Gauri Viswanathan, *Masks of Conquest: Literary Study and British Rule in India* (New York: Columbia University Press, 1989); Henry Schwarz, "Aesthetic Imperialism: Literature and the Conquest of India," *MLQ: Modern Language Quarterly* 61.4 (2000), pp. 563–86.

3 E. P. Thompson, *The Making of the English Working Class* (New York: Pantheon, 1964), p. 12.

4 Katie Trumpener, *Bardic Nationalism: The Romantic Novel and the British Empire* (Princeton, NJ: Princeton University Press, 1997), p. 12.

5 Ian Watt, *The Rise of the Novel: Studies in Defoe, Richardson, and Fielding* (London: Chatto and Windus, 1957).

6 Trumpener, *Bardic Nationalism*, p. 14.

7 For an excellent account of the complexities and transformations of the term "creole," including its different usage in the context of Louisiana, see Carolyn Vellenga Berman, *Creole Crossings: Domestic Fiction and the Reform of Colonial Slavery* (Ithaca, NY: Cornell University Press, 2006), esp. ch. 1, "Creoles and Creolified," pp. 27–56.

8 Benedict Anderson, *Imagined Communities: Reflections on the Origin and Spread of Nationalism*, 2nd ed. (London: Verso, 1991).

9 Sean X. Goudie, *Creole America: The West Indies and the Formation of Literature and Culture in the New Republic* (Philadelphia: University of Pennsylvania Press, 2006).

10 John Galt, *Bogle Corbet; or, The Emigrants*, 3 vols. (London: Henry Colburn and Richard Bentley, 1831), vol. 1, p. iii.

11 For example, the results of such a search for the year 1800 can be found here: www.british-fiction.cf.ac.uk/searchAdvResults.asp?srchAuthTrans=&srchTitle=&srchGender=&srchPubLocn=&srchPublisher=&srchPubFrom=1800&srchPubTo=1800&srchNotes=&AdvSrchGo=Search (accessed March 14, 2013).

12 Georg Lukács, *The Theory of the Novel* (1920; Cambridge, MA: MIT Press, 1971).

13 Anderson, *Imagined Communities*, p. 50, emphases in original.

14 Cynric R. Williams, *Hamel, the Obeah Man*, ed. Candace Ward and Tim Watson (Peterborough, ON: Broadview, 2010), p. 100.

15 James Fenimore Cooper, *The Pioneers; or, The Sources of the Susquehanna*, 2 vols. (New York: Stringer and Townsend, 1853), vol. 1, pp. 105–6.

16 Siraj Ahmed, *The Stillbirth of Capital: Enlightenment Writing and Colonial India* (Stanford, CT: Stanford University Press, 2012).

17 Williams, *Hamel*.

18 Patrick Brantlinger, *Victorian Literature and Postcolonial Studies* (Edinburgh: Edinburgh University Press, 2009); Brantlinger, *Rule of Darkness: British Literature and Imperialism, 1830–1914* (Ithaca, NY: Cornell University Press, 1988);

Said, *Culture and Imperialism*; Deirdre David, *Rule Britannia: Women, Empire, and Victorian Writing* (Ithaca, NY: Cornell University Press, 1995); Viswanathan, *Masks of Conquest*; Suvendrini Perera, *Reaches of Empire: The English Novel from Edgeworth to Dickens* (New York: Columbia University Press, 1991).

19 J. R. Seeley, *The Expansion of England* (1883; Chicago, IL: University of Chicago Press, 1971), p. 12.

20 Jed Esty, *Unseasonable Youth: Modernism, Colonialism, and the Fiction of Development* (New York: Oxford University Press, 2012).

21 Olive Schreiner, *The Story of an African Farm*, ed. Joseph Bristow (Oxford: Oxford University Press, 1992), p. xlii.

22 Frantz Fanon, *The Wretched of the Earth*, tr. Constance Farrington (New York: Grove, 1968), p. 227.

23 Joseph Conrad, *Lord Jim*, ed. Jacques Berthoud (Oxford: Oxford University Press, 2002), p. 205. Further references given parenthetically in the body of the chapter.

24 E. M. Forster, *A Passage to India* (San Diego: Harcourt Brace, 1924), p. 65. Further references given parenthetically in the body of the chapter.

25 Graham Greene, *The Heart of the Matter* (New York: Viking, 1948), p. 14. Further references given parenthetically in the body of the chapter.

26 Rudyard Kipling, *Kim*, ed. Edward W. Said (London: Penguin, 1987), p. 49. Further references given parenthetically in the body of the chapter.

27 Jean Rhys, *Voyage in the Dark* (New York: Norton, 1982), p. 45. Further references given parenthetically in the body of the chapter.

28 Claude McKay, *Banana Bottom* (San Diego: Harcourt Brace, 1922), p. 313.

29 Simon Gikandi, "Postcolonialism's Ethical (Re)Turn," interview with David Jefferess, *Postcolonial Text*, 2.1 (2006), www.postcolonial.org/index.php/pct/article/viewArticle/464/845 (accessed March 31, 2013): "If you see decolonization as that search for a new humanism, driven by powerful ethical concerns about the status of the human, and the status of culture, and the status of moral well-being, then perhaps we need to go back to that moment and see how that ethical project could somehow politically and ethically be sustained and indeed, be debated. ... Because I don't want to make a choice between colonialism and nation, because I don't want to see one as a reflection of the other, I've been calling attention to that middle space, and that's what I'm calling, perhaps for lack of a better word, decolonization."

3

DEBJANI GANGULY
Australian National University

The Postcolonial Novel in the Wake of 1989

Postcolonialism's Afterlife

"Rushdie in his Manhattan retreat is no longer a Third World or postcolonial writer but a bard of the grim *one world* we all, in a state of some dread, inhabit"; so wrote John Updike in what was one of the earliest reviews of Rushdie's elegiac narrative on Kashmir, *Shalimar the Clown*.[1] Novelistic work on this "grim one world" of interconnected hoops of violence interlaced with the proliferation of graphic digital images and an emergent global humanitarian imagination is the subject of my chapter. In the wake of the stupendous domination of literary critical imaginaries by the postcolonial novel from Marquez and Achebe to Rushdie, a significantly new kind of *world* novel has, I contend, emerged around the world-transforming events of 1989 and the waning of the Cold World Order. The year 1989 as a temporal threshold here features not just as an imaginary of a post-Communist world, but also as a critical threshold of crisis of the "liberal contract" that was forged in the erstwhile First World in the spring of 1968 and extended until 1989 after which it was rapidly fractured by the excesses of a neoliberal world order that culminated in the occupation of Iraq. The year 1989 in my analysis also features as a technological threshold with the creation of the World Wide Web by Sir Tim Berners-Lee who put a proposal to a Geneva firm CERN in March 1989 to create a service feature on the Internet that would, for the first time in human history, enable human informational connectivity on a global scale.

If the postcolonial novel has imagined (and continues to imagine) human futures at the intersection of post-Second World War; anticolonial and nationalist movements across Africa, Asia, and Latin America; and the social identity movements of the 1960s, the new *world* novel has begun to take shape at the conjuncture of four critical post-1989 phenomena: geographies of violence since the end of the Cold War, hyperconnectivity through advances in information technology, the financial exuberance and excesses of the information economy, and the emergence of a new humanitarian sensibility in a context where suffering has a presence in everyday life through the immediacy of digital images.

Whether it is Gary Shteyngart's hyperbolic black satire on both the collapse of the Soviet Empire and the maximalist consumption credo of a new America in *Absurdistan*, Joseph O'Neill's luminous and sad rendition of a twenty-first-century diasporic Great Gatsby amidst the world-shattering effects of 9/11 in *Netherland*, Don De Lillo's spectacular capture of the lure of hypercapitalism in a cybernetic age in his *Cosmopolis*, Janette Turner Hospital's poetic conjoining of music and terror in the aftermath of Guantanamo Bay and the wars of Iraq and Afghanistan in her *Orpheus Lost*, or even Ian McEwan's Mrs. Dalloway-inspired depiction of a day in the life of a hyperanxious neurosurgeon in London on the eve of the Iraq war in his *Saturday*, the new world novel is a distinct product of the age of informational capitalism in the sense that its capacity to be world oriented is inextricably linked to the capacity of a global informational economy to work as "a unit in real time on a planetary scale."[2] This does not mean that it encompasses the world as a whole in its spatial and affective orientation, even if Shteyngart's comic hero–villain, Misha Vainberg, extravagantly declares, "I swallow the World!" It is rather that the novel now evinces a capacity, predominantly through a global informational infrastructure, to imagine the human condition on a scale larger than ever before in history and certainly beyond national and regional configurations, which latter have traditionally marked both its conditions of possibility and its limits. The compulsion that McEwan's anxious neurosurgeon in *Saturday* feels in the aftermath of 9/11 and on the eve of the Iraq War to understand where he stands with the *world*, a nervous compulsion born out of a habit to turn to the only-too-accessible information networks he is surrounded by, networks that feed his absorption with global violence that threatens to engulf *his* world – it is this compulsion to *visualize* his condition on a hitherto unprecedented scale – with no less than the world as its measure – that marks Henry Perowne as a quintessential inhabitant of a post-1989 world imaginary.[3]

If the industrial age saw the rise of the novel as a genre representing a new space-time configuration enabled by print capitalism that then created the conditions under which the "nation" could be imagined (as Benedict Anderson has taught us), the radical spatiotemporal shifts generated by the information age produce the new post-1989 novel that helps imagine the "world." The information age, of course, began much before 1989 – historians date it to the 1950s with the invention of the computer at the height of the Cold War – but the age of informational capitalism that has seen rise of the World Wide Web and various forms of social media under a largely capitalist world system, and all of which in turn have forged such compelling virtual communities around the world, is an indelible feature of the post-1989 world. As Vija Kinski, the tycoon Eric Packer's chief financial advisor in De Lillo's *Cosmopolis*, exults on the marvels of a liquid crystal cyberglobalism while her boss traverses Manhattan in the year 2000 in his stretch limousine: "I love the screens. The glow of cyber-capital. So radiant and seductive" (78). Only in this age of informational capitalism and the global nature of post-Cold War conflicts could Rushdie write immediately after the release of *Shalimar the Clown*: "It used to be possible to write a novel about, say London or Kashmir or Strasbourg or California, without any sense of connection. But now it's all one story. . . . Now I feel more and more that if you're telling a story of a murder in California, you end up having to tell the story of many other places and many other times in order to make sense of that event and that place. To try to show how these stories join."[4] Updike's reference of Rushdie's "Manhattan retreat" and Rushdie's own reference to California as an epicenter of world historical connections might appear to play right into the hands of the critics who decry the emergent debates on world making and ecumenical imaginaries as nothing more than the globalization of an American way of life; as yet another imperial paradigm.[5] However, far from being an alibi for U.S. global dominance, *Shalimar the Clown*'s allegorical structure of interconnected histories evokes many worlds in the making from the Second World War to the rise of Islamic fundamentalism at the end of the twentieth century. In fact, the rise of America in this saga becomes a subplot to the novelist's epic lament of the loss of Kashmir's transcendent beauty in the catastrophic vortex of Indian partition and post-War world history. It is a novel that painstakingly narrates the relationship between multiple worlds, highlights collisions between them, and undertakes a melancholic reconstruction of those irrevocably lost in a cycle of unrelenting violence and global neglect.

If 1947 was the historical threshold for Rushdie's postcolonial saga, *Midnight's Children*, 1989 is the temporal fulcrum on which Rushdie's world historical allegory hangs. The significance of this year, however, unfolds not in the political epicenter of post-Cold War eruptions, the Soviet Union, but in Kashmir, the disputed Himalayan territory that both India and Pakistan continue to covet at the cost of cataclysmic military upheaval on the subcontinent. As is well known to historians of South Asia, in the redistribution of Hindu and Muslim-majority territories during the Partition, Kashmir was an anomaly. It had a Muslim majority but a Hindu king who wanted Kashmir to be part of India, not Pakistan. When Pakistan attacked Kashmir in 1947 with every intention of annexing it, Maharaja Hari Singh sought help from Nehru's government. The Indian army intervened and managed to beat back the Pakistani troops to the line that now constitutes the border between Indian Kashmir and Pakistan-occupied Kashmir. The war was halted with the intervention of United Nations. The status of Kashmir, it was resolved then, would be determined by a referendum to be undertaken by the Indian state at a future date. The referendum never took place and Kashmir continues to be a disputed territory torn apart by skirmishes between the two partitioned nations.

What then of the significance of 1989 in this tale of subcontinental fractures? Unnoticed by the rest of the world too caught up in the euphoria of the fall of the Berlin Wall, the Kashmiris staged their first ever insurgency against both Indian and Pakistani occupation in that very year. The uprising failed comprehensively against the military might of both nations and clarified for all that an independent Kashmir was not viable. Until this time, the Kashmir dispute had remained a regional problem: a postcolonial casualty of half-baked colonial plans for partition and a hasty British departure. Not until the post-1989 transformation of Soviet-era *mujahideens* into global warriors of Islam, and their adoption of Kashmir as a site of global jihad, did Kashmir feature in the international political radar as yet another site of global battle against Islamic fundamentalism. It is significant that while Rushdie's *Midnight's Children* – a novel completed in 1980 and published in 1981 – featured Kashmir as only a small part of the narrative of the coming into being of an amorphous postcolonial India, in *Shalimar the Crown*, Kashmir is a whole world. Every other recognizably world historical event in the novel features in relation to it: the build up to the Second World War, the Cold War antipathy between India and America, Vietnam, the fall of the Berlin Wall, the radicalization of Islam, and the rise of diasporic networks of terrorists.

The year 1989, of course, features as a literary, temporal, and political threshold for Rushdie in yet another way. It was the year of his fatwa, and the first visible global eruption of an ominously *worldly* response to Rushdie's controversial depiction of the Prophet in *The Satanic Verses*. As more than one scholar has argued, the Khomeini fatwa was really the beginning of the rise of a visible fundamentalist global mobilization in the name of Islam.[6] The transition of Rushdie from a *postcolonial* to a *world* novelist, one might well argue, began not in 2005 with his Kashmir and California saga as Updike suggests, but in 1989. The significance of Rushdie's oeuvre from 1981 to 2005 is, however, not exactly the focus of this chapter. To me, rather, this preliminary discussion of Rushdie serves as a critical opening to think about the changed world view and morphology of the novel as one moves from the era of the postcolonial to the global in world literary history.

Unlike many recent scholars of literary modernism who have displayed an exuberant enthusiasm for the idea of "world" in literature without much meaningful engagement with the history of postcolonial literary production,[7] I cannot possibly treat the idea of the "world novel" as a radically new form that has had scarcely anything to do with the efflorescence of its postcolonial counterpart, and certainly not in a volume where every other preceding chapter is *about* the postcolonial novel. Wasn't the moment of the postcolonial, after all, the first push toward bringing the non-Euroamerican *world* into literary theoretical reckoning? At the same time, I cannot settle for readings that continue to see all contemporary novelistic productions from the erstwhile postcolonial world as invariably a combination of "western form, local material and local form" as Moretti described in his 2000 chapter, "Conjectures on World Literature." This modular approach scarcely captures the novel directions that many of these works have taken in the era of literary globalization after 1989 and that by no means merely generate only *local* realities. Writing about contemporary Latin America in a forum on "The Futures of the Novel" organized by Duke University in 2011, Carlos Alonso, for instance, notes:

> This understanding of the third-world novel as an artifact rent down its middle – as a novel invariably manqué – will not help us navigate the non-Western novel in the age of globalization. ... The foreign form–local materials distinction on which our understanding of the third-world novel was articulated has been challenged to the core since the 1990s with the widespread publication of novels written in Spanish by Latin American writers ... that nevertheless do not incorporate Latin American "reality" in any meaningful fashion. Novels such as those of Alan Pauls, Santiago Gamboa, Ignacio Padilla, Jorge Volpi, etc. mark their distance from the preceding novels of the Boom by taking leave from Latin American history and circumstance and *suffusing their texts with paradigms, categories and even plots derived from mass media, the new digital technologies and global networks of circulation and meaning.*[8]

My focus in this chapter is on the worlding of both the postcolonial novel and the so-called western novel form in ways described by Alonso. Since the term "world" has featured so prominently thus far, it is worthwhile to contemplate some aspects of its usage in modern literary theory and philosophy, especially in ways that are relevant to the concerns of this chapter.

Worlds in Literary Thought

While one hears the term "world" all too frequently in literary critical circles now,[9] and in ways that mark our current conjuncture as perhaps the most apposite historical *moment* for its circulation, "world" as a concept has carried considerable philosophical and literary weight in modern intellectual history. Let us, to start with, turn to an apposite *postcolonial* usage. Over three decades ago, in his celebrated work *The World, The Text, and the Critic*, Edward Said questioned the insulation of canonical texts of English Literature from the world historical imperatives of their times.[10] His historical frame was the period of high European imperialism from the mid-eighteenth century until the end of the Second World War. The task of the critic, he said, was to prize open the "worldliness" of the literary text, to situate it as a product of its material allegiances and historical affiliations. At the time of Said's writing, the category "world" in relation to literature did not quite circulate with the charge it does today. The noisy, strident presence of *globalization* as an intellectual exchange alley was still a decade away, as were ways of imagining the world as maximal connectivity through information technology – all of which give the idea of "world literature" and the "world" in literature today an inflection not exactly available to Said's protean intellect and imagination in the late seventies and early eighties.

Literary worldmaking as the travel of genres and textual patterns, as the elliptical reception of texts in different regions of the globe, as translated worlds that haunt or echo other literary imaginaries – such celebratory accounts of contemporary literary approaches liberated from national, nationalistic, and Cold War-era geopolitical boundaries abound. Not surprisingly, so do contentious and skeptical accounts. The contentions are aplenty for a view that paradoxically condemns the idea of "world" to a constitutive singularity: world literature as a handmaiden of the forces of globalization; as a posthistorical triumphal narrative of an enforced unification of the world; as conscription of the imagination to dangerously polarized worldviews, or even to an "image capitalism" that perpetuates in the name of an ecumenical vision what is, in fact, the "US Empire's particular national mythology."[11]

The most trenchant attacks on the category are a throwback to a neomaterialist idiom that characterized the rise of postcolonial literary studies in the 1970s. "World" and "worlding" in the early postcolonial disciplinary context categorically meant an orientation to the material reality outside the literary text (as we saw with Said) and often even a position of radical antiaestheticism that denounced any intellectual gesture that hinted at literary and cultural autonomy from the realm of imperial interest. In *Culture and Imperialism* Edward Said wrote: "Cultural experience or indeed every cultural form is radically, quintessentially hybrid, and if it has been the practice in the West since Immanuel Kant to isolate cultural and aesthetic realms from the worldly domain, it is now time to rejoin them."[12] This polarization between "cultural materialism" and "cultural immunity," to use Leela Gandhi's terms, often times led literary studies down an antiliterary path; as if the only legitimate way to read a text produced during the period of high European colonization was to unmask its aesthetic features as signs of imperial intent.[13] This is not to suggest there were no rich literary critical studies produced under this rubric or that the discipline as a whole was afflicted by a materialist determinism. It is rather to draw a point of comparison with current circulations of the idea of "world" in literary productions of our globalized era, and the contentions that the category has generated. The "world" for Said, as it is for scholars currently deeply critical of globalization's cultural hegemony, was primarily the material domain of economic and political interests.

My reading of the relationship between the world and its relationship to the novel in this chapter is at significant variance from Said's for it resists his overwhelming emphasis on the novel's extradiegetic dimensions, and his "one-world" mimetic argument about the role of the critic in evaluating the novel. The "human" in the novel, as both Bakhtin and Lukács remind us, is a surplus, an entity that signifies modes of world making irreducible to empirical truths. Or as Lukacs puts it: "The dissonance special to the novel, the refusal of the immanence of being to enter into empirical life, produces a problem of form."[14] The novel, in other words, is the only genre in which form and content are "radically heterogeneous."[15] Its relationship to its extradiegetic worlds is extremely complex. To follow this logic through, the world novel of our times – and this is my primary contention in this chapter – while being a product of our global age, is not reducible to the *realism* of globalization. The "global," I contend, is an empirical category in the Saidian sense; it is the domain of territorial and material expansion. The "world," on the other hand, can be conceptually distinguished from the "globe" through a phenomenological apprehension of the work of the human in making worlds through language and through an orientation critically attuned to the *surplus* of humanness that Bakhtin talks of. In fact, in his chapter "Forms of Time and Chronotope in the Novel" Bakhtin invokes the idea of precisely such a distinct *aesthetic world*, when he writes that the world of a novel's reader or writer is

> set off by a sharp and categorical boundary from the *represented* world of the text. Therefore, we may call this world the world that *creates* the text, for all its aspects ... participate equally in the creation of the represented world in the text. Out of the actual chronotopes of our world (which serve as a source of representation) emerge the reflected and *created* chronotopes of the world represented in the work.[16]

Such an understanding of the "world" as *related to but nonsynonymous with its material and chronotopical coordinates* has an exciting genealogy going back to Leibniz and his idea of "possible worlds" in the analytic philosophy tradition on the one hand, and the existential thought of Heidegger, Arendt, Eugene Fink, and more recently Jean Luc Nancy on the other. There is no space in this chapter to explicate this rich body of thought in any detail. In brief, I take from Leibniz a minimalist reading of "world" as a linguistically finite set of entities and relations marked off by worlds made up of other finite sets of entities and relations. The novel in such a reading is a world-enclosing total system and its various degrees of *realism* derive primarily not from its correspondence with the *actual* world out there, but from the ways in which the entities within its demarcated set relate plausibly to each other, or Leibniz put it, are "compossible" with each other.[17] The actual world is but one of the conditions of possibility for the creation of the fictional world and not the sole determinant of its *realism*. A recent parallel iteration of this point can be found in literary theorizations of the world-systems model in the works of Franco Moretti and Pascale Casanova. For them, the "world" is not the actual world of material and territorial expansion but a world-constituting system of literary production and consumption whose myriad patterns can only be grasped by a system of analysis that scales up way beyond an individual text, author, nation, and region. Further, such literary world-systems operate at a remove from political and economic ones. While this metaliterary approach is not the preferred method in this chapter – for I do invest in close reading of symptomatic texts that capture of the force of the world I am explicating – I take from these positions their investment in a fundamental difference between *ontological* and *ontic* understandings of the world, a distinction that Eric Hayot in his recent book *On Literary Worlds* usefully highlights. It is important, he suggests, to

clarify the difference between the ontological status of worlds in world-systems and their material or ontic ground with respect to the planet (... rendered as globe). World systems *are* worlds in the sense they constitute a self-organizing, self-enclosed, and self-referential totality, but they are not to be confused with *the* actual world which – though it is also, of course, a world – is the only world whose geographical scope coincides exactly with that of the Earth.[18]

This distinction between the ontic and the ontological is, of course, quintessentially Heideggerian and Heidegger's celebrated difference between the "earth" and "world" is the source of much writing on the *world* in recent times. From this rich existential tradition, I take the idea of the world and human as mutually enclosing and disclosing each other through language. A stone is world poor, as Heidegger famously said, while the human is world rich. Technology objectifies the world, Heidegger tells us, while the human dwells "in" the world through language.[19] The distinction that Heidegger poses between *world-making* in art and *picturing* the world that modern science enables – that is, the placing of the world "before us" to be "looked at," which for him is what distinguishes "the essence of the modern techno-logical age" – actually weaves together two complementary ideas of the world that add immense value to my train of argument. In reading the world as I do in literary works that critically manifest a global humanitarian sensibility digitally mediated through the power of *visually* witnessing sites of violence, I subscribe to *both* Heidegger's invocation of aesthetics as the most powerful ground of world creation *and* his idea of the force of "world picturing" in our modern era. Not that Heidegger had much to say about the actual status of the "picture" or visual stimulus of any kind in his philosoph-ical work, but the charge of his idea of "world picture" can scarcely be underestimated in our image-saturated age. The technological sublime of world-transforming digital imagery – whether in the spectacular horror of terrorist acts or in the liquid shimmer of financial wizardry – is palpably experienced by the writer, Bill Gray, in De Lillo's *Mao II* as the death knell of the craft of narration. In a startlingly prescient pre-9/11 vision, images of spectacular annihilation are seen by Bill Gray as the new domain of aesthetic world-making: "Beckett is the last writer to shape the way we think and see. After him, the major work involves midair explosions and crumbled build-ings. This is the new tragic narrative" (157). Again, technological wizardry as the new source of disembodied rapture is what De Lillo's neocapitalist tycoon protagonist, Eric Packer, experiences in *Cosmopolis* as he is about to be assassinated. His subliminal mind functions

> as data, in whirl, in radiant spin, a consciousness saved from void. The technology was imminent or not. It was semi-mythical. It was the natural next step ... an evolutionary advance that needed only the practical mapping of the nervous system onto digital memory. It would be the master thrust of cyber-capital, to extend the human experience toward infinity as a medium for corporate growth and investment, for the accumulation of profits and vigorous reinvestment (*Cosmopolis*, 206–7).

The subject–object bifurcation aside – which for Heidegger was the essence of the technological revolution – the modern human's predilection to visualize the world as object is now also intimately tied to a saturated consciousness of the world as an affective entity and a zone of immanence. It is precisely this affective and immanent dimension of the "world" as opposed to a more materialist, object-like "globe" that Jean Luc Nancy highlights in his recent exposition of the tension between "globalization" and "world-making."[20] Nancy plays on the availability of the term "mon-dialization" in French and its semantic range that captures both ideas.

"World," in Nancy's reading, escapes all horizons of speculation and calcul-ability; it is immanence itself, containing every expansive potential of human creativity and empathetic connection beyond the abstract, speculative calcu-lus of finance capital and its political coordinates. He defines the death drive of contemporary globalization as "the conjunction of an unlimited process of eco-technological enframing and a vanishing of forms of life and/or of common ground" (95). The logic of this quest for a life-imbued "com-mons" – a singularity – is the obverse of the principle of general equivalence that characterizes the space-time continuum of late capitalism. Or as Nancy puts it, the French term *monde*, "by keeping the horizon of a "world" as a space for possible meaning for the whole of human relations ... gives a different indication than that [given by the globe] of an enclosure in the undifferentiated sphere of totality."[21] The meaning of "world" I invoke in this chapter – a world of hyperconnected humans sensitized as witnesses to the depredations of gruesome global violence and the excesses of a liquid capitalism – has substantial affinities with Nancy's in that it is invested with an aesthetic and normative capacity to enter into yet another compact with humankind in this era of violent wars and intense connectivity; a kind of relationality that is informed but not overdetermined by the economic and political systems of globalization. The new world novel, I argue, is a signifi-cant cultural corpus that captures this disjunction. Thus far, I have been talking about the world novel and the semantic hypertrophy of the concept "world" without taking the measure of the morphological, narrative, and ideological heft of the post-1989 novel, except perhaps in my brief account of Rushdie's *Shalimar the Clown*. In what follows, I visit the works of Shteyngart, O'Neill, Spiegelman, McEwan, De Lillo, and Turner Hospital to understand better the makings of this new world novel.

The Tragicomic Poetics of Capital

In an interview in 2009, Gary Shteyngart had this to say about his acclaimed second novel: "In some ways, *Absurdistan* was really in the throes of what happens to globalism when the whole deck of card collapses."[22] As an effervescent black comedy on the collapse of the Soviet Union and the treacherous glitter of American-style capitalism, not to mention the devas-tating fragmentation of Russian, Slavic, and Central Asian lifeworlds, *Absurdistan* is the first global Anglophone novel to capture the vicissitudes of the post-Cold War era from both sides of the divide. With audacious allegorical surfeit, the novel oscillates between the two worlds even as it settles for an implausible nonplace, *Absurdistan*, as a mediating chronotope and the site of much catastrophic action. Located rather vaguely between

Russia, East Europe, and Central Asia, *Absurdistan* is a composite nonnation of global ruins, the detritus of post-Cold War dreams gone askew: at once Afghanistan, Iraq, Kazakhstan, the Baltic states, the Balkans, and a worn-down Russia. As an outpost of the military-industrial complex of the United States and the last frontier of avaricious Russian oligarchs' endless quest for lucrative energy sources, this hapless new world country allegorizes the absurdity of the very idea of a post-Cold War world as one: etymologically "stan" is "place" in Sanskrit, Persian, and Arabic. Shteyngart's satire is Swiftian:

> This place is strategically located. Iran is next door. What about an air force base? Well you've got a problem. The Russians still see Absurdistan as their backyard. They might get mad. And anyway how much can you skim off a little base like that? You need something big. You need as huge US Army presence doing peacekeeping and humanitarian work. Now KBR was set to score a ten-year LOGCAP contract starting in 2002, but what good is all that if there's no heart-wrenching genocide around the corner? "Think Bosnia" became everyone's motto. "How can we make this place more like Bosnia?" I mean you've got to hand it to Halliburton. If Joseph Heller were still alive, they'd probably ask him to be on their board. (307)

The son of Russian immigrants who migrated to the United States when Shteyngart was seven, and as someone who has made frequent trips back home, the author is superbly placed to give us firsthand accounts of the humiliation of the Soviet Empire and the subsequent thrall of American style capitalism in the collapsed Second World. Significantly, he becomes a chronicler of a degraded post-Cold War Russia, a sad and ironic literary figure coming after a generation of Russian literary giants of the Cold War – Pasternak, Solzhenitsyn, and Nabokov. The Russian immigrant writer in the novel, Jerry Shteynfarb, and the contempt by which he is held by the protagonist Misha Vainberg, is but one instance of Gary Shteyngart's deprecatory sense of his own insignificance as a post-Cold War Russian immigrant writer. Misha brands Jerry as "an upper middle-class phony who came to States as a kid and is now playing the professional immigrant game" (81). The undertone of this novel in respect to both his political and literary abjectness is clear. It is captured well in these lines from *Absurdistan*:

> Let's be certain: the Cold War was won by one side and lost by another. And the losing side, like any other in history, had its countryside scorched, its gold plundered, its men forced to dig trenches in far away capital cities, its women conscripted to service of the victorious army. From my plane window, I saw defeat on the ground. Windstrewn, deserted suburban fields. The gray shell of a factory sliced in two by some unnameable force, its chimney leaning

precariously. A circle of seventies apartment houses, each sinking toward the circular courtyard that separated them, like old men huddled together in conversation (57).

The chronicler in the novel is Misha Vainberg, the obscenely obese son of a rich Russian oligarch who is the face of new petrocapitalism in Russia after the Cold War Rich beyond measure, Misha studies in an exclusive American college and after graduation moves into a Manhattan penthouse from where he has full views of the twin towers and the Manhattan cityscape. His primary desire, he declares in a biting Swiftian twist of language, was to actually rent a place at the World Trade Center:

> I was still a Soviet citizen at heart, afflicted with a kind of Stalinist gigantamania, so that when I looked at the topography of Manhattan, I naturally settled my gaze on the Twin Towers of the World Trade Center, those emblematic honeycombed 110-story giants that glowed white gold in the afternoon sun. They looked to me like the promise of socialist realism fulfilled, boyhood science fiction extended to near-infinity. (27)

The novel begins on 15 June 2001, scarcely three months before the spectacular razing of the twin towers to Ground Zero. It is Misha's observations from his plane of a ravaged Russia we saw earlier, and one that propels the narrative toward a future in a no man's land that for this privileged Russian will be far darker than he could imagine in his extravagant and licentious days in the United States. The novelist is ruthless in his parody of the notion of post-Cold War America as the capitalist supremacist, as the face of the World, so to say. But he is even more brutal in his capture of the lawless land-and-resource-grabbling kleptocracy of Putin's Russia. Misha with his enormous girth becomes an emblem of both. In the United States he is the king of consumption and literally eats his way into its capitalist belly. When he declares, at one point, "I swallow the World," the allusion is all but literal but hardly grandiose. The World with which he is engorged is the tawdry trans fat-, alcohol-, sex-, and pill-driven dreg of the West laid bare. Correspondingly, the vulgar misogyny of the protagonist is confronting but hardly surprising. American womanhood is Rouenna – the busty, black-brown barmaid from Bronx with whom he is fixated beyond measure and who in an utterly improbable fantasy is always willing to give him the best possible sex. She is also not quite improbably the flesh-and-blood incarnation of a futuristic mixed-race humanity that could potentially make the world One: "Half Puerto Rican. And half German. And half Mexican and Irish ... raised Dominican" (32). The twenty-one-year-old Russian daughter of another oligarch whom he meets on the other side of the Cold War divide is, however, blonde, curvy, and promiscuity epitomized. The racial prototype of a now-waning world, Nana is, like Misha, "another American trapped in a foreigner's body." They both crave a home in the United States and at one point Misha muses: "Perhaps the generals in charge of the INS, in their Noahlike wisdom, would make an exception for *two* hungry and fully consumerist post-Soviet bears" (188). Misha's widowed youthful step-mother decked in her designer gear lures him to her bed soon after his father's murder. Other women characters are either painted snobs or tramps. Misha's ubercapitalist ambitions require nubile expression much like the transnational culture of global marketing. But here is youth distorted, grotesque, no longer the promise of modernity as in the classical *Bildungsroman*.

Shteyngart's post-Cold War dystopic *Bildungsroman* takes Misha from his boyhood days to the hoary wisdom of thirty by which time he is in the throes of a massive psychosis. His journey as a "holy fool" is recorded at the start of his narration in a series of "dedications" to Russian literary forebears. The deprecating tone notwithstanding, one cannot here miss the narrative of the "exceptional" individual, a point, as we shall go on to see, is critical to the tragicomic poetics of capital in the history of the novel:

> As you read about my life and my struggles in these pages, you will see certain similarities with Oblomov, the famously large gentleman who refuses to stir from his couch in the nineteenth-century novel of the same name. I won't try to sway you from this analogy ... but may I suggest another possibility: Prince Myshkin from Dostoyevsky's *The Idiot*. Like the prince, I am something of a *holy fool*. I am an innocent surrounded by schemers. I am a puppy deposited in a den of wolves. ... Like Prince Myshkin, I am not perfect. In the next 318 pages, you may occasionally see me box the ears of my manservant or drinking one of Laphroaig too man. But you will also see me attempt to save an entire race from genocide; you will see me become a benefactor to St. Petersburg's miserable children; and you will watch me make love to fallen women with the childlike passion of the pure   (15).

The lure of capitalism, Franco Moretti noted in one of his earliest works, *The Way of the World*, is the one powerful source left in the novel for a reprisal of aristocratic values, a genre that is otherwise overwhelmingly democratic:

> The "common" hero is ... an essential component of a *democratic* culture. ... As de Tocqueville, John Stuart Mill and Burkhardt realized early on [democracy] does not aim at furthering great individualities. These latter are able to look after themselves, and, in any case, capitalism (which is not the same as democracy) offers them a new and immense field of application. For its part, democracy is anti-heroic. ... It aims at reducing the rate of "adventure" in our lives while expanding the jurisdiction ... of "security."[23]

Extrapolated on to Hegel's famously contemptuous phrase, "prose of the world" – that domain of the ordinary, everyday, contingent, and finite, in short, everything that thwarts transcendence – Moretti's "democracy" and quest for "security" are the novel's *prosaic* destiny. What occasionally enables this genre to showcase exceptional individuals is the *poetic* force of capitalism as the last great enchanter in an otherwise disenchanted world, a world from which the gods have disappeared, as the young Lukács once lamented. Scott Fitzgerald's *The Great Gatsby* is the redoubtable early twentieth-century exemplar here. The ultimate materialist and aesthete, Gatsby and his wife Daisy channel the expressive power of capital to its zenith, so much so that her voice is compared to the "exhaustible charm ... the jingle ... the cymbals' song" of money itself.[24] As for him, he is the Platonic ideal of capitalist aesthetics. The "luminosity of his pink suit under the moon," we are told by his chronicler Nick Carraway, "sprang from his Platonic conception of himself. He was a son of God – a phrase if it means anything, means just that." (104). This "son of God" is no moral exemplar, but he presides over his worldly domain with immense *élan*. His shadowy emergence from a world of crime and illicit wealth to the aristocracy of Long Island is hinted at several times in the novel by Gatsby's chronicler, Nick Carraway, the perfect "normalizing" foil to Gatsby's dazzle.

The world novels under discussion feature several such amoral capitalist aesthetes now in radically changed global circumstances. Capital is infinitely more liquid and virtual in this hypergauzy world as it spreads its networks wide through a million nodes. We already saw De Lillo's Eric Packer in *Cosmopolis*, the billionaire financial tycoon who kills his way to the top, whose dealings affect the value of currencies around the globe, and who watches with glee as his monetary wizardry leads to the fall of the Japanese yen at one point of the novel. The dazzle of his digital screen feeds his supreme narcissism. Even the President of the United States, who rides in a motorcade which temporarily stalls Packer's drive through Manhattan, appears "gynecoid" on his flat screen that dominates his view from inside his long white stretch limousine. The President, we're told, appears "undead. He lived in a state of occult repose, waiting to be reanimated" (*Cosmopolis*, 77), presumably by Packer's cybercapitalist magic. Rushdie's flamboyant Maximilian Ophuls in *Shalimar the Clown* is yet another such novelistic creation who revels in the enchantments of a hypercapitalist world after the fall of the Berlin Wall. He "celebrat[es] the junk food of America and wax [es] lyrical about the new banality of diet cola." He "admir[es] the strip malls for their neon and chain stores for their ubiquity" (*Shalimar the Clown*, 22).

The novel that comes closest to creating a twenty-first century Great Gatsby is Joseph O'Neill's *Netherland*. Chuck Ramkissoon, a colorful product of his Indo-Caribbean heritage and his Bronx habitation, is the ultimate postcolonial Gatsby in a world city of limitless possibilities. "Think fantastic" is his motto, he tells his own Nick Carraway, Hans, as the two drive around the seedier parts of New York City. While Hans as an equity broker on Wall Street is the "legitimate" creator of wealth of the kind that our global systems recognize, Chuck Ramkissoon is the underbelly entrepreneur always looking for gaps in the market that he can exploit with the help of "mezzanine" finance, his own metaphor for money that is neither white nor black. The ironies of the 2008 global financial crisis aside, which revealed how "mezzanine" even the finances of Wall Street banking were, Chuck is seen by Hans as his complete antithesis. Hans, the boring, strait-laced, self-deprecating, family loving, upper middle class inhabitant of Manhattan; Chuck, the charismatic world player channelling the crooked energies of his multicontinental bearings to think and play hard on any field that opens up for him, including developing a cricket industry for America:

> Chuck valued craftiness and indirection. He found the ordinary run of dealings between people boring and insufficiently advantageous to him at the deep level of strategy at which he liked to operate. He believed in owning the impetus of a situation, in keeping the other guy off balance, in proceeding by way of sidesteps. If he saw an opportunity to act with suddenness or take you by surprise or push you into the dark, he'd take it, almost as a matter of principle. (71)

Hans encounters Chuck in a local cricket match, but soon realizes that Chuck's aspiration for the game in the greatest country on earth far exceeds winning on weekends. In a fantastic reversal of colonial game-play, Chuck with sly grandiose suggests that the only way he can "civilize" America is by aggressively promoting cricket, the game of gentlemen. This is the America after 9/11. "What's the first thing that happens," he asks the bemused Hans, "when Pakistan and India make peace? They play a cricket match." Then he launches forth and Hans is spellbound by the "Napoleonic excess" of Chuck's peroration:

> Cricket is instructive, Hans. It has a moral angle. . . . Everybody who plays the game benefits from it. So I say, why not Americans. . . . Americans really cannot see the world. They think they can. But they can't. I don't need to tell you that. Look at the problems we're having. It's a mess, and it's going to get worse. I say, we want to have something in common with Hindus and Muslims? *Chuck Ramkissoon is going to make it happen.* With the New York Cricket Club, we could start a whole new chapter in US history. Why not? Why not say so if it's true. Why hold back? I'm going to open our eyes. And that's what I have to tell the Park Service. . . . If I tell them I'm going to build a playground

for minorities, they're going to blow me away. But if I tell them we're starting something big, tell them we're bringing back an ancient national sport, with new leagues, new franchises, new horizons.   (211)

Chuck's impudent dazzle makes Hans overlook his mysterious visits to various dark corners of the city in search of "mezzanine" finance. The criminal shadows that hover over Chuck eventually hound him to his death. By the time his decomposed body is hauled up from the defunct depths of the Gowanus Canal in Brooklyn, Hans is back in England with his child and estranged wife. But he hasn't forgotten his dark, flamboyant friend. Chuck's death haunts him and when he cannot break through the indifference of the New York police in treating the death as a legitimate investigation, all Hans is left with in his silent mourning are occasional virtual journeys on Google Earth to their old cricket haunts in unfashionable Brooklyn.

Despite Hans's narrative of an irrevocable chasm – cultural, professional, moral – between his world and Chuck's, the novel adroitly weaves their stories into an allegory of the perils of speculative finance of which, of course, the Wall Street (Hans's professional world) cannot but be emblematic. Both are inveterate gamblers in a hypercapitalist era of extreme speculation. Hans, we are told quite early on in the novel, is an equities analyst for oil and gas stocks and has just been rewarded by his bank for being ranked number four in the sector by *Institutional Investor*, the reputed publication in the world of equities and hedge funds. On the very day that his bank celebrates his success, his wife gives him notice about their marriage and leaves for England. The difference between Hans and Chuck is that the latter, notwithstanding his flamboyant entrepreneurial predilections, is out of joint with the white-gold world of liquid finance and cybercapital. Chuck is Hans' *doppelganger*, hedging bets in the grubby grey world of mezzanine finance. New York's underbelly is his zone of transaction. Hans recognizes their mutual affinity all too late when his now-reconciled lawyer wife admonishes him even as she reminds him of the distance between their worlds:

"You drive him around while he runs his numbers game? What were you thinking?". . . . "Darling, this man was a gangster. No wonder he ended up the way he did."   (238)

It is telling that, far from distancing himself from the taint of Chuck's death, Hans seeks out another personage from the world of speculative finance, Faruk Patel, as his comrade in sorrow. Patel is the millionaire businessman who promised to finance Chuck's cricket dreams but on his own terms in the world of roving cybercapital:

"The New York Cricket Club," Faruk says, raising his eyebrows, "was a splendid idea – a gymkhana in New York. We had a chance there. But would the big project have worked? No. There's a limit to what Americans understand. The limit is cricket. ... My idea was different. My idea was, you don't need America. Why would you? You have the TV, Internet markets in India, England. These days, that's plenty." (251)

Hans and Faruk depart after acknowledging their mutual bereavement: "It's a tragedy ... Ramkissoon was a rare bird." Faruk's succinct eulogy sums up the sordid grandeur of Chuck's life and death in our twenty-first century world of spectral and speculative capital, that one remaining domain of exceptional and the enchanted, as we saw, in the novelistic worlds of our times. But this is no epic enchantment and Chuck is no tragic hero; there can be none in this amoral universe. In such a cosmopolis "the logical extension of business is murder," as De Lillo's tycoon hero, Eric Packer, states as if uttering the most prosaic of truths (*Cosmopolis*, 113). The narrative poetics of this dazzling yet murderous tragicomic world of cybercapital finds its correlate in the narrative screen of terror to which we now briefly turn.

The Narrative Screen of Terror

"The terrorists were the first to have waged an information war," noted Paul Virilio with frightening prescience in 1982; "the explosion only existed because it was simultaneously coupled to a multimedia explosion."[25] Yet another anticipatory remark by a character in De Lillo's *Underworld* likens the terrorist act to a radically new kind of screen authorship, one that shakes up the world in ways that conventional literature is not able to anymore in this era of spectacular technology. The technologized terror script, it appears, began to be graphed onto our collective imaginations before the *event* finally happened. The global spectacle of the 9/11 explosions were but the inevitable fulfillment of a technological momentum that has been gathering steady pace since the rationalistic accelerations of a super-technologized Cold War. One remembers Hannah Arendt's wondrous yet tremulous thoughts, in *The Human Condition*, on the fragility of human habitation on earth after the Sputnik phenomenon.[26] The atomic explosion in Japan and the phenomenon of automation in general had already exposed her anxieties about the annihilative potential of technology. While Arendt's dystopic vision in 1958 of an apocalyptic space and nuclear warfare did not quite materialize on the scale she feared, less than half a century later the world witnessed a startling conjoining of modern technology and an almost medieval "fire of aggrieved belief" (De Lillo) to create a multimedia explosion of near-apocalyptic proportions. The spectacular nature of the 9/11 attacks has been commented on often enough. As Richard Schechner, observes: "What makes 9/11 different is that it was mediated from the outset and intended to be mediated. Its authors' purpose was not to conquer or occupy territory, or even slaughter as many civilians as possible, but to stage a stunning media event, photo op and real-life show – a terrifying, sublime event."[27]

Novelistic remediations of this event repeatedly draw on the motifs of the spectacle and the spectacular. At the same time they are not *contiguous* with contemporary cinematic or televisual or new media genres in representing the *immediacy* of violence, but are rather texts that register the sedimented and recursive, history of such mediation. Among the most magnificent instances of such remediation is, of course, Art Spiegelman's graphic masterpiece, *In the Shadow of No Towers*, in which the famous plate number six is a particularly powerful example of the formal processes at work. The skeletal frame of the glowing North Tower looms across the left column of the entire page. We see five falling figures across the length of the Tower, each of them resembling Spiegelman, and no doubt commemorating one of the most iconically disturbing images of the 9/11 catastrophe. The "falling" Spiegelman figure symbolizes all at once the history of his personal trauma as a child of holocaust survivors, his own terrifying experience of the attack on the Towers as a resident of lower Manhattan, and his identification with the fateful death-leaps of the inhabitants of the Twin Towers. This vertical telescoping, across the ashen frame of the burnt North Tower, of multiple temporalities of trauma, both personal and historical, is then replicated breadth-wise in a series of violent palimpsests across eleven other panels more conventionally associated with a comic book. Holocaust history, the history of Arab anti-Semitism, and 9/11 "smash" into each other in these panels. The key encounter here is between Spiegelman and a homeless Russian woman who daily hurls anti-Semitic abuses at him in her native tongue as he walks down the street. On the afternoon of 9/11 she disappears from the street only to reappear as a demonic spectre right at the center of the entire plate. The reader is confronted by a flaming rectangular panel featuring her devilish profile, framed by iconography from Nazi-era history, Biblical Hell, and the familiar glowing skeletal frames of the Twin Towers. The boxed caption reads, "Her inner demons had broken loose and take over our shared reality." Interestingly she is back on the streets after the fatal day, and this time in a series of three panels we see her spouting her anti-Semitic venom in English, not Russian. The panels become charged with her hate-filled invectives. "You Damn Kikes, You Did It!" she screams in one of them. This dangerous coalescing of the histories of Nazi and Arab hatred of the Jews in the figure of this woman shakes Spiegelman out of his stupor. In his preface to the book, memorably entitled "The Sky is Falling!," he notes his own predilection for conspiracy theories and his realization of their limits during 9/11:

> In those first few days after 9/11 I got lost constructing conspiracy theories about my government's complicity in what happened that would have done a Frenchman proud. (My own susceptibility for conspiracy goes back a long way but had reached its previous peak after the 2000 elections.) Only when I heard paranoid Arab Americans blaming it all on the Jews did I reel myself back in.

We see this position graphically hypostatized in panel nine where the home-less Russian woman is physically thrown back by the force of his retaliation: "Damn it, Lady! If You Don't Stop Blaming Everything on the Jews, People Are Gonna Think You're CRAZY!" Panel ten shows him striding off after his successful knockdown of the specter of conspiracy, except the sequence ends recursively with a throwback to his figuration as the little son in *Maus*, suffering a nightmare and being consoled by his mother, "Hush, You Fell Out of Bed Sweetie." In the space of a single plate with twelve panels in all – *windows*, he calls them – Speigelman manages brilliantly to compress mul-tiple histories of personal trauma and political catastrophes.

The burning north tower is also the product of the artist's first-hand experience: seeing the collapse of the north tower, inhaling the toxic dust clouds as he runs to rescue his son, then attending the United Nations school. "It took a long time to put the burning towers behind me," Speigelman says in the preface to the book. One image in particular is an original. It is the one that iconicizes his "eyewitness" experience and that recurs throughout *In the Shadow of No Towers*: that of the glowing skeletal remnants of the north tower. 9/11 is by far the most photographed and televised of world catas-trophes; but there are no publicly consumed images of the "glowing bones" of the north tower that Speigelman captures in his comic book:

> The pivotal image from my 9/11 morning – one that didn't get photographed or videotaped into public memory but still remains burned onto the inside of my eyelids several years later – was the image of the looming north tower's glowing bones just before it vaporized. I repeatedly tried to paint this with humiliating results but eventually came close to capturing the vision of disinte-gration digitally on my computer. I managed to place some sequences of my most vivid memories around that central image but never got to draw others.[28]

Apart from this iconic original, most other remediation in *In the Shadow of No Towers* occurs through an interweaving of textual material: newspaper clips from exactly one hundred years ago of the capture of an anarchist accused of murdering President McKinley, cartoon strips from the 1920s to the postwar period, the official 9/11 report, news coverage of the wars in Afghanistan and Iraq, and even *Maus*.

In the staggeringly lethal conjoining of terror and technology at the epicenter of American-style hypercapitalism, one has never felt more acutely the imagistic force of Bakhtin's idea of the "chronotope" as a spatiotemporal matrix in a literary work, a narrative conjuncture of a specific space-time continuum that "takes on flesh," that makes "palpable and visible" particular world views.[29] The novel words of 9/11 become coextensive as it were with the visual unfolding of this spectacular theatre of cruelty on the site of one of the most visible global icons of capitalism's grandeur. The iconography of the "falling man" against the collapsing Twin Towers on 9/11, combined with a cataclysmic "time and space of falling ash and near night" that transforms the "street" into the "world," provide the chronotopical frame of Don DeLillo's *Falling Man*:

> The world was this as well, figures in windows a thousand feet up, dropping into free space, and the stink of fuel fire, and the steady rip of sirens in the air … there was something else then, outside all this, not belonging to this, aloft. He watched it coming down. A shirt came down out of the high smoke, a shirt lifted and drifted in the scant light and then falling again, down toward the river. … He closed his eyes and drank, feeling the water pass into his body taking dust and soot down with it … there was an aftertaste of blood in the long draft of water. (4–5).

That terror of this kind can literally take on "flesh" becomes evident to the survivor protagonist, Keith Neudecker, when he visits a makeshift clinic to have shards of glass extracted from his flesh. The doctor tells him that survivors of suicide bombing catastrophes often come back months later with "bumps" under their skin that are literally "tiny fragments of the suicide bomber's body … that come flying outward with such force and velocity that they get wedged … in the body of anyone who's in striking range" (16). These are "organic shrapnels," pellets of flesh that appear as bumps under the skin.

The novel, in narrating the impact of this catastrophe in meticulous material and corporeal detail, carries the burden of so much nonliterary narratives of effects unleashed by the September 11 attacks. One critical affective transformation has been the emergence of a new temporality of fear. The 9/11 fireballs and falling bodies in the foreground of the collapsing Twin Towers undoubtedly fulfilled the attackers' desire to create a global *spectacle* of terror. But the monumental *stealth* of the attack by unconventional enemy combatants from the shadows of ominous caves thousands of miles away has given rise to an everyday fear of "the evil of a malice knowing neither measure nor ground,"[30] as Derrida put it with such prescience years before the catastrophe. This has temporalized fear less as a reaction to a past occurrence than to a future possibility, which in its turn has generated a newer form of state intervention that is proleptically violent. After 9/11 and on the eve of the Iraq War, McEwan's neurosurgeon in *Saturday* finds himself up in the middle of the night gazing fearfully from his window frame as a flaming aircraft zooms across the dark London horizon:

> It's already eighteen months since half the planet watched, and watched again the unseen captives driven through the sky to slaughter, at which time there gathered round the innocent silhouette of any jet plane a novel association. Everyone agrees, airliners look different in the sky these days, predatory or doomed. (16)

This *felt* reality of a menace that *will have happened* no matter what the nature of the evidence one has in the present is an experience that is symptomatic of many novels of our times. This experience is not always an individualized one of conscious threat perception, but often a distributed feeling simmering under the surface of the everyday. An illustration of this appears in the following passage from Janette Turner Hospital's *Orpheus Lost*:

> People had begun to speak of incidents the way they spoke of accidents on the pike: the frequency was distressing, but such things always happened to someone else. There was a certain *frisson*, a low-level hum of anxiety that was more or less constant, especially in crowds, especially at sporting events, or in concert halls, or in the subway. (92–3)

This "menace-potential" is aggravated by the commanding logic of a preemptive politics that has nothing to do with the materialization of threat. A *felt* threat is judged to be as real as an actualized one. This again is illustrated in the way Leela, the Eurydice-like character in *Orpheus Lost* and a postdoctoral fellow at MIT working on the mathematics of music, is picked up peremptorily for interrogation without a warrant because her boyfriend, Mishka, a musical genius and a Harvard graduate student, is seen to visit a mosque frequently. She is dropped home as abruptly with a warning:

> "When your boyfriend asks where you've been," he said, "remember we'll be listening in." He got back into the car. "Now that you've followed your boyfriend to the mosque, you are radioactive. Every Boston incident, from last year's Prudential bombing to this week's big bang at Park Street, has been traced to that mosque. Think about it. We've got you both under surveillance." (84)

The second aspect of such a political ontology of threat is the performative dimension of the *sign* of menace on which the operative logic of preemption critically depends: the mosque here, for instance. Such a sign is indexed not to *facts* but to *affects* and to the body's becoming alert. Hints, instincts, unaccountable apprehension, set off by a single sign of threat, all mark the performative semiosis of preemption. Coextensive with the body's perpetual state of alertness, such semiosis dissolves the distinction between agent and patient. Drawing on Peirce's work on the indexical force of the sign, Brian Massumi, in his chapter "The Future Birth of Affective Threat," highlights the critical force of this zone of indistinction "between the body reactivating and the action of the sign," which then extends to the environment around.[31] The indexical for Peirce, we might remember, is the sign's force on the body before the latter's conscious awakening to signification. Massumi works with Peirce to philosophically foreground an affective field of surplus danger that operates with such indexical force; one that is always already felt as *real*, before being consciously experienced as such; "a world of infinitely seriating menace-potential made actual experience ... [through] sign's formative performance."[32] The fallout of the foundational threat event in *Orpheus Lost*, a bomb blast in Prudential Tower, and its recursive patterning through the semiosis of both preemption and the sentient world of music to which the protagonists belong, are classic manifestations of this two-fold affective ontology of political threat.

This chapter has sought to give a *world* to novels that mediate the precariousness and shared vulnerabilities of our war-torn and image-saturated age. The hypercapitalist present is more a mirage in these works than a golden now that can forever be extrapolated on to a predictable future. What, I have sought to ask, happens to the humanitarian narrative when compassion has as its object not a singular body in pain or at the threshold of death, but a network of effects generated by horrific media spectacles of war and violence? That is, when the image is not individuating and thus humanizing, but rather an exposure to the corporeal anonymity of mass violence? The humanitarian horizon toward which these works glance is not so much predicated on a benevolent liberalism that looks sympathetically at extreme suffering at a distance, but on an anxiety-ridden solidarity. As Butler notes in *Frames of* War, "over and against an existential concept of finitude that singularizes our relation to death and to life, precariousness underscores our radical substitutability and anonymity in relation to death and to life."[33] Massive mediatization of war underscores our radical substitutability and anonymity in relation to death. It is only on the basis of anonymity and substitutability that a bond of obligation can be formed among strangers. Such a bond is conditioned by a "grievability" that inheres in a mood of apprehension, anxiety, and vulnerability pertaining to the structure of a certain kind of image, beyond and prior to the very possibility of recognizing an individual life. The anxiety, this "common corporeal vulnerability," is marked by an anticipatory temporality, a constant awareness of the imminence of terror and violence that binds us all, an affect that McEwan captures brilliantly in *Saturday*. I close this chapter with the Henry Perowne's ruminations on the shattering of his liberal humanitarian certitudes:

> London, his small part of it, lies wide open, impossible to defend, waiting for its bomb, like a hundred other cities. Rush hour will be a convenient time ... the authorities agree, an attack's inevitable. He lives in different times – because the newspapers say so doesn't mean it isn't true ... this is a future that is harder to read, a horizon indistinct with possibilities ... Baghdad is waiting for its bombs. Where's his appetite for removing a tyrant now? ... Will be revive his hopes for firm action in the morning? All he feels now is fear. He's weak and ignorant, scared of the way consequences of an action leap away from your control and breed new events, new consequences, until you're led to a place you never dreamed of and would never choose. (*Saturday* 276–7)

Notes

1 John Updike, "Paradises Lost: Rushdie's *Shalimar the Clown*," Review in *New Yorker*, 5 September 2005, www.newyorker.com/archive/2005/09/05/050905crbo_books?printable=true&currentPage=all, accessed November 2005.
2 Manuel Castells, *Rise of the Network Society*, vol. 1 (New York: Blackwell), p. 101.
3 On the eve of the 2003 Iraq War, Henry Perowne, the neurosurgeon protagonist of Ian McEwan's novel, *Saturday*, ponders the pervading sense of anxiety and vulnerability across the world, a feeling aggravated by incessant exposure to electronic images of violent global flashpoints: "He takes a step towards the CD player, then changes his mind for he's feeling the pull, like gravity, of the approaching TV news. It's *the condition of the times, this compulsion to hear how it stands with the world*, and be joined to a generality, to a community of anxiety ... the television networks stand ready to deliver, and their audiences wait. Bigger, grosser, next time. Please don't let it happen. But let me see it all the same, as it's happening and from every angle, and let me be among the first to know" (176, italics added).
4 Salman Rushdie, "In the Incredible Lightness of Salman," Interview with Ginny Dougari, *The Times*, 20 August 2005, http://entertainment.timesonline.co.uk/tol/arts_and_entertainment/books/article1081011.ece, accessed 29 September 2009.
5 See Timothy Brennan's "The Subtlety of Caesar," *Interventions* 5:2 (2003), pp. 200–6; and Djelal Kadir's critique of the idea of world literature in "To World, to Globalize: Comparative Literature's Crossroads," *Comparative Literature Studies* 41:1 (2004), pp. 1–9.

6 See, for instance, Faisal Devji's *The Terrorist in Search of Humanity: Militant Islam and Global Politics* (New York: Columbia University Press, 2009); Mahmood Mamdani, *Good Muslim, Bad Muslim* (New York: Pantheon, 2005).

7 I am thinking here especially of the recent enthusiasm of modernism scholars for world models. See Rebecca Walkowitz's *Cosmopolitan Style: Modernism Beyond the Nation* (New York: Columbia University Press, 2006) and Eric Hayot's *On Literary Worlds.*

8 See Carlos J. Alonso piece "The Novel without Literature" in special issue "Futures of the Novel" published in *Novel: A Forum on Fiction* 44: 1 (2011), p. 3–5; emphasis added.

9 Eric Hayot in his 2012 publication *On Literary Worlds* categorically talks of the "rhetorically unmatched prestige" of the concept of "world" in literary criticism of the twenty-first century, p. 30.

10 Edward Said, *The World, the Text, and the Critic* (Cambridge, MA: Harvard University Press, 1984).

11 Timothy Brennan, "The Subtlety of Caesar," *Interventions* 5.2 (2003), pp. 201, 200–6.

12 Edward Said, *Culture and Imperialism*, p. 69

13 Leela Gandhi, "Art," *Affective Communities: Anticolonial Thought, Fin-de-Siecle Radicalism and the Politics of Friendship* (Durham, NC: Duke University Press, 2006), p. 152.

14 Georg Lukács, *The Theory of the Novel*, trans. Anna Bostock (1920; Cambridge, MA: MIT Press, 1971), p. 71.

15 Timothy Bewes does an excellent reading of Lukács in his brief intervention at a Duke "Futures of the Novel" forum, "The Novel Problematic," published in *Novel: A Forum on Fiction* 44:1 (2011), pp. 17–19.

16 M Bakhtin, "Forms of Time and Chronotope in the Novel,"*The Dialogic Imagination: Four Chapters*, trans. Caryl Emerson and Michael Holquist (Austin: University of Texas Press, 1981), p. 253, emphasis original.

17 See Ruth Ronen *Possible Worlds* (Cambridge: Cambridge University Press, 1994), and Thomas G. Pavel's *Fictional Worlds* (Cambridge: Cambridge University Press, 1989) on the operation of set logic in literary theory.

18 Eric Hayot, *On Literary Worlds*, p. 32.

19 Heidegger, "The Age of the World Picture," *Questions Concerning Technology and Other Chapters*, trans. William Lovitt (New York: Harper and Row, 1977).

20 Jean Luc Nancy, *The Creation of the World, or Globalization*, trans. Francois Raffoul and David Pettigrew (New York: SUNY Press, 2007).

21 Nancy, *Creation of the World*, p. 28.

22 "I am the World, I'll Eat the World: A conversation with Gary Shteyngart," Sarah Brown and Armando Celayo in *World Literature Today* 83:2 (2009), p. 30.

23 Franco Moretti, *The Way of the World: The Bildungsroman in European Culture* (London: Verso, 2000), pp. 191–2.

24 F. Scott Fitzgerald, *The Great Gatsby* (1925; New York: Collier, 1992), p. 127.

25 Paul Virilio, *Pure War* (New York: Semiotexte, 1982), p. 174.

26 Hannah Arendt, *The Human Condition* (Chicago, IL: Chicago University Press, 1958).

27 Richard Schechner, "9/11 as Avante-Garde Art?" *PMLA* 124.5 (2009), p. 1827.

28 Preface, *In the Shadow of No Towers* (New York: Pantheon Books, 2004). Page not numbered.
29 Mikhail Bakhtin, "Form of Time and the Chronotope in the Novel: Notes Towards a Historical Poetics," in *The Dialogic Imagination: Four Chapters*, ed. Michael Holquist, trans. Caryl Emerson and Michael Holquist (Austin: University of Texas Press, 1981), p. 250.
30 Jacques Derrida, *The Politics of Friendship*, trans. George Collins (New York: Verso, 1997), p. 83.
31 Massumi, "The Future Birth of the Affective Threat," eds. Melissa Gregg and Gregory Siegworth, *The Affect Theory Reader* (Durham, NC: Duke University Press, 2010), pp. 65–6.
32 Massumi, "Future Birth," p. 65.
33 Judith Butler, *Frames of War: When Is Life Grievable?* (London: Verso, 2009), p. 14.

4

ZOE NORRIDGE

King's College London

Magical/Realist Novels and "The Politics of the Possible"

London was emerging from the war and the oppressive atmosphere of
the Victorian era. I got to know the pubs of Chelsea, the clubs of
Hampstead, and the gatherings of Bloomsbury. I would read poetry, talk
of religion and philosophy, discuss paintings and say things about the
spirituality of the East. ... The women I enticed to my bed included girls
from the Salvation Army, Quaker societies and Fabian gatherings. When
the Liberals, the Conservatives, Labour or the Communists, held a
meeting, I would saddle my camel and go.

Tayeb Salih, *Season of Migration to the North*, translated by Denys
Johnson-Davies (Oxford: Heineman, 1970, first published 1966), p. 30.

In 1969, the African Writers Series published *Season of Migration to the
North* – Denys Johnson-Davies' English translation of Tayeb Salih's novel,
which appeared in Arabic three years earlier. Through the eyes of a Sudanese
man who has studied in London and then returned home, the novel recounts
the journeys of both the narrator and a mysterious man – Mustafa Sa'eed, also
returning from England. James Currey, then editor of the African Writers
Series, comments that "The village scenes on the banks of the Nile are warm
and realistic. The London scenes, set in the 1920s, are cold, harsh and violent;
they parody the mythologies held by Westerners about the Arab world."[1]

I open my chapter with a quotation from this extraordinary work in order
to foreground the ways in which the "real" has *always* been mediated in the
postcolonial novel. Literary realism refers to a body of writing that engages
in a particular way with what we might term the "real world." This engagement is characterized by both *mimesis* and *verisimilitude* – by the way in
which the literary text *reflects* reality on the one hand, and by the ways in
which it gives the *appearance* of being realistic (that is to say convincing) on
the other. This inevitably asks readers to agree on certain codes of reading
and on what, within the format of a novel, is probable. When James Currey
writes that *Season*'s village scenes are "warm and realistic" he does so not
because he spent his own childhood summers on the banks of the Nile but
because they align with emerging literary descriptions about what North
Africa is *like*. Salih may parody European writing about the Orient when he

saddles up his camel but he also produces new novelistic *versions* of "real" London and the Sudan. This writing is mediated by his editor (James Currey), the translator (Denys Johnson-Davies), the publishing series (*African Writers Series, Arab Authors, Penguin Modern Classics*), and the texts the novel is placed alongside, be that in bookshops, in review pages, or on the university curriculum.

As we will see in this chapter the postcolonial novel is both interested in a corresponding referent in reality – *real* societies, geographies, political regimes, and histories – and wary of taking for granted any possibility that such a relationship might be established without being framed through individual and group subjectivities, colored with prejudice and prevailing ideologies. Derek Attridge has commented that "to respond in full responsibility to the act of a realist work is to respond to its unique staging of meaning, and therefore to its otherness." He continues: "It could even be said that the realist work is more, not less, demanding than the modernist work, in that its otherness is often disguised, and requires an even more scrupulous responsiveness."[2] Postcolonial novels are inherently self-conscious, a self-consciousness born out of uneasy cultural encounters and an awareness that the gatekeepers of international publishing firms (and their targeted readers) are still, in far too many cases, based in the "West." Realist postcolonial novels encourage encounters with a "staging of meaning" that is often cross-cultural and always ethically complex.

Writing about the intersections between realism and postcolonialism is a mammoth task. While I might be able to *imagine* the pillars of the realist tradition in Anglophone African literature, say, by conjuring up images of university shelves filled with the orange spines of the African Writers Series,[3] the breadth and scope of the postcolonial novel – crossing the world's continents – proves impossible to hold in my mind. Instead, in this chapter we will shift our focus from one example to another and between countries and continents, offering partial glimpses of national traditions with an approach best illustrated by Rushdie's image of the perforated sheet, which allows the looker to see only parts of a whole and never the body in its integrity.[4] My own field is African literature and my examples spring spontaneously from across this continent. But I will also draw on writing from many of the other rich postcolonial traditions, including novels from India, Sri Lanka, Papua New Guinea, New Zealand, Jamaica, and Canada.

Finding Realism: Unheard Voices

Realism as a term suggests both a distinct period of (predominantly) European literary history and a set of stylistic qualities associated with works from this time that have since been traced to writing that both precedes and follows realism's heyday. Accounts of the stylistic features of realism tend to include thick description, attention to landscape and material details, evocation of a logical world in which actions lead to expected consequences, an interest in the working classes, and a focus on the individual navigating his or her own journey toward self-awareness and knowledge. To examine how ideas relating to realism are applied to postcolonial novels, I will first locate the term within two national traditions before considering how these intersect with the history of colonialism and its aftermath.

As Pam Morris points out, France is seen as the country in which "the realist novel genre was most consciously pursued, debated, acclaimed and denounced."[5] In the nineteenth century the novel was still a relatively new form and its rise was tied to the growth and increasing economic power of the bourgeoisie. As is often the case, realist writers defined themselves in relation to their literary predecessors – in opposition to the logic of neoclassicism and in dialogue with romanticism. Key realist novelists whose sustained use of form, character development, and description would influence later writers include Stendhal, Gustave Flaubert, George Sand, and Honoré de Balzac. From a postcolonial perspective it is also important to note two writers most conventionally seen as romantic – François-René de Chateaubriand and Gérard de Nerval – because their interest in autobiography and psychological complexity (respectively) presages the sense of loss, isolation, and disillusionment found in the myriad forms of later twentieth-century realism. From the 1860s onward, we also see the advent of naturalism – an extension of realism allegedly coined and certainly epitomized by Émile Zola, and marked by pessimism, the harshness of life, and a fascination with "science."

While France was still grappling with the aftermath of the French Revolution (1789–99) and the strictures of the Académie Française (restored by Napoleon in 1803), British history was somewhat less turbulent and the writing consequently arguably less political. The origins of literary realism on the British side of the channel can be traced to eighteenth-century writers such as Daniel Defoe, Samuel Richardson, and Henry Fielding. The nineteenth-century novelists who took up and developed this style include Jane Austen, the Brontë sisters, Charles Dickens, George Eliot, Elizabeth Gaskell, and Thomas Hardy. Female novelists had a more prominent role in Britain, although of course many of the French novels by male writers include detailed studies of the restrictions faced by women (*Madame Bovary*, *Thérèse Raquin*). Common to both groups is an ongoing interest in the middle and working classes, a strong sense of social engagement and the development of new narrative techniques. While Morris suggests that one key difference was the British "skepticism towards any claim that novels can provide faithful or accurate representations of reality" (80), I would argue that Flaubert was also well aware of the mimetic constrictions of his craft.

From the postcolonial perspective, it is notable that many of these realist novelists in the nineteenth century were explicitly engaging with the project of colonialism. Said includes Flaubert's *Salammbô*, Chateaubriand's *Itinéraire de Paris à Jérusalem*, and Nerval's *Voyage en Orient* as key proponents of European Orientalism.[6] Much fascinating recent work has explored the legacies of colonialism, both in terms of material goods and the migration of people, in the work of Dickens, Eliot, the Brontës, and Austen. Increasing literary interest in social conditions at "home" coincides with the rise of Empire but not with a growth of writing about people in the colonized countries. A growing awareness of and unease about the possibilities of representing anything approaching an "objective" reality is not reflected in the consideration of representations of non-European people. And finally, mounting sympathy with the complexities of personal perception, psychosis, and illusions, particular to novelists such as Nerval (so rich in potential overlap with later magical realism), *isn't* reflected in attempts to understand alternative world views from the colonies.

This is the source of much criticism of realism as a mode of writing – with detractors arguing that it was fundamentally implicated in the colonial project. Two of the most criticized texts – Daniel Defoe's *Robinson Crusoe* and Joseph Conrad's *Heart of Darkness* – fall on either side of the period of high realism. Peter Hulme has argued that *Robinson Crusoe*, as one of the earliest realist novels, links the advent of this style of writing with the imperial project. Arguing that the island functions as an allegory of the colonial encounter between the British and the Caribs, he shows how Defoe dramatizes the "education" of the "savage" and "cannibal" Friday.[7] The detail in the novel serves to render this imperial gesture more believable, both in the sense that it can be imagined and that it is figured as the natural order of things. It is similarly the realist detail that Achebe finds so preposterous in Conrad's example of late realism shifting toward modernism, *Heart of Darkness*.[8] Developing Leavis' observation of Conrad's "adjectival insistence upon the inexpressible," Achebe argues that Conrad is engaged in "inducing hypnotic stupor in his readers through a bombardment of emotive words and other forms of trickery." Conrad similarly stands accused of naturalizing the depiction of the complex white mind, set against a background of the simultaneously empty and mysterious African landscape, peopled only by the suffering "black savage." Such writing then is dangerous, because it normalizes imperial ideology, because it takes a specific perspective on the world and encourages the reader to believe that this is the *only* plausible viewpoint.

It is perhaps unsurprising that in response to over a hundred years of realist European novels that sidelined, contorted, or denied the voices of colonized people, writers from colonized countries would adapt the tools of realist narrative to their own advantage in contesting and redressing a long-established mimetic imbalance. Such reframing of realism, often referred to as "writing back,"[9] particularly when the text in question is responding to a specific European precursor, doesn't *begin* with the start of decolonization. Meenakshi Mukherjee, for example, writes lucidly about the many varied forms of the realist Indian novel from the mid-nineteenth to the early twentieth century.[10] But for the purposes of this collection, I will focus my discussion on postcolonial novels emerging from the 1950s to the present day. Many of these novels, while writing to address the perspectival gaps and reductive ideologies of imperialism, also share similar stylistic and ethical preoccupations, apparent in their interest in the growing middle classes, women's perspectives, and the narrative of the individual, embedded in his or her social and historical situation.

If classic postcolonial realism reclaims the history of (formerly) colonized people, then Chinua Achebe's *Things Fall Apart* is the realist novel *par excellence*. As Achebe comments in "The Novelist as Teacher": "I would be quite satisfied if my novels (especially the ones I set in the past) did no more than teach my readers that their past – with all its imperfections – was not one long night of savagery from which the first Europeans acting on God's behalf delivered them."[11] Achebe achieves such a realization through the detailed and sympathetic depiction of an Igbo man – Okonkwo – and his extended family, living in the fictional village of Umuofia. While his concern with the workings of society and the full depiction of character development over time resonates with classic nineteenth-century realism, many critics have observed that the novel is stylistically innovative in its inclusion of elements of oral literature and Igbo language. With his typically simple yet evocative prose, Achebe both depicts both the longevity of local traditions and their increasing interruption by the arrival of white missionaries.

Narratives that recuperate past history while also evoking the speed of change and challenges to indigenous culture in the aftermath of imperial contact can be found in formally colonized countries across the world. So, for example, Vincent Eri's *The Crocodile*, the first novel published by a Papua New Guinean in 1970, five years before independence from Australia, has many elements in common with *Things Fall Apart*.[12] It is also set in a remote village, centered on the narrative of a young man, Hoiri, trying to understand the arrival of the white men. Eri reverses the ubiquitous anthropological gaze on the Pacific islands, rendering the missionaries strange and normalizing the customs and culture of the village. Again this is accompanied with the inclusion of oral elements alongside the ongoing presence of traditional beliefs in the supernatural. As we will see later, the literary depiction of such traditional beliefs, grounded in early realist novels, is foundational for the work of postcolonial magical realism. This is abundantly apparent in Chantal Spitz's *L'île des rêves écrasés* (*Island of Shattered Dreams*) – the first novel published by a Mā'ohi (indigenous Tahitian) writer in 1991. Drawing on real events and people, this novel explores the meaning of enduring colonial relationships with the French from World War II to the late twentieth century, grounded in traditional beliefs (the novel opens with the Mā'ohi account of the foundation of the world) yet critiquing contemporary events such as nuclear testing in the Pacific.

Since the wave of decolonization that began in the 1950s, increasingly sophisticated and ambitious novels have been written exploring histories lost through the imposition of imperialism. Such writing spans decades or even centuries, and aims to make sense of the currents of history through the detailed examination of personal experience. Key examples might include Guadeloupian novelist Maryse Condé's two-volume novel *Ségou*, written in French, which traces the decline of the Bambara empire in Mali across the eighteenth and nineteenth centuries through the story of the Traoré family and the scattering of their descendants across the world. More urban in setting yet similar in its focus on multiple generations of one family, *The Cairo Trilogy* by Naguib Mahfouz is composed of three classic realist novels in Arabic that depict life in Cairo from the Egyptian Revolution (1919) to the end of the Second World War (1945).[13] Drawing on the legacy of Mafouz, Ibrahim Nasrallah's *The Time of White Horses* describes three generations of one family in a fictional Palestinian village before the establishment of Israel – the family's tragedy reflecting that of the nation. Traveling east, another epic saga, spanning a full century of history (from the fall of the Konbaung Dynasty to World War II) and reaching across geographies (Burma, India, the United States) is *The Glass Palace* by Amitav Ghosh. We might also add Sri Lankan novelist and activist Ambalavaner Sivanandan's *When Memory Dies*.

Echoing the nineteenth-century movement toward the reevaluation of more diverse social classes, while contesting these novelists' obfuscation of colonized people's perspectives, both male and female postcolonial novelists, like their European predecessors, have also used the realist novel to explore the experiences of women. In South Asia, Indian women writers have a particularly long history of pathbreaking realist novels. Relatively recent examples include *Difficult Daughters* by Manju Kapur and *Rich Like Us* by Nayantara Sahgal – both foregrounding the challenges faced by women against a backdrop of political upheaval. Turning to Samoa, Sia Figiel's *Where We Once Belonged* is yet another novel that examines women's responses to political and economic upheaval – exploring young women coming of age in the twentieth century, expanding the parameters of the now ubiquitous accounts by cultural anthropologist Margaret Mead. In Africa, Nigerian literature has proved particularly rich in such writing. Classic examples include Flora Nwapa's *Efuru* and Buchi Emecheta's *The Joys of Motherhood*, both of which specifically examine the challenges of infertility and child-rearing.

Many of the postcolonial realist novels written by women focus on one individual (see the two Nigerian examples) and could be aligned with the popular nineteenth-century *Bildungsroman*. This genre might be briefly glossed as the novel of development, a form in which the narrative follows the maturation of a single protagonist as they face the tensions and challenges of their age and establish themselves through the growth of their own personality and incorporation into their society. In *Human Rights Inc.*, Joseph Slaughter traces the intersections between the rise of human rights discourse and the evolution of the *Bildungsroman* as a genre, beginning his study with a discussion of *Robinson Crusoe*.[14] He later goes on to characterize the postcolonial *bildungsroman* as in many ways functioning as an anti-*bildung*. He explains:

> Contemporary first-person postcolonial *Bildungsromane* tend to be novels of disillusionment, in which the promises of developmentalism and self-determination are revealed to be empty, or at least exaggerated; *Bildung* thus becomes the process of recognising the limits of personal development and the sociohistorically contingent condition of the idea and project of the *Bildung* itself. (215–16)

The classic example discussed in *Human Rights Inc.* and offered in many postcolonial literature courses is Tsitsi Dangarembga's *Nervous Conditions*. As Slaughter suggests, the novel recounts the process by which the young Tambudzai becomes aware of the empty promises of development offered by the colonial novels she consumes as a child and instead learns to manage the limitations of living within both colonial and patriarchal systems of domination (228–45). The result is a profound dissatisfaction whereby the protagonist both believes in the possibility of the "free and full development" of his or her personality, while also recognizing the concrete limitations enforced by his or her society. It is this dissatisfaction that perhaps separates the protagonists of classic nineteenth-century novels from their postcolonial successors. The genre is found across the global spread of countries formerly occupied by European powers. Antiguan novelist Jamaica Kincaid's *Lucy* is a classic example. It depicts a young woman, who is attracted by the myth of self-determination, as she travels to the United States to work as an au pair. But ultimately she is disappointed by the limitations of ongoing racism and economic marginalization she encounters at home and overseas. The genre isn't of course limited to stories of women. Recent male-centered examples from South Asia include Khaled Hosseini's *The Kite Runner* and Aravind Adiga's *The White Tiger*.

These classically realist postcolonial novels, with their focus on reclaiming lost perspectives and giving voice to those who were previously unheard, all function against the backdrop of history. But their focus remains on the individual or individuals making up a family, who navigate a complex social world through their own astute insights and well-developed personalities. While this is fascinating in itself, to understand the relationship of the postcolonial novel to realism in more depth, it is also necessary to examine both historical novels which engage with the particularities of history and those texts that explore individuals' responses to the traumas of colonialism and its aftermath in a manner that departs from traditional conceptions of realism and offers a link instead to what is widely termed "magical realism."

Considering Conflict: Alternatives in Realism

As with all periodization, the temporal parameters of postcolonialism are contested. But if we ground our discussion of the postcolonial realist novel in the years following the official dissolution of European, Australian, and American empires in the second half of the twentieth century, we notice that this was a time marked by widespread and catastrophic violence on a global scale. Still recovering from the aftermath of the Second World War, the ways in which independence was mapped and managed by Britain, France, Portugal, Belgium, the Netherlands, Spain, the United States, the Soviet Union, and Australia often led to conflict, in some cases delayed, in others immediate. Realist responses to the process of decolonization necessarily negotiate appalling violence, from accounts of the bloody partition of India and Pakistan (1947) to the brutal Algerian war of Independence (1954–62), from the civil war in Nigeria/Biafra (1967–70) to Bougainville's struggle for secession from Papua New Guinea (1987–97). Even in countries where there was no immediate bloodshed, such as Ghana or Côte d'Ivoire, we see an overwhelming disappointment and disillusionment with Independence, as depicted in novels such as Ayi Kwei Armah's *The Beautyful Ones Are Not Yet Born* and Ahmadou Kourouma's *Les Soleils des indépendences*. Literature set during this period necessarily engages with the nuances of violence in both a manner akin to realism and, increasingly over the course of the second half of the twentieth century, with stylistic features that reflect the subjective experience of violence – an experience that often seems to depart from the detailed, linear, logical sequences of high realism and instead move toward intense sensuality and fragmentation.

While postcolonial writers have resisted being seen as producing only socially relevant work, critics have pointed out that postcolonial novels tend to be more engaged with history than their European counterparts.[15] This is unsurprising if we consider the troubled history of the postcolony. What remains remarkable is the conviction that literature is somehow relevant, that the novel has work to do, in describing and responding to real world events. In a 1987 essay on realism and naturalism Neil Lazarus comments on two realist narrative modes proposed by Njabulo Ndebele: the *spectacular* – which depicts the situation of oppression mimetically; and the *ordinary* – more "dynamic and disclosive," offering "methods" for the situation's "redemptive transformation."[16] Lazarus then maps these terms onto Lukács's distinction between naturalism and realism. Naturalism, concerned with replicating reality in detail to show the ways in which social context determines the development of personality, Lazarus links to Ndebele's *spectacular*, since "in its concern to replicate the look – the 'spectacle' – of everyday life" it fetishizes the visual – "mistaking its surface for deep meaning." The *ordinary* on the other hand is aligned with *realism* as an "expressive avatar of truth" – an "analytical mode, not a documentary one, concerned to portray and not merely to report" (55). Lazarus illustrates his case with two Kenyan novels: Ngũgĩ's *Petals of Blood* and Meja Mwangi's *Going Down River Road*. The former he aligns with the realist text, ending as it does with an evocation of "the vigor and purpose of working-class militancy" – a depiction of and prescription for life in the postcolony. The more pessimistic *Going Down River Road* is instead seen as naturalist in its suggestion of the interminable suffering of the laborers' existence. However, with a radical twist in the story, Lazarus finally argues that the naturalist narrative *is* still ideologically engaged, that the most radical postcolonial writing might not echo the "progressivist ideologies that sustain realism as a discourse" but instead depart from the promise of nationalism in favor of an "oppositional politics whose content, unspecifiable in advance, will yet not be reducible to the centering categories ... of class and nation" (58).

Two and a half decades later we still see postcolonial novelists asking crucial questions about literary realism's engagement with the world. Arguably, Lazarus has been proved right in that naturalism seems less dated than the "recommendations" of social (and socialist) realism, grounded as they were in a particular idea of the nation-state that has since so often been seen to fail. The new realist genre for the twenty-first century is arguably the literature of human rights. In 2002, Michael Ignatieff posited that "since the cold war, human rights has become the dominant moral vocabulary in foreign affairs"[17] and this vocabulary has also increasingly inflected both writers' and publishers' approach to ongoing violence and inequalities. Let us remember that several theorists of literature and human rights have traced the advent of thinking about rights to the rise of the *Bildungsroman*[18] and life-writing[19] – both of which grew exponentially through and alongside the advent of literary realism. Novelists engaging with human rights issues today ground their narratives in detailed descriptions of social context and historical events and considerations of how these external factors shape the development of individual personalities.

We could date human rights inflected naturalist realism back to the post-independence conflicts I discussed earlier – to the new role of writers and the media say in protesting embargoes placed on Biafra (Achebe, Nwapa, Emecheta) or early literary resistance to the plight of the Palestinian people (Sahar Kalifeh, Ghassan Kanafani). But there has also been an upsurge in this form of writing in recent times. The 1994 genocide in Rwanda, for example, inspired a new generation of African writers, including Boubacar Boris Diop (Senegal), Véronique Tadjo (Côte d'Ivoire), and Tierno Monénembo (Guinea) to *bear witness* to the aftermath of mass violence. Their responses are indeed spectacular – grounded in the visual and offering descriptions of violent acts that have a photojournalistic feel, while also foregrounding the experiences and emotions of the individual. Such writing has a tendency to circle the graphically wounded body, the displaced community and the scarred landscape. But they do not remain solely within the realm of the spectacular – instead encouraging both empathy and, ultimately, action, through complex character development. Further examples might encompass a wide range of issues including contested land (see, for example, Palestinian Elias Khoury's *Gate of the Sun* or Maori writer Patricia Grace's *Potiki*), the enduring horror of poverty (Chris Abani's *Graceland*), and the human cost of environmental degradation (Indra Sinha's *Animal's People* about the 1984 Bhopal gas disaster). The shared objective of these writers is to bear witness to what has happened or what happens. To provide evidence, albeit in a fictional form, to build a case for (unspecified) change.

Alongside this quasi-naturalist literature of witnessing in recent years we have also seen a growing range of aesthetic strategies that depart from conventional realist writing in foregrounding both intense sensuality (pleasurable and negative) and the temporal ellipses that are characteristic of real world responses to trauma. A prime example of the first category is Chimamanda Ngozi Adichie's *Half of a Yellow Sun*. Adichie, drawing on a rich inheritance of writing about Biafra, composes a novel told from three distinct viewpoints: a wealthy young Nigerian woman, a houseboy transiting through puberty, and a rather ineffectual English writer. All of the narration is grounded not solely in the visual appearance of the world but also through depictions of the other senses, and in particular touch. I have written about how Adichie draws upon the sensuality of sex to evoke an intimacy that then provides a physical vocabulary to depict the intensity of hunger, loss, and serious wounding.[20] She is not the only writer of her generation to do so. Aminatta Forna, in her account of the aftermath of civil war in Sierra Leone *The Memory of Love*, also revels in the pleasures of consensual sex in order to create a discomforting juxtaposition with the sexual violence perpetrated against both women and men during the fighting. Similarly, Kamila Shamsie in *Burnt Shadows* articulates the physicality of suffering related to the bombing of Nagasaki and the partition of India and Pakistan, through careful description of sexual contact, epitomized in a scene in New Delhi when the Urdu-speaking Muslim protagonist Sajjad touches the burn marks on atomic bomb survivor Hiroko's back, both moved and aroused.

The writer who has captured the sensuality and temporal disconnection of trauma perhaps more than any other is the Zimbabwean novelist Yvonne Vera. Her work engages with the extremes of anticolonial and postcolonial violence through deeply personal and sensual narratives that slide between different time periods in a looping nonchronological manner. Epitomized by her discussion of postindependence violence in Matabeleland, *The Stone Virgins*, in their fragmentation, these novels echo the structure of trauma itself, which, as Cathy Caruth among others has pointed out, is characterized by gaps in memory and missing information in narratives of events, alongside involuntary flashbacks and disturbing linkages between past and present.[21] Such writing is not confined to African novels. Regis Stella's *Gutsini Posa*, for example, explores the disintegrating mental health of a young man returning to the island of his childhood (thinly veiled references to Bougainville, Stella's own birthplace), and the islanders he finds existing in a haunting state of "psychological death" engendered by extended suffering. The collapse of linear narrative and distortion of chronological time in such narratives reflects both the experience of the victims of such violence and deprivation and also the official silences that surround these difficult histories. Michael Ondaatje's *Anil's Ghost* is another case in point.[22] Evoking the challenges in ever achieving a full account of the civil war in Sri Lanka, the novel demonstrates to what extent the later postcolonial novels of conflict are uneasy about any possibility of full knowledge of events.

Here we begin to perceive a series of linkages between the many forms of realism in the postcolonial novel. The most traditional realist novels foregrounded stories of individual development alongside the restitution of voices and the contestation of history. Through the encounter with conflict, growing disillusionment with the aftermath of colonialism, and mounting caution about the optimism of Marxist or nationalist ideology, the realist novel arguably turns toward more naturalist techniques. These techniques intersect with growing global social and political interest in the human rights narrative, leading to an ethics of "witnessing" that, while it has its roots in representations of earlier conflicts, seems to be aesthetically particularly tied to the contemporary period. Attempts to further engage readers with the realities of ongoing suffering lead to aesthetic innovation that departs from conventional realist narrative techniques but, in its objective – to capture the quality of the lived experience in art – also remains consonant with both realism and the tenets of modernism. The other major current in postcolonial writing that intersects with this complex history is the advent of magical realism.

Magical Realism and "the politics of the possible"

Toward the opening of Rushdie's *Midnight's Children* the narrator, Saleem Sinai, after tying his birth inexorably to the moment of Indian Independence and partition from Pakistan, declares:

> I must work fast, faster than Scheherazade, if I am to end up meaning – yes, meaning – something. I admit it: above all things, I fear absurdity.
> There are so many stories to tell, too many, such an excess of intertwined lives events miracles places rumours, so dense a commingling of the improbable and the mundane! I have been a swallower of lives; and to know me, just the one of me, you'll have to swallow the lot as well. (9)

As with the multiple forms of realist responses to conflict, the storyteller here seeks a purpose for his narrative. And it is a purpose that falls between two spheres of meaning: the real world (as seen in the precise manner with which he ties elements of the plot to specific historical events) and the world of literature where the *story* – the tales spun by Scheherazade over a thousand and one nights – is a lifeline in itself. The excessive stories of "intertwined lives events miracles places rumours" map from the outset the intricate webs of connections in the novel to come. The phrase, without commas, spoken in one breath, also defies the usual boundaries of classification – the outlandish miracle nestling beside the concrete event, the salacious rumor alongside the firm ground of place. All of this spun through the metaphor of consumption – of absorbing other lives.

This novel, published in 1981, exemplifies the "commingling of the improbable and the mundane" – the characteristics of a literary mode referred to as magical realism that in the 1980s moved beyond its first full flourishing in Latin America and emerged as one of the key forms of post-colonial writing. Nearly every critic writing about "magical realism" observes that the term is an oxymoron – that there is an inherent tension between the magical and the real. But it is precisely this contradiction that proves so alluring for writers and theorists. Definitions of magical realism usually stress that the mode manifests an *equivalence* between the supernatural and the real. That is to say neither the world of magic nor the empirical reality we might expect to see in a realist novel is given the upper hand over the other realm and indeed they often "commingle" as Rushdie so provocatively suggests. In addition, there is no attempt to "explain away" the existence of the magical – it is not for example shown to be tied to the hallucinations of trauma or the imaginative wonderings of a child (although both trauma and children appear recurrently in all of these texts).[23] These novels also often exhibit elements of oral literature and emphasize sensory experiences alongside a proliferation of details that contribute to the reality effect of the narrative.

Chris Warnes has traced the origins of the term "magical realism" to the writings of the German romantic poet and philosopher Novalis.[24] He intriguingly dates the first use of this combination of words to 1798, the year in which Napoleon landed in Egypt and *Lyrical Ballads* was published by Wordsworth and Coleridge. This marks the beginning of romanticism, before the full advent of nineteenth-century realism. The term did not seem to gain traction and resurfaces only much later in the work of art historian Franz Roh and the writing of Italian critic Massimo Bontempelli. By the late forties and early fifties Ulsar-Pietri and Angel Flores are applying the term to Latin American authors, joined by Luis Leal in the late sixties. Influential early authors coming out of Latin America writing in this mode include Alejo Carpentier (Cuba) and Miguel Angel Asturias (Guatemala). But the most famous Latin American magical realist is of course the Colombian writer Gabriel García Márquez whose classic novel *One Hundred Years of Solitude* was published in 1967.

In the 1980s a range of international magical realist novels appeared, including *Midnight's Children*, Angela Carter's *Nights at the Circus*, and Toni Morrison's *Beloved*. By 1988, Stephen Slemon was suggesting, drawing on Canadian examples of magical realism, that postcolonialism and magical realism were fundamentally intertwined. Slemon argues that in magical realist work the specific site of narration "becomes a metonymy of the postcolonial culture as a whole" – that is to say that the postcolonial magical realist novel can be read as relevant to all postcolonial contexts. In addition the novel both foreshortens history in order to contain "the long process of colonization and its aftermath" and foregrounds the "gaps, absences, and silences produced by the colonial encounter and reflected in the text's disjunctive language of narration."[25] This is an ambitious assertion. But it is echoed in the writing of Wendy Faris, who argues that magical realism's suspension between the supernatural and the real fundamentally "resembles the colonial subject's suspension between two – or more – cultural systems." She claims it therefore plays a "decolonizing role, one in which new voices have emerged, an alternative to European realism."[26] These new voices, both literary and theoretical, are brought together in Faris and Zamora's globally conceived path-breaking collection *Magical Realism: Theory, History and Community*.[27]

While I agree that magical realism offers a particularly fertile aesthetic approach to postcolonial material, the grounding of its value in opposition to the supposed straitjacket of realism is problematic, as we saw through examining the complexities of postcolonial realist novels earlier in this chapter. There may also be a danger, as several critics have pointed out, that magical realism merely reenacts dominant power structures. Faris herself cites Taussig's objection that the wonder of magical realism is presented in accordance with "a long-standing tradition of folklore, the exotic and *indigenismo*" that she argues "in oscillating between the cute and the romantic is little more than the standard ruling class appropriation of what is held to be the sensual vitality of the common people and their fantasy life" (104). On a related note, Kumkum Sangari, in an essay from which I borrow the second part of this chapter heading, argues that:

> Though forged within the insistent specificity of a localized relation, the very differences of such fiction are read as techniques of "novelty" and "surprise" in the West. Novelty guarantees assimilation into the line of postmodern writers not only because the principle of innovation is also the principle of the market in general, but also because the postmodern obsession with antimimetic forms is always on the lookout for new modes of "self" fracture, for new versions of the self-locating, self-disrupting text.[28]

The "fashionable" nature of magical realism in the late twentieth and early twenty-first century then is arguably linked as much to Western consumer patterns as it is to any internationally coherent protest against the enduring forms of (neo)colonialism. But while such reservations do encourage a note of caution when making assertions about relevance and resistance, they don't detract from the quality of the texts themselves or from the careful scholarship on magical realism. Let us turn then to novels themselves to probe the qualities of magical realism further.

Rushdie's *Midnight's Children* is still upheld as *the* classic postcolonial magical realist novel. Recounting three generations of the Sinai family and Saleem Sinai's links with the 1,001 other children born at the moment of India's independence, the narrative spins through detailed machinations of history alongside mysterious everyday occurrences. In common with many other magical realist texts this is often mediated through evocative accounts of physical sensation, particularly smell (repeated references to Sinai's nose) and taste (cooking, pickles). Such phenomenological descriptions ground a narrative that otherwise swoops (Rushdie's word) between different locations and perspectives, circling and spiraling through time in the manner of oral literature. These textual maneuvers have multiple regionally grounded sources of inspiration, not least Hindu mythology and the *One Thousand and One Nights*. But Rushdie also overtly points to international intertexts that consciously locate the novel within the field of magical realism: namely, Gunter Grass's *The Tin Drum* and Márquez's *One Hundred Years of Solitude*. In his review of *Chronicle of a Death Foretold* Rushdie comments that:

> *El realismo magical*, "magical realism," at least as practised by García Márquez, is a development of Surrealism that expresses a genuinely "Third World" consciousness. It deals with what Naipaul has called "half-made" societies, in which the impossibly old struggles against the appallingly new, in which public corruptions and private anguishes are more garish and extreme than they ever get in the so-called "North," where centuries of wealth and power have formed thick layers over the surface of what's really going on.[29]

Such observations are also clearly applicable to *Midnight's Children* and further align the novel, both with the international mode of magical realism *and* with those realist novels of disillusionment and conflict we discussed earlier. Rushdie also perceptively comments that in Latin America "the damage to reality was – is – at least as much political as cultural." That is to say the literary depictions of reality by Márquez, and by extension Rushdie, grapple with boundaries between the real and unreal not solely because of a rich cultural tradition of such blurring, but also as a reflection of ongoing political unease, manifest in descriptions of the Amritsar massacre, the Bangladesh war, and Indira Gandhi's Emergency. Magical realism here reflects the impossibility of ascertaining the truth of a particularly dystopic political situation, despite Sinai's protestations that he is not "speaking metaphorically" and instead recounts "nothing less than the literal, by-the-hairs-of-my-mother's-head truth" (200).

Chris Warnes, trying to ascertain the purpose of the magical in such novels, offers two possible interpretations. On the one hand he suggests the text may generate, "in postmodern fashion, the effect of unmasking the real, showing up its claims to truth to be provisional and contingent on consensus." On the other hand, "the magical may seek to force its way into the company of the real" with the hope of sharing "the privileged claim the language of realism has to representing the world" (9). The two approaches he describes as *irreverence* and *faith*. In his later monograph he clarifies that:

> In faith-based magical realism, the supernatural event or presence may stand synecdochically or metonymically for an alternative way of conceiving of reality usually derived from a non-Western belief system or world view. By contrast, in the irreverent strands of magical realism such an event or presence, which is not rationalized or explained away, nonetheless stands in place of an idea or a set of ideas, say, about the ways language constructs reality, or about the incapacities of binaristic thinking.[30]

Warnes gives *The Satanic Verses* as his key example of irreverence and then goes on to give another key postcolonial text – Ben Okri's *The Famished Road* as his example of faith. Citing Okri himself, he suggests the magical elements in this novel of the early nineties reflect not the surrealism of Rushdie but instead a West-African perspective on reality: "This is just the way the world is seen: the dead are not really dead, the ancestors are still part of the living community and there are innumerable gradations of reality, and so on."[31]

The Famished Road has long been taken as the key example of magical realism from Africa. The novel – Nigerian author Ben Okri's third – tells the story of an *abiku* child. Such a child, inhabited by an *abiku* spirit, traditionally dies before puberty only to return later as another child, destined to die prematurely once more. However, the novel's young protagonist, Azaro, wishes to remain within the world of the living, tied to his parents by their love and ongoing suffering. His is a liminal position – he sees the spirits of the dead and can pass into realms beyond this world – but it is also one grounded in the detail of poverty and childhood desires. Such suspension between worlds necessarily echoes the tenets of magical realism. As Elleke Boehmer observes: "In contrast both to the colonial writing which placed Africa as signifier of the exotic and the forbidden, and to early nationalist writing which sought to reverse colonial stereotypes, Okri's worlds have absorbed the extremes of the exotic and the real."[32] Ato Quayson, in "Magical Realism and the African Novel," traces this to the influence of West African oral traditions. Pointing out that orality is not merely a manner of communication but instead a way of perceiving and interpreting the world, which structures "reality" through proverbs, myths, and legends, Quayson draws on Garuba's suggestion that "within the animist worldview ... the physical world of phenomena is spiritualized" (159–60). This doesn't signal a "return" to an imagined precolonial. Instead, in Garuba and Quayson's terms, animist realism offers the opportunity to "appropriate the tools of both traditionalism and modernity for explicitly strategic contemporary purposes" and magical realism is read as a "subspeciate" of animist realism (161). In some ways this doesn't seem very different from Warnes' distinction between irreverence (grounded as it is in the play of the postmodern) and faith. What both readings point toward is the multiplicity of influences on this form of writing alongside the belief that at least some elements of such aesthetic strategies can be compared across cultures synchronically.[33]

For our final examples, then, let us turn our attention to the other side of the world and writing from New Zealand. Keri Hulme's *The Bone People* is sometimes included in the canon of magical realist world literature – as much by lay readers trying to find words to describe the spiritual Maori elements of the novel as by critics working with the mode in any strictly defined sense. Winner of the Booker Prize (in the company of *Midnight's Children* and *The Famished Road*), the novel relates the story of Kerewin, a reclusive artist; Simon/Haimona, a young, apparently orphaned boy; and his Maori foster-father Joe. The narrative engages with very real social problems including what appears to be a form of alcoholism and horrific ensuing violence directed at the young child. It also explores the mixing and comingling of Maori and Pakeha (white) identities in contemporary Aotearoa – an angle for which it has gained international acclaim. But at its core it is a novel of friendship and love across generations and languages. Much of the mystery of the novel is grounded in incomplete information only partially shared between the characters so that each person remains uncertain about the others' experiences and feelings. The elements readers have referred to as magical include a perennial sense of foreboding, disorientating swapping between third- and first-person narrative voices (which might more accurately be interpreted as a postmodern trait), and descriptions of contact with Maori ancestors. Simon, the only one of the three with no indigenous heritage, sees a "little brown man with blue lines across his face" during their stay at Moerangi who sings to him in Maori (215, 305). Kerewin is later mysteriously helped by an unknown visitor while dying of cancer in the same place (515–16) and Joe is finally instructed by an elder, Kaumatua, that he must assume a particular sacred role (440).

The Bone People is not however a magical realist text in the strictest sense of the term, primarily because the novel doesn't form a sense of equivalence between the worlds of the real and the supernatural. Instead, Kerewin, Joe, and Haimona are grounded in a material sense of the real, only unequivocally moving outside of this realm during distinct encounters. That said, the novel is written through with local traditional oral sources and the supernatural incidents do suggest an "alternative way of conceiving reality ... derived from a non-Western belief system."[34] We might then suggest that *The Bone People* could be placed somewhere on a continuum between realism and magical realism, as indeed can many postcolonial realist texts, incorporating as they do elements of religious belief and local practices. Works by leading Maori writers including Witi Ihimaera (*The Whale Rider*) and Patricia Grace (*Potiki*) might also fall along such a continuum. As would Kim Scott's *Benang*, a novel exploring the author's own dual Aboriginal and white settler heritage and in particular the horrors of the stolen generations of children using magical techniques (flight, spirituality) to overcome gaps in the official history. Similarly, African writing comes in many shades of the supernatural. Amos Tutuola's overtly otherworldly *The Palm Wine Drinkard* is unequivocally "magical" even if critics have excluded it from the strictest definitions of "magical realism." At the other end of the spectrum, Achebe's classic realist novel *Things Fall Apart* also includes an *ogbanje* (Igbo for the Yoruba term *abiku*) child even if the spiritual beliefs about the child are treated in a sympathetic ethnographic rather than fantastical manner.

Magical realism is perhaps more porous than critics would like to think. In drawing on local mythologies and oral narratives, novels with "magical realist" elements call into question the "politics of the possible" or what we (whoever "we" might be) choose to believe is (un)likely. Certain practices (particularly fragmentation, emphasis on the illusion of meaning, and self-authoring) also align with contemporary trends in postmodern writing. Magical realist novels, strictly defined, tend to combine these practices with the aforementioned *equivalence* between the magical and the real. But arguably nearly all texts within the realist postcolonial canon include allusions to the supernatural, alongside references to experiences that fall outside of the "ordinary" realm of Euro-American experience.

Concluding Thoughts

In *The Singularity of Literature* Derek Attridge argues that:

> The tradition of realist fiction should be understood – in so far as it is literature and not a type of history read for its vivid representation of past events – as a staging of objectivity, an invitation to experience the knowability of the world. We learn from literature not truth, but what the telling (or denying) of the truth is.[35]

Attridge goes on to talk about recent critical interest in literature's ability to "witness" historical traumas. It is the "staging" of witnessing, of truth-telling, of testimony, that is so fascinating for the reader. And it is in this "staging" that the reader encounters the unique challenges posed by literature in relation to the extent to which we can ever access the subjectivity of other human minds.

Realist and magical realist postcolonial novels invite the reader to engage with the politics of representation and the limits of perception. By the nineteenth century, realist novelists were already calling into question the extent to which literature could ever provide an accurate "reflection" of reality. Postcolonial novelists inherited a set of formal characteristics and literary questions that they then developed in new manners, ever conscious of the ways in which those same eighteenth and nineteenth-century novelists obscured the perspectives of peoples colonized by their Empires. We have seen how a great deal of this writing is concerned with reclaiming histories and marginalized subject positions, with responding to conflict and with challenging dominant assumptions about the boundaries of perception.

The realist mode shows no signs of ill health. And indeed recent realist postcolonial offerings have carried the boundaries of the novel ever further. Many demonstrate virtuosity in their shifts between realist approaches to individual perspectives. Examples include highly successful recent novels from India such as Kiran Desai's *The Inheritance of Loss* or Ghosh's *Sea of Poppies* where the narrative moves between radically different protagonists, across class and geographies. Jamaican novelist Diana McCaulay's *Dog-Heart* is another case in point – swapping as it does between the viewpoint of the "ghetto" child Dexter and the uptown "brown" woman Sahara. Here, as in many postcolonial novels, the differences are manifested not only in the parameters of experience but also in the language used by the first-person narrators. Dexter speaks a version of Jamaican patois adapted for international readership, Sahara a standardized, but nevertheless resolutely Jamaican English. Such linguistic realism of course has many precedents, not least from the Caribbean context Sam Selvon's *The Lonely Londoners*. But the movement between contrasting linguistically framed subjectivities – seen in other contemporary novels such as Adichie's *Half of a Yellow Sun* and Andrea Levy's *Small Island* – remains fresh and compelling.

There are of course many more manifestations of the (magical) realist novel I have not been able to discuss; for example, recent novels from the perspectives of animals such as José Eduardo's *The Book of Chameleons* or *Dog Days* by Patrice Nganang.[36] There is also a great deal more critical work to be done understanding the fluid boundaries between the literary representation of trauma and magical realism, examining for instance the extraordinary schizophrenia-inflected *A Question of Power* by Bessie Head or Delia Jarret-McCaulay's dreamlike account of the aftermath of the civil war in Sierra Leone, *Moses, Citizen and Me*. Further afield in world literature, exciting work is taking place mapping socialist realism and exchanges of theory and narrative between China, Japan, the then Soviet Union and East Germany. Such scholarship is of course likely to span outward to literatures of revolution across the Pacific, Indian, and Atlantic oceans. This chapter then is avowedly (and necessarily) incomplete, but I hope it may participate in expanding the conversation.

Notes

1 James Currey, *Africa Writes Back* (Oxford: James Currey, 2008), p. 177.

2 Derek Attridge, "Literary Form and the Demands of Politics: Otherness in J.M. Coetzee's *Age of Iron*," in ed. George Levine, *Aesthetics and Ideology* (New Brunswick, NJ: Rutgers University Press, 1994), p. 262.

3 This would of course be incomplete given the variety of publishers printing African novels both inside and outside the continent.

4 Salman Rushdie, *Midnight's Children* (London: Vintage, 1995, first published 1981), pp. 23–9.

5 Pam Morris, *Realism* (London & New York: Routledge, 2003), p. 47.

6 Edward Said, *Orientalism* (London: Penguin Books, 1991, first published 1978).

7 Peter Hulme, *Colonial Encounters: Europe and the Native Caribbean, 1492–1797* (London & New York: Methuen, 1986), p. 216.

8 Chinua Achebe, "An Image of Africa: Racism in Conrad's Heart of Darkness," *Research in African Literatures* 9:1 (Spring 1978, first published 1977).

9 Bill Ashcroft, Gareth Griffiths, and Helen Tiffin, *The Empire Writes Back* (London: Routledge, 2002, first published 1989).

10 Meenakshi Mukherjee, *Realism and Reality: The Novel and Society in India* (Delhi: Oxford University Press, 1994).

11 Chinua Achebe, "The Novelist as Teacher," in *Hopes and Impediments: Selected Essays, 1965–1987* (London: Heinemann, 1988, first published 1965), pp. 27–31.

12 Vincent Eri, *The Crocodile* (Brisbane: Jacaranda Press, 1970).

13 Najīb Maḥfūẓ, *The Cairo Trilogy* (New York: Alfred A. Knopf, 2001).

14 Joseph Slaughter, *Human Rights, Inc.: The World Novel, Narrative Form, and International Law* (New York: Fordham University Press, 2007).

15 Keith Booker, "The African Historical Novel," ed. Abiola Irele, *The Cambridge Companion to the African Novel* (Cambridge: Cambridge University Press, 2009), p. 141.

16 Neil Lazarus, "The Retrieval of Naturalism: The Politics of Narrative in Radical African Fiction," *Critical Exchange* 22 (Spring 1987), p. 55.

17 Michael Ignatieff, "Is the Human Rights Era Ending?," The *New York Times*, 5 February 2002, www.nytimes.com/2002/02/05/opinion/is-the-human-rights-era-ending.html?pagewanted=all&src=pm, accessed 1 April 2012.

18 Slaughter, *Human Rights, Inc.*

19 Kay Scaffer and Sidonie Smith, *Human Rights and Narrated Lives: The Ethics of Recognition* (New York: Palgrave Macmillan, 2004).

20 Zoe Norridge, "Sex as Synecdoche: Intimate Languages of Violence in Chimananda Ngozi Adichie's *Half of a Yellow Sun* and Aminatta Forna's *The Memory of Love*," *Research in African Literatures* 43:2 (2012), pp. 18–39.

21 Cathy Caruth, *Unclaimed Experience: Trauma, Narrative, and History* (Baltimore, MD: John Hopkins Press, 1996); Roger Luckhurst, *The Trauma Question* (London: Routledge, 2008).

22 Michael Ondaatje, *Anil's Ghost* (London: Bloomsbury, 2011, first published 2000).

23 For more on these criteria, see Ato Quayson, "Magical Realism and the African Novel," in ed. Abiola Irele, *The Cambridge Companion to the African Novel* (Cambridge: Cambridge University Press, 2009), pp. 159–76.

24 Chris Warnes, "Naturalizing the Supernatural: Faith, Irreverence and Magical Realism," *Literature Compass* 2 (2005), p. 2.

25 Stephen Slemon, "Magic Realism as Post-Colonial Discourse," *Canadian Literature* 116 (Spring 1988), p. 13.

26 Wendy Faris, "The Question of the Other: Cultural Critiques of Magical Realism," *Janus Head* 5:2 (Fall 2002), p. 103.

27 Lois Parkinson Zamora and Wendy Faris (eds.), *Magical Realism: Theory, History, Community* (Durham, NC: Duke University Press, 1995).

28 Kumkum Sangari, "The Politics of the Possible" *Cultural Critique* 7 (Autumn 1987), p. 181.

29 Salman Rushdie, "Angel Gabriel," *London Review of Books* 4:17 (16 September 1982), p. 4.

30 Chris Warnes, *Magical Realism and the Postcolonial Novel: Between Faith and Irreverence* (London: Palgrave, 2009), pp. 14–15.

31 Jean Ross "Contemporary Author Interview with Ben Okri" in ed. Donna Olendorf, *Contemporary Authors* 138 (Detroit, MI: Gale Research, 1993), p. 338.

32 Elleke Boehmer, *Stories of Women: Gender and Narrative in the Postcolonial Nation* (Manchester: Manchester University Press, 2005), p. 142.

33 For a much more detailed discussion of magical realism in Syl Cheney-Coker, Ben Okri, and Kojo Laing see Brenda Cooper, *Magical Realism in West African Fiction* (London: Routledge, 1998).

34 Warnes, *Magical Realism*, p. 15.

35 Derek Attridge, *The Singularity of Literature* (London: Routledge, 2004), p. 97.

36 José Eduardo, *The Book of Chameleons* (London: Arcadia Books, 2006, translated by Daniel Hahn, first published 2004). Patrice Nganang, *Dog Days*, translated by Amy Baram Reid (Charlottesville: University of Virginia Press, 2006, first published 2001).

5

ANTHONY CARRIGAN

University of Leeds

Nature, Ecocriticism, and the Postcolonial Novel

One of the most compelling developments in postcolonial studies over the last decade has been the explosion of interest in literature and the environment. It is not difficult to see why ecological concerns should be central to postcolonial thought: as Edward Said famously asserted, imperialism is predicated on "an act of geographical violence,"[1] and regaining sovereignty over land and natural resources has been vital to decolonization movements worldwide. Experiences of environmental conflict and recuperation are similarly core concerns for postcolonial writers, who have dealt with such highly charged subjects as resource wars, land and animal rights, development and urbanization, conservation, food security, tourism, militarism, and waste. If the environment has been rather more understated in the development of postcolonial literary studies, the recent emergence of postcolonial ecocriticism has brought ecological issues to the fore, presenting renewed possibilities for ecocritical analysis within and beyond the postcolonial field. This chapter builds on this exciting work by examining what the postcolonial novel has to say about the effects of imperialism and globalization in a range of different environments. Drawing on examples from Africa, Australasia, the Caribbean, North America, and India, the chapter shows how postcolonial novelists depict nature in ways that are culturally localized and globally engaged, inflected by specific colonial histories and contemporary neocolonial concerns. In so doing, they highlight the importance of narrative in helping us to imagine foundations for environmental equity in a world marked by deepening ecological crises.

Contested Natures

One of the first things to address in approaching postcolonial ecologies – and environmental criticism more broadly – is the fraught and potentially misleading idea of nature. This is because, much like "race," "nature" is a social construct, whose definition depends partly on separating it from "culture" or the human world. Nature is often portrayed as a universal entity, but as Kate Soper puts it pithily, "the one thing that is not 'natural' is 'nature' itself,"[2] and ecofeminists and environmental philosophers have identified it as a product of Enlightenment traditions that divided the world into categories to be surveyed, ordered, governed, and possessed.[3] It is telling that many cultures – and indigenous peoples in particular – do not have separate words for nature or the environment, while the nature/culture divide in western thought relies on similarly dualistic thinking to that which underpins imperialism and patriarchy. Moreover, as Val Plumwood observes, imperial constructions of "nature" often included "what are thought of as less ideal or more primitive forms of the human. This included women and supposedly "backward" or "primitive" people, who were seen as exemplifying an earlier and more animal stage of human development."[4] Such hierarchies underpin what Alfred Crosby has termed "ecological imperialism," which describes an array of practices from appropriation of indigenous land to the introduction of new biological species that have reconfigured global ecosystems.[5]

Given the plurality of how nature has been constructed over time, it seems safest to follow Phil Macnaghten and John Urry's claim that "there is no singular 'nature' ... only a diversity of contested natures ... constituted through a variety of socio-cultural processes."[6] We need to be open to a plurality of environmental understandings that are shaped by local worldviews and global processes, and see nature as both a discursive construct and material fact that is bound up with issues of power, difference, and domination. This is a feature of political ecology and environmental justice scholarship, which has helped expand understandings of ecological imperialism to include, for instance, "biocolonialism" or the corporatization of nature through movements such as the Green Revolution and gene patenting, and "environmental racism," which refers to how the exploitation of ethnic groups and natural environments can be mutually reinforcing.[7] These processes are also key for postcolonial ecocriticism, which has drawn attention to how literary texts represent power relations as environmentally embedded, and has extended ecocriticism's horizons by connecting global ecological transformation to histories of colonialism.[8]

Ecocriticism is often simply defined as the study of literature and the environment, but it is motivated by a refusal to treat the nonhuman world as passive "setting" or backdrop in literary texts. Rather, ecocritics are interested in how writers and artists depict the nonhuman world as constitutive of human endeavors. Ecocriticism shares postcolonial studies' interest in interdisciplinarity and political critique, conveying a broadly green agenda and a commitment to thinking through issues of rights and responsibilities from nonanthropocentric perspectives. The development of postcolonial ecocriticism has helped telescope – and in some cases transcend – points of conflict between anticolonial and environmental politics while exploring the many "varieties of environmentalism" portrayed in global texts, which often exhibit different priorities to western environmentalisms.[9]

While early ecocritics were drawn to identifying "environmental" genres (e.g., nature writing, ecopoetry, animal fables), most now agree that *all* literary texts can be read ecocritically. The novel's capacity for environmental representation has, however, been regarded with added suspicion because its canonical development is so closely tied to the rise of capitalism, industrialization, and bourgeois individualism, which have endangered the planet at large. Dominic Head, for instance, has emphasized the novel's environmental limitations due to its focus on individual development within social contexts, its address to increasingly urbanized populations, and its focus on time over place, and he reserves most scepticism for the *realist* novel's capacity for ecological thought due to its perceived anthropocentrism.[10] The counterargument to this is that all texts carry a sense of "environmentality," and that the novel's perceived inadequacy for conveying green ideas does not preclude examination of the insights it offers into the politics of space, place, and ecology over time.[11]

Certainly in the hands of postcolonial writers, the novel has proved a major form for portraying social *and* environmental justice concerns. This has involved not simply rejecting but also building on the legacies of social realism, which in its canonical form is by no means divorced from broader ecological and economic processes. As Elleke Boehmer observes, "Empire enters the nineteenth-century novel chiefly as commodity, in images of riches and trade,"[12] and Robert Marzec has also examined how the novel developed alongside and engaged with the rise of the Enclosure Movement, a "nationwide and eventually worldwide restructuring of humanity's relation to the land" based on transferring agricultural commons to private ownership.[13] The various natural and built environments depicted in the form over time therefore provide gateways to broader discussions of how the physical world has been organized, and how urban and metropolitan environments are internationally and ecologically networked.

The generic innovations postcolonial writers have used to represent environmental concerns overlap significantly with how they have negotiated the novel's implication in industrial capitalism and high imperialism. They also reflect how the novel as a relatively "long" form has been adapted to portray decolonization as a protracted process, which has been compromised by new and resurgent colonialisms, and the often violent demands of globalization. If political and economic decolonization has been distinctly uneven in many contexts, yielding benefits to some while continuing to oppress others, the decolonization of nature has been even more partial, with ongoing disputes over environmental sovereignty, resource use, and pollution exemplifying the colonial politics that underpin planetary crisis – points that the following sections will now address.

Exploration and Environmental Knowledges

Colonialism has long been legitimized through celebratory narratives, emphasizing heroic voyages of discovery, exploration, and possession, with land and ocean territories either being considered "empty" – and therefore ripe for settlement – or in need of "cultivation" and "improvement," justifying external administration and control.[14] A stark example is the settlement of Australia, which was designated "terra nullius" or "empty land" by Europeans who claimed sovereignty on the basis that Aboriginal peoples were "uncivilized" and lacked recognizable land titles. These claims were in themselves fictions, underwritten by military power and the will to govern, and encoded in law. Postcolonial representations of the environment frequently expose this logic of domination, asserting alternative epistemologies of place habitation and exploring how, as Said puts it, "geographical identity" might be "restored."[15] Yet the complexity of postcolonial identity means this is no simple task. In settler colony contexts, for instance, populations have competing claims to being "native" and often very different ideologies of land use that must be negotiated. Similarly, in transcultural regions such as the Caribbean, slavery and the plantation industry produced such profound ruptures that environmental "restoration" can only be conceived through acts of collective imagination.[16]

These points become legible if we consider two mid-century examples that critique the mythos of colonial exploration and environmental appropriation in Australia and the Caribbean, Patrick White's *Voss* (1957) and Wilson Harris's *Palace of the Peacock* (1960). *Voss* was White's breakthrough novel, and it looks back to nineteenth-century expeditions into Australia's interior. The title character, Johann Ulrich Voss, is a fictionalization of German naturalist Ludwig Leichhardt, and the novel's epic scope, following Voss's similarly epic attempt "to cross the continent from one end to the other," satirizes his desire to lay claim to "this country of which he had become possessed by implicit right."[17] While Voss boasts that he will "make" the map rather than study it, the narrative is mordantly critical of his aspirations to environmental mastery, and functions as an alternative form of "mapping" that focuses as much on Voss's disturbed psyche as it does on the Northern Australian interior.

This suggests an obvious affinity with Joseph Conrad's *Heart of Darkness*, which famously uses the voyage into the literal and symbolic "interior" to critique the monomania of resource extraction and environmental violence.[18] Whereas the ivory trade prompts the events of Conrad's narrative, Voss's expedition is supported by private investment from farmers and merchants who hope to lay stake to productive land. The result is what John Kinsella describes as a form of "sub-pastoral," claiming that "[m]apping as a means to pastoralising land is the sub-pastoral aesthetic of Australian nationalism,"[19] and that *Voss* stands in ironic tension with this tradition due to its protagonist's ultimate demise (echoing Leichhardt's mysterious disappearance in 1848). White therefore reworks the historical novel to present a sense of monumental endeavor – literally, as the novel ends with a statue of Voss being unveiled – which is destabilized through failed confrontation with an environment charted in awe but with little insight.

As Voss and his companions venture into the bush, their brand of European-derived naturalism falls short in the face of the interior's ecological rhythms, and they struggle against drought and heavy rain without the cultural coordinates to adapt. The potential for more inclusive environmental interpretations is further undermined by conflicts between the company and a shadowy cast of Aboriginal supporting characters, who are conflated with nonhuman nature as "animals" (338) or "trees" (342). This forms part of *Voss*'s uneven satire on nineteenth-century racism, which reads all the more uncomfortably given that Aboriginal peoples continued to be classed legally as "fauna" until a decade after its publication.[20] The unevenness derives from the novel's inability to depict indigenous ecological knowledge or place understanding, which constitutes an enduring challenge for settler writing about the environment,[21] and brings *Voss* closer to the limitations of its antihero than the narrative's ironic distance would seemingly allow.

Contrast this with Wilson Harris's first novel, *Palace of the Peacock*, published three years after *Voss* and the first in a similarly epic series known as *The Guyana Quartet*. Harris writes from the position of having worked as a government surveyor, and the Guyanese landscape is a major presence in his work. Like numerous ecocritics, he has argued that "a civilization which is geared towards progressive realism cannot solve the hazards and dangers and the pollution which it has inflicted upon the globe."[22] His alternative has been to produce fictions that operate in "parallel with profound myth that lies apparently eclipsed in ... so-called savage cultures,"[23] and to incorporate this as part of an allusive style that blends Amerindian culture, the surveyor's eye for detail, and a deeply poetic sensibility, resulting in a transcultural vision of the Guyanese environment that remains shaped by the collision between colonialism and indigenous habitation.

There is a beautiful example of this in Harris's "A Note on the Genesis of *The Guyana Quartet*":

> A great magical web born of the music of the elements is how one may respond perhaps to a detailed map of Guyana seen rotating in space with its numerous etched rivers, numerous lines and tributaries, interior rivers, coastal rivers, the arteries of God's spider. Guyana is derived from an Amerindian root word, which means "land of waters." The spirit-bone of water that sings in the dense, interior rainforests is as invaluable a resource in the coastal savannahs which have long been subject to drought as to floodwaters that stretched like a sea from coastal river to coastal river yet remained unharnessed and wasted; subject also to the rapacity of moneylenders, miserable loans, inflated interest. (7)

Here, the syntax and imagery combine to present Guyana's ecology as resplendently animate: the riverine "map" is not static but moves in space and time, revealing an ecological matrix that is powerful yet vulnerable to exploitation. It is also keenly relational and inlaid with different cultural histories, responding to how the postcolonial environment is constituted at once by indigenous place understandings, transcultural interactions, and the "rapacity" of colonial and capitalist prospectors. This composite vision reflects the interplay between form and content in *Palace of the Peacock*.

Despite its stylistic difference from *Voss*, *Palace of the Peacock* performs a comparable "remapping" with respect to colonial history and environmental domination. It depicts a journey by river into the Guyanese interior led by Donne, a callous plantation owner aiming to conscript indigenous laborers, who also recalls explorers such as Walter Raleigh (author of *The Discovery of Guiana* in 1595). While Donne represents the violent extreme of colonial endeavor – content to "fight everything in nature" while staking a claim to "No-man's land" (22) – Harris rejects the linear quest narrative and singularity of character. Instead, we are presented with a series of thresholds that transcend the boundaries between life and death, "human" and "nature," and transport us toward a renewed vision of environmental agency.

Consider, for instance, the following example toward the end of the novel:

> The sun rolled in the grasses waving in the wind and grew on the solitary tree. It was a vast impression and canvas of nature wherein everything looked perfect and yet at the same time unfinished and insubstantial. One had an intuitive feeling that the savannahs—though empty—were crowded. ... Across the crowded creation of the invisible savannahs the newborn wind of spirit blew the sun making light of everything curious hands and feet, neck, shoulder, forehead, material twin shutter and eye. They drifted, half-finished sketches in the air, until they were filled suddenly from within to become living and alive. (111–12)

The brilliant modulations of this passage – whose rolling cadences and metamorphic imagery continue over several pages – exemplify Harris's method of representing a highly agential and networked environment, "crowded" with human and extrahuman interactions that connect across space and time. The prose here is necessarily mythic, offering a linguistic correlative to the web of life and what the narrator describes as the "musical passage" between elements in the "dark corridor and summons and call in the network of the day" (111). This last description applies equally to the form of *Palace of the Peacock*, which initiated a sustained work of ecological imagination for Harris in which he sought "not just to re-map geographical boundaries" imposed by colonialism but also to "provide a template from which we can re-map our perceptions of the living earth."[24] This transcends the limitations seen in *Voss*, and gestures toward the institution of what Richard Peet and Michael Watts term "liberation ecologies," which they see as dependent on anticolonial politics and creative practice.[25] Yet it is a vision that remains compromised by the "progressive realism" of environmental exploitation, territorialization, and developmentalism that has shadowed political decolonization in many postcolonial states, and undermined movements toward environmental equity. As such, we need to balance the revelatory optimism of Harris's work with the only partially ironized struggles portrayed in novels such as *Voss* in order to imagine the shifting grounds on which liberation ecologies must be based.

Conservation, Sustainability, and Development

The tenacity of racial conflict is a clear instance of how colonialism's historical structures continue to be perpetuated, and coincide with environmental sovereignty disputes and the pressures of economic globalization. An obvious example is apartheid in South Africa, which involved a system of spatial enclosures that attempted to confine black South Africans to supposed "homeland" territories, leaving white South Africans in control of the land. The resulting entanglement of environmental and racial politics is given vivid treatment in Nadine Gordimer's novel *The Conservationist* (1974). This was published during a period of growing labor unrest and incipient black nationalism, and gestures beyond sovereignty claims to consider what an emancipatory pastoralism might look like following decades of colonial abuse.[26] Mehring, the novel's protagonist, is a successful white industrialist who buys a farm as an antidote to his role as an investment fund director, following the example of other "well-off city men" who sought "to make contact with the land" and render themselves "fully human and capable of enjoying the simple things in life."[27] These "things," we discover,

include predictably instrumental ideas of women and the natural environment; "[a] farm is not beautiful unless it is productive" (18), Mehring muses,
and he soon becomes "possessed only by the brilliant idea of the farm-house
as a place to bring a woman" (41). But the novel's focus is as much on the
threat to white landowners from the black labor force, whose role as
potential owners or custodians is impeded by economic repression and the
ruptures of colonialism and apartheid.

The novel's commitment to imagining the (literal) grounds for resistant
black agency is symbolized from the outset by the body of an unidentified
black man who is found dead on one of Mehring's pastures and buried in a
shallow grave following lack of police interest. Over the course of the
narrative, environmental events such as storms and floods return the body
to the surface, locating it a haunting material counterpart to Mehring's
neurosis about entitlement to the land. Nature here plays an active role in
creating the conditions for black repossession, and paves the way for the
farm laborers to transcend their lack of ancestral pastoral knowledge as they
eventually come together to enact a ritual burial for one who "had come
back" and "took possession of this earth, theirs; one of them" (323). This
evokes not only a figurative "blackening" of the land, but also a new
inflection to the "conservationism" of the novel's title, which functions as
the indirect object for liberation ecology in this case.[28]

The novel's focalization positions Mehring as claimant to the titular role,
which is none-too-subtly undercut by his investment in sexual, economic,
and environmental exploitation. At the same time, he exhibits moments of
ecological sensitivity, such as when he feels his black laborers do not appre-
ciate the extent of fire damage to the vlei: "the way the vast sponge of earth
held in place by the reeds in turn holds the run-off when the rains come, the
way the reeds filter, shelter" (109–10). This appreciation reflects how the
movement toward black repossession represents a form of "conservation" –
protecting or restoring the environment from spatial segregation and colonial abuse – but one which is complicated by how "there is no black
pastoral" or land ethic "to supplant Mehring's story,"[29] and by the hegemony of capitalist resource management. If Mehring is archetypically concerned with "conserving" environmental supremacy within the context of
apartheid and globalization, what space does this leave for an anticolonial
conservationism to emerge, and how might this address the demands of
social justice and economic need?

As a principle for liberation, conservation harbors similar ambivalences to
the key environmental watchword of recent decades, sustainability, which
classically relies on safeguarding biodiversity and intergenerational equity,
but is compromised by its annexation to the "sustainable development"

88

paradigm, which generally prioritizes the "conservation of development" over nature.[30] Mehring exemplifies this logic in *The Conservationist* when he considers how unearthing a "uranium deposit ... can raise the gross national product to a level where development – viability – becomes a reality, not a dream that depends on "justice," wherever you're expecting to find that" (174). Here, not only is the "dirty" industry of mining held up as a passport to development, but development is conflated with social sustainability or "viability," with "justice" a chimerical distraction, and the destructive nuclear and military uses of uranium going unmentioned. Mining has, unsurprisingly, provoked widespread resistance in global contexts due to its many ecologically damaging and socially exploitative operations, but postcolonial novelists have also grappled with more ambivalent industries that bring economic development, conservation, and social "viability" into tension. Tourism is a prominent example, providing much-needed income while often exacerbating environmental conflicts, not least as it transforms the very cultures and environments it fetishizes.

Patricia Grace's novels *Potiki* (1986) and *Dogside Story* (2001) explore these concerns in the context of coastal Aotearoa New Zealand, with *Potiki* depicting the struggles of a Māori family against developers who want to convert their ancestral land into a resort, and *Dogside Story* focusing on a millennial tourism enterprise managed by a Māori community. While short shrift is given to the avarice of white (Pākehā) developers, Grace uses the polyvocality of the novel form to present a nuanced picture of the pressures and possibilities of postcolonial tourism. On one level, the two novels seem to engage with different political moments in the struggle for Māori self-determination and sustainability. *Potiki* portrays an entrenched conflict between tourism developers and the Tamihana family, whose victory in the face of brutal aggression affirms indigenous values during a period of sustained Māori activism that spanned the 1970s and 1980s. By contrast, the indigenization of tourism in *Dogside Story* arguably reflects the improving social and economic position for Māori communities, and an acceptance that development initiatives may be made consonant with cultural sustainability even as environmental rights issues remain live.

Yet the distinction is not as sharp as it appears. The family in *Potiki* is well aware, for example, that the changing demands and opportunities presented by urbanization place a limit on their role as environmental custodians for whom "the land and the sea and the shores" represent "our science and our sustenance."[31] The "chosen poverty" (146) that underpins self-sufficiency cuts against younger generations' demands for less sparse lifestyles, and the elder family members' commitment to nonviolent resistance is superseded by their university-educated daughter's confrontational and ultimately successful approach to repelling the developers. This provokes the question of whether the escalating destruction – including desecration of their "sacred places" (176), the "scarring" of the landscape (169), and the murder of their youngest son – could have been avoided through a form of resistance that went beyond their principled assertion, essential as it is, that the "land does not belong to people, but ... people belong to the land" (110). *Dogside Story* raises comparable concerns, as while the endogenous tourism venture is economically successful, it unearths a series of tensions that test the limits of community cohesion. In both cases, the relationship between increasingly heterogeneous communities and their ancestral environments is portrayed as simultaneously vulnerable and resilient to the pressures of development and globalization.[32]

Crucially, Grace's innovative use of the novel functions as a correlative to the process of cultural adaptation she depicts with respect to tourism and environmental agency. Her work indigenizes the form by blending aspects of social realism with communal storytelling practices and indigenous mythology, and in so doing highlights the false dichotomy that often accompanies approaches to conservation and sustainability. Both novels suggest that the choice is not between "conserving" postcolonial cultures and environments as static objects or permitting them to be transformed by the forces of modernity. Rather, sustainability – and the process of conservation on which it depends – requires a similarly adaptive approach to how Grace treats the novel form. This involves renewing ecocultural values that counter development's repressive dimensions, while leaving space to respond to changing economic opportunities that can provide a necessary – if always questionable – basis for environmental sovereignty.

Slow Violence, Disaster, and Climate Change

If Grace's novels imagine the localized challenges of negotiating tourism development and conservation, the climatic impact of mass travel through carbon emissions presents a clear limit to site-specific sustainability claims. It also lays down a serious challenge for postcolonial novelists who take on the subject of catastrophic environmental damage that unfolds over decades or even centuries. Rob Nixon has coined the term "slow violence" to describe the "attritional" yet "exponential" calamities caused by pollution, desertification, climate change, and toxic drift.[33] These are important concerns for postcolonial writers who have helped give "imaginative definition" to protracted crises, and to the structural factors that make the world's poorest communities particularly vulnerable to slow violence.[34] In some cases, this has involved turning to what Margaret Atwood calls "speculative fiction" – the creation of scenarios that could conceivably come to pass – which she has done to great effect through her dystopian novel, *The Handmaid's Tale* (1985), and the more recent post-pandemic trilogy, *Oryx and Crake* (2003), *The Year of the Flood* (2009), and *MaddAddam* (2013).

The Handmaid's Tale is set in the military-authoritarian state of Gilead, a Christian theocracy in the former United States. The narrative focuses on the oppression of women in a rigidly patriarchal state, but it also reads as a "postapocalyptic" fiction, in Frederick Buell's terms, which is less interested in representing full-blown environmental destruction than the experience of "a very *slow* apocalypse," with "no clear path out of crisis."[35] In this case, Atwood draws attention to the compound effects of environmental degradation in providing the context for a gendered caste system. This is made evident from the novel's focus on fertility: the titular handmaids are conscripted to bear children for the ruling class in response to the widespread reproductive disorders caused by global pollution. As the protagonist, Offred, considers of a fellow handmaiden:

> What will Ofwarren give birth to? A baby, as we all hope? Or something else, an Unbaby, with a pinhead or a snout like a dog's, or two bodies, or a hole in its heart or no arms, or webbed hands and feet? . . . The chances are one in four, we learned that at the Centre. The air got too full, once, of chemicals, rays, radiation, the water swarmed with toxic molecules, all of that takes years to clean up, and meanwhile they creep into your body, camp out in your fatty cells. Who knows, your very flesh may be polluted, dirty as an oily beach, sure death to shored birds and unborn babies.[36]

This description captures fears about the slow violence of ecological toxicity on people and environments as a result of planetary crisis. Yet the novel also emphasizes how such poisoning is unevenly distributed, with its most extreme effects already realized in "the Colonies." These shadow regions map obliquely onto contemporary postcolonial states and function as forced labor camps for socially dissident "Unwomen." Some remain agriculturally productive, acting as plantation-style resource peripheries; others have borne the brunt of global environmental damage, and host groups of Unwomen condemned to the fatal task of cleaning up "toxic dumps and radiations spills" in what are now ecological wastelands (248).

This portrayal of toxic ecological imperialism is by no means purely speculative: the irradiation of islands in the Pacific through nuclear testing is an obvious point of comparison,[37] and we might think back further to how the environmental exhaustion of island colonies prompted the beginnings of conservationism or "green imperialism," as Richard Grove has argued.[38] More recently, the conversion of postcolonial states to "toxic dumps" has been mooted as global economic policy, with the president of the World Bank, Lawrence Summers, claiming in 1991 that "the economic logic behind dumping a load of toxic waste in the lowest-wage country is impeccable": "countries in Africa are vastly under polluted; their air quality is probably vastly inefficiently low compared to Los Angeles," so "shouldn't the World Bank be encouraging more migration of the dirty industries to the Least Developed Countries?"[39] The tenacity of these destructive processes is a significant concern in *The Handmaid's Tale*, and the novel remains prescient in connecting deepening social and environmental crises to the reentrenchment of elite power, with the ruling class claiming: "All we've done is return things to Nature's norm" (220). The "norm" in this context is of course anything but "natural"; rather it extends preexisting patriarchal dominance and postcolonial inequality through a deliberately uneven distribution of risk.

This comes into even sharper focus if we consider another real-world example, the Bhopal gas disaster, which occurred the year before *The Handmaid's Tale* was published and whose ongoing aftermath is powerfully depicted in Indra Sinha's novel, *Animal's People* (2007). The Bhopal disaster resulted from an explosion in the American-owned Union Carbide pesticide factory situated in the slum district of the city. The very presence of Union Carbide in India forms part of the wider framework of post-World War II developmentalism discussed in this chapter, which led to the "Green Revolution" in many postcolonial states. The ostensible aim of the Green Revolution was to increase agricultural production through modernization, but it was also a neocolonial endeavor of mass environmental corporatization. In the case of Bhopal, Union Carbide's failure to understand the specificity of Indian ecology and agricultural practices rendered the factory unprofitable, so the company began to reduce safety standards while preparing to close down. This resulted in the toxic gas release on the night of 2–3 December 1984, killing thousands of people immediately and injuring over half a million more in the following decades. Despite its manifest culpability, Union Carbide (now owned by Dow Chemical) continues to evade trial in India, and the site remains contaminated, causing birth defects and widespread health problems for the city's poorest inhabitants.

Animal's People refracts the lived experience of environmental violence through the consciousness of nineteen-year-old Animal, who lost his parents "that night" and is forced to walk on all fours due to the toxin-induced "smelting in [his] spine."[40] The story opens with Animal stating "I used to be human once" (1), inhabiting a reconfigured understanding of selfhood that rejects concepts of the "human" as rights-bearing subject – which underpin the international legal structures that have failed Bhopal – in favor of "transpersonality and collectivity in response to the toxic degradation of a postcolonial environment."[41] Animal comes to accept himself as "especially abled" (23), both in terms of his sensory perceptiveness and skilful negotiation of the urban landscape, and through his considerable talents as a storyteller. Resisting voyeuristic reporters who continuously fetishize the events of "that night" (5), his narrative presents a singular yet communally responsive perspective on the disaster, drawing attention to renewed forms of environmental agency in a context where the corporation saw little "difference," as one character observes, between "making poisons to kill insects" and "kill[ing] us instead" (306). The novel does this by defying the disaster's common designation as "gas tragedy," along with the sentimental narratives of pity this evokes, in favor of combining a range of narrative influences including crime fiction, the picaresque, magical realism, social realism, *Bildungsroman*, melodrama, and the gothic, among others.[42] This generic hybridity reflects how the disaster's toxic legacy respects neither borders nor conventional narrative frames, and presents an analogue for the blend of registers, influences, and perspectives that are needed to understand the disaster's ramifications over time.

The novel depicts the disaster not as a singular event but as a *process* that is compounded by colonial history, capitalist exploitation, and state mismanagement, and which has differential but collectively damaging effects throughout the "bastis" or slums. Unlike the "Colonies" in *The Handmaid's Tale*, the poor in Bhopal are not condemned to isolated, terminal wastelands, but represent "the real face of globalization," both in terms of transnational capitalism's toxic effects and the vitality of activist response.[43] The slum community is internally variegated yet able to see itself as part of an abused collective that is being placed in harm's way on a global scale, not least through exposure to disasters.[44] As Animal identifies in the restorative conclusion to the novel, "All things must pass but the poor remain. We are the people of the Apokalis [apocalypse]. Tomorrow there will be more of us" (366). This resistant energy in the face of environmental violence reflects a horizon of hope that is reflected across a wide range of postcolonial novels, which continue to confront the most heinous abuses of power while representing – and in a sense embodying – the creative negotiations needed to survive in the context of monumental economic disparity and ecological crisis.

Perhaps the appropriate novel to end on in this context is one that embodies environmental resistance and creative negotiation at multiple scales, and which returns us to where we began the chapter in Northern Australia – in fact, to the very region where the Leichhardt River flows today. Alexis Wright's epic novel *Carpentaria* intersects with many of the issues addressed here – from conflicting environmental epistemologies through to economic development initiatives and climate change – and it illustrates both the changing nature of ecological imperialism over time and its deep-set continuities. Like several other novels discussed in this chapter, *Carpentaria* presents a multilayered narrative that is epic in scope, engaging with mythic modes of storytelling to represent the ecological specificity of the Gulf of Carpentaria in ways that are responsive both to indigenous cosmology and to the "progressive realism" of capitalist industry. Set in the coastal town of Desperance, a fictional hinterland "fraught with modernity,"[45] the narrative opens by depicting the indigenous Pricklebush clan residing "in a human dumping ground next to the town tip" (4), and engaged in a range of disputes with the town's white settler population and a multinational mining corporation.

The inevitable sense of history repeating is evoked in the novel's opening line, which imagines "a nation" chanting: "*But we know your story already*" (1; original emphasis). Yet, as in *Potiki* and *Animal's People*, "hope" comes from the vitality of response to oppression and environmental racism, and from how the many "stories" in *Carpentaria* incorporate changing cultural and ecological circumstances (12). Not least among these is the connection between development and climate change. We can see this in the slippage Wright depicts between indigenous-led resistance and environmental agency. As with the resort construction in *Potiki*, the mine in *Carpenteria* is eventually destroyed by indigenous activists. In this case, though, it takes a "miracle ... whirly wind" (394) to precipitate its final conflagration, which is in keeping with how the novel presents the elements as major actors in an epic drama, culminating in the complete destruction of Desperance by a cyclone that shows "how history could be obliterated when the Gods move the country" (473).

This agential interpretation of environmental forces evokes precisely the indigenous cosmologies that are absent from *Voss*, locating place understanding at the intersection of mythological and "inside knowledge about this river and coastal region," which has been "handed down through the ages since time began" by people who "[k]now the moment of climatic change better than they know themselves" (3). Rather than treating "inside knowledge" as static, the narrative emphasizes its flexibility in relation to what the indigenous characters characterize as "[a]ll that scientify stuff" (238), exemplified in scenes such as the following when fisherman Norm Phantom recognizes, on seeing a "long tubular cloud" on the ocean's horizon, that

> the birds were travelling along a special route made from the evaporation left
> by the heat in the cooling atmosphere by the trail made by the big fish on their

journeys into the sky world of summer.... Then when the heavy rains finally stopped and the waters became calmer the following year, the big fish would return, as was the natural cycle of things.   (248)

This supple blending of "scientify" understanding (evaporation, atmospheric "cooling") with mythic journeys to the "sky world" symbolizes the process of adaptive knowledge combination that characterizes the novel's storytelling technique as a whole. But it also creates a tension with "the moment of climatic change" beyond the horizon – not least atmospheric *warming* – which is fundamentally altering "the natural cycle of things."

Northern Australia is prone to periodic cyclones and flooding as well as drought, and the powerful environmental events depicted *Carpentaria* are presented as part of the indigenous characters' "ordinary" understanding of Gulf country weather, conditioned as it is by the deep time of cultural memory and myth. At the same time, the "miraculous" nature of the "whirly wind" that destroys the mine, and the extreme impact of the cyclone that razes the town and leaves one character floating on "an extraordinary island of rubbish" out to sea (475), hint at the need to reconfigure "inside knowledge" systems in light of the environmental havoc that is being wreaked on a global scale. Wright's interests in climate change are exemplified in her recent novel, *The Swan Book*, which like *The Handmaid's Tale* is set in a dystopian future ravaged by environmental degradation. However, *Carpentaria* is no less engaged with this process: its creative integration of many factors that have driven global warming – from colonialism to extractive industry – permit us to read *for* climate change at multiple narrative levels, and in ways that reflect the culturally differentiated responses that are needed to address climate change in reality.

At this point, we may begin to discern some of the parameters for a postcolonial engagement with climate change and contested natures that focuses not just on the depiction of extreme events but also on the long-term processes of environmental exploitation that have led to humanity becoming a geological force (indicated most prominently by the proposed shift from the Holocene epoch to the "Anthropocence").[46] This is evidently a fertile area for further research, and one that will be most instructive if it draws on histories of imperialism and globalization, and emphasizes the lived experience of ecological change in postcolonial contexts as much as imagined future scenarios. As this chapter has argued, the postcolonial novel is an indispensable form for mediating these concerns, along with the myriad tensions between social and environmental justice that accompany oppressive power relations. Through creative manipulations of form and genre, through polyvocality and the blending of cultural storytelling techniques, and through attention to the importance of time as well as space in comprehending environmental change, postcolonial novels provide vital perspectives on how we narrate, understand, and respond to environmental conflicts. The challenge is to continue analyzing and sharing these insights as a means of enhancing their restorative potential for an ecologically endangered world.

Notes

1 Edward Said, *Culture and Imperialism* (London: Vintage), p. 271. See also Elizabeth DeLoughrey and George B. Handley, "Introduction: Toward an Aesthetics of the Earth," in *Postcolonial Ecologies: Literatures of the Environment*, eds. Elizabeth DeLoughrey and George B. Handley (Oxford: Oxford University Press, 2011), pp. 3–39.

2 Kate Soper, *What Is Nature? Culture, Politics and the Non-Human* (Oxford: Blackwell, 1995), p. 7.

3 See Carolyn Merchant, *The Death of Nature: Women, Ecology, and the Scientific Revolution* (San Francisco: Harper and Row, 1980); Val Plumwood, *Feminism and the Mastery of Nature* (London and New York: Routledge, 1993).

4 Val Plumwood, "Decolonizing Relationships with Nature," in *Decolonizing Nature: Strategies for Conservation in a Post-colonial Era*, eds. William Adams and Martin Mulligan (London: Earthscan, 2003), pp. 51–78 (p. 52).

5 Alfred W. Crosby, *Ecological Imperialism: The Biological Expansion of Europe 900–1900*, 2nd ed. (Cambridge: Cambridge University Press, 2004).

6 Phil Macnaghten and John Urry, *Contested Natures* (London: Sage, 1998), p. 1.

7 See Graham Huggan and Helen Tiffin, *Postcolonial Ecocriticism: Literature, Animals, Environment* (London and New York: Routledge, 2010), pp. 3–4.

8 For further discussion, see Elizabeth DeLoughrey, Jill Didur, and Anthony Carrigan, "Introduction: A Postcolonial Environmental Humanities," in *Global Ecologies and the Environmental Humanities: Postcolonial Approaches*, eds. Elizabeth DeLoughrey, Jill Didur, and Anthony Carrigan (London and New York: Routledge, 2015), pp. 1–32.

9 See Joan Martínez-Alier, *The Environmentalism of the Poor: A Study of Ecological Conflicts and Valuation* (Cheltenham: Edward Elgar, 2002).

10 Dominic Head, "The (Im)possibility of Ecocriticism," in *Writing the Environment: Ecocriticism and Literature*, eds. Richard Kerridge and Neil Sammells (London and New York: Zed, 1998), pp. 27–39.

11 See also Upamanyu Pablo Mukherjee, *Postcolonial Environments: Nature, Culture and the Contemporary Indian Novel in English* (Basingstoke: Palgrave Macmillan, 2010); Astrid Bracke, "The Contemporary English Novel and Its Challenges to Ecocriticism," in *The Oxford Handbook of Ecocriticism*, ed. Greg Garrard (Oxford: Oxford University Press, 2014), pp. 423–39.

12 Elleke Boehmer, *Colonial and Postcolonial Literature: Migrant Metaphors*, 2nd ed. (Oxford: Oxford University Press, 2005), p. 26.

13 Robert P. Marzec, *An Ecological and Postcolonial Study of Literature: From Daniel Defoe to Salman Rushdie* (Basingstoke: Palgrave Macmillan, 2007), p. 1.

14 Colonialism is linked etymologically to settlement and agriculture, deriving from the Latin *colōnia* (farm, landed estate, settlement) and *colōnus* (tiller, farmer, cultivator, planter, settler in a new country) (*OED*, colony, n.).

15 Said, *Culture and Imperialism*, p. 271.

16 For more on settler colonial environments, see, e.g., Travis Mason, Lisa Szabo-Jones, and Elzette Steenkamp, eds., "Postcolonial Ecocriticism among Settler-Colonial Nations," special issue of *ARIEL* 44.4 (2013); on the Caribbean, see Elizabeth M. DeLoughrey, Renée K. Gosson, and George B. Handley, eds., *Caribbean Literature and the Environment: Between Nature and Culture* (Charlottesville: University of Virginia Press, 2005).

17 Patrick White, *Voss* (London: Vintage, 1994, first published 1957), p. 33. Further page references to novels will be included in the text.

18 See Huggan and Tiffin, *Postcolonial Ecocriticism*, pp. 141–7.

19 John Kinsella, *Contrary Rhetoric: Lectures on Landscape and Language*, eds. Glen Phillips and Andrew Taylor (Fremantle: Fremantle Press, 2008), p. 143.

20 DeLoughrey and Handley, "Introduction," p. 12.

21 Cf., e.g., Kate Grenville's more recent subpastoral novel, *The Secret River* (2005).

22 Wilson Harris, *The Radical Imagination: Lectures and Talks*, eds. Alan Riach and Mark Williams (Liège: Liège Language and Literature, 1992), p. 73. See also DeLoughrey and Handley, "Introduction," p. 4.

23 Wilson Harris, *The Guyana Quartet* (London: Faber and Faber, 1985), p. 7.

24 Chris Campbell, *World-Creating Jungles: Wilson Harris, Derek Walcott and the Caribbean Environment* (Amsterdam: Rodopi, in press), ch. 2.

25 Richard Peet and Michael Watts, eds., *Liberation Ecologies: Environment, Development, Social Movements*, 2nd ed. (London and New York: Routledge, 2004).

26 See James Graham, *Land and Nationalism in Fictions from Southern Africa* (London and New York: Routledge, 2009), pp. 61–9.

27 Nadine Gordimer, *The Conservationist* (London: Jonathan Cape, 2005, first published in 1974), p. 17.

28 Graham, *Land and Nationalism*, p. 63.

29 Dominic Head, *Nadine Gordimer* (Cambridge: Cambridge University Press, 2004), p. 101.

30 Wolfgang Sachs, "Global Ecology and the Shadow of 'Development,'" in *Global Ecology: A New Arena of Political Conflict*, ed. Wolfgang Sach (London and New Jersey: Zed, 1993), pp. 3–21 (pp. 9–10). See also Anthony Carrigan, *Postcolonial Tourism: Literature, Culture, and Environment* (London and New York: Routledge, 2011), pp. 6–8; 57–59.

31 Patricia Grace, *Potiki* (Auckland: Penguin, 1986), p. 104.

32 See Carrigan, *Postcolonial Tourism*, ch. 2 and ch. 8, for further discussion.

33 Rob Nixon, *Slow Violence and the Environmentalism of the Poor* (Cambridge, MA: Harvard University Press, 2011), p. 3.

34 Nixon, *Slow Violence*, p. 6.

35 Frederick Buell, *From Apocalypse to Way of Life: Four Decades of Environmental Crisis in the U.S.* (London and New York: Routledge, 2003), p. 105; 322.

36 Margaret Atwood, *The Handmaid's Tale* (London: Vintage, 1996, first published in 1985), p. 110.

37 See, e.g., Elizabeth DeLoughrey, "Radiation Ecologies and the Wars of Light," *Modern Fiction Studies* 55.3 (2009), pp. 468–95.

38 Richard Grove, *Green Imperialism: Colonial Expansion, Tropical Island Edens and the Origins of Environmentalism, 1600–1860* (Cambridge: Cambridge University Press, 1995).

39 Cited in Nixon, *Slow Violence*, p. 1.

40 Indra Sinha, *Animal's People* (London: Simon and Schuster, 2007), p. 15.

41 Pablo Mukherjee, "'Tomorrow there will be more of us': Toxic Postcoloniality in *Animal's People*," in *Postcolonial Ecologies: Literatures of the Environment*, eds. Elizabeth DeLoughrey and George B. Handley (Oxford and New York: Oxford University Press), pp. 216–31 (p. 228).

42 For further generic discussion, see Rob Nixon, "Neoliberalism, Slow Violence, and the Environmental Picaresque," *Modern Fiction Studies* 55.3 (2009), pp. 443–67; Anthony Carrigan, "'Justice is on our side'? *Animal's People*, Generic Hybridity, and Eco-Crime," *Journal of Commonwealth Literature* 47.2 (2012), 159–74.

43 Stephen Zavestoski, "The struggle for Justice in Bhopal: A New/Old Breed of Transnational Social Movement," *Global Social Policy* 9.3 (2009), pp. 383–407 (p. 384).

44 For further discussion, see Anthony Carrigan, "Towards a Postcolonial Disaster Studies," in *Global Ecologies and the Environmental Humanities: Postcolonial Approaches*, eds. Elizabeth DeLoughrey, Jill Didur, and Anthony Carrigan (London and New York: Routledge, 2015), pp. 117–39.

45 Alexis Wright, *Carpentaria* (London: Constable, 2006), p. 55.

46 For further discussion, see, e.g., Dipesh Chakrabarty, "Postcolonial Studies and the Challenge of Climate Change," *New Literary History* 43.1 (2012), pp. 1–18.

6

CLARE BARKER

University of Leeds

Disability and the Postcolonial Novel

Ngũgĩ wa Thiong'o's African dictator novel *Wizard of the Crow* begins with a mystery: "There were many theories about the strange illness of the second Ruler of the Free Republic of Aburĩria, but the most frequent on people's lips were five."[1] A description of the Ruler's symptoms is withheld until almost 500 pages later, so the fact that the illness is speculated upon at the very start of the text presents it as an interpretative dilemma both to the novel's characters and to the reader. Some people in the fictional nation of Aburĩria, we are told, suspect the Ruler's condition has emotional causes: it results from a build-up of intense anger, or manifests the unshed tears of his ill-treated wife. Others favor supernatural explanations – the malady is a curse, or the work of demons – while still others conjecture that it is symbolic, "something to do with the aging of his rule" (5). The reader of this novel is plunged into uncertainty regarding how to negotiate this complex fictional world: what types of knowledge should we privilege? Which rumors point to the "truth"? Immediately, then, the unaccounted-for illness demands an explanation – it requires a story to be told – and in doing so, it performs several important narrative functions. First, the contrasting "diagnoses" of the Ruler's condition demonstrate how a diversity of worldviews and interpretative frameworks abound in Aburĩria. This is important because the demotic force of the rumors (many of which are not complimentary) destabilizes the Ruler's claims to omnipotence, since he cannot fully control the thoughts and beliefs within the populace. Second, the mysterious illness further undermines the despot's all-powerful facade by exposing corporeal vulnerability: he is revealed from the outset as being all-too-human, inhabiting a body that is as fragile as anyone else's. When the narrative later reveals that the Ruler's body has "started puffing up like a balloon" (496) during a diplomatic visit to the United States, his condition turns into a stand-off between "Science versus Sorcery" (493) as Harvard professor Din Furyk and the enigmatic Wizard of the Crow vie for the role of potential healers. This larger-than-life polarization of biomedicine and "traditional" healing parodies stereotypes of an Africa steeped in superstition and the rational, modern "west," contributing to Ngũgĩ's satirical dramatization of the overbearing neocolonialism of the United States and African nations' subordinated positions within global international politics. Finally, the Ruler's unruly, ailing body brings to mind the notion of a body politic – a nation-state – that is dysfunctional or under pressure: if the Ruler's body stands in metonymically for the nation of Aburĩria itself, the inexplicable disorder of this body points toward wider *national* pathologies of corruption, oppression, and social disorder, "symptoms" of both the horror and the impossibility of absolute power in this postcolonial African dictatorship.

I have chosen to begin with this reading of *Wizard of the Crow* because it shows how the extraordinary bodies of disabled or sick characters can be completely central to the workings of postcolonial novels. The Ruler's condition allows many things to happen: it creates the impetus for a story to be told; it aids in the characterization of the Ruler and those around him; it provides the principal strand of symbolism to the novel, in which Aburĩria is figured as "a body monstrously bloated with absolute power";[2] and it creates a scenario enabling Ngũgĩ's critique of oppressive power structures – both within the dictatorship and globally. This movement between individual body and national or global political concerns is typical of how disability functions in postcolonial novels. Like the despotic Ruler's bloated body, disability lends postcolonial fiction some of its most potent and pervasive images and metaphors: dismembered nation-states; silenced subaltern subjects; economies crippled by international debt; healing through decolonization and the reclamation of indigenous knowledge. As a trope, a narrative device, disability enables postcolonial writers to tell vivid stories about colonialism and its aftermath, stories that resonate outward from a character's disabled body to address "damage," inequality, and power and its abuses in the postcolonial world. Besides these metaphorical connections, though, postcolonial novels also tell stories about disability and ill health in which the material body is intimately entangled with postcolonial politics. The disabilities of countless people around the globe are *produced by* the effects of colonial oppression and postcolonial conflict – wars, forced migrations, violence, poverty, and malnutrition – while others' experience of disability is shaped by the economic and social conditions, the institutions, services, and attitudes that have emerged from colonial relations in their homelands. It is important to have an awareness of disability when reading postcolonial literature for the simple reason that disability is a huge presence in many postcolonial texts, as it is within many postcolonial communities.[3]

"Disability" is a fluid term, which can encompass diverse forms of bodily variation: physical and sensory impairments, cognitive and learning differences, mental illness, chronic conditions, and differences in appearance (birthmarks, for example) that may not limit a person's functions but subject them to stigma and discrimination from others. This follows what disability scholars call the "social model of disability," which distinguishes between impairment, a medicalized term denoting a difference or limitation of the body, and disability, which refers to the forms of oppression, restricted activity, exclusion, and discrimination that people with impairments might face, from inaccessible environments to prejudice and hate crime. According to this model, disability is socially constructed rather than residing in the body.[4] Crucial to our understandings of what constitutes "disability" is a notion of difference from what is perceived to be "normal" in terms of health and embodiment. In this respect, postcolonial novels tend to complicate how we understand disability, as they often foreground forms of cultural relativity that bring the concept of normalcy into question. Like other hegemonic identity categories such as whiteness or masculinity, the "normate" – Rosemarie Garland-Thomson's term for the "proto-ordinary body" that "we think of as normal or call able-bodied"[5] – is often assumed to be self-explanatory, transparent, obvious. When we look for normality in postcolonial literature, however, it can prove itself to be a slippery concept that shifts according to cultural location and features of the local society and environment. For instance, it is with wonder that Adah Price, the hemiplegic daughter of an American missionary to the Congo in Barbara Kingsolver's *The Poisonwood Bible*, realizes that:

> Here, bodily damage is more or less considered to be a by-product of living, not a disgrace. In the way of the body and other people's judgment I enjoy a benign approval in Kilanga that I have never, ever known in Bethlehem, Georgia.[6]

In the United States, Adah's paralysis, unusual gait, and elective muteness are decidedly nonnormative, eliciting stares and exclusion. But in 1960s Kilanga, where many people are disabled as a result of disease, hard labor, accidents, and malnourishment, Adah's differences are unremarkable and disability more generally is quite a "normal" state of affairs – the whiteness of Adah and her family actually proves to be more exceptional and stare-worthy. Adah has to readjust her understanding of her body in Kilanga; no longer is she seen as a tragic or "disgraceful" figure, because here disability tends to be apprehended as a fact of living within that community rather than as an individual's stigma or burden. While Adah's pleasure in this revelation verges on romanticizing the hardships in Kilanga, it is certainly the case that postcolonial novels reveal cultural differences in the way that disabilities are interpreted, understood, treated, and managed; and disability representations can offer insights into communities' metaphysical beliefs, structures of care, and attitudes to minorities. The very ordinariness of disability in many postcolonial novels can require a reorientation of perspective from "western" readers, unsettling what we assume "normalcy" to be.

National Allegory and the Body Politic

Just as the Ruler's body in *Wizard of the Crow* anchors the novel's exploration of nation and power, many other novels use disability as an allegory for colonial "damage" and the "dysfunctionality" of postcolonial nation-states. One prevalent trope is to conceive of colonialism as a disease infecting the national body. In Tsitsi Dangarembga's *Nervous Conditions*, set in colonial Rhodesia, for instance, Ma'Shingayi diagnoses "the Englishness" as the cause of her niece Nyasha's eating disorder, darkly predicting that "It'll kill them all if they aren't careful."[7] Similarly, the child protagonist Lenny in Bapsi Sidhwa's *Cracking India* understands her polio as a "'dastardly' ... instance of British treachery" and interprets the surgery on her leg as her "first personal involvement with Indian politics: the Quit-India sentiment that has fired the imagination of a subject people and will soon sweep away the Raj!"[8] In such statements, postcolonial nations are presented as "wounded" by their colonial histories, and the process of decolonization is perceived as "purging" the body of infection. Conversely, in the sequel to *Nervous Conditions*, *The Book of Not*, Nyasha's father Babamukuru is symbolically disabled at the moment of Zimbabwe's independence, sustaining spinal damage when he is "struck by a stray bullet that ricocheted off a flag post during the twenty-one gun salute while they lowered the Union Jack and raised the Zimbabwean flag at the Independence celebrations."[9] This act of disablement portends how Robert Mugabe's independent Zimbabwe would bring its own forms of "damage," rather than the promised "cure" for black Zimbabweans' prolonged subjugation under the colonial regime. Tropes such as these are a form of what disability theorists David Mitchell and Sharon Snyder call "narrative prosthesis," referring to instances when disability functions as a "crutch upon which literary narratives lean for their representational power, disruptive potentiality, and analytical insight."[10] Frequently, they point out, disability provides a convenient metaphor for notions of breakdown or disorder located *outside* of the body – in the family, society, or nation. In postcolonial novels' national allegories, disabled characters can be crucial to the texts' critiques of the "deformations" of political, social, and cultural structures and practices that occur under and in response to colonialism.[11]

Salman Rushdie's *Shame* gives us a powerful example of narrative prosthesis at work in the postcolonial novel. This text contains a metafictional commentary in which the narrator struggles with the challenge of how to represent Pakistan, a newly constructed and perhaps *"insufficiently imagined"* postcolonial nation where, under the military regime of General Mohammad Zia-ul-Haq in the 1970s and 1980s, censorship was routine and dissent brutally punished.[12] To get around this dilemma, the narrator composes a "modern fairy-tale" (70) centering on the figure of Sufiya Zinobia Shakil, the daughter of General Raza Hyder, the country's military leader (and a thinly veiled stand-in for General Zia-ul-Haq). As a child, Sufiya contracts "a case of brain fever that turned her into an idiot" (100), and becomes a figure of shame within her high-profile family. This novel is centrally preoccupied with exploring the multiple facets of shame (or *sharam*) and shamelessness, concepts that Rushdie sees as integral to Pakistani culture and politics. Sufiya, "for so long burdened with being a miracle-gone-wrong, a family's shame made flesh" (139), comes to embody, and suffer from, all the many occasions for shame in Rushdie's highly critical postcolonial allegory: Pakistan's corrupt and brutal leadership, patriarchal oppression in Islamic culture, and ultimately the shame of Pakistan's birth in a bloody act of partition characterized by sectarian violence.

Rushdie's self-reflexive narrator meditates on why Sufiya's brain damage is necessary for the novel's plot and symbolic economy:

> I did it to her, I think, to make her pure. Couldn't think of another way of creating purity in what is supposed to be the Land of the Pure ... and idiots are, by definition, innocent. Too romantic a use to make of mental disability? Perhaps; but it's too late for such doubts. (120)

Here, Sufiya's cognitive difference is self-consciously employed as a trope that enables a representation of Pakistan, aslant from reality, to take shape; it is the "prosthesis" that the narrator relies upon in order to bring the story into being. But his professed uneasiness about instrumentalizing disability in this way might also cause us to question the ethics of such a representation. Allegorical uses of disability can be highly problematic as they reinforce the association between disability and negative conditions such as disorder, deviance, or dehumanization.[13] This is certainly the case in *Shame*, where, at moments of stress and humiliation, Sufiya becomes a barely human "beast" and embarks on a vengeful series of supernaturally violent acts, decapitating turkeys, raping and beheading men, and ravaging the countryside.

When analyzing disability representations, though, it is important to consider the generic conventions that influence them and "situate the disabled characters differently from genre to genre."[14] As a figure in a fairy tale, Sufiya is an archetype, a stock character who performs a useful textual function in driving the allegorical critique of the postcolonial nation. *Shame*, we are told, is "a novel about Sufiya Zinobia ... [but] perhaps it would be more accurate, if also more opaque, to say that Sufiya Zinobia is about this novel" (59). In other words, the narrator's main concern is with the novel itself, rather than with Sufiya per se; with the questions of political expression, authorial validity, and the right to represent that the form of the postcolonial novel raises. The narrator self-avowedly suppresses his ethical concerns about the effects of Sufiya's demonization to achieve the primary goal of telling a story of shame and shamelessness. This itself is perhaps a shameful act – and this sometimes brutal wielding of narratorial power is something that Rushdie's metafictional novels of the 1980s specifically ask us to interrogate: how the power to narrate a version of a postcolonial national history might exclude or oppress those it represents. Disability, then, can facilitate postcolonial allegories that critique power imbalances based on race, religion, and nationality, but in doing so it "oscillates uneasily between the aesthetic and the ethical domains,"[15] prompting consideration of the ethics of putting disabled bodies – so often subjected to deprivation and abuse – to this narrative purpose.

"The wounds of war, which no one can heal": Disability and Violence

There are, of course, many representations of disability in postcolonial novels that are not primarily allegorical, but instead deal with the everyday realities of disabled experience. Amongst these are numerous novels depicting characters whose disabilities are brought about by violence. Frantz Fanon famously wrote that colonialism "is violence in its natural state, and it will only yield when confronted with greater violence"; for him, "decolonization is always a violent phenomenon."[16] If we see colonial histories as histories of violence in this way, they are also inevitably histories of mass disablement, and numerous contemporary postcolonial communities are still dealing with the violent fallout of colonial relations. This means that many postcolonial novels, whether representing the colonial period, decolonization, or new postcolonial state formations, are set in what we might describe as disabling environments – spaces where human bodies and minds are rendered especially vulnerable by ongoing states of sociopolitical disorder (war, human rights violations, autocratic or racist forms of government), by economic factors (poverty, uneven distribution of food, and resources), and by infrastructural problems (inadequate healthcare systems).[17] The presence of disability in novels of conflict often raises questions about citizenship, belonging, and state care following destructive and traumatic events, enabling an indictment of violent regimes and their impact upon individuals and communities.

As one of the most tangible consequences of violence, disability often features in postcolonial novels' negotiations of postconflict aftermath and social reconstruction. This is the case with Ngũgĩ's realist novels from the 1960s and 1970s, works dealing with Kenya's violent struggle for independence and the transition to self-rule in 1963. In *Petals of Blood* (1977), Ngũgĩ traces this history through to the abusive neocolonial regime that governed following independence, and presents a "vision of Kenyan peoples' ... collective identity" as an identity of "resistance."[18] To do so, the novel relates the tale of Abdulla, an ex-freedom fighter who has lost a leg in the Mau Mau uprising and now lives in a "hovel,"[19] mired in poverty. This novel gives a powerful account of the socioeconomic plight of disabled war veterans, and mobilizes Abdulla's disability as a material sign of the new government's corruption and neglect of its citizens. Abdulla recounts that:

> "I said: let me go from office to office. I will go back to the factory where I used to work. All I wanted was a job.
> "I went to the office.
> "Well, I said: I only wanted a job.
> "They said: a cripple?
> "I said: a cripple: must he not eat?
> "They looked at one another.
> "They said: he who has ears should hear: he who has eyes should see.
> "This is New Kenya.
> "No Free Things." (254–5)

This abandonment by the new regime, "so bitter a betrayal" as Abdulla terms it (255), is exposed more starkly when juxtaposed with the idealized vision of a "New Kenya" – a more equal society – that prompted his participation in the uprising. Before independence, Abdulla sees himself within a genealogy of African freedom fighters (including Toussaint, Nkrumah, and Cabral) and understands Mau Mau as "a link in the chain in the long struggle of African people through different times at different places" (137). Abdulla's friends later honor his leg stump as a "badge of courage indelibly imprinted on his body" (139), and he believes that he "carr[ies] the memory" of the liberation struggle and its ideals "on [his] leg" (254). Abdulla's disability therefore operates as an ambivalent marker of "the struggle betrayed,"[20] at once a positive symbol of honorable resistance and clear-headed idealism and a material reminder of a history of dispossession and loss, part of the cost and the disillusionment of independence.

Beyond the period of decolonization, disability is employed in some post-colonial novels as part of a critique of transnational power-brokering, casting light on how geopolitical maneuverings at the highest levels of power impact upon the lives and bodies of ordinary people. In "Necropolitics," Achille Mbembe outlines how, in postcolonial states of emergency such as apartheid South Africa, Rwanda, and the Palestinian occupation, "life, death, and the human body (in particular the wounded or slain body) ... are inscribed in the order of power."[21] Human lives and bodies are "instrumentaliz[ed]" within regimes of terror, and in contemporary warfare,

> weapons are deployed in the interest of maximum destruction of persons and the creation of *death-worlds*, new and unique forms of social existence in which vast populations are subjected to conditions of life conferring upon them the status of *living dead*.[22]

In such "death-worlds," the disablement of the populace is often part of military strategy, designed to debilitate the enemy's fighting forces while stretching their spirit and their resources – in terms of healthcare, welfare, and unemployment support – to the limit.

We see this dynamic at work in Michael Ondaatje's 2001 novel *Anil's Ghost*, set in war-torn Sri Lanka in the 1980s. In the midst of ethnic conflict between the Sinhalese-majority national government and the Liberation Tigers of Tamil Eelam (or "Tamil Tigers"), Ondaatje presents disability as being completely imbricated in both the domestic politics of postcolonial civil war and in processes of global political, military, and economic exploitation. We glimpse these complexities through the perspective of Gamini, an emergency doctor at a base hospital in an area going through "waves of violence":[23]

> The victims of "intentional violence" had started appearing in March 1984. They were nearly all male, in their twenties, damaged by mines, grenades, mortar shells. ... The guerrillas had international weaponry smuggled into the country by arms dealers, and they also had homemade bombs.
> The doctors saved the lives first, then the limbs. There were mostly grenade injuries. An antipersonnel mine the size of an inkwell would destroy most of a person's feet. ... There was a need for rehabilitation programmes, and the making of what came to be known as the "Jaipur Limb." In Europe a new artificial foot cost 2,500 pounds. Here the Jaipur Limb was made for 30 pounds – cheaper because Asian victims could walk without a shoe.   (118)

In this matter-of-fact passage, Ondaatje alludes to the global health marketplace and its entanglement with the "military-industrial complex": international arms dealers supply the guerrillas with the means to disable their enemies, simultaneously creating the need for new commodities tailored to local markets – mobility devices and rehabilitation services – which may shore up foreign economies while Sri Lanka remains "crippled" by war. When seen in the context of globalization, as Michael Davidson writes, disability is "as much about national and cultural power differentials as it is a matter of medicine and bodies."[24] Here in Sri Lanka, Ondaatje shows how national and global forces operate on the bodies of local citizens and determine the nature of their medical treatment. By utilizing Gamini's per-spective, this passage combines the documentation of the facts and injustices of war with its less tangible human consequences – assaults on comfort, faith, well-being – both for victims of grenades and for their carers. Gamini feels he is "without self" during intense periods of suffering, "lost among the screaming" when the hospital runs out of painkillers:

> This was when he stopped believing in man's rule on earth. He turned away from every person who stood up for a war. Or the principle of one's land, or pride of ownership, or even personal rights. All of those motives ended up somehow in the arms of careless power. (118–19)

It is such "careless power" that forms the target of Ondaatje's critique, and this is realized through the juxtaposition of those who profit from war – such as distant arms dealers – with the caring professions left impotent through lack of resources ("care-less"). In a novel that explores multiple forms of postcolonial biopolitics, these ongoing acts of disablement form an import-ant backdrop, exposing how human bodies are all too frequently rendered "disposable," reduced to insignificant cogs in the "war machines" of con-temporary geopolitics.[25]

In response to the dehumanizing effects of conflict, many postcolonial novels are concerned with excavating the psychological trauma that accom-panies violence and exploring the possibilities of healing. Any account of disability in postcolonial conflict novels must both consider trauma *as* a disabling condition and situate disability within a context of wider traumatic losses.[26] Yvonne Vera's *The Stone Virgins* (2002) focuses on a period of catastrophic violence that occurred in Matabeleland, Zimbabwe, in the 1980s, the early days of independence under Mugabe's regime. Conflict between government military forces and veterans of the rival nationalist group, the Zimbabwe People's Revolutionary Army (ZIPRA), resulted in widespread terror against civilians. *The Stone Virgins* gives an intimate portrait of horrific acts of violence inflicted on two sisters, Thenjiwe and Nonceba, and in doing so it depicts disability as inseparable from trauma and grief. The fragmented, impressionistic narrative gradually yields the story of how Sibaso, an ex-ZIPRA soldier who sees himself only as "an instrument of war,"[27] beheads Thenjiwe in front of her sister, then proceeds to rape Nonceba and mutilate her face, cutting off her lips. A year later, Nonceba's injuries are healing and she is being cared for by Cephas, Thenjiwe's former lover. The narrative makes it clear that her facial disfigurement, serious as it is, represents only a fraction of the damage done by Sibaso's violence: "She carries visible scars; he [Cephas] shields her from the invisible ones" (172). What is more, the fallout from the liberation struggle is collectively felt: Cephas is carrying his own "absolute hurt ... like a quiet flame" (172), and Sibaso is himself depicted as intensely disturbed by his wartime experiences. Individuals' disabilities signify differently in such environments of mass brutalization. Rather than being a hypervisible marker of difference or stigma, Nonceba's scars are apprehended in an understated manner: "With some powder on, she looks almost unharmed. Almost. At least no one stares. No one turns to look. No one asks questions" (170). This muted response testifies to both the omnipresence of injury and the collectivity of trauma in Bulawayo City; here, Nonceba's scars are a reminder of the horrors experienced in the countryside, from which many people have fled and are now attempting to forget.

For Nonceba herself, the embodied effects of disfigurement are represented tangibly and intimately: "Everything has changed, and changed her way of seeing, of inhabiting her own body, of being alive" (91). However, her sense of dismemberment extends beyond her own body to encompass the loss of Thenjiwe as well, since "There had always been two of them" (91). Skin grafts may repair some of the damage to Nonceba's face, but this is purely cosmetic, and throws into relief the depth of psychological trauma, which is represented as enduring, incurable: "These are the wounds of war, which no one can heal; bandages and stitches cannot restore a human being with a memory intact and true inside the bone. Only the skin heals" (95). There is therefore no resolution in *The Stone Virgins*. Nonceba finds ways to live on, with her scars, after atrocity, but Vera's novel makes it clear that there is no real "cure" for the invisible "wounds of war." The work of healing is represented as an unachievable but ongoing process in the aftermath of extreme violence.

Interdependence, Community, and Care

With damage, fragility, and healing acting as such powerful tropes in postcolonial literature, it is no surprise that many novels are concerned with structures of care and community support. As we saw in *The Poisonwood Bible*, in some contexts disability is recognized as part of the texture of community life rather than as an individual's personal stigma. Indigenous cultures in particular often value the interdependence of community members over independence, which affects how the forms of dependency that might accompany disability are understood. In novels emerging from these cultural perspectives, "[i]mpairment" does not necessarily "diminish personhood,"[28] but can instead provide a focal point for emphasizing communal strength, inclusivity, and solidarity. Narratives that focus on interdependence therefore often contest the notion that postcolonial communities are disordered, incapable of self-governance, or lacking in some essential way – or, as Mbembe memorably writes of perceptions of Africa, "quite innocent of any notion of center, hierarchy, or stability."[29] Instead, they represent creative modes of care and the accommodation of difference, while often presenting critical examinations of the state services – education, healthcare, and social services – available for minority groups.

In New Zealand writer Keri Hulme's *The Bone People*, the presence of the disabled child Simon Gillayley provides a platform for Hulme's critique of monocultural and spiritually lacking care services in New Zealand. The novel presents an alternative vision, not yet realized, of more holistic care that incorporates Māori understandings of health and interdependence. Simon is a victim of child abuse, scarred from multiple attacks, who is mute and communicates in a sign language of his own invention. By the end of the novel, he is also deafened (at least temporarily) after a final beating from his Māori foster father Joe, who is represented in this ethically complex novel as troubled and violent, but also as a loving father who understands and cares deeply for Simon. Simon's disabilities are typically read by critics in symbolic terms: he is understood as a Christlike sacrificial figure, or a trickster like the Polynesian cultural hero Maui.[30] But the novel also has a lot to say about Simon's *experiences* as a disabled child, and the failings of New Zealand's health and social welfare institutions in the period Hulme was writing (from the 1960s to the early 1980s). These institutions – schools, hospitals, care homes, and the police – struggle to adequately care for this unusual child. Their responses to Simon's communicational and behavioral differences are procedural and uncreative, and they do not tailor their practices to account for his needs. In the care home he is sent to, Simon is beaten for misbehaving – a stunningly inappropriate and unimaginative way of dealing with a traumatized victim of abuse. After the beating from Joe, Simon's nurse suggests that all he requires is "a good stable place to grow up in, a place of kind authority, a normal background at last,"[31] but these standards (stability, authority, and normalcy) reflect the ideals of what Hulme presents as the conformist dominant culture. Implicitly, for these services, "normalcy" is based on European-derived notions of what family and stability look like, and exclude the kinds of communal care that Simon's Māori foster family can offer, and which, crucially, he desires.

The challenge that Simon poses to the health authorities exposes most starkly a lack of spiritual and emotional care within the system. As Kerewin (Simon's adult friend) analyzes, "medicine is in a queer state of ignorance. . . . There is no holistic treatment. Doctor does not confer with religious who does not confer with dietician who does not confer with psychologist" (505). The novel finds an answer to this lack in Māori communal structures and conceptions of holistic wellbeing. Both Kerewin and Joe have to reconnect with their Māori heritage before they can become worthy carers for Simon, and the end of the novel sees the whole whānau (extended family) coming together, taking responsibility for protecting Simon and helping Joe to address his violent behavior, in a newly configured, interdependent, space of home. This is an arrangement that Kerewin calls "commensalism" (528), and it restores Māori epistemologies at the foundations of an alternative model of communal care. In *The Bone People*, Simon's predicament triggers a crisis point that requires family and community to reorient themselves around the complex care needs of a vulnerable child. Commensalism has allegorical resonances, as the New Zealand nation was developing bicultural institutions and services in the 1980s – essentially learning to live as two peoples in the same space. It also establishes the value of Māori ways of living that were then lacking in New Zealand institutions, making a compelling case for including these within a truly bicultural nation-space.[32]

In a very different way, Australian author Tim Winton's novel *Cloudstreet* offers another reconfiguration of postcolonial community that is catalyzed by the presence, and care, of a disabled character. Like in *The Bone People*, this resonates on a national level but also explores the intimate dynamics of family and community, this time for white working-class families in mid-twentieth-century Australia. The novel focuses on two families, the Pickleses and the Lambs, who are brought together by disabling accidents. Sam Pickles cuts off the fingers of one hand – his "bloody working hand," as his wife realizes with horror – in an industrial accident, and Sam's new "crip" status has huge implications for his family's income: "They were done for; stuffed, cactus."[33] Meanwhile, nine-year-old Fish Lamb almost drowns when fishing, and while his survival is considered a miracle by his Christian family, they soon realize that "not all of Fish Lamb had come back" (29). In medical, realist terms, Fish experiences brain damage that limits his cognitive development, but as a function of the narrative, which allows the surreal and otherworldly to pierce the social realist framework, Fish is granted a kind of split consciousness, whereby the part of him that has not "come back" from near death becomes the novel's transcendent, philosophical narrative voice. When the two accidents result in the families sharing a rambling old house on Cloud Street in Perth, a "great continent of a house" in which they initially feel "lost" (39), their jarring coexistence prompts an exploration of luck and faith, home and belonging, that intersects with debates about Australian national identity in the mid-twentieth century.

The Cloud Street house functions as a symbolic nation-space, and the families' initial discomfort stems in part from its traumatic history. The house has previously been inhabited by a woman who runs a mission home for aboriginal girls, aiming "to make ladies of them so they could set a standard for the rest of their sorry race" (33), and is haunted by her ghost and that of one of the aboriginal girls who has committed suicide. Fish Lamb's liminal position "half in and half out" (68) of the living world gives rise to an intuitive awareness of this painful past: he alone is able to see the "shadow girl" (287) and informs his family that "The house hurts, you know. ... Some people cry" (311). This is an example of the kind of alternative "phenomenological perspective" that embodied or cognitive difference can bring,[34] and Fish's access to both the mundane and the numinous in the novel facilitates Winton's wider exploration of hurt and healing, both within the two families and on a national level. Fish's father Lester expresses a sense of dislocation that is ultimately related to the fraught history of settlement and its legacy for white Australians: "You think maybe we don't belong here, like we're out of our depth, out of our country?" (235). Reaching some kind of peace with this uneasy sense of emplacement and belonging is the families' overarching quest. They have to learn to become a "new tribe" (425), accepting their differences and frailties, sharing the space of the house, and enabling its history to be aired rather than suppressed. As an Australian "Bicentennial" novel,[35] *Cloudstreet* explores Australian identity, community, and history at a significant moment of national reflection, and like *The Bone People* it places the disabled figure at the center of a vision of a reconfigured nation-space.

The "Wounded Storyteller"

Fish Lamb and Simon Gillayley drive their respective narratives and enable transformations in community and care regimes, not only because of their vulnerability as disabled child characters but also due to the particular kinds of knowledge and imagination that are brought about by their disabled difference – the alternative stories they allow to be told. This chimes with the trope of the "wounded storyteller," a figure whose insight and storytelling ability derive from bodily or cognitive exceptionality. Arthur Frank asserts that stories have healing powers, since they create empathic bonds between the storyteller and the reader or listener, and writes that the "injuries" of wounded storytellers consequently "become the source of the potency of their stories," enabling them to make connections and "care for others" through their narrative ability: "The ill and all those who suffer, can also be healers."[36] The trope of the wounded storyteller is prominent across literatures and cultures – Frank traces it back to the blind seer Tiresias in Greek mythology[37] – but has particular inflections in postcolonial novels, where it contributes to the exposure of global inequalities and injustices that arise so often in these narratives, and the critical perspectives on healing (physical, cultural, and national) that they frequently offer.

Adah in *The Poisonwood Bible* is a "wounded" storyteller who provides the most subversive narrative perspective in that novel. She embraces the poet Emily Dickinson's imperative to *"Tell all the truth but tell it slant,"* interpreting this in relation to her disability: "And really what choice do I have? I am a *crooked* little person, obsessed with balance" (461; italics in original). In Adah's case, her "slant" perspective on the world causes her to see in sharp focus the undesirable nature of ableist, racist, and exclusionary aspects of "Western" culture. This informs her development into a "doctor poet" (195), a healer and storyteller whose narrative embraces and celebrates cultural and disabled difference. She reflects:

> Don't we have a cheerful, simple morality here in Western Civilization: expect perfection, and revile the missed mark! ... If you are whole, you will argue: ... Don't the poor miserable buggers all want to be like me?
> Not necessarily, no. The arrogance of the able-bodied is staggering. Yes, maybe we'd like to be able to get places quickly, and carry things in both hands, but only because we have to keep up with the rest of you. ... We would rather be just like *us*, and have that be all right. (559; italics in original)

This culture of perfectionism, as Adah sees it, is based on wealth and privilege: the availability of medical treatment and levels of consumerism that are the norm in the United States. When Adah returns to America and receives treatment that allows her to coordinate her body in a more normative way, she grieves for the lost version of herself. Her "two unmatched halves," she explains, "used to add up to more than one whole," a duality that she believes was accepted in the Congo and encapsulated in the Congolese term *"bënd-uka,"* meaning both the "bent-sideways girl who walks slowly" and "a fast-flying bird" (335). In the United States, treatment deprives her of the slant perspective – the "gift" (559), as she sees it – that her disability bestows on her. The pressures of normalization quash exceptionality and eradicate the benefits as well as the disadvantages that disability can bring.

In questioning the efficacy of "Western civilization's" obsession with cure and in valuing cultural, linguistic, and disabled difference, Adah is a postcolonial "wounded storyteller" who destabilizes some of the most ingrained narratives about the disabled body in "western" culture. As Lennard J. Davis explains, the novel as a literary genre arose in the context of Euro-American modernity, and intersects with all the forms of standardization and normalization that accompanied industrialisation, the rise of statistics, and the professionalization of medicine.[38] For Davis, the novel is historically invested in the idea of normalcy and consequently tends to rely upon a structure in which "[a] normal situation becomes abnormal and, by the end of the novel, normality or some variant on it is restored." Or, put another way, "the novel must have a wound [and] the wound must be healed or cured."[39] It is certainly the case that, through "tragic death or sudden cure,"[40] the fate of disabled characters may be instrumental in resolving the plotlines of many novels. However, Adah's ambivalence toward her "cure" points to just how many postcolonial novels complicate this pattern and unsettle the closure that a restoration of normalcy can bring: in *The Stone Virgins*, Nonceba's skin grafts only touch the surface of healing, leaving her psychological trauma raw and intact; the cure of Lenny's limp in *Cracking India* enhances her prospects of marriageability, but substitutes the clinical gaze for an equally oppressive sexualized gaze; and for Adah, bodily normalization shuts down forms of physical and intellectual difference that are productive, insightful, and valued. The wounded storyteller in the postcolonial novel therefore tends to offer a "slant," sceptical perspective on normalcy and cure, instead offering visions of the future, beyond the end of a text, that continue to include and to value disabled difference.

If postcolonial novels do not tend to "cure" wounds or resolve the social and cultural "deformations" they represent, this is, perhaps, tied up with the precarity of existence in many postcolonial locations, where many collective and cultural "wounds" remain unhealed or prove incurable. Postcolonial histories are still unfolding, conflicts are still unresolved, and injustices are still uncompensated, meaning that postcolonial novels rarely offer neat forms of closure. This translates into representations that are generally more interested in imagining possible futures where disability may continue to exist than in eradicating it. The aesthetics of representing disability – the choices novelists make about plot, characterization, symbolism, denouement – are therefore very much contingent on postcolonial politics in the contemporary world, and disability is often foundational to the dramatization and critique of colonial and neocolonial modes of oppression. As a significant presence in postcolonial spaces, disability has had, and will continue to have, a central role to play in postcolonial writing.

Notes

1 Ngũgĩ wa Thiong'o, *Wizard of the Crow* (London: Vintage, 2006), p. 3. Further page references to novels will be included in the text.
2 Brendon Nicholls, *Ngugi wa Thiong'o, Gender, and the Ethics of Postcolonial Reading* (Farnham: Ashgate, 2010), p. 178.
3 For an extended discussion of disability in postcolonial literature, see Clare Barker, *Postcolonial Fiction and Disability: Exceptional Children, Metaphor, and Materiality* (Basingstoke: Palgrave Macmillan, 2011).
4 See Tom Shakespeare, "The Social Model of Disability," in *The Disability Studies Reader*, ed. Lennard J. Davis, 4th ed. (London: Routledge, 2013), pp. 214–21. On the much-debated relationship between illness and disability, see Susan Wendell, "Unhealthy Disabled: Treating Chronic Illnesses as Disabilities," *Hypatia* 16.4 (2001), pp. 17–33.
5 Rosemarie Garland-Thomson, *Staring: How We Look* (Oxford: Oxford University Press, 2009), p. 45.
6 Barbara Kingsolver, *The Poisonwood Bible* (London: Faber & Faber, 1998), p. 84.
7 Tsitsi Dangarembga, *Nervous Conditions* (Banbury: Ayebia, 2004), p. 207.
8 Bapsi Sidhwa, *Cracking India: A Novel* (Minneapolis, MN: Milkweed, 1991), p. 26.
9 Tsitsi Dangarembga, *The Book of Not* (Banbury: Ayebia, 2006), pp. 197–8.
10 David T. Mitchell and Sharon L. Snyder, *Narrative Prosthesis: Disability and the Dependencies of Discourse* (Ann Arbor: University of Michigan Press, 2000), p. 49.
11 See Ato Quayson, *Aesthetic Nervousness: Disability and the Crisis of Representation* (New York: Columbia University Press, 2007), pp. 20–22, for a discussion of how disability fuels plots of "social deformation."
12 Salman Rushdie, *Shame* (London: Vintage, 1995), p. 87. Italics in original.
13 Mitchell and Snyder, *Narrative Prosthesis*, ch. 2.
14 Quayson, *Aesthetic Nervousness*, p. 35.
15 Quayson, *Aesthetic Nervousness*, p. 19.
16 Frantz Fanon, *The Wretched of the Earth* (Harmondsworth: Penguin, 1967), p. 48, 27.
17 See Anthony Carrigan, "Postcolonial Disaster, Pacific Nuclearization, and Disabling Environments," *Journal of Literary and Cultural Disability Studies* 4.3 (2010), pp. 255–72.
18 Patrick Williams, *Ngugi wa Thiong'o* (Manchester: Manchester University Press, 1999), p. 19.
19 Ngũgĩ wa Thiong'o, *Petals of Blood* (Oxford: Heinemann, 1986), p. 3. "Mau Mau" is a contested term with a complex history; the Kikuyu-majority freedom fighters referred to themselves as the Kenya Land and Freedom Army (KLFA).
20 Williams, *Ngugi wa Thiong'o*, ch. 3.
21 Achille Mbembe, "Necropolitics," trans. Libby Meintjes, *Public Culture* 15.1 (2003), pp. 11–40 (11).
22 Mbembe, "Necropolitics," p. 14, 40. Italics in original.
23 Michael Ondaatje, *Anil's Ghost* (London: Picador, 2000), pp. 117–18.

24 Michael Davidson, *Concerto for the Left Hand: Disability and the Defamiliar Body* (Ann Arbor: University of Michigan Press, 2008), p. 175.

25 Mbembe, "Necropolitics," p. 27, 30.

26 Clare Barker and Stuart Murray, "Disabling Postcolonialism: Global Disability Cultures and Democratic Criticism," in *The Disability Studies Reader*, 4th ed., pp. 61–73. On trauma in postcolonial literature, see Stef Craps, *Postcolonial Witnessing: Trauma Out of Bounds* (Basingstoke: Palgrave Macmillan, 2013).

27 Yvonne Vera, *The Stone Virgins* (New York: Farrar, Straus and Giroux, 2002), p. 141.

28 Susan Reynolds Whyte and Benedicte Ingstad, "Disability and Culture: An Overview", in *Disability and Culture*, eds. Benedicte Ingstad and Susan Reynolds Whyte (Berkeley: University of California Press, 1995), pp. 3–32 (p. 11).

29 Achille Mbembe, *On the Postcolony* (Berkeley: University of California Press, 2001), p. 3.

30 See, e.g., Val Melhop, "The Making of Ho(l)mes: A Symbolic Reading of *the bone people*," *Journal of New Zealand Literature* 17 (1999), pp. 99–109. For a disability-focused reading of the novel, see Ato Quayson, "Looking Awry: Tropes of Disability in Postcolonial Writing," in *Relocating Postcolonialism*, ed. David Theo Goldberg and Ato Quayson (Oxford: Blackwell, 2002), pp. 217–30.

31 Keri Hulme, *The Bone People* (London: Picador, 2001), p. 477.

32 Since the publication of *The Bone People*, health policy in New Zealand has developed along bicultural lines, and there is now an established Māori Health Strategy based on Māori models of health and well-being. See Ministry of Health/ Manatū Hauora, *Māori Health Models* (2014), www.health.govt.nz/our-work/ populations/maori-health/maori-health-models.

33 Tim Winton, *Cloudstreet* (London: Picador, 2008), p. 13, 16.

34 Sharon L. Snyder and David T. Mitchell, *Cultural Locations of Disability* (Chicago, IL: University of Chicago Press, 2006), p. 10.

35 In 1988, the bicentennial anniversary of the arrival of the first fleet of British convict ships in Sydney prompted reflection on Australian national identity, community, and the traumatic history of colonization. See Robert Dixon, "Tim Winton, *Cloudstreet* and the Field of Australian Literature," *Westerly* 50 (2005), pp. 240–60, for a discussion of *Cloudstreet* in this context.

36 Arthur Frank, *The Wounded Storyteller: Body, Illness, and Ethics* (Chicago, IL: Chicago University Press, 1995), p. xii.

37 Frank, *The Wounded Storyteller*, p. xi.

38 See Lennard J. Davis, *Enforcing Normalcy: Disability, Deafness, and the Body* (New York: Verso, 1995), and Lennard J. Davis, "Who Put the *the* in *the Novel*? Identity Politics and Disability in Novel Studies," in *Bending Over Backwards: Disability, Dismodernism, and other Difficult Positions* (New York and London: New York University Press, 2002), pp. 79–101.

39 Davis, "Who put the *the*," 98. Davis's analysis is based on eighteenth- and nineteenth-century novels by canonical European writers.

40 Mitchell and Snyder, *Cultural Locations*, 169.

7

EVAN MWANGI

Northwestern University

Gender, Sexuality, and the Postcolonial Novel

Introduction

Since the mid-1980s, a slew of important works have examined gender in individual texts or specific sets of postcolonial novels, signaling the shifts and circulations of paradigms of gender and sexuality in writing from the global south.[1] Although drawing mainly on African literatures, I refer to texts from Europe, the Caribbean, South Asia, the Pacific region, and New Zealand to survey the shifts from representation of mothers as symbols of the nation toward production of images that signal societies no longer enamored of the historical metaphors of the family institution or the sanctity of the nation-state. The chapter also examines the inclusion of gay-themed writing since the mid-1990s. Exploring how ideas related to gender and sexuality have traveled across markers of time and space as manifested in novels, I use as my underlying theoretical assumption Eve Kosofsky Sedgwick's view in *Between Men* that sexuality is an important "signifier of power relations" which interacts with other "historically variable power asymmetries."[2] Sedgwick has been criticized in postcolonial scholarship for limiting her readings to European and American literatures, but it is good to note that the representation of sexual and gender roles in postcolonial novels signify similar kinds of power relations to those Sedgwick describes, in which what is viewed as normative sexual expression has deeper and broader social and political implications.[3]

By "gender" I mean the socially constructed power relations between female and male members presented in the texts surveyed, while by "sexuality" I refer to sexual practices, identities, thoughts, fears, longings, and lifestyles that suggest the existence of diverse expressions of desire outside the normative human heterosexual practices (e.g., gay, lesbian, and transsexual desires, interspecies sex even if they are not labeled using these terms in the texts). It is also imperative to acknowledge that in a cluster of scholarly works published since the mid-1980s, several postcolonial theorists are uncomfortable with such labels as "gay," "lesbian," "queer," and "feminist" to describe nonwestern sexual practices and gender ideologies.[4] But one thing that unites postcolonial scholarship is that the critics in this field variously point out that nonwestern creative works about sex-related topics do not duplicate western sensibilities, terms of reference, or theories; rather, displaying cultural disjuncture, postcolonial texts are read as depicting local gender practices and forms of eroticism while at the same time acknowledging the interconnectedness between discrete postcolonial societies with the rest of the world. The novels highlighted here draw attention to the parallels between current sex-based inequalities and past colonial practices, as well as suggest that there do not exist in the postcolonial era pure autochthonous precolonial identities that have not been touched by colonial influences and varied models of subjectivity.

Like Sedgwick, postcolonial theorists have since the 1990s noted the centrality of sexuality to the understanding of postcolonial power relations because these relations are expressed in sexed terms. The theme keeps recurring in postcolonial theorists' attempts to explain different forms of power dynamics.[5] In the fictions from the global south, bodies serve as locations of encoding both individualized desires and collective memory of colonial experiences. It is also important to mention at the outset that in most postcolonial societies, homosexuality is a serious crime. This has a number of implications. Most postcolonial writers cannot declare their support for homosexuality openly without comprising their safety or risking state harassment. In spite of gay activism in these societies, even critics (with a few exceptions) have avoided discussing gay themes in postcolonial literature. Novels that openly present gay issues are either ignored or have at times been discussed without any reference to the same-sex themes in the text.[6] Sexual minorities are tolerated in most postcolonial societies only if, as Rosamond King observes about the Caribbean, "those individuals adhere to traditional gender codes and to the parameters mandated by el secreto abierto."[7] Thus the majority of postcolonial writers who have treated the theme of homosexuality sympathetically live in Europe or North America, outside their countries of origin. Critics have further noticed that the treatment of gay themes is more likely to be in short forms than in novels.[8] However, the different ways in which sexuality is presented in the postcolonial novel is what makes it truly diverse. It is also while treating taboo sexual themes that the postcolonial novel is in its most experimental mode, embedding the themes in antirealist passages.

Erotic References in Foundational Novels

Historians of the British Empire, such as Ronald Hyam, have stressed some of the sexual interests that underpinned colonialism.[9] In literary scholarship, the gendered representations of imperial desires in colonial fiction have also received a sizeable amount of criticism since the 1990s. Literary historians seem unanimous that colonial male novelists from the eighteenth century (e.g., Daniel Defoe in *Robinson Crusoe*) through the late nineteenth century (e.g., Henry Rider Haggard *King Solomon's Mines*) used tropes of femininity to represent the colonized territories.[10] Although there were differences among these texts and internal contradictions within an individual narrative, in the novels, to use Ania Loomba's words, "female bodies symbolize conquered lands."[11] The colonies also served as sites where sexual freedoms Europeans were denied at home could be explored. Even those texts that use modernistic techniques to signal their ambivalence toward imperialism (e.g., Joseph Conrad's *Heart of Darkness*) imagined the colonized cultures as feminine.[12] Behind this imagery was the imperialist desire to rationalize the dispossession of indigenous people of their land, as the land was presented as idle, unclaimed, unoccupied, and in need of cultivation.[13]

Women colonial writers in the nineteenth century (e.g., Flora Annie Steel, in her 1896 *On the Face of the Waters*) undermined the masculinist foundations of colonialism but tended to justify colonial domination by presenting anticolonial natives as wicked. However, around the same period some female novelists born in the colonies, such as the South African Olive Schreiner (1855–1920), sought to disrupt Victorian mores in narratives that also experimented with form. Schreiner's first novel, *The Story of an African Farm* (1883), exemplifies an early African text that is at once anticolonial and feminist. First published under the masculine nom de plume of "Ralph Iron," the novel explores colonialism's disempowerment of white women and treats taboo themes such as premarital sex. It is a precursor of novels that use modernistic styles, as it deploys the stream of consciousness to depict women's desire to come out of the restrictive environment in which they found themselves in colonial South Africa. Schreiner was also interested in Victorian ideas about women's liberation, which highlighted the possibilities for self-determination among educated women, who were no longer interested in marriage and children. In the novel, she presents in her character Lyndall a prototype of the "new woman" – a free-spirited and educated individual, who regards colonialism and Victorian mores as restricting and degrading to women.

The most influential foundational anticolonial fiction came out in the 1950s. These works were largely realist, but they avoided detailed treatment of sexual themes. One reason given for the reluctance of these writers to include sexual themes is the fear of reinforcing the "negative stereotyping" of the nonwestern subject as hypersexual, a stereotype "that emerged from a history of slavery and colonialism."[14] Another reason is that the novels were usually written in the *Bildungsroman* form, ending at a juncture where the young characters are about to enter the threshold of puberty.[15] Further, the nationalist texts circulated in the global south as pedagogical tools for use in the classroom and therefore avoided broaching themes that would be considered inappropriate. It is not surprising that the few serious novels that explored some sexual themes from the perspective of a child (e.g., the Guyanese Jan Carew's *Black Midas)* had the sex-themed parts edited out in school editions.[16]

With the exception of Somali's Nuruddin Farah, African male writers tended not only to tell their story from the perspective of male characters and narrators but also to sideline women's issues. Female characters were subordinated to male anticolonial heroes. In Achebe's *Things Fall Apart,* for instance, Okonkwo is censured not for beating his wife, but for beating her during the week of peace. In the novel, the masculinity of the traditional African man is counterpoised against the effeminate Europeans and indigenous people who cannot stand up to colonialism, a reversal of the colonial representations that coded the colonized as essentially effeminate. In Achebe's novel and others from the period, women characters are not as fully developed as their male counterparts. Colonialism, Western education, and Christianity are seen as emasculating the African male or as accentuating the alienation of effeminate boys, such as Achebe's Nwoye, from the desired masculine ideals. The "writing back" to the European canon therefore produces anticolonial narratives that mostly celebrate African hyper-masculinity and male sexual prowess at the expense of women's issues.

Also seeking to revalue the denigrated cultures of the colonized, postcolonial fiction of the 1950s and 1970s bemoaned in sexed and gendered ways the threatened masculinity of the male colonial subject but avoided overt sexual descriptions. When these works mentioned sex, it was mainly to emphasize that it should be heterosexual and within the family setup, mainly for the purposes of reproduction. While the plight of women in the material world was largely ignored, women characters were glorified as symbols of the nation in images that saw the nation as analogous to a heterosexual family.[17] In such settings, citizens are supposed to be sexually active. For example, in the first Papua New Guinean novel, Vincent Eri's *The Crocodile,* the life of an individual without "one's own children, children from one's own liquid" is bound to end in tragedy, as is the case of the childless old man Ivurisa. The impotent man is silenced in the narrative; we only hear about him as the narrator briefly tells us about his suicide. A superfluous presence in the plot, Ivurisa's significance in the story is to contrast his impotence and old age to the youthful fecundity of the novel's protagonist.

The 1950s and 1960s saw the publication of important women writers from the postcolonial world. These include Jean Rhys, Shashi Deshpande, Kamala Markandaya, Anita Desai, and Flora Nwapa. The novels of female self-definition emphasized gender as a category of analysis, and situations were narrated either by a female narrator or were focalized through female characters. While Rhys's *Wide Sargasso Sea* responded to the stereotypes about creole women in Charlotte Brontë's *Jane Eyre*, later women writers such as the Trinidadian Merle Hodge in the 1970s and the Haitian-American Edwidge Danticat in the twenty-first century were careful not to compound the silencing of black women in the work of Rhys, even when exploring the unstable creolized and relational models that reject identitarian conventions. But it is the male novels that dominated because of their inclusion in the school curriculum.[18] Novels such as Rebeka Njau's *Ripples in the Pool,* which explored lesbian desire, were included in the canonizing African Writers Series for some time, but were later dropped.

Disillusionment: Rape and Prostitution of the New Nation

In colonial novels such as E. M. Forster's *A Passage to India,* the prostitution motif is used to demonize male anticolonial characters, in this case Dr. Aziz, who are supposedly morally corrupt. In contrast, postcolonial novels presented prostitution as a form of exploitation of native women. For example, written in the 1920s, the Afro-Trinidadian historian C. L. R James's *Minty Alley* bemoaned the fact that it was only through prostitution that its most prominent female character could have a chance of improving her life under colonialism. But it is in the 1960s and 1970s that prostitution becomes a recurrent motif in postcolonial literature. This is a period when disillusionment defined postindependence nations. Despite flag freedom in individual nations, life in the former colonies did not improve substantively for the general populations. Prostitution becomes a metaphor for the moral rot eating at the vitals of the new nation, thanks to the widely spreading global capitalist exploitation. The prostitute figure features in popular urban novels of Meja Mwangi, such as *The Cockroach Dance,* as well as in works sympathetic to women's plight, such as Nuruddin Farah's *From a Crooked Rib,* but the most famous of the "prostitute" African novels is Cyprian Ekwensi's *Jagua Nana,* a melodramatic work about a woman who abandons her husband to work as a prostitute in the city. Ngũgĩ's works written in the 1970s and 1980s (such as his 1977 novel *Petals of Blood*) also include a prostitution motif to crystallize his view that the nationalist leaders in the postcolonial nations have prostituted their societies to neoimperialists. The prostitute is usually contrasted with an unchanging rural woman character, regarded in the fiction as the custodian of national ideals and the repository of the kind of traditions the currently corrupt nation should be restored to. In these novels, the prostitute is naïve and, if at all, has to be saved from her situation by the male heroes of the narrative. The prostitute also enjoyed varied degrees of sympathy. Like Warĩĩnga in Ngũgĩ's *Devil on the Cross,* the prostitute is sometimes transformed into a male-like figure who will liberate Africa from the shackles of neocolonialism. But while most of the prostitute characters in the male novels lack female agency, when prostitutes appear in women's novels such as Buchi Emecheta's *The Joys of Motherhood,* Marjorie Oludhe-Macgoye's *Coming to Birth,* and Genga-Idowu's *Lady in Chains,* they are not passive victims; they are depicted as working among themselves out of their condition or, indeed, using the proceeds from prostitution to better their lives.

The male prostitute has briefly featured in works such as V. S. Naipaul's *In a Free State* but it was in the 1990s and the twenty-first century that male prostitutes started to be explored in depth in works such as the *Dogeaters* by Jessica Tarahata Hagedorn and *Thirteen Cents* and *The Quiet Violence of Dreams* by the South African K. Sello Duiker. The presence of male prostitutes in these novels implies that gender identities are fluid, whereby men in decadent urban centers take up roles traditionally played by women. In Naipaul's *In a Free State,* a novel about the failure of the new postcolonial nations to take off at independence because of external meddling, the Zulu male prostitute the white man Bobby meets in a hotel bar considers himself essentially heterosexual although Bobby sees him as gay and tries to seduce him. It is suggested that the African youth might not be gay; it is the perverted Bobby who constructs him as homosexual because the white man's mission in Africa is selfish and exploitative. By contrast, in the novels by Hagedorn and Duiker, the prostitutes are more complex and dynamic. The abandoned child of a black American serviceman and prostitute, the gay prostitute in Hagedorn's *Dogeaters,* Joey Sands, is depicted as a product of the economic and political events that have shaped the twentieth-century Philippines, including American cultural and political imperialism.

Rape featured as a motif in European works about the colonies, but rarely did these authors present the historical sexual assault of colonized women by European colonialists.[19] However, postcolonial writers, such as James Ngugi (later Ngũgĩ wa Thiong'o) in *A Grain of Wheat* (1967), presented incidents of rape at the hands of white colonial officers.[20] They also occasionally presented nationalist characters raping Europeans or imagining carnal violence against white women. In such anticolonial novels, rape of European women was seen as providing "the opportunity both for vengeance and for the assertion of an anti-colonial masculinity that was under threat of emasculation by the colonizer's violation."²¹ Ngũgĩ revised his novel in 1986 to remove the scenes in which black characters gang rape a white woman and in which one of them fantasizes about raping Queen Elizabeth. This seems to be to avoid entrenching the stereotype about the colonized subject as oversexed and atavistic. However, novels by women, such as Edwidge Danticat's *Breath, Eyes, Memory* and Yvonne Vera's *Without a Name* and *The Stone Virgins*, bear witness to the traumatic instances in which nationalist male insurgents raped native women during the fight for independence. Written after independence, these women's novels use motifs of black-on-black rape to crystalize the disillusionment with the nationalist cadres that took over from colonialists.

Some Earlier Potential Queer Futures

It has been noted that although same-sex desire features prominently in precolonial texts, in the foundational nationalist novels, homosexuality is discretely hidden in the subtexts.²² But even without dealing with homosexual themes, the foundational postcolonial novel suggests what Jason Edwards, in a study of Sedgwick's readings of Charles Dickens and Henry James, calls "potential queer erotic resonances."²³ There is in these works recognition of the possibility of a queer future/presence, where sex would be different from the prevailing normative practices. For example, sexual relations in Eri's *The Crocodile* are heterosexual. Even if colonial Papua New Guinea is one of the Melanesian islands where, according to Robert Aldrich, "homosexual acts played an important role in rites of initiation,"²⁴ there is no depiction of homosexuality in *The Crocodile*. But a minor character in the novel hypothesizes that the village Councilor Morafeae cannot take time off from his colonial duties to do basic duties at home because "he is probably frightened that the Government officer might push his finger up his black bottom."²⁵ A similar reference to anal sex is repeated a moment later. The statements are declared to be a "joke" in the text, but they hint at an awareness that such sexual acts happen or could happen.

Similarly, numerous novels depicting heterosexual desire suggested that there is a potential for same-sex erotic relationships, resonating with Michael Warner's observation, following Judith Butler, that humans are intrinsically "resistant to the normal."²⁶ For example, the characters in Achebe's *No Longer at Ease* are heterosexual, including those that epitomize an unprecedented break with traditions. If there is any sexual bonding between the young male characters, it is homosocial, not homosexual. But in their utopian world of absolute freedom from the shackles of tribal rules that bar the protagonist Obi Okonkwo from getting married to Clara because she is an *osu* (outcast), the characters seem to include, though probably unconsciously, the freedom to be gay. The enigmatic Joseph Okeke suggests a utopian future when people who cannot marry one another today would be able to do that because, "in future, when we are all civilized, anybody may marry anybody." This time has not come yet, but it is possible.[27]

Queer Fluidity and a New Mesh of Possibilities

In the 1980s, European fiction touching on postcolonial themes was critical of European hegemony in a way that was not registered in works published at the turn of the twentieth century. For example, Alan Hollinghurst's *The Swimming Pool Library* satirizes the sexual exploitation of black gay people in Europe.[28] Like Hanif Kureishi's exploration of the intersection of race, class, and sexuality in *Buddha of Suburbia*, Hollinghurst's novel suggests that its gay upper-class characters are participants in exploitative networks that reproduce structures of oppression that have governed the relationship between English colonizers and the black colonized even after the end of formal colonialism. Novels from the global south have also imagined colonialism and its aftermath in male homosexual terms. If the European penetration of the colonial interior is figured as an act of regenerative heterosexual conquest in European male writing of the nineteenth century and early twentieth century, some post-independence writers evoke colonialism as homosexual exploitation of African males by European men. A notorious example is the Ghanaian Ayi Kwei Armah's *Two Thousand Seasons*, which portrays Arabic and European colonization of Africa as perverted homosexual predation of Africans. However, without embracing gay identities as part of the postcolonial cultural fabric, some writers condemned irrational hatred of people considered to be gay. Wole Soyinka's *The Interpreters* indirectly criticized homophobia as an attitude based on rumors and innuendos against the suspected character. Even if these novels were antihomophobic, we are not quite sure if the characters labeled gay by others are actually gay or just suspected to be so.

The 1990s saw an upsurge of gay-themed novels about Caribbean, African, and Asian diasporas in America and Europe. As if to counter the argument among postcolonial critics at the time that homosexuality was not an important issue in societies of the global south as it was in the Western conceptions of gender and sexuality, in the 1990s some postcolonial novelists depicted the centrality of same-sex to the negotiation of identity.[29]

In these novels, homosexuality was no longer a foreign import or something
that the postcolonial subject experiences among foreigners as happens to
Sissie, the Ghanaian Ama Ata Aidoo's young African girl in *Our Sister
Killjoy*; rather, in post-1990s gay-themed novels, same-sex desire was given
to the most Afrocentric characters in the narratives. Same-sex desire was also
depicted as not a transitory experience that only teenagers experimenting
with sexuality go through; the novels depict the evolution of homosexual
consciousness in the characters as they grew past pubescence into
adulthood.[30]
    An excellent example of fiction depicting same-sex desire as an integral
part of African reality is H. Nigel Thomas's *Spirits in the Dark*, a *Bildungsroman* about a black underclass boy, Jerome Quashee, in the fictional island
of St. Isabella. One of the earliest Caribbean novels written from a gay male
perspective, it is a coming out story in which Jerome, energized by his
growing African spirituality, accepts his identity as a gay black person.
Earlier Caribbean novels had captured the alienated split personality that
colonial education produces. But Jerome in Thomas's novel eventually
understands that part of his alienation emanates from his failure to come
to terms with his desire for fellow men. Pretending to be heterosexual when
one is gay is equated with racial passing, analogous to living in "the South o'
United States" and painting "yo'self white."[31] Such passing culminates in
madness.
    Other important works treating same-sex desire published in the 1990s
include the Sri Lankan Shyam Selvadurai's *Funny Boy*, which suggests the
easier acceptance of lesbianism in hypermasculinist cultures, in the sense that
the main character is considered "funny" because he plays feminine roles,
while no punitive action is taken against the girl who tells on him to adults,
in spite of the fact that her behavior is masculine. For its part, Mootoo's
Cereus Blooms at Night celebrates individual autonomy that allows one to
embrace one's sexuality even if it is unconventional. Although lesbian desire
had been hinted at in earlier novels by male authors (e.g., Alfred Mendes'
Black Fauns), it in the 1990s that female writers such as Mootoo started to
explore the theme with obvious sympathy. The presence of same-sex desire
in the fictions inspired critical attention into lesbian experiences in texts,
even when this desire is not explicit in the narratives.[32]
    The late 1990s also witnessed some graphic treatment of queer themes in
works by a diverse set of writers from the global south. For example, the
London-based Trinidadian novelist Lawrence Scott's *Aelred's Sin* uses explicit paragraphs to present taboo issues such as gay sex and anal rape. The
novel also covers other queer themes, including cross-dressing and transsexuality, to imply that gender identities are constructed and performative,

as opposed to being immutable and natural.[33] Never before had male gay love, including sex, been as openly presented as it is depicted in *Aelred's Sin*, in which Jean Marc engages in sex in the Caribbean amid homophobia before joining a monastery in England. Even as an adult, he continues to explore his nonnormative desires.[34]

Individual writers have also changed over time with regard to their attitude toward gay themes. The gay Māori author Witi Ihimaera's novels of the 1970s and 1980s were discreet about homosexuality, but the ones he wrote since the 1990s explored the theme more openly. The novels he published in the 1970s and 1980s investigate the effects of European colonialism in New Zealand from the Māori cultural nationalist perspective, but in *The Whale Rider* he criticizes the Māori culture for marginalizing women. Homosexuality features in the novel in the form of comical scenes, such as the spectacle of a drag queen Rawiri encounters in Sydney or when, back home, his grandfather mistakes the young narrator for a woman as they share a bed. Heterosexual unions in the novel are presented as potentially dysfunctional, and the friendship between a bull whale and the male ancestor of the Māori is suggestively coded as homoerotic. Ihimaera's later novels present the experiences of homosexual people among ethnic minorities in New Zealand, trying to find a common ground between precolonial Māori masculinity and gay practices in the postcolonial world. Written shortly before he came out as gay, *Nights in the Gardens of Spain* is a roman à clef that mentions a middle-aged married man with children who realizes that he is gay. Ihimaera's *The Uncle's Story* follows two generations of gay Māori men to challenge the essentializing homophobia among the indigenous Māori. Although he tends to present the Māori as patriarchal and homophobic, Ihimaera also suggests in his fiction that the codes of behavior among the Māori gay people are different from those among the Pakeha (Europeans) in the sense that among the Māori the dichotomy between homosexuality and heterosexuality is fluid and flexible.[35]

Remarkable also is the intensive use of experimental techniques to represent gay and other sex themes taboo. Before the explosion of antirealist writing in the 1980s, novels such as Bessie Head's *Maru* used localized moments of dreamy, magical descriptions to signify madness and hint at the existence of homosexuality in African societies. In the 1980s experimental women's novels by Erna Brodber and Michelle Cliff insert women's and gay people's experiences in the reconstruction of national history through similarly hallucinatory devices, while Yvonne Vera uses dense modernistic prose to depict sexual violence, including incest. In the work of the twenty-first century, experimental forms, especially science fiction and fantasy, are used in more sustained way to explore dissident sexual practices.

The novels exemplify queer works that present what Sedgwick would call "the open mesh of possibilities, gaps, overlaps, dissonances and resonances, lapses and excesses of meaning when the constituent elements of anyone's gender, of anyone's sexuality aren't made (or can't be made) to signify monolithically."[36] For example, Nalo Hopkinson's *Brown Girl in the Ring*, *Midnight Robber*, *The Salt Roads*, and *The New Moon's Arms* explore through linguistic experimentation the experiences of transgender people, suggesting that gender identities are far from fixed; the identities form a continuum, the extremes of which are not superior or inferior to other extremes or any identity in between. Hopkinson's works, thus, are part of a trajectory begun in the 1990s, in which writers examined the multiple intersections of the Caribbean identity through the figure of a transgender individual whose gender is as ambivalent as his/her others forms of belonging. Such characters include Nurse Tyler and Otoh Mohanty in Shani Mootoo's *Cereus Blooms at Night*, Harry/Harriet in Michelle Cliff's *No Telephone to Heaven*, and Mr. Lowe in Patricia Powell's *The Pagoda*, whom the authors use to showcase the multiplicities and contradictions within a single individual at the contact zone of different cultural heritages.

Conclusions

From reading various postcolonial novels, it is apparent that the representation of gender and sexuality has changed over time. While only a handful of African, Caribbean, and Asian women writers were published in the 1950s, in the twenty-first century the situation has changed, with "more women writers being published than men."[37] Male writers have also evolved. Although feminist close readings are likely to reveal contradictions and patriarchal subtexts in newer writing by men, male novelists whose initial novels focused almost exclusively on men have started incorporating strong women characters in works published since the late 1970s.[38] Male and female writers have also been inclusive regarding homosexuality. Chimamanda Ngozi Adichie's novels are about heterosexual desire, but her *Americanah* includes instances where homophobia among African men is made fun of.

This survey might give the impression that same-sex desire is addressed only in works, such as Adichie's and Nigel Thomas's, published in Western capitals. Although this is largely the case, there have been a handful of texts by local publishers. These include the Nigerian Jude Dibia's *Walking with Shadows*, the South African K. Sello Duiker's *The Quiet Violence of Dreams* and Phaswane Mpe's *Welcome to Our Hillbrow*, and the Zimbabwean Tendai Huchu's *The Hairdresser of Harare*. These novels differ in many ways, but they question compulsory heterosexuality and see it as equivalent to xenophobic nationalism. While Duiker seems to see homosexuality as resulting from economic and political developments in postapartheid South Africa, Dibia's novel suggests that some individuals are predisposed to engage in same-sex activities from their childhood.

Interspecies sex is largely presented as a perversion and featured in choice insults, usually expressed in anger through a character's stream of consciousness, implying that the thoughts about such a taboo sexual relationship are unspeakable. For instance, in Eri's *The Crocodile,* the evil sorcerer behind the death of the main character's wife is described from the character's center of consciousness as a "bastard" who "must have been produced when his mother was mating with a dog."[39] In Lauren Beukes's dystopian *Zoo City,* it is suggested that a girl has sex with a snake. But this happens in a stage performance presented as contemptible even within the context of the outlandish things that happen in the narrative. When interspecies sexual desire is alluded to positively in works such as Suniti Namjoshi's *The Conversations of Cow,* Witi Ihimaera's *The Whale Rider,* and Zakes Mda's *The Whale Caller,* it is in the form of a mythical romance that does not literally involve physical sex with an animal. Mda's novel has a scene in which the eponymous Whale Caller experiences orgasm while performing for a whale he is in love with. But the act is masturbatory because he does not come into contact with an animal as is presented to have happened between humans and apes in the American Bernard Malamud's *God's Grace* or the Danish Peter Høeg's *The Woman and the Ape.*

As we have observed earlier, the "writing back" to the Western canon in the early fiction also tended to focus on nationalism. But later transnational rewritings of the Euro-American canon (e.g., Robert Antoni's rewriting of Hemingway's *The Sun also Rises* in *Carnival* and David Dabydeen's rewriting of Conrad's *Heart of Darkness* in *The Intended*) insert gender and sexuality as a key component of the texts, expressing the fluidity of postcolonial identities, including sexual orientations. For their part, when rewriting the Western canon, women writers are not adversarial in their attitude toward the western canon. Rather than seeking to overthrow it, they have given agency to female characters that lacked it in the colonial ur-texts, with novelists like Michelle Cliff in *No Telephone to Heaven* giving more complexity to Ariel and Miranda than Shakespeare gave these women characters in *The Tempest.*

It cannot be stressed enough that gender and sexuality themes in the postcolonial novel have rarely been presented in a political vacuum; they have been placed at the intersection of other historical and social concerns, including colonialism, racism, ethnicity, and class differences. The other themes are also presented in gendered language. This means that sexual leitmotifs have been recurrent components in postcolonial writing even when they were subordinated to these other thematic interests. Indeed, going by recent studies of the history of postcolonial sexualities (e.g., Zabus's *Out in Africa*, Andrade's *The Nation Writ Small*, Gopinath's *Impossible Desires*, and Munro's *South Africa and the Dream of Love to Come*), it appears the analysis of sexuality in postcolonial literature will continue being done from interdisciplinary perspectives that draw on sociology, anthropology, political science, and feminist and queer theories to tease out cultural differences in sexual practices and demonstrate colonialism's impact on ideas about sex. This is because in the novels under study, gender and sexuality issues have been explored within a web of other political and social themes, such as race, citizenship, class, and migration. The aesthetics and formal properties of the novels, however, still need systematic analysis, as same-sex desire is encoded in subtexts that cannot be fully appreciated through the homogenizing distant-reading surveys that inform most studies of gender and sexuality in postcolonial texts.

Notes

1 Works studying women's postcolonial novels in English and the images of postcolonial women in male and female fiction include: Carole Boyce-Davies and Anne Adams Graves (eds.), *Ngambika Studies of Women in African Literature* (Trenton, N.J.: Africa World Press, 1986); Susheila Nasta (ed.), *Motherlands: Black Women's Writing from the Caribbean, Africa, and South Asia* (New Brunswick, N.J.: Rutgers University Press, 1992); Florence Stratton, *Contemporary African Literature and the Politics of Gender* (London: Routledge, 1994); Ketu H. Katrak, *Politics of the Female Body Postcolonial Women Writers of the Third World* (New Brunswick, N.J.: Rutgers University Press, 2006); Susan Z. Andrade, *The Nation Writ Small: African Fictions and Feminisms, 1958–1988*, (Durham, N.C.: Duke University Press, 2011). I discuss works on same-sex desire presently.
2 Eve Kosofsky Sedgwick, *Between Men: English Literature and Male Homosocial Desire* (New York: Columbia Press, 1985), p. 7.
3 For a critique of Sedgwick's disregard for nonwhite sexualities, see, for example, Keja Valens, *Desire between Women* (Basingstoke: Palgrave Macmillan, 2013), pp. 6–9; Omise'eke Natasha Tinsley, "Black Atlantic, queer Atlantic: queer imaginings of the middle passage," *GLQ: A Journal of Lesbian and Gay Studies* 14. 2–3 (2008), p. 204.
4 For example, Keja Valens has misgivings about calling Caribbean women who desire other women "queer." Keja Valens, *Desire between Women in Caribbean Literature* (Basingstoke: Palgrave Macmillan, 2013), p. 5. See also Omise'eke Natasha Tinsley, *Thiefing Sugar: Eroticism between Women in Caribbean Literature* (Durham, N.C.: Duke University Press, 2010). For a discussion on whether postcolonial scholars should use western or indigenous terms in the study of local forms of eroticism, see J. Neil C. Garcia, *Philippine Gay Culture: Binabae*

to Bakla, Silahis to MSM (Hong Kong: Hong Kong University Press, 2009). In West African cultural studies, Oyèrónkẹ́ Oyěwùmí claimed in 1997 that the gender distinctions upon which feminism as practiced in western institutions is based are not as pronounced in African societies as western feminists would have us believe. Oyèrónkẹ́ Oyěwùmí, *The Invention of Women: Making an African Sense of Western Gender Discourses* (Bloomington: Indiana University Press, 1997).

5 Dipesh Chakrabarty, "Postcoloniality and the Artifice of History: Who Speaks for 'Indian' Pasts?," *Representations* 37 (Winter, 1992), p. 12, explains the link between Indian nationalism and notions of sexuality. Also see Rosamond S. King, "Sex and Sexuality in English Caribbean Novels: A Survey from 1950," *Journal of West Indian Literature*, 11.1 (2002), p. 24, for an outline of the treatment of sexuality in Caribbean literature. For an exploration of how "sex and gender norms have historically been central to the structure of power relations" in Africa, see Achille Mbembe, "Ways of Seeing: Beyond the New Nativism," *African Studies Review* 44.2 (2001), p. 7; Achille Mbembe, *On Postcolony* (Berkeley: University of California Press, 2001), pp. 102–41.

6 The willful silencing of homosexual references in postcolonial scholarship has been noted in Timothy Chin, "'Bullers' and 'Battymen' Contesting Homophobia in Black Popular Culture and Contemporary Caribbean literature," *Callaloo* 20.1 (1997), pp. 127–41; Ronald Cummings, "Queer Theory and Caribbean Writing," in Michael A. Bucknor and Alison Donnell (eds.), *The Routledge Companion to Anglophone Caribbean Literature*, New York: Routledge, 2011), pp. 323–31; Ruth Vanita, "Same-Sex in India," in Brinda Bose (ed.), *Translating Desire* (Katha Publications, New Delhi, 2002), pp. 166–81; Rosemary Marangoly George, "'Queernesses All Mine': Same-Sex Desire in Kamala Das' poetry and fiction," in Ruth Vanita (ed.), *Queering India* (London: Routledge, 2002), pp. 111–26.

7 Rosamond S. King, *Island Bodies: Transgressive Sexualities in the Caribbean Imagination* (Gainesville: University Press of Florida, 2014), p. 90.

8 See, for example, King, *Island Bodies*, p. 74.

9 Ronald Hyam, *Empire and Sexuality: The British Experience* (Manchester: Manchester University Press, 1990).

10 Rebecca Stott, "The Dark Continent: Africa as Female Body in Haggard's Adventure Fiction," *Feminist Review* 32 (1989), pp. 69–89, reads the use of feminine tropes in Haggard's presentation of the colonized.

11 Ania Loomba, *Colonialism/Postcolonialism* (London: Routledge, 1998) p. 152.

12 For a reading that sees Conrad's *Heart of Darkness* as presenting the colonized as feminine, see Bette London, "Reading Race and Gender in Conrad's Dark Continent," *Criticism* 31.3 (1989), pp. 235–52.

13 Scholars who have examined the eroticized representation of colonized societies as female figures in need of penetration by the masculine, rational, colonial male include Doris Sommer, *Foundational Fictions: The National Romances of Latin America* (Berkeley: University of California Press, 1991); Anne McClintock, *Imperial Leather: Race, Gender, and Sexuality in the Colonial Contest* (New York Routledge, 1995); Jenny Sharpe, *Allegories of Empire: The Figure of Woman in the Colonial Text* (Minneapolis: University of Minnesota Press, 1993); Rachel Lee, *The Americas of Asian American Literature: Gendered*

EVAN MWANGI

Fictions of Nation and Transnation (Princeton, N.J.: Princeton University Press, 1999).
14 Jenny Sharpe and Samantha Pinto, "The Sweetest Taboo: Studies of Caribbean Sexualities," *Signs* 32.1 (2006), p. 247.
15 For a discussion of this tendency in works by George Lamming, Paule Marshall, and Jamaica Kincaid, see Alison Donnell, *Twentieth Century Caribbean Literature* (London: Routledge, 2006), p. 182.
16 In Jan Carew's *Black Midas,* the boy narrator Aaron Smart visits brothels in Georgetown. Passages describing his sexual encounters are left out of an edition of the work Sylvia Wynter adapted for schools in the late 1960s.
17 This tendency is discussed in Ketu Katrak, "Indian Nationalism, Gandhian Satyagraha, and Representations of Female Sexuality," in Andrew Parker, Mary Russo, Doris Sommer, and Patricia Yaeger (eds.), *Nationalisms and Sexualities,* (New York: Routledge, 1991), pp. 395–406; Sangeeta Ray, *En-Gendering India: Woman and Nation in Colonial and Postcolonial Narratives* (Durham, N.C.: Duke University Press, 2000); Mineke Schipper, "Mother Africa on a Pedestal: The Male Heritage in African Literature and Criticism," *African Literature Today* 15 (1987), pp. 35–53. For a discussion of similar images of women in Irish and African nationalist literature, see C.L. Innes, "Virgin Territories and Motherlands: Colonial and nationalist Representations of Africa and Ireland," *Feminist Review* 47 (1994), pp. 1–14.
18 For a discussion of the male dominance of the Caribbean literature of 1950–1965, see Alison Donnell and Sarah Lawson Welsh's "1950–65: Introduction," in Alison Donnell and Sarah Lawson Welsh (eds.), *The Routledge Reader in Caribbean Literature* (London: Routledge 1996), p. 218.
19 These works include E.M. Forster's *A Passage to India* and Paul Scott's *The Jewel in the Crown.*
20 Black men's infatuation with white women is also seen in the early migrant novels, for example, those written by Roger Mais, Samuel Selvon, Austine Clarke, George Lamming, and V.S. Naipaul. For a discussion of such works, see King, "Sex and sexuality," p. 28.
21 Faith Smith, "Caribbean Literature and Sexuality," in Michael A. Bucknor and Alison Donnell (eds.), *The Routledge Companion to Anglophone Caribbean Literature* (New York: Routledge, 2011), p. 405.
22 Texts that discuss same-sex erotic representations in precolonial work include Ruth Vanita and Saleem Kidwai (eds.), *Same-Sex Love in India: Readings from Literature* (New York: St. Martin's Press, 2000); Ruth Vanita (ed.), *Queering India: Same Sex Love and Eroticism in Indian Culture and Society* (New York: Routledge, 2002), pp. 1–14; Ruth Vanita, *Love's Rite: Same-Sex Marriage in India and the West* (Houndmills: Palgrave Macmillan, 2005). Leela Gandhi goes as far as to say that its colonialism that introduced to India "a virulent strain of homosexual anxiety/homophobia." Leela Gandhi, "A Case of Radical Kinship: Edward Carpenter and the Politics of Anti-Colonial Dissidence," in Brinda Bose and Subhabrata Bhattacharyya (eds.), *The Phobic and the Erotic: The Politics of Sexualities in Contemporary India* (Calcutta: Seagull, 2007), p. 92.
23 Jason Edwards, *Eve Kosofsky Sedgwick* (London: Routledge, 2009), p. 60.
24 Robert Aldrich, *Colonialism and Homosexuality* (London: Routledge, 2003), p.246.

25 Eri, *Crocodile*, pp. 17–18.
26 Michael Warner, *The Trouble with Normal Sex, Politics, and the Ethics of Queer Life* (New York Free Press, 1999), p. 142.
27 Stephanie Newell reads "queer" subtexts in Achebe's and Ifi Amadiume's works about the Igbo, even if these authors seem to disavow the existence of homosexuality in pre-colonial Igbo culture. Stephanie Newell, *The Forger's Tale: The Search for Odeziaku* (Athens: Ohio University Press, 2006), pp. 12–14.
28 For an examination of anticolonial critique in Hollinghurst's novel, see James N. Brown and Patricia Sant, "Race, Class, and the Homoerotics of *The Swimming-Pool Library*," in John Hawley (ed.), *Postcolonial and Queer Theories: Intersections and Essays* (Westport, Conn.: Greenwood Press, 2001), p. 113. For readings of European homosexuality as sometimes exploitative, see Robert Aldrich's *Colonialism and Homosexuality* (London: Routledge, 2003), p. 9; Joseph A. Boone, "Vacation Cruises; or, the Homoerotics of Orientalism," *PMLA* 110.1 (1995), p. 100.
29 Gwendolyn Mikell, "African Feminism: Toward a New Politics of Representation," *Feminist Studies* 21.2 (1995), p. 412. Gwendolyn Mikell, "Introduction," in Gwendolyn Mikell (ed.), *African Feminism* (Philadelphia: University of Pennsylvania Press, 1997), p. 4. See also Abena Busia, "Words Whispered Over Voids: A Context For Black Women's Rebellious Voices in the Novel of the African Diaspora," in Joe Weixlmann and Houston A. Baker, Jr. (eds.) *Studies in Black American Literature*, Vol. 3 (Greenwood, Fla: Penkevill Publishing, 1988), p. 9. For her part, Olabisi Aina argues that homosexuality is an "abomination" peripheral to African feminism. Olabisi Aina, "African Women at the Grassroots: the Silent Partners of the Women's Movement," in Obioma Nnaemeka (ed.), *Sisterhood: Feminisms & Power: From Africa to the Diaspora* (Trenton, N.J.: Africa World Press), p. 72.
30 Although same-sex desire in postcolonial fiction has not received the systematic analysis it deserves, some of the critics who have examined homosexuality include Neville Wallace Hoad, *African Intimacies: Race, Homosexuality, and Globalization* (Minneapolis: University of Minnesota Press, 2007); John C. Hawley (ed.), *Postcolonial, Queer: Theoretical Intersections*, (Albany: State University of New York Press, 2001); Cheryl Stobie, *Somewhere in the Double Rainbow: Representations of Bisexuality in Post-Apartheid Novels* (Scottsville, South Africa: University of KwaZulu-Natal Press, 2007); Brenna M. Munro, *South Africa and the Dream of Love to Come: Queer Sexuality and the Struggle for Freedom* (Minneapolis: University of Minnesota Press, 2012); Chantal J. Zabus, *Out in Africa: Same-Sex Desire in Sub-Saharan Literatures and Cultures* (Oxford: James Currey, 2013).
31 H. Nigel Thomas, *Spirits in the Dark* (Toronto: Anansi, 1993), p. 198.
32 Keja Valens's *Desire between Women* (Basingstoke: Palgrave Macmillan, 2013) is a book-length exploration of the treatment of female same-sex desire in Caribbean literature, interrogating the works of Jamaica Kincaid and Patricia Powell. See also Omise'eke Natasha Tinsley, *Thiefing Sugar: Eroticism between Women in Caribbean Literature* (Durham, N.C.: Duke University Press, 2010) for a discussion of erotic relations between women in the Caribbean. Also Gayatri Gopinath, *Impossible Desire* (Durham, N.C.: Duke University Press, 2005) for an

examination of queer desire among women in works by male and female authors from the Caribbean, including V.S. Naipaul.

33 For a detailed discussion of cross-dressing in the Caribbean fiction, such as novels by Michelle Cliff, Nalo Hopkinson, and Lawrence Scott, see Maria Cristina Fumagalli, Bénédicte Ledent, Roberto del Valle Alcalá (eds.), *The Cross-Dressed Caribbean: Writing, Politics, Sexualities* (Charlottesville: University of Virginia Press, 2013). See also Zoran Pecic, *Queer Narratives of the Caribbean Diaspora* (New York: Palgrave Macmillan, 2013), p. 170.

34 For a discussion of homoeroticism in Lawrence Scott and other Caribbean writers, see Alison Donnell's *Twentieth Century Caribbean Literature* (London: Routledge, 2006), pp. 208–14; Charleston Thomas, "Male Same-Sex Relationality as Critical Trauma," in Michael A. Bucknor and Alison Donnell (eds.), *The Routledge Companion to Anglophone Caribbean Literature* (New York: Routledge, 2011), p. 420.

35 For a study of Māori sexuality as more diverse than Ihimaera presents it, see Clive Aspin and Jessica Hutchings, "Māori sexuality," in Malcolm Mulholland (ed.), *State of the Māori Nation: Twenty-First-Century Issues in Aotearoa* (Auckland: Reed, 2006), p. 228.

36 Eve Kosofsky Sedgwick, *Tendencies*. (Durham, N.C.: Duke University Press, 1993), p. 8. For a reading of cross-dressing in the context of stylistic experimentation, see Knepper's analysis of Hopkinson's *Midnight Robber*: Wendy Knepper, "Cross Dressing and the Caribbean Imaginary in Nalo Hopkinson's *Midnight Robber*," in Maria Cristina Fumagalli, Bénédicte Ledent, and Roberto del Valle Alcalá (eds.), *The Cross-Dressed Caribbean: Writing, Politics, Sexualities* (Charlottesville: University of Virginia Press), pp. 140–56.

37 Emily Taylor, "Introduction: Reading Desire between Women in Caribbean Literature," *Contemporary Women's Writing* 6.3 (2012), p. 191.

38 One of the women critics' works that laud male writers' shifts in gender focus over time is Ciarunji Chesaina Swinimer, *Perspectives on Women in African Literature* (Nairobi, Kenya: Impact Associates, 1994).

39 Eri, *Crocodile*, p. 119.

8

YOON SUN LEE

Wellesley College

The Postcolonial Novel and Diaspora

Dispersal, disintegration, and the "affirmation of a distance" lie at the heart of the novel as a literary form. In his *Theory of the Novel*, Georg Lukács suggested that the genre emerges from the collapse of what he calls "integrated civilisations." "Our world has become infinitely large ... our thinking follows the endless path of an approximation that is never fully accomplished."[1] The homelessness that Lukács describes is transcendental, consisting of a rupture between the external world given to experience and the sphere of essence or eternal truth. Yet Lukács's account holds even truer for diasporic novels, which literalize his spatial metaphors. As the novel assumes the formal task of representing migration and dislocation, it continues to pursue its destiny as a genre. Through embracing the diasporic imaginary, the novel finds new ways to affirm unbridgeable distances in the world.

The idea of a diasporic condition is both ancient and new. To the concept of Jewish diaspora has been added the array of displacements, both forced and voluntary, that have been experienced by ethnically, racially, or religiously defined groups across the modern world. Shaped and scaled by the conjoined projects of capitalism and empire, such migrations have produced new forms of subjectivity and sociality, and new relations to space and place. Diasporic consciousness is not always as recent as that of the post-1960s influx of immigrants to former metropolitan centers, nor is it limited to the effects of British empire. Two brief examples illustrate some of the complex layers and intersections of the global history of diaspora. In the Filipino novelist José Rizal's 1887 novel, *Noli me Tangere*, first published in Berlin, the protagonist, returned to Manila from Europe, finds his surroundings "shadowed automatically ... and inescapably," in Benedict Anderson's words, "by images of [phenomena] in Europe."[2] In a 1937 novel published in the United States, the Korean diasporic writer Younghill Kang locates in the Japanese conquest of East Asia the cause of his own journey to New York. The diasporic Korean community in 1920s New York City "floated insecurely, in the rootless groping fashion of men hung between two

133

worlds," seeking each other like a "flock of homesick birds. . . . Yet there was no home . . . all they got was the only the sound of a tongue that had been heard since the days of the cradle until they left their native land."[3] The entanglements of East and West, North and South, imperial ambition and individual aspiration are neither recent nor simple. Most of the texts mentioned in this essay emerge from the upheavals of the twentieth century: war, decolonization, globalization. Some also reflect the older diasporas that brought slaves and laborers as well as colonial elites of different races across the seas.

Theorists have extensively examined the relation of diasporic social formations to hegemonic ideologies, including those of nation-state and empire. My concern here is not to discover a political orientation inherent in diasporic identity; rather, I will examine the structures of feeling and imagination found in novels written by and about populations characterized by a conscious, persistent sense of displacement. The key aspects of the diasporic imaginary highlighted in sociological and theoretical accounts can also be found in the novels of diaspora. Most important is the dialectic of host nation and homeland, the recursive mutual structuring of memory and discovery, the myth of the homeland and the experience of the host nation. This dialectic structures space, identity, and attitudes toward the material world, including the body.[4] These dimensions, which this essay will examine, can be aligned with traditional aspects of the realist novel: its setting or what Fredric Jameson has called its floor plan, the models of subjectivity and sociality that underlie its character system, and its overall plot trajectory. But the diasporic novel is more deeply marked by the recursive shaping of here and there, former selves and future selves. These features allow us to see in it the heir to the cultural revolution that Jameson identifies with the nineteenth-century realist novel. If the prose of Balzac and Flaubert helped to bring about the disenchantment or "desacralization of the older precapitalist life world," undoing hierarchies and erasing pluralities of qualitative experience, the diasporic novel carries on that work.[5] This is not to say that the diasporic novel portrays the world as uniform. In fact, it is driven by the discovery in the host nation of deeply embedded, highly consequential forms of difference, whether racial, gendered, or socioeconomic. But what results from this discovery is far from the reassertion of fixed relations, identities, or locations. Instead, the diasporic novel questions the hierarchy of center and periphery, uncouples movement from space in an era of accelerating travel, and articulates a striking ambivalence toward identity, property, and even material embodiment. In its more radical moments, its aim even appears to be dissolution: a dissolving of the bonds that hold bodies together.

The diasporic imaginary rests on space: space traversed, experienced, and registered as distance. As such, it constitutes a particularly rich and complex dimension of this genre: space is rarely if ever a simple backdrop, setting, or container. Uncoupled from actual place, space is often oddly impervious to experience or knowledge. It is marked by internal divisions, invisible barriers as well as impossible contiguities. Labyrinths, a frequent figure in these novels, are as intensive as they are extensive, a matter of a private inability either to escape or to enter a place. To begin to illuminate this dimension of the diasporic novel, we can turn to the idea of the nonplace described by the anthropologist Marc Augé. Anthropological place, Augé argues, provides a stable principle of meaning: associated with origin and identity, it encodes social relations both internal and external to a group, and constitutes a link with the past.[6] Nonplaces, by contrast, result from the hypermobility, eventfulness, and individualism of what Augé calls "supermodernity." Empirical nonplaces, which include "air, rail, and motorway routes, the mobile cabins called 'means of transport' ... airports and railway stations, hotel chains, leisure parks, large retail outlets," create a "solitary contractuality," in which the individual enjoys a temporary anonymity in her role as simply customer, user, or passenger. As Augé argues, the nonplace "creates neither singular identity nor relations; only solitude and similitude."[7] Nonplaces, in other words, belong to the realm of seriality and superficial resemblance, while anthropological places reinforce singular identities.

If anthropological places as well as theoretical world systems are internally ordered around central nodes, diasporic novels reflect serial displacement, entrapment, and dissolution. The diasporic imaginary often lacks the sense of a center through which peripheralized locations or persons can mediate their identity. By way of contrast, the centrality of the metropolis can be clearly felt in Samuel Selvon's *The Lonely Londoners*, for example: "just to say 'Charing Cross' have a lot of romance in it ... that place that everybody in the world know about." The clock in Piccadilly Circus, likewise, "what does tell the time of places all over the world," is "a place that everybody know ... a meeting place," where "the big life" can be experienced.[8] In Naipaul's *A Bend in the River*, likewise, the "colonial rage" that fills a character as he enters India House in Trafalgar Square reflects a similar sense of a place that defines his own identity as a postcolonial subject: "in that building ... I had been granted the most cruel knowledge of where I stood in the world."[9] Many diasporic novels of more recent decades, however, find in the host nation a series of nonplaces, as defined by Augé. Train and subway station platforms, subway cars, supermarkets, strip malls, and other serialized places define the landscape. Airports and fast-food franchises offer little sense of where one stands in the world. Dinaw

Mengestu's Ethiopian immigrants inhabit "twenty-story slabs of gray concrete apartment buildings [that] line an overly congested road developed to
the point of breaking with a dozen strip malls" in a suburb of Washington,
D.C.[10] Ha Jin's *A Free Life* carefully locates its immigrant protagonist's
Chinese restaurant in "a half-deserted shopping center" in a suburb of
Georgia containing "a fabric store, a Laundromat, a photo studio, a pawn-
shop, and a fitness center" together with a supermarket that comes to be
replaced by a Goodwill store – a small inventory of nonplaces in which
aspiration and failure, the unmade and the discarded blur together.[11] Le Thi
Diem Thuy's *The Gangster We Are All Looking For* jumps from one nonplace to another, from a refugee camp in Singapore to the deserted midnight
aisles of a Safeway supermarket in San Diego. The "fluorescent-lit city bus,"
and the series of apartments that the novel's Vietnamese family occupies
in southern California are equally devoid of the characteristics of
anthropological place.

Monuments are rarely seen in this diasporic landscape. The Statue of
Liberty, for example, that most famous American landmark, is not even
mentioned when the narrator of Younghill Kang's *East Goes West* arrives in
New York harbor; in Teju Cole's *Open City*, it is glimpsed first as a
"glimmering green figurine" in the distance, and then described only as a
fatal hazard for migrating birds in the novel's final sentence.[12] Fallen centers
of power, ruins, hold more appeal, for both Cole and Mengestu, but more
often there is an ongoing substitution of one place for another. Spaces
acquire significance not because of their public history but through contingent personal associations, resemblances, or echoes. One city or a park
reminds you of another, or a nonplace stands in for a dream of identity.
André Aciman's *Harvard Square*, for example, centers on a cafe named
Algiers, a provisional, inauthentic substitute for an imaginary pan-
Mediterranean place: "it was ... part dreamplace for the displaced, and
always part-something-from-somewhere-else for those who were neither
quite here nor altogether elsewhere."[13]

But the nonplaces of diasporic novels are not those of Augé's privileged
traveler, who enjoys a temporary suspension of identity for the sake of
leisure or consumption. Nor do they merely signify a condition of supermodernity. Rather, nonplaces are often defined by state power, even in an
age of globalization, and they can be places to which persons and collectives
are too often relegated or confined by force. Robert Davidson notes that
"[t]he ratified state of ... having arrived, experienced by one who travels by
choice, is precisely what is denied the migrant or refugee either through ...
contraction of state space through excision or the state's management of
specific non-places, or both."[14] The World War II internment camp first

described by Japanese Canadian writer Joy Kogawa in her novel *Obasan* still figures prominently in novels written by Japanese Americans. The long train ride described in Julie Otsuka's *When the Emperor Was Divine*, for example, takes the characters to an internment camp in the middle of the Utah desert, a supreme example of a governmental nonspace. Ha Jin's *War Trash* shuttles its protagonist from one UN prisoner-of-war camp to another during the Korean War. Detention centers and temporary holding facilities remain important sites, as in Teju Cole's *Open City* and Chimamanda Adichie's *Americanah*.

For many migrants, the "impossibility of arrival," in Pnina Werbner's words, marks the spaces of everyday life with risk and precarity, if they manage to stay at all.[15] In Maxine Hong Kingston's 1989 *China Men*, migrants from China work incessantly and collectively to transform the landscape of the American West and Hawaii; yet even as they lay down railroads, reshape mountains, expand plantations, they fail to acquire a permanent relation to the land, even a sentimental one. Constantly "driven out" by legal and extralegal forms of persecution, the migrants, in Kingston's telling, "slid down mountains, leapt across valleys and streams, crossed plains," and scatter themselves surreptitiously across the country, always in hiding and constantly ready to leave.[16] Places themselves become elusive, as faceless as Kingston's migrants, unable to be fully entered, known, or possessed.

Invisible as well as visible planes of separation often divide space in these novels, bringing to mind Robert Davidson's observation that states create "selectively porous" spaces: "traversable spaces for some, impenetrable membranes for others."[17] In many diasporic novels, windows, vitrines, and other transparent partitions determine one's relation not only to space but to other people and things. Internet and telephone shops seem to reinforce rather than overcome this sense of untotalizable space.[18] In many novels, an invisible plane of separation marks off the spectacle of European or American bourgeois domesticity. Characters such as Mengestu's narrator walk around the city at night, peering through the "curtains provocatively peeled back to reveal a warmly lit room with forest green couches ... I stared into the living rooms of others ... paintings on the wall ... long, elegant dining tables."[19] Even when inside such spaces, diasporic narrators feel themselves admitted only temporarily to a "dark, rather sacred" temple filled with "great silence," as Kang's narrator describes wealthy American homes.[20] The space of the host nation can be not only indifferent but impervious, striated most notably by race as well as class. A Vietnamese immigrant in Linh Dinh's *Love Like Hate* finds in all American cities "the same remoteness and blankness. ... She reminded herself that assimilation was a gradual process: You learned English, met people, learned the country's history, its pastimes and perversions, then doors were opened and you were allowed in. Only slowly did she realize that America was always a flat and transparent surface, with all desirable things just on the other side."[21] The racial barrier of separation is emphasized in novels such as Sandra Cisneros's *The House on Mango Street* as well as novels such as Faye Ng's *Bone* and Frank Chin's *Donald Duk* – novels that take as their setting the diasporic ethnic enclave. Entering and exiting such places cannot be done freely by all.

Diasporic space is layered as well as divided. Underground spaces such as train stations, subway platforms, and subway cars suggest that spaces become layered with the idea of history as a forgotten accumulation of disasters. In Cole's *Open City*, New York City always verges on becoming a catacomb, a labyrinth hollowed out by and for the dead. It provides a remarkable anatomy of nonintersecting and buried spaces that are connected in occult ways: overpasses, bridges, barriers, overlooked plaques, small-scale models, two-dimensional representations of places, the empty place that used to be filled with the World Trade Center. In his most mundane yet resonant example, the air-conditioning vents that the narrator notices in the subway cars remind him of "the final terrible moments in the camps" of the Holocaust.[22] Any place or nonplace is infiltrated by the air of another. Such connections cannot be represented on a map, yet they are more than purely private associations. In Rushdie's *Satanic Verses*, as the character Gibreel undertakes his Blakean wanderings through London's streets, the city metamorphoses, tropicalizes around him. The small-scale re-creation of Dickensian London at the movie studio where Gibreel goes on "a night of dreadful heat" again reveals the intricate pathways of diasporic imagination.[23]

Though such dreams are not fully abandoned, characters in these novels cannot seem to express themselves through owning or inhabiting a space, whether individually or collectively. As Kiran Desai's *The Inheritance of Loss* suggests, the dream of a space saturated by identity and intention is shifted into the past and the future. That novel juxtaposes three types of spaces: the colonial space of the past, the nationalist space of the future, and the American space of the present. Both the promise of the desired future nation-state, "Gorkhaland for Gorkhas," and the charisma of the crumbling colonial estate, Cho Oyu, are empty. Yet they are only enhanced by the novel's exploration of the basement kitchens, restaurants, and apartments in which its American story unfolds. In the diasporic novel, space signifies differently, taking on an allegorical dimension: space itself becomes full of time and distance, anteriority and alterity. Susan Choi's *The Foreign Student* evokes two contrasting and apparently unrelated worlds, Korea at the end of

Japanese occupation, and Sewanee, Tennessee, where the Korean protagonist, Chang, arrives as a student in 1955 to encounter Katherine, an American woman. Yet both places are equally saturated and defined for these characters by a loss of innocence. That moral and political process warps the novel's spaces and fills them with otherness. For Chang, the usual relation of body and space is inverted; rather than living in a home, he experiences even at the end of the novel "the great space within him where his home had to live."[24]

In many diasporic novels, movement figures a permanent state or relation rather than an event. Rather than simply going from one point to another, expressing intention or desire, bringing about change, or mapping out the lineaments of a world, such movements simply prolong a condition of dislocation and can even collapse a Cartesian sense of space. Choi's two primary characters find themselves most at home only in Katherine's car, while driving, often aimlessly. Cole's narrator, in his ceaseless walks, experiences motion through space as an illusion.[25] Le's characters in *The Gangster We Are All Looking For* note how "how sky and sea follow you from place to place as if they too were traveling."[26] At times the persistence of homeland spaces results through the actions of the diasporic coethnic community, the "villagers" as Maxine Hong Kingston calls them. In this uncanny condition of permanent dislocation, ideas of homeland become at best "mythologies of home."[27] The transformation of movement into stasis appears to be a product of history itself. Mengestu's narrator sees his Congolese friend Joseph at his job as a waiter inside a restaurant named "the Colonial Grill": "He stands there frozen in the middle of a busy restaurant designed to look like a nineteenth-century English dining room."[28] Acts of accounting, of remembering particular temporal or spatial locations, feel outdated. Maps and globes feel obsolete in a condition of permanent movement. The spaces that are most strikingly rendered cannot be given coordinates – as in the extraordinary internal and external placelessness experienced by the protagonist of John Okada's *No-No Boy* (1956), banished both from the imaginary homeland of his Japanese parents and from the American nation that has rejected him for his refusal to participate in its war. In the diasporic imaginary, space has less to do with external coordinates than with the intensive experience of movement, relocation, recollection.

As Ato Quayson has pointed out, "the question of identity – who am I? – is necessarily entangled with that of place" in the diasporic novel.[29] But identity is not determined by spatial location in any simple manner. Space and place are themselves extraordinarily complex, as we have seen: divided, layered, unmappable. Through the pressures of diaspora, other social wholes undergo a similar stretching and distortion. As nations and families are spread apart, the question of belonging becomes both urgent and difficult to ascertain. In the host nation, class undergoes a reshuffling, and unfamiliar categories of racial difference make themselves impossible to ignore. Identities are sometimes assigned to you, and just as often denied. Belonging to a larger whole cannot be taken for granted. In these novels, identity emerges as something radically contingent on performance, on performing certain types of acts, gestures, or styles. Yet to do so is not to earn admission to some predefined collective entity. What is striking is the absence of a part–whole dialectic, as will be argued in the following. Rather than thinking of themselves as a part of something complete or absolute, characters find themselves more often than not confronting a possible double, a mirror figure whose performance seems to hold a clue to selfhood or belonging. Diasporic identity seems to comprise ceaseless performances by means of which selves with gender, class, and even racial characteristics emerge temporarily.

The idea that seems to be notably missing in diasporic novels is the notion that everything belongs necessarily to a larger whole. The latter idea is brilliantly embodied in Rushdie's consideration of postcolonial identity in *Midnight's Children*. That novel's treatment of identity rests on the part–whole dialectic. By anchoring itself to the trope of birth, the novel offers the ideal of a whole body that is simultaneously that of the individual, the family, the nation, and the narrative itself. That wholeness is, of course, both playfully withheld and more seriously denied; the recurring image of the perforated sheet does the former work, while the frame of narratorial disintegration performs the latter. Nevertheless, the novel rests on the question of what it means to be a part: whether a body part, a part of a family or tribe, or a part of a nation. The dialectic is inescapable: to reject the whole is still to belong to it conceptually. To lose a part is still to assert the whole. For instance, nothing bespeaks the body's essential wholeness more than to lose a part – something that happens multiple times to the narrator. The novel's reenactments of scenes of birth draw attention to the illusory nature of natality. Birth and the emergence of a body only appear to present something new; larger, older, and more entangled wholes have already ruled out complete independence. At the same time, the wholeness of the body, family, or nation is constantly challenged by the unruliness and entropy of its parts. In the end, only obsessive repeating, reminding, and anticipation create wholeness at the narrative level, there to remain as a formal ideal.

Rushdie's *Satanic Verses*, by contrast, inhabits the apparently limitless space in which its first chapter opens: "air-space ... that soft, imperceptible field which had been made possible by the century ... most insecure and transitory of zones, illusory, discontinuous, metamorphic."[30] Boundaries between elements, species, lives, genres, and modalities are routinely crossed in this novel of diaspora. Yet the negation of boundaries does not create the sense of a dialectical movement toward a greater whole; characters and elements stubbornly refuse to be sublated or incorporated into something larger, even as they cycle through their various permutations. The distinction between metamorphosis and performance comes into question and remains unresolved. A preference for the performative, however, can be detected. Though the novel seems at the end to abjure the state of "rootless limbo," Saladin Chamcha, the "Man of a Thousand Voices," still needs to continue the performances that have been his life, only in a different voice and mode, in a homeland that is also in the process of reinvention. Contingent combinations and temporary transmutations fill this novel of migration; but even when patterns are repeated, they create, instead of wholeness, an overwhelming sense of variability.

The question of identity in diasporic novels points to the relation or tension between narrative form and sociological vision. The bonds formed by characters, whether bonds of friendship, fraternity, or romantic love, can take shape through the discovery of a common essence, that is to say with a sense of necessity; or they can be formed simply through the collective performance of certain actions or contingent gestures. It is necessary to look, then, not only at what relationships seem to lend identities to characters but with what degree of narrative necessity or emplotment they are created. Carlos Bulosan's 1946 novel, *America is in the Heart*, one of the first important works of the Filipino-American diaspora, explores the basis of a larger identity. Bulosan's narrative is divided into two parts; the first tells of the narrator's childhood in the Philippines, as it became a U.S. territorial possession. The second part relates his experiences in the United States as a migrant agricultural worker and, eventually, his self-education and transformation into a writer, teacher, and labor organizer. Bulosan's novel tries to affirm a collective identity based on class, as when he discovers that "this was the one and only common thread that bound us together, white and black and brown in America."[31] But Bulosan experiences this "feeling of growing with a huge life," this collective identity, most powerfully only when he "walked silently with the men, listening to their angry voices and to the magic of their marching feet."[32] Away from such performances, the novel continually disintegrates, showing recursiveness without awareness, forgetting constantly and remembering only contingently. America as a whole cannot be imagined; the homeland of the Philippines, likewise, is neither part nor whole, caught in its own nondialectical trap as a U.S. territory.[33]

In diasporic novels of the past decade, social class remains an elusive and reluctant axis of identification; class differences not only fail to provide a vehicle of collectivization but disjoint diasporic communities from within. Successful members leave behind or fail to recognize their diasporic coethnics, and new arrivals find themselves in an unfamiliar class as well as nation. The "shadow class" of undocumented workers, as in Desai's *Inheritance of Loss*, cannot unite itself for long or in public: "You lived intensely with others, only to have them disappear overnight, since the shadow class was condemned to movement. The men left for other jobs, towns, got deported, returned home, changed names."[34] Class consciousness is barely imaginable. The middle-class diaspora seems to fare better, as in the South Asian immigrant communities of Jhumpa Lahiri; yet shared class and cultural identities provide only a fragile and backward-looking bond between characters, as in *The Namesake* or *Unaccustomed Earth*.

The Western first-world concept of race, anchored for minorities in the indignities of everyday discrimination, might appear to hold out a more secure identity for third-world migrants to the United States or Europe. In diasporic novels, however, race is often rejected as a meaningless and empty form of collective identity. Julie Otsuka's *The Buddha in the Attic* offers a particularly interesting case. The novel, which describes the everyday lives of Japanese picture brides as they arrive in the United States, build lives, and eventually leave for the internment camps of World War II, is narrated in the first-person plural voice. Yet the entire rhythm, the narrative and ethical drive of the novel, works to dismantle a collective identity. Through fast-moving anaphoric repetition, Otsuka dwells on the singularities that set apart each individual. The chapter called "Last Day," for instance, consists entirely of naming and noting differences as the Japanese Americans on the West Coast leave for internment camps in 1942: "One man left East First Street ... with a white wooden box filled with his wife's ashes. ... One man left downtown Hayward with a tin of chocolates given to him. ... One man left Sacramento shaking and empty-handed."[35] Women are also named, given one sentence each and not mentioned again: "Miyoshi left pining for her big horse. ... Satsuyo left looking for her neighbors. ... Tsugino left with a clear conscience after shouting a long-held and ugly secret down into a well."[36] Children are noted and described singly or in small groups, their various hometowns, clothing, gestures, varying emotions, and expectations concisely described, again in one sentence each. The narrative disassembles the collective, cutting just at the point at which its members differ. Its point is that these individuals, now classified as an enemy race, can only be conceived as a group through an erasure of singularity that amounts to a gross abuse of power.

Race as a source of collective identity continues to provoke confusion and resistance. In Adichie's *Americanah*, African international students in the

United States mock African Americans for their apparent obsession with race. Her protagonist's experiences in America consist largely of the bemused discovery of race in both intimate and public settings. This character wonders whether her experience of racialization is shared: "she longed to hear the stories of others. How many other people chose silence? How many other people had become black in America?"[37] She starts a successful blog, drawing readers "by the thousands from all over the world;" "Dear Non-American Black," she writes, "when you make the choice to come to America, you become black. Stop arguing."[38] Yet the readers are only known to her and represented in the novel as traces, clicks, virtual signs of approval, and fragments of comments. The only occasion on which her readers are imagined as a collective entity is in a nightmare vision of them as "a judgmental angry mob waiting for her, biding their time until they could attack her, unmask her."[39] What the blog offers is not a collective identity but the illusion of intimacy, an invitation to reveal private experiences. As a private experience anonymously shared with the world, race can only become the basis of a blurry, virtual community.

The diasporic novel frequently explores how performance becomes the refuge and source of identity. Masculinity appears to be the dimension of identity that becomes most strenuously performative. Louis Chu's 1961 *Eat a Bowl of Tea*, set in the diasporic enclave of New York's Chinatown, revolves around the impotence of its young newly married protagonist: his inability to perform sexually as a man. Ha Jin's *A Free Life* represents the lives of diasporic Chinese men in the United States as a constant assault on their masculinity from all sides. Exiles in possession of a "significant past" can continue to imagine their own importance through their relationship with "the central power that had banished [them] from China," but ordinary diasporic Chinese men become "enervated and diminished" by their lack of money, power, and cultural knowledge. Their women derisively use the term "small man" to describe "male Chinese immigrants who ... made no effort to blend into American society."[40] Ha Jin's novel suggests that diasporic life leaves Chinese men "mentally dwarfed and socially handicapped," lacking any viable ideal of masculinity.[41] Even characters established as part of a diasporic community still need to acquire their gendered identities through learned performances. Often, gestures comprise the substance of the lessons. In Frank Chin's *Donald Duk*, the eponymous hero, a fifth-generation Chinese American boy living in San Francisco's Chinatown amidst newly arrived immigrants, must learn how to act like a man: "Don't hunch your shoulders. ... Keep your head up. ... Walk like you know where you're going."[42] Not coincidentally, the mentor, the father, as well as the presiding deity in Chin's novel, are all revealed to be actors. Junot Díaz's *The Brief*

Wondrous Life of Oscar Wao offers a more elaborate version of this relationship between Oscar Wao and its primary narrator, Yunior, who attempts to instruct Oscar in the performance of diasporic Dominican masculinity. Oscar's appearance, manners, and behavior, however, precisely delineate the antithesis of this masculine ideal. Instead of attracting women, he repels them, despite Yunior's efforts to reform and reshape him. Díaz's novel suggests that a exaggerated heterosexual masculinity arises as both a legacy of and a response to the historical colonization of the homeland and the social marginalization of the U.S. Dominican diaspora. Chin has a similar point to make about the racial oppression of Asian males in the United States. The ironies involved can be seen in Díaz's tongue-in-cheek footnote about the term "parigüayo," which he explains "came into common usage during the First American Occupation of the DR," to denote Marines who would stand at parties and simply watch, but which came to mean a person like Oscar, who "stands outside and watches while other people scoop up the girls."[43] The aggressive performance of masculinity in these diasporic novels can be said both to ignore and to compensate for these larger factors of inequality.

The dyadic relationship figures more dramatically than the condition of belonging to a larger collective in the diasporic novel. A curiously intimate relation can develop when a previously arrived and better-assimilated friend instructs a newcomer in the performance of identity in this new setting. In Younghill Kang's *East Goes West*, the Korean protagonist receives instruction from his friend in dressing, flirting, and all the arts of appealing to women. In Desai's *Inheritance of Loss*, an anticolonial nationalist masculinity, achieved by learning "to stand tall and be rough ... good firm gestures," is learned through joining a political independence movement in India. But in its diasporic plot, the protagonist finds his ego ideal in the performance of sincerity offered by his friend, an undocumented worker from Zanzibar, "the man he admired most in the United States of America," who "charmed [the country], cajoled it, cheated it ... he would pledge emotional allegiance to the flag with tears in his eyes and conviction in his voice."[44] In Aciman's *Harvard Square*, the narrator, a privileged Alexandrian-born graduate student, obsessively studies an undocumented Tunisian cab-driver, Kalaj: "I wanted to learn from him. He was a man." The narrator finds in him "my screen, my mentor, my voice."[45] Chang-rae Lee's *Native Speaker* also focuses on the relationship between its young Korean American narrator and an older Korean man, a successful New York politician. Maxine Hong Kingston's 1975 *Woman Warrior* offers a memorable variant of this relationship in an episode in which the narrator confronts her double, another Chinese American girl, and proceeds to torture her, childishly interrogating and physically abusing her, in what is clearly an attempt to learn if there is in fact an essence, an essential identity rather than a performative one. Mohsin Hamid's *The Reluctant Fundamentalist*, written in the second person throughout, makes inventive use of this dyadic or mirroring relationship. The narrator, an American-educated Afghan who has recently returned to his homeland, addresses his counterpart, an American whose identity as a covert agent is only hinted. But the airless and aggressive intimacy of this relationship, as well as its uneasy, ambiguous imbalance of power, suggest that narrator and narratee are more alike than opposite.

Rather than revealing how a whole emerges out of multiple parts, then, diasporic novels seem to focus more on the performativity of social dimensions of identity. Jessica Hagedorn's *Gangster of Love* rests on a notion of identity as a series of performances, some of which are stylized versions of former selves, while others are clearly attempts to rebel against lingering homeland ideologies. The narrator, Rocky, pursues a "stylish and dangerous" life in a rock band, while her Filipina mother "reigns from her run-down San Francisco apartment as if she were still the privileged wife." The unnamed elderly Filipino immigrants on Kearny Street follow the unwritten diasporic rule of theatricalizing identity: "they exude gangster flash and style, chewing on fat cigars ... acting like millionaires and preening like peacocks. ... Fiercely determined to keep up appearances at any cost, strutting proudly to their graves. ... All that bragging and pretending, all that posturing and face-saving."[46] Whether identity at its deepest level can be considered performance, however, remains a question, as the trope of nostos suggests. The desire to return to the homeland, as well as the struggle to negate that desire, suggest a self that may reside at a deeper level. Chang-rae Lee's novel *A Gesture Life* explores this question of performative identity from a different angle. Its narrator, an ethnic Korean Japanese who had been a medic in the Japanese Imperial Army and has long been settled in a quiet suburban American existence, comes to realize that the notion of merely performing his duty, on which he had relied in complex and contradictory ways during the war, has left him without a sense of self: "I sometimes forget who I really am. ... I forget what it is I do, the regular activity of my walk and my swim and my taking of tea, the minor trappings and doings of my days, what I've made up to be the token flags of my life. I forget why it is I do such things, why they give me interest or solace or pleasure."[47] Performance can be a temporary escape from questions of identity as well as an answer to those questions. It can take the place of essence in more permanent ways.

Whether moving in space or performing gestures that signify an identity, the body can be an embarrassment. With its stubborn, resistant materiality, the body is itself a place, and demands to be tended as such, to be given a proper setting, adequate acknowledgment and extension. Its fabric also has its own story, its temporal trajectory of physical development, maturity, and decline. The diasporic imaginary lingers over this dimension of the world. But its attitude is ambivalent, and its approach broad. Bodiliness is made continuous with other forms of materiality, including property and money. Often conflated through the trope of weight or of hunger, material things and the material properties of persons can engender a distinct revulsion. The body seems ineluctably to prefer proximity to distance, repletion to void, and this is often experienced as a betrayal of the diasporic imagination. Instead of moving as realist novels do toward material improvement or solid acquisition, toward a permanent shelter for characters who have been shaped and rounded by a history of engagement with the social world, diasporic novels appear to seek dissolution, erasure, divestment from concrete, material existence. Their primary allegiance is to distance and to space.

The rejection of the body takes complex forms in diasporic novels but seems to base itself on negating the simplest claim that bodily existence makes: that material presence is primary. A novel such as Joy Kogawa's *Obasan* explicitly maps its Japanese Canadian protagonist's maturity through her dawning understanding of her mother's absence from her life. Her mother's unexplained failure to return from a visit to Japan was both part of a larger historical tragedy, the American bombing of Nagasaki, and also an act of love and enduring connection to her children, as she kept from them the knowledge of the disfigurement and disease she suffered as a result of that event. The narrator remarks at the end, "because I am no longer a child I can know your presence through you are not here."[48] The novel's hostility to the claims of the flesh and to the world of materiality emerges through an elaborate system of images. Proximity and accumulation are rejected in favor of disembodied memory and sensation – arguably, a response as well to the dispossession and internment of Japanese Canadians that the novel memorably depicts. Nora Keller's *Comfort Woman* likewise makes of the body mere temporary housing for immaterial forces. Its protagonist, a former Korean comfort woman living in Hawaii, works as a shaman; as her daughter, the novel's other narrator, remarks, "the mother I knew turned off, checked out, and someone else came to rent the space . . . the body of my mother would float through our one-bedroom apartment, slamming into walls and bookshelves."[49] The Korean woman radically disavows her own body as a site of exploitation because of her experiences in the military camps; yet her American-born daughter also experiences her growing adolescent body with profound alienation. That novel as well as others repeatedly articulates a fantasy of dissolution.

The body's problem is not simply its interiority but the way in which it can internalize hostile or damaging ideologies of the host nation. The way that bodies betray their owners by self-naturalizing a selective hatred of the flesh appears dramatically in Toni Morrison's first novel, *The Bluest Eye*. Morrison evokes a subset of African American women in the deep South who learn a particular lesson in "how to do the white man's work with refinement ... how to behave." The lesson consists in the disciplining of the now-fully-racialized body, the textures, sounds, movements, dimensions, or passions now identified as black: "how to get rid of the funkiness ... they wipe it away; where it crusts, they dissolve it; wherever it drips, flowers, or clings, they find it and fight it until it dies."[50] Whiteness, disguised as beauty, as "order, precision, and constancy," becomes the norm that rules and ruins their lives.

An ambivalent attitude toward the flesh expresses itself through characters of exaggerated size and appetite. One character in Morrison's novel, nicknamed The Maginot Line, is described as "[a] mountain of flesh ... massive legs like tree stumps parted wide at the knees. ... A dark-brown root-beer bottle, like a burned limb, grew out of her dimpled hand."[51] A similar "mountainous woman" in Gish Jen's *The Love Wife*, is described in a scene of eating: "We ate. Sue's pace was not abnormal, only the placid way she kept at it, eating and eating and eating."[52] What the scene suggests is an invisible void within. Another version of this idea appears in Catherine Chung's *Forgotten Country*, a novel that moves beyond diaspora to disavow place and bodiliness altogether. Chung's novel traces a Korean family's movements to the United States and back again to Korea as the father dies of cancer; the daughter-narrator emphasizes the slow dissolution of his body, his gradual vanishing from physical existence. After he is brought back to his natal village, and as she watches over his death, the narrator blames herself: "it is you who have forced on him again and again the foolish, impossible weight of your wanting."[53] A graduate student in mathematics, she makes clear why she has chosen this path: "how reassuring it could be to live in the world of abstract ideas: how it untethered you from the physical world."[54] The decline of the body and the boundedness of place seem to be the most tragic qualities of this rejected physical world.

Yet the flesh also functions as a metaphor for history in complex ways: the personal history that clings and subsists in the subject, or the world-historical developments that also shape subjects' desires and appetites. Ha Jin's first novel, *Waiting*, makes this latter connection extraordinarily intimate; set in China during and after the Cultural Revolution, the novel focuses on one hapless and indecisive character who waits for more than a decade to marry his girlfriend. The nation's slow turn toward capitalist values manifests itself in small details and in many scenes of eating and other bodily functions. The protagonist notably recoils from the appetitive and acquisitive forces that gather momentum through the novel. He wonders "how [his wife's] body could generate so much desire," and, waiting miserably in the hospital for her to give birth, he asks bitterly, "Why do people have to live like animals eating and reproducing, possessed by the instinct for survival?"[55] But the novel suggests that eating and other forms of acquisition are not so much driven by instinct as spurred by history's unseen larger forces.

In Junot Díaz's *The Brief Wondrous Life of Oscar Wao*, the recurrent nightmares of history are expressed through and recorded on the body. The dictatorship of Trujillo is represented as an sexual domination of the country by one male and his surrogates; yet the diasporic narrator Yunior's unflagging emphasis on the beauty, the desirability, the fertility and frailty of female bodies naturalizes that as well as other social forms of domination. Bodies bear the literal scars of history; they are burned, beaten, and broken. Oscar's obesity, his sheer material bulk, is emphasized to the very end, when three laborers are required to move his body from the sugarcane field where he is killed. The novel's pathos derives largely from Oscar's unsuccessful attempts not only to escape the world but to negate the world in which these bodies exist, to defy gravity through fantasy and the insubstantiality of fiction. Not only the diasporic imagination but also the diasporic body finds escape from the dialectic of homeland and host country only in the otherworldly, weightless fictive space of fantasy, science fiction, comic books, and similar genres. At the end, the novel's ideal seems to be expressed in the impossible injunction to "travel light," to leave behind colonial history and to shed nature itself: "he felt light on his feet, he felt weightless."[56]

The rejection of materiality is an enduring theme in diasporic novels. In Ha Jin's *A Free Life*, the protagonist achieves material success in America and then radically disavows it in favor of pursuing his dream of writing poetry; poetry is valued for its immateriality, its weightless transparency, and most of all, it seems, for its unprofitability: "What was the meaning of an existence that was altogether bodily?"[57] In the final scene, he gives away all his money to a homeless man. Chang-rae Lee's *Aloft* expresses a similar uneasiness about the ties of both flesh and property, and an ethical preference for the barest or merest forms of life as it emerges at the very beginning or the end of life. Asceticism is acknowledged as an ideology, a salutary way of life, albeit an unfamiliar one to American families, in Gish Jen's *Love Wife*. Its newly arrived Chinese nanny states, "Better to want nothing. ... Then nothing means nothing," and the novel ultimately affirms this "wanting to want nothing."[58]

Plots of divestiture are frequent in diasporic novels. In Jhumpa Lahiri's *The Namesake*, for example, "diasporic life" is constituted by a permanent suspension. The novel is punctuated by scenes in which apartments and houses are emptied of their belongings. The many scenes of methodical preparation, often preparation for social events, seem in the end merely to rehearse the novel's final leave-taking, in which the woman who had arrived as a young bride in 1968 prepares, thirty-two years later, to return to India. She methodically sorts through her possessions, discarding and donating all of them, erasing the traces of her family's life. Through this austere sentimental inventory, the occasional scrap of connection to past identities is "salvaged ... by chance."[59]

Yet the deaccessioning of both materiality and meaning is rarely complete. In a familiar paradox, distance and emptiness reveal themselves to be full. Anzia Yezierska's *Bread Givers* begins in an apartment "packed with furniture ... packed with Father's books," with "junk."[60] Leaving behind the crowded, over-stuffed environment and bulging bodies of these immigrant tenements, the protagonist finally acquires her own space, which she leaves conspicuously empty: "No carpet. ... No pictures on the wall. Nothing but a clean, airy emptiness."[61] But she realizes that "this beautiful, clean emptiness I had created for myself" is still full of "the crowded dirt from where I came." Returning to see her family at the end, she still feels "the generations who made my father whose weight was still upon me."[62] Jamaica Kincaid's *Lucy* likewise traces a girl's deliberate attempt to leave behind her homeland. Her solitude at the end of the novel is described as an achievement: "I was alone in the world. It was not a small accomplishment." Desire has apparently been replaced with freedom; she tells her former employer, "I wanted nothing ... everything she had reminded me ... of the weight of the world."[63] Yet such announcements are performative failures. "The object of my life now was to put as much distance between myself and [my mother] as I could manage. For I felt that if I could put enough miles between me and the place from which that letter came ... would I not be free to take everything just as it came and not see hundreds of years in every gesture, every word spoken, every face?"[64] The question is never answered.

The diasporic novel is capacious in its imagination and equally generous in its disavowals. The ideal of place, narratives of accomplished movement, collective forms of shared essence, and the material burdens and gains of history are disavowed but never completely denied or forgotten. Diasporic novels seem to represent a mature dialectical engagement with the formal horizons of the novel as a genre. They remind us of a longer history of novel writing about coerced and willful travel of subjects to all corners of the globe.

Notes

1 Georg Lukács, *The Theory of the Novel*, trans. Anna Bostock (Cambridge, MA: MIT Press, 1971), pp. 34, 72.
2 Benedict Anderson, *The Spectre of Comparisons* (London: Verso, 1998), p. 2.
3 Younghill Kang, *East Goes West* (New York: Kaya, 1997), pp. 69–70.
4 See Ato Quayson and Girish Daswani, "Introduction," in *A Companion to Diaspora and Transnationalism*, ed. Ato Quayson and Girish Daswani (New York: Blackwell, 2013), p. 3, as well as *The Cambridge Companion to Post-colonial Literary Studies*, ed. Neil Lazarus (Cambridge: Cambridge University Press, 2004).
5 Fredric Jameson, "The Realist Floor-Plan," in *On Signs*, ed. Marshall Blonsky (Baltimore, MD: Johns Hopkins University Press, 1985), pp. 373–383, 379.
6 Marc Augé, *Non-Places: An Introduction to Supermodernity* (London: Verso, 1995), p. 44.
7 Augé, *Non-Places*, pp. 64, 76, 83. Despite his references to refugee camps as well as luxury hotels, Augé's paradigm is clearly that of the privileged traveler in possession of passport and credit card, rather than the undocumented migrant. Augé's insistence that nonplaces are defined by economic rather than political function is usefully criticized by R. Davidson.
8 Samuel Selvon, *The Lonely Londoners* (New York: Longman, 1956), pp. 84–5.
9 V.S. Naipaul, *A Bend in the River* (New York: Random House, 1989, c. 1979), p. 146.
10 Dinaw Mengestu, *The Beautiful Things That Heaven Bears* (New York: Penguin, 2007), p. 96.
11 Ha Jin, *A Free Life* (New York: Random House, 2007), p. 169.
12 Teju Cole, *Open City* (New York: Random House, 2012), pp. 162, 259.
13 Andre Aciman, *Harvard Square* (New York: Norton, 2013), p. 125.
14 Robert Davidson, "Spaces of Immigrant 'Prevention': Interdiction and the Non-place," *diacritics* 33, 3–4 (2003), pp. 3–18, 11.
15 Pnina Werbner, "Migration and Transnational Studies: Between Simultaneity and Rupture," in Quayson and Daswani, *A Companion*, pp. 106–24, 113.
16 Maxine Hong Kingston, *China Men*, (New York: Vintage International, 1989), p. 146.
17 Davidson, "Spaces of Immigrant 'Prevention,'" p. 15.
18 Cole, *Open City*, p. 101.
19 Mengestu, *Beautiful Things*, p. 52.
20 Kang, *East Goes West*, pp. 241, 300.
21 Linh Dinh, *Love Like Hate* (New York: Seven Stories Press, 2012), pp. 22–3.
22 Cole, *Open City*, pp. 228–9.
23 Salman Rushdie, *Satanic Verses* (Delaware: The Consortium, 1992, c. 1988), p. 421.
24 Susan Choi, *The Foreign Student* (New York: Harper Collins, 1998), p. 323.
25 Cole, *Open City*, p. 52.
26 Le Thi Diem Thuy, *The Gangster We Are All Looking for* (New York: Alfred A. Knopf, 2003), p. 89.
27 Chimamanda Adichie, *Americanah* (New York: Alfred A. Knopf, 2013), p. 118.
28 Mengestu, *Beautiful Things*, p. 172.

29 Ato Quayson, "Postcolonialism and the Diasporic Imaginary," in Quayson and Daswani, *A Companion*, pp. 140–59, 148.
30 Rushdie, *Satanic Verses*, p. 5.
31 Carlos Bulosan, *America Is in the Heart* (Seattle: University of Washington Press, 1973), p. 313.
32 Bulosan, *America*, p. 196.
33 See Allan Isaac, *American Tropics: Articulating Filipino America* (Minneapolis: University of Minnesota Press, 2006).
34 Kiran Desai, *The Inheritance of Loss* (New York: Grove Atlantic, 2006), p. 112.
35 Julie Otsuka, *The Buddha in the Attic* (New York: Vintage, 2011), p. 107.
36 Otsuka, *The Buddha*, p. 108.
37 Adichie, *Americanah*, p. 298.
38 Ibid., p. 222.
39 Ibid., pp. 306, 308.
40 Ha Jin, *Waiting* (New York: Random House, 1999), pp. 356, 140.
41 Ha Jin, *Waiting*, p. 286.
42 Frank Chin, *Donald Duk* (Minneapolis, MN: Coffee House Press, 1991), p. 4.
43 Junot Díaz, *The Brief Wondrous Life of Oscar Wao* (New York: Riverhead, 2007), pp. 20–1.
44 Desai, *The Inheritance*, pp. 59, 88–9, 284.
45 Aciman, *Harvard Square*, pp. 50, 52, 69.
46 Jessica Hagedorn, *The Gangster of Love* (New York: Penguin, 1997), pp. 67, 210, 200, 211.
47 Chang-rae Lee, *A Gesture Life* (New York: Riverhead, 1999), p. 285.
48 Joy Kogawa, *Obasan* (New York: Doubleday, 1981), p. 292.
49 Nora Okja Keller, *Comfort Woman* (New York: Penguin, 1997), p. 4.
50 Toni Morrison, *The Bluest Eye* (New York: Penguin, 1994), p. 83.
51 Ibid., p. 102.
52 Gish Jen, *The Love Wife* (New York: Alfred A. Knopf, 2004), p. 332.
53 Catherine Chung, *Forgotten Country* (New York: Riverhead, 2012), p. 271.
54 Ibid., p. 206.
55 Ha Jin, *Waiting*, pp. 246, 273.
56 Díaz, *Wondrous Life*, pp. 290, 286.
57 Ha Jin, *Waiting*, p. 520.
58 Gish Jen, *The Love Wife*, pp. 86–7.
59 Jhumpa Lahiri, *The Namesake* (Boston: Houghton Mifflin, 2003), p. 291.
60 Anzia Yezierska, *Bread Givers* (New York: Persea Books, 2003), p. 8.
61 Ibid., p. 240.
62 Ibid., 297.
63 Jamaica Kincaid, *Lucy* (New York: Penguin, 1990), pp. 161–2.
64 Ibid., 31.

9

PHILIP DICKINSON

Columbia University

Itineraries of the Sublime
in the Postcolonial Novel

There are at least two ways of tracing the presence of the sublime in postcolonial representations, which together reflect the doubleness of the sublime
as a critical concept. On the one hand, the sublime is a representational
language, at least minimally conventional and with a history of appearances
in literature and in art that can be traced genealogically or inventoried
according to its manifold iterations. According to this understanding, we
can locate the sublime by the presence or modulation of an assemblage of
particular descriptors: the sublime is "there" wherever such phenomena as
vastness, intensity, power, or obscurity, for example, are in privileged representational play. On the other hand, the sublime has been the object of
sustained philosophical consideration since the eighteenth century precisely
insofar as it denotes a category of aesthetic or phenomenological experience
that exceeds available (re)presentational languages that would process such
experience.[1] In this sense, the sublime appears exactly where predictable or
familiar descriptors fall away or fail, where they lose their meanings, associations, and coherences; as Jean-François Lyotard puts it in his postmodern
theorization of the sublime, "[w]hen the sublime is 'there' (where?), the mind
is not there."[2] The sublime, therefore, can be read through the history of its
"saying" and as the category of the "unsayable." In the postcolonial novel,
my focus in this chapter, the sublime appears in both of these senses: it exists
as a mechanism for the representation of space, associated with the history
of literature and painting and with the long history of the imperial gaze; but
it also appears as a problem or tension within representation and aesthetic
"presentation" themselves.

While the sublime is not usually considered as a postcolonial concept, it
has a significant history in imperialist discourse, and the writings of Edmund
Burke provide an important reference point for tracing this history.[3] Sara
Suleri has shown how Burke's investment in the sublime, as displayed in his
Enquiry of 1757, leaks into his writings and speeches about India.[4] For
Suleri, Burke's discussions of India exhibit a tendency to itemize and list

aspects of India in an epistemological movement dependent upon India's prior conception as a place of bewildering complexity and uncontainable heterogeneity. Burke's writings on the sublime and his writings about India both reflect a fascination with what, in the words of the *Enquiry*, is "dark, uncertain, confused, terrible," even though they both respond to and, in a way, resist the concomitant affective astonishment by enumerating, often in an incongruously pedestrian idiom, the features that add up – or fail to add up – to the sublime object.[5] Suleri's reading of Burke has a broader significance. In the larger body of colonial discourse, those qualities that Burke saw as generative of the sublime – obscurity, vastness, terror – are often projected onto colonial space in ways that supplement the apparently anti-sublime representations of colonial space that function through various taxonomic discourses, including those of anthropology, botany, zoology, geology, and cartography. These are elements of what Mary Louise Pratt calls the discourse of "anti-conquest," in which an apparently benign observational imperative serves to encode the sovereignty of the imperial imagination.[6] The very representability of colonial space makes it available for epistemological conquest prior to the material entrenchment and institutionalization of colonial power. But the language of "anti-conquest" functions hand in hand with the apparently opposing language of the sublime, which suggests the negative ground over which such knowledge must be built. The presence of the sublime in colonial discourse suggests a threat, the liability of knowledge to fall into the abyss of nonknowledge or the unrepresentable.

While the sublime has a history as long and itinerant as aesthetic discourse itself, it is this tension between the imperative to represent, on the one hand, and the possible encounter with unrepresentability, on the other, that is most visible in its colonial manifestations. This is akin to the conflict or "agitation" that Kant describes in *Critique of Judgment*, between the apprehension of an abyss in which the mind is afraid to lose itself and the compensatory movement of reason that proves the mind's "supersensible" vocation. But while for Kant the sublime is properly the feeling of the mind's supersensible power, and thus ultimately functions to monumentalize the rational, perceiving subject, in colonial discourse what we often see is the anxious operation of the agitation itself, whereby the spectre of the unrepresentable object of colonial discourse persists in a haunting relationship with that discourse. When Homi Bhabha talks of the "colonial nonsense" as that which announces the "extinction of the recognisable object of culture in the disturbed artifice of its signification," he is talking about the sublime in this way, even though he doesn't use the term.[7] The sublime can be said to appear as a locus of instability within colonial representation; it might even be that the sublime, in colonial writing, already has an incipient *postcolonial* valency by virtue of its destabilization of the epistemological claims of colonial discourse – although this is a claim to which I shall return.

The two most important examples of the sublime in the colonial novel occur in Joseph Conrad's *Heart of Darkness* and E. M. Forster's *A Passage to India*, two of the texts Bhabha considers in the chapter from which I have quoted. Marlow's evocation of the Congo could hardly be more Burkean: the "dark continent," in Marlow's generalizing and racist vocabulary, is characterized by its "tenebrous immensity," its terrifying obscurity, by sudden sounds and also sudden privations of sound and visibility. The extent of Marlow's recapitulation of the aesthetic of the sublime reflects its discursive entrenchment within the language of colonial conquest but also brings the sublime to a pitch of racialized fear and colonial anxiety that is almost parodic. Indeed, the sublime and the ridiculous appear in such proximity in the novel that Marlow's attempts to assert the semantic integrity of Kurtz's famous words – "the horror, the horror" – are inevitably contaminated by the failure of representation that these words seem to mark. Forster's version of the Conradian "horror" is associated with the Marabar caves and the confused events that take place within them. The caves are a metonym for the otherness of India: they are "readily described" – "eight feet long, five feet high, three feet wide" – and yet a visitor finds it "difficult to discuss the caves, or to keep them apart in his mind": "Nothing, nothing attaches to them"; they are "dark caves," there is "little to see," there is "nothing" inside them.[8] The caves can be described, their shapes and sizes measured and tabulated, but their "nothingness," it seems, will always escape description. They mark an obscurity, a blankness, and a kind of disappointment that spoils the grandeur of the Himalayan prospect, the vision of the hills "older than anything in the world" on which the imperial imagination wants to feed (138). Both novels display a ramification of the sublime: the sublime operates in these novels through the presence of particular descriptors, but also as a larger aesthetic of unrepresentability. And if these novels reflect the migration of the sublime into colonial discourse, they also transpose the sublime back into an aesthetic key: only in this way does the sublime become interesting in these texts, reflective of the operation of something less certain than a programmatic colonial ideology and racism.

For Kant, the pleasure of the sublime feeling is linked to the supersensible moment within the "agitation" I mention earlier; we feel pleasure at the evidence of a mental capacity "transcending every standard of the senses."[9] An analogous claim might be made about the sublime as it works in these two novels: there is an ambiguous (imperialist?) pleasure to be drawn from the fact that language can code – just – that which is at the very threshold of comprehensibility. Of course, one might read the tenuousness of this "just" exactly as that to which colonial representation tends in its effort to *produce* an alien, threatening other. Does the sublime really undermine colonial representation from within, or does it just reflect a form of cultured racism? One of the obvious responses of the postcolonial novel to the imbrication of the sublime with colonial representation is, after all, simply to reject the sublime as fundamentally racist. Chinua Achebe's novels with pre- and early colonial settings are exemplary in this regard, as they reclaim the history of colonized places by showing them to be full of a lived plenitude incommensurable with European landscape aesthetics and accessible to the postcolonial imagination. *Things Fall Apart* and *Arrow of God* are both concerned with presenting precolonial Africa in a way that not only refutes the pigmented language of the "dark continent" but also undermines the very idea of Africa as a generalizable space, as a continent with certain characteristic features that can be indiscriminately projected onto any African terrain. Thus, *Things Fall Apart* might be considered as something other than a novel about Africa, Nigeria, and even the Igbo: it is a novel about a particular fictional clan, Umuofia, composed of nine distinct villages, that the novel is at pains to represent in its sociocultural and historical singularity. When characters in the novel wonder about the different customs of unfamiliar villages, the point ought to be clear: *Things Fall Apart* is concerned with the tragic story of a distinct *polis*, with a fullness of life and a uniqueness of political culture that can never be abstracted within European aesthetics. If the story of Umuofia is to be considered representative of the story of precolonial Africa, it should only be in a negative sense: the novel suggests, sometimes despite itself, the irreducible nonrepresentativeness of even the most pedagogical and apparently world-historical of stories.

Of Achebe's novels, *Things Fall Apart* and *Arrow of God* especially "write back" to *Heart of Darkness*, but they also produce the possibility of a retroactive transformation of Conrad's novel for postcolonial readers, precisely through their antagonistic relationship with the sublime. More than protesting the co-implication of European aesthetics and European imperialism, these novels function to fill out analeptically the "dark places" of the imperial imagination with subaltern presence and subaltern agency. The tenebrousness and obscurity posited by the colonial sublime itself opens up this possibility, marking an opening – or an epistemological event horizon – within which the seeds of an alternative history of imperial conquest reside. The sounds of the drums that Marlow hears, his sense of a presence that exceeds its troping, are not simply indications of colonial "nonsense," as Bhabha claims. They mark sites of a possible counterreading, whereby the colonial novel signals, however unwittingly, the limits of its own readings of space and time. It is not just that the sublime, in the postcolonial novel, should be read in relation to the history of this aesthetic in colonial discourse, but also that the interest the postcolonial novel takes in the sublime gives us new possibilities for reading these colonial novels and the colonial archive more broadly.

The dispositions of the sublime in the postcolonial novel, though, are as manifold as anywhere else and reflect the manifold representational politics of the postcolonial text. Wilson Harris's fiction offers one of the most strange and striking mobilizations of the sublime, not so much critiquing as extending and reinscribing it. The protagonist of *The Secret Ladder*, a government land surveyor investigating a stretch of the Canje river for a development project, is a kind of postcolonial Marlow transplanted to Guyana: South America, now, is the "continent of mystery," the place of a threatening obscurity in which, "within a hundred yards of where one stood ... the jungle turned blind as a shuttered place and the eye learnt to relinquish the neighbouring sun for a tenebrous, almost electrical gloom."[10] The oppositions the novel mobilizes are clear: the clearing stands against the jungle, the measurements of the gauge against the jungle's immeasurable and nonnavigable terrain, the dam-building project against both the resistant autonomy of nature and the resistance of the Canje people (the representation of the two is aesthetically confused in proper Conradian fashion, raising questions about the primitivist representational politics of the book). Perhaps above all, these oppositions enunciate a tension between the developmental ambitions of the postcolonial state and the true "spirit" of the nation, associated with a noninstrumentalizable nature, a nonurban, nonelite "nation people," as well as with the deep history of the land of Guyana: the leader of the resistance in the novel, Poseidon, is descended from a resistant band of black slaves; and all of the characters in the novel associated with the survey are ambiguously implicated in the history Poseidon embodies, even Fenwick, the surveyor himself, whose racial ancestry neatly (too neatly?) reflects the multiple, intermingled ethnicities of Guyana.

The thematic and narrative conflicts in the novel reflect the ontological seam marked by the hyphen in the word "nation-state," and the sublime is a representational mechanism for signaling the priority of the first term in the couple: it implies a presence or a spirit that always exceeds the representational technologies of the government survey. In this sense, the sublime landscape is once again metonymic, but metonymic of an otherness that ought not to be opposed but rather embraced. Any synthesis, though, between representation and the spirit of place, in the teleology of Harris's fiction, can only be achieved through the power of imagination, resulting in narrative conclusions that move toward the transcendence of the contingencies and conflicts of the given world (the conclusion of *Palace of the Peacock* describes an ascension onto a plane transcendent of time and place, as each character finds "what he had been for ever seeking and what he had eternally possessed").[11] In such visions, the difficulties and indeterminacies that characterize the language of the sublime are left behind, as Harris's novels enact, or yearn to enact, what Peter Hallward has seen as one of the most problematic movements of postcolonial writing: they disengage from the domain of the "specific" and access the plane of the "singular," a kind of divine plane that is aspecific, ahistorical, and fundamentally nonrelational.[12]

Indeed, if the sublime foregrounds anything in colonial and postcolonial contexts, it is the problem of relation itself, the problem of relating with other people (Conrad, Forster), with the traumas of contemporary history (Conrad, Harris), and also with the past (Harris, Malouf, Kincaid, as we shall see). If a novel like *Palace of the Peacock* does not relate, so much as triumphantly *sub*late, the histories of encounter, genocide, slavery, indenture, colonial rule, and ecological exploitation *through,* in Harris's own Romantic terms, imagination, then it is not alone in doing so: David Malouf's *Remembering Babylon* offers a similar movement of transcendence at its conclusion that is just as historically burdened and politically problematic, as the violence of Australian settlement is absorbed into a vision of continental sympathy. Malouf's novel engages with the white settlement of Australia, representing a small community in Queensland in the middle of the nineteenth century struggling to sustain itself. The settlement is founded in precarious opposition to a continent that is described in Burkean terms as "dark," "impenetrable," "illimitable" (7).[13] The settlers, rather like the surveyors in *The Secret Ladder*, must translate the threatening otherness of the land, "ringbarking and clearing and reducing it," exerting mastery over the land and space to make it productive and, moreover, "like home": defined as property and, above all, rid of "every vestige of the native" (8). The novel is interested in exploring the collective psyche of the early settlers of Australia and presents their historical predicament as a kind of explanation for the white racism that still informs much Australian political discourse. But the novel is also interested in offering an alternative image of community, one that is not founded upon mastery and exclusion but that works toward a radically inclusive ethic, a sympathetic embrace of the "vast continent" and all that lives there and has lived there, including the past and present victims of historical violence and marginalization.

As with Harris, this interest suggests a revision of the sublime, from the sublime as something that menaces and problematizes relation to the sublime as an experience of pure (and therefore nonrelational) relation, as an experience of ecstatic transpersonal communion that leaves behind the social world. Malouf's novel concludes some years after the events that are described in the earlier sections of the text, and the closing scene is focalized through the perspective of a single character, Janet. Sitting at her window in the fading light, she looks out to see the "one-roomed shacks on low stumps" where the children who visit her live, the yards "strewn with rubbish, old bed frames ... old beer and castor-oil bottles, charred stick-ends, broken bricks" (180). Her mind "drifts so far, then further," beyond the "muddy, stinking flats" to the bay; she sees the sea coming in, "as we approach prayer," knowledge, and one another:

> It glows in fullness till the tide is high and the light almost, but not quite, unbearable, as the moon plucks at our world and all the waters of the earth ache towards it, and the light, running in fast now, reaches the edge of the shore, just so far in its order, and all the muddy margin of the bay is alive, and in a line of running fire all the outline of the vast continent appears, in touch now with its other life. (182)

Janet's vision of harmony is also a harmonizing of diverse epistemologies: the "communication" of the bees, the Aboriginal understanding of the "dream-time" of the land, and the Christian prayer all come together to articulate a powerful vision of continental sympathy, an Australia "in touch" in a moment of spiritual communion and reconciliation. This moment appears as a triumph of the Romantic sublime – as the fulfillment of its usually deferred promise of reconciliation between subject and object – as it moves beyond the picturesque observation of shacks, the Christian prayer for renewal and community, the indigenous or bee-like apprehension of unity, and *performs* that unity, putting everything in touch with everything else in an act of transcendent imagination underpinned by a panoramic visual perspective.

It is as clear in Malouf as in Harris that the sublime experience reflects a necessary transcendence of the legacies of colonial and postcolonial violence. Janet's vision is immediately preceded by the novel's first and only allusion to the practice of "dispersal," where punitive expeditions would attack Aboriginal groups in order to further entrench white settlement. As part of a government road gang surveying land in the north, Janet's brother, Lachlan, comes across what he thinks must be word of Gemmy, the "black white man" (9) raised by an Aboriginal group whose arrival in the settlement and subsequent disappearance form the main stuff of the narrative. Lachlan hears of a dispersal six years previously, "too slight an affair to be called a massacre," and is guided to the bones of the "eight or nine" victims. He looks at the bundles of bones and sees that they are not distinguishable, feeling nothing more for one than for any of them. But he decides "without proof" that this was "the place," that one of these parcels contained the bones of Gemmy (179). This "decision" reflects a logic of substitutability, where one death can mark any other and tie up the "loose ends" in the lives of the survivors, giving Lachlan the sense, that he knows is fictitious, that he can lay the dead to rest. In the fifty years separating this discovery and his reconciliation with Janet, Lachlan learns that they were "inextricably joined [with Gemmy] and would always be." But while the novel contrasts Lachlan's projection of Gemmy's name onto a pile of bones with an alternative sense of Gemmy's more spiritual, or spectral, survival, Lachlan's logic of substitution still obtains. Gemmy comes to be metonymically connected with the "eight or nine" victims of this specific incident and even with all of the victims of settler violence. When Lachlan hears the story of the dispersal he notes that it "had elements in common with others he had heard," but these similarities make Lachlan wonder whether "they were all one story." These uncertainties are left behind, as the events are "gathered now into the dreamtime of the land itself." The past is brought into the present through a transcendence of its violence, through a process of disengagement that refuses to allow past violence to fracture the present imaginary and that, as Jean-Luc Nancy would put it in *Inoperative Community*, "makes a work" of the singular death.[14] This movement is all the more uncomfortable given the appropriation of indigenous epistemologies that enables the novel's closing prayer of memory and community, which absorbs and overcomes that which might threaten the community's legitimacy. The "dreamtime" of the land, or the "communication" of the bees, suggest an alternative archive of community to Australian nationalism, but one that performs, conveniently, a translation of trauma into peace, violence into spirit, socioeconomic destitution (Janet notes the shacks) into aesthetic communion.

Harris's and Malouf's novels reflect many of the features of the postcolonial sublime, as they enunciate a representational circuit involving landscape, history, and the presenting subject. Whether the concluding movements of these novels are themselves "rigorously" sublime is open to question, however, since they leave behind the problem of what Lyotard calls the "unpresentable" in "presentation itself," a problem, for Lyotard, central to postmodern writing but equally central, I would argue, to postcolonial writing.[15] Harris's and Malouf's novels develop but also dispose of this problem in their synthetic teleologies, but the postcolonial novel has more often questioned its own ability to bear witness to, let alone totalize, the often multilayered histories of postcolonial space. The Antiguan writer Jamaica Kincaid provides a countervoice to these projects in her novel *The Autobiography of My Mother*. This text develops an aesthetic of the sublime linked with blankness, blankness here configured not as a threat to the sovereign imagination but as the informing condition of Caribbean historical consciousness. The "mother" at the supposed center of this text registers only as a spectral presence; the novel's narrator, Xuela, can only relate to her mother, who "died at the moment" Xuela was born, as an absence, a fact that has special significance since her mother was Carib. Her mother's absence, and the absence of the "autobiography" that the text promises, thus becomes a metaphor for the nonrecoverable nature of the history of the Caribbean, especially the history of the indigenous peoples of the islands. This absence is reflected in Xuela's perception of the inhuman indifference of the landscape and the sea, "the big sea ... so gray, so without mercy, so powerful and without thought," at the sight of which, "so unpitying," she would "exhaust [her]self in tears."[16] The landscape, in this novel, is that which inscribes Caribbean history negatively: its very blankness bespeaks the limits of what can be "presented" – said, thought, or even felt (Xuela's tears suggest the breakdown of sense as much as affective response) – and in this sense is sublime, taking the novel up to the limits of its representational capacities.[17]

Kincaid's novels often trace the infection of postcolonial subjectivity with phenomenological schemas derived from the corpus of European aesthetics – especially from the canon of English literature. In *Annie John*, the eponymous protagonist expresses her love for *Jane Eyre*, in a way that exemplifies the role of colonial education in *de*-forming as much as in forming the consciousness of the subject of the Caribbean *Bildungsroman*. And in *Lucy,* the experience of perception itself is contaminated by Lucy's readings and the history they signify: Lucy yearns to explain to her American employer what the daffodils they stumble upon together really mean to her, to communicate her urge to "kill" them and the fact that they are forever tied, in her mind, to a "scene of conquered and conquests."[18] When I talk of the sublime in *Autobiography*, though, I am not talking of just another inherited framework of perception with a problematic colonial history, but of what I see as something approaching a *postcolonial sublime*. For while the sublime is a specific representational convention that is rejected and contested and even recapitulated in the postcolonial novel, it is also the name for a difficulty in perception and in representation that is symptomatic of the concern of the postcolonial text with the violence of totalizing perceptual and epistemological schemas.

In a different context, the fiction of J. M. Coetzee similarly represents the sublime as an experience of a certain aesthetic – that is, sensory – blankness, but the objects of relation that precipitate these experiences are not victims of past violence but bodies that inhabit the same time and the same political space as the presenting subject. Coetzee finds in the sublime a way of articulating in aesthetic terms the pathological orientations of white

subjectivity in South Africa. His novels generally represent privileged protagonists – often white and relatively enfranchised men – encountering the
limitations of their worlds. This concern is present in his very first novel,
Dusklands, the second part of which, "The Narrative of Jacobus Coetzee,"
offers a fictionalized document of the travels of an early settler–explorer in
the interior of what came to be South Africa in the mid-1700s (edited by S. J.
Coetzee and translated, we are told, by J. M. Coetzee). In this text, the
otherness of the expanse of the "wild" must be imaginatively annihilated;
Jacobus Coetzee dreams of exerting a visual sovereignty that conquers all
alien presence:

> Only the eyes have power. The eyes are free, they reach out to the horizon all
> around. Nothing is hidden from the eyes. As the other senses grow numb or
> dumb my eyes flex and extend themselves. I become a spherical reflecting eye
> moving through the wilderness and ingesting it. Destroyer of the wilderness,
> I move through the land cutting a devouring path from horizon to horizon.
> There is nothing from which my eye turns, I am all that I see.[19]

We are again in the realm of dark parody and monomania, here: if Harris's
surveyor is a version of Marlow, then Coetzee's Coetzee is a version of
Kurtz. The fact that the first part of this novel engages with the Vietnam
war lends a disturbing historical resonance to the imagery of destructive
paths moving from "horizon to horizon" and to the apparent Emersonian
language internal to this imperial egoism: "what is there that is not me?"
Jacobus asks, his "spherical reflecting eye" echoing Emerson's "transparent
eye-ball." But Jacobus Coetzee can only enact these fantasies from his bed,
and Coetzee's novels are more often concerned with encounters with otherness that generate epistemological lacunae and interrupt the subject's capacity to recreate the world.

Coetzee's work eschews the "literature of vastness," or the experience of
the "horizontal sublime" in which Jacobus is invested, in favor of presenting
another, equally sublime category of aesthetic experience associated with
blockage and stupor.[20] In his study *White Writing*, Coetzee considers the
possibility that the sublime has not had the same presence in white South
African writing as the picturesque because of its valuation of "verticality"
above "horizontality," the horizontal plane being more dominant in South
African landscape.[21] David Lurie, the protagonist of Coetzee's 1999 Booker
Prize-winning novel *Disgrace*, is a teacher of Wordsworth's poetry, and in
his lecture on *The Prelude* tries, and fails, to assert the viable migration of
Romantic aesthetic schemas into South African terrain: "We don't have Alps
in this country, but we have the Drakensberg, or on a smaller scale Table
Mountain," Lurie asserts, but he is "just talking, covering up," as "sick of

the sound" of his voice as his bored, blank students.[22] The point, though, is not that the vertical demands of the European sublime cannot be so easily satisfied in South Africa (we have seen that the colonial sublime and its postcolonial inheritors have no particular need of the vertical), but that the very appropriateness of the passage Lurie discusses resides in the experience of disappointment and sensory estrangement of which it tells:

> we also first beheld
> Unveiled the summit of Mont Blanc, and grieved
> To have a soulless image on the eye
> That had usurped upon a living thought
> That never more could be.   (21)

The physical mountain presents itself to the poet, in this passage, as a soulless image "burned upon the retina," as Lurie puts it, "usurp[ing] upon" and threatening to destroy the prior plenitude of the "living thought" of the summit. While Lurie argues for the possibility of a reconciliation between image and idea, reality and imagination, the aesthetic disappointment described by Wordsworth in fact anticipates Lurie's experiences of aesthetic stupor throughout the novel. Coetzee's novels often take their protagonists to the limits of what might be called their aesthetic "enclosures," their familiar sensory and imaginative terrains, which are also reflective of the "enclosures" – aesthetic and material – that protect white liberal subjectivity in apartheid and post-apartheid South Africa. When Lurie mysteriously falls asleep with Katy the bulldog, or while watching the football with Petrus, or when he breaks into tears driving home from a round of "killings" at the animal welfare clinic, he experiences an opening onto an otherness that resists "presentation," that cannot be encapsulated by the supersensible schemas of the mind.

Lurie, in his lecture, talks of keeping "the beloved" alive somewhere between reality and ideality, by throwing a "veil over the gaze." It is precisely this movement of aesthetic veiling that becomes untenable in a novel that, at key moments, seems to be interested in what Giorgio Agamben, reading Heidegger, calls the "simply living being." [23] Agamben's figure of "bare" or "animal" life is the figure that inhabits a zone of political nonrecognizability, but we might elaborate this to develop an idea of *aesthetic* nonrecognizability, to denote those bodies that are excluded from the sensory order and cannot be apprehended by the senses, bodies that do not inhabit our sensible landscape, that leave Lurie, as Lucy cries on his shoulder, feeling listless, indifferent, even weightless (*Disgrace*, 156).

I would argue that Coetzee's novels present one of the most striking contemporary articulations of the sublime, and this interest clearly cannot be separated from the "politics of aesthetics," understood less as the politics of particular representational practices than as the politics involved in the very ways in which the postcolonial (postapartheid) subject apprehends the world – a world of others and otherness – on a phenomenological level. To talk of the sublime in Coetzee is to talk of these breakdowns in sense and sensibility, and his protagonists, far from transcending this zone of aesthetic confusion, generally arrive at points of failure and disappointment: the Magistrate of *Waiting for the Barbarians* ends the novel thinking that "this is not the scene [he] dreamed of," finding himself feeling "stupid," pressing on along a "road that may lead nowhere";[24] Coetzee's Dostoevsky ends *The Master of Petersburg* with an "empty heart," feeling a "dull absence of torment," recognizing "nothing of himself";[25] Lurie, similarly, loses himself in an aimless enterprise, writing an opera that will never be performed, that "does not come from the heart" (181), the kind of work "a sleepwalker might write" (214). If the blankness of Kincaid's sublime appropriately refutes the violence of representation, then the same might be said here: Lurie constantly wants to represent in (usually gendered) artistic terms the world he inhabits, and the moments of subjective collapse he experiences function in counterpoint to this reproductive project; the Magistrate's emergent "stupidity" blocks his similar efforts to interpret the ruins buried under the dunes or to interpret the body of the "barbarian girl," to read her history in her scars and wounds. All of these novels are focalized through single characters, but they indicate not only the breakdowns suffered by the imagination of the subject but also the interruption of the novel's own totalizing power, the limitations of its own ability to bear witness to the traumatic autonomy of the world.

In a way, the sublime has always been about this traumatic autonomy, whether the sublime is considered a mode of representation in art that aims to render something at the edges of representability, or whether it is considered a feeling, or a kind of affective response that can't quite be called a "feeling," generated by an encounter with an alienating world. In postcolonial contexts, the interest in such feelings is also an interest in the trials and uncertain destinations of postcolonial subjectivity in a world that might loosely be described as "given," as disappointingly nonamenable to the shaping power of imagination and as noncompliant with the narratives of collectivity and freedom that might, from one critical perspective, be considered the proper concern of the postcolonial novel. Indeed, if the sublime in colonial discourse registers the strangeness of the colonial or racial other, in the postcolonial text it often seems to mark an otherness internal to the polity, whether it be an otherness that is alien to the surveys of the new state, to the narratives of Australian nationalism, to the imaginary of the Antiguan schoolchild, or to the world view of the white, liberal university professor in South Africa. Does the sublime, then, not mark the failure of community, or the postcolonial novel's abdication of its vocation to represent the social and reproduce a functional social imaginary? The sublime, after all, always reinscribes borders: it is the experience of the border itself. I would like to suggest an alternative possibility, namely that in proximity to the horizon of the sublime, it becomes clear, in the Jamaican novelist Erna Brodber's words, that there are "ways and ways of knowing." The sublime indicates the limitations of singular, self-contained perspectives and always renders inoperative totalizing narratives and story forms. For this reason it finds a place in the postcolonial novel.

Notes

1 The apparent contradiction between these two ways of understanding the sublime reflects a divergence internal to the critical usage of the phrase "the aesthetic," which can mean both the world of art – a concern with form – and the world of experience – a concern with *aisthēsis* (lit. sensory perception).
2 Lyotard, Jean-François, "Answering the Question: What is Postmodernism?," *Postmodernism: A Reader,* ed. Thomas Docherty (Hemel Hempstead: Harvester and Wheatsheaf, 1993), p. 32.
3 Edmund Burke, *A Philosophical Enquiry into the Origin of Our Ideas of the Sublime and the Beautiful,* ed. James Boulton (London: Routledge and Paul, 1958), pp. 41, 51–2.
4 Sara Suleri, *The Rhetoric of English India* (Chicago, IL: Chicago University Press, 1992), p. 45.
5 Burke's itemization of the qualities that generate the sublime suggests a desperation to describe that accrues a kind of banality: he deals in turn with terror, obscurity, privation, vastness, infinity, and then succession and uniformity, sound and loudness, suddenness, "intermitting" [sic], even "the cries of animals." He asserts that "length" strikes less than "height," but that "height" is less grand than "depth" – but of that, he concedes, he is "not very positive" (51–2).
6 Mary Louise Pratt, *Imperial Eyes: Travel Writing and Transculturation* (London and New York: Routledge, 1992), pp. 38–68.
7 Homi K. Bhabha, *The Location of Culture* (London: Routledge, 2004), p. 180.
8 E.M. Forster, *A Passage to India* (London: Penguin, 2000), pp. 138–9. Subsequent page references to be cited in the main text.
9 Immanuel Kant, *Critique of Judgment,* trans. Nicholas Walker (Oxford: Oxford University Press, 2007), p. 81. Subsequent references to be provided in the main text.
10 Wilson Harris, *The Secret Ladder* (London: Faber and Faber, 1963), pp. 20, 11.
11 Wilson Harris, *Palace of the Peacock* (London: Faber and Faber, 1998), p. 117
12 Peter Hallward, *Absolutely Postcolonial: Writing between the Singular and the Specific* (Manchester: Manchester University Press, 2001).
13 David Malouf, *Remembering Babylon* (London: Vintage, 1994), p. 7. All subsequent references to be provided in the main text.

14 Jean-Luc Nancy, *The Inoperative Community*, ed. Peter Connor, trans. Peter Connor, Lisa Garbus, Michael Holland, and Simona Sawhney (Minneapolis: University of Minnesota Press, 1991), p. 15.

15 Lyotard, "Answering," p. 46.

16 Jamaica Kincaid, *The Autobiography of My Mother* (New York: Penguin, 1997), pp. 106, 5.

17 This idea of the negative materiality of history as reflected in the landscape can be seen elsewhere in Caribbean writing, most significantly in Derek Walcott's poetry. In poems such as "Air," "The Castaway," or "The Sea is History," there is "too much nothing" inscribed in the antimemorial archive of the landscape or the sea.

18 Jamaica Kincaid, *Lucy* (New York: Farrar, Straus and Giroux, 1990), p. 30.

19 J.M. Coetzee, *Dusklands* (New York: Penguin, 1985), p. 78

20 Coetzee discusses the South African "literature of vastness" in his Jerusalem Prize Acceptance Speech. See J.M. Coetzee, *Doubling the Point: Chapters and Interviews*, ed. David Attwell (Cambridge, Mass.: Harvard University Press, 1992), p. 98.

21 J.M. Coetzee, *White Writing: On the Culture of Letters in South Africa* (New Haven, CT: Yale University Press, 1988), p. 52.

22 J.M. Coetzee, *Disgrace* (London: Vintage, 1999), p. 23.

23 Giorgio Agamben, *The Open: Man and Animal*, trans. Kevin Attell (Stanford, CT: Stanford University Press, 2004), p. 50.

24 J.M. Coetzee, *Waiting for the Barbarians* (London: Penguin, 1999), p. 152.

25 J.M. Coetzee, *The Master of Petersburg* (London: Vintage, 1999), p. 250.

10

STEPHEN KNIGHT
University of Melbourne

The Postcolonial Crime Novel

Colonial Beginnings

Crime fiction is both massively popular and worldwide: it seems inevitable that such a force would interact with postcolonialism, but this has not been a simple relationship. Some texts resist the reality or memory of imperial power, while others, notably recently, see the major threat as modern imperialist capitalism. Powerful novels have used crime fiction patterns to critique the present racial oppressions either in formerly colonial states or in modern countries with tensions developed by immigration. Yet other writers have, in the past or even the present, spoken up for empire, settler culture, or even modern forms of touristic neocolonialism.

Commentaries have varied in their understanding of the term "postcolonial" in this context. At times all texts set in a formerly colonial country have been included, whether they resist empire or not, and neocolonial or settler texts are sometimes discussed as if not incompatible with firmly antiimperial statements made in the same genre. Here the preposition "post" will be taken to imply at least some resistance to empire, though in some cases it may be to modern mercantile versions of exploitation rather than the original forms of empire.

Crime fiction as a narrative form, especially in its detective-focused mode, has had quasi-imperial power in the publishing market and also possessed originary links to colonialism. An argument has been offered for an unmediated link between the crime fiction and imperialism during the rise of the genre in the early nineteenth century. Reitz claims a "relationship between the rise of domestic police power and the expansion of the British Empire," and the "omnipresence of an imperial narrative within the detective story."[1] This is too assertive: a list of some ten thousand plays staged in London between 1800 and 1850[2] reveals almost none dealing with the empire but many dealing with murder, robbery, and fraud in England.

166

A less sweeping argument is offered by Mukherjee, seeing separation but also parallelism between empire and crime fiction. He shows that Indian authorities were interested in Peel's 1829 model of new policing in London, especially to resist the phenomenon of Thuggee in the 1820s and 1830s, and he identifies in early crime fiction "a connection between the colonized and the domestic oppressed."[3] But even Mukherjee is relying on atypical texts, principally Philip Meadows Taylor *Confessions of a Thug* (1839), a unique project from India itself, and Wilkie Collins's *The Moonstone* (1868), which essentially dissents from post-Mutiny attitudes to empire, as discussed in the following.

The connection between empire and genre is not so overt as Reitz and Mukherjee argue, and is therefore potentially more pervasive. As a genre, crime fiction developed when older narratives, showing rural crimes identified by local knowledge or sometimes Christian guilt, were felt out of date, and a professional investigator was required to trace credibly the deceptive threats to property and life among the teeming masses of the modern city.[4] As Foucault envisaged in *Discipline and Punish*, police and then detectives were instituted as disciplinary operatives in both reality and fiction. The new processes of individual competition could readily generate crime or its detection, as they did other forms of self-advancement, and the new forms of crime and writing about crime are in these ways evidently coextensive with the rise of empire, itself so dependent on individual mercantile and urban competitiveness.

But the new genre had very limited direct topical interest in empire. A returned imperial soldier threatens order in "Circumstantial Evidence," one of the 1850 *Experiences of a Barrister* stories in *Chambers' Journal*; Captain Burt, a "grim Indian sun-bronzed villain," is trapped by Waters the police detective in an 1856 story by "William Russell." Ticket-of-leave men, convicts returning from Australia, occur among the criminals in G. M. W. Reynolds's detective-free *The Mysteries of London* (1844–6), before they were held to be ringleaders in the garrroting panics of the 1850s, well before they were partially redeemed by Dickens through Magwitch in *Great Expectations* (1860–1).

The specifically imperial early texts are special variants of crime fiction rather than structural to it. *The Confessions of a Thug* is in part an exercise in the new policing, as the narrator listens patiently to Ameer Ali's account of the crimes and beliefs of the Thugs, but it was also, like the *Mémoires of Vidocq* (1828), very popular as book and play, confessional crime fiction as a spectator sport. *The Moonstone* is interrogative crime fiction as well as a rejection of post-Mutiny jingoism. A brutal and acquisitive English imperial officer has stolen from a temple the very valuable "Moonstone" diamond, and its theft from an English country house brings serious tensions to the family and their servants. Complexities follow: the police detective fails, and the only inquirer to make headway is Ezra Jennings, a nervous and humble man of mixed race. It was not the Indians seen in the neighborhood who took the stone but an apparently very respectable Englishman, whom the Indians, it seems justifiably, kill, and then repatriate the stone. Though, as Mukherjee notes, the novel never overtly criticizes the operations of empire, just deplores the domestic disruption foreign wealth brings to English tranquillity, he also identifies its "radical credentials,"[5] including the racial hostility of English characters to the Indians, the poor treatment of the hybrid Jennings, the courage and fidelity of the three Indians.

However, most crime fiction continued its uninterrogative way in the Anglophone (and Francophone) system of world management, including detection, and soon found room for the naïve antiforeigner plotting of turn-of-the-century spy stories by authors such as William Le Queux, dealing with German threats but ready to include Asian, Russian, and generally non-English agents of threat to the prosperity of the empire.

This is not uniformly the case with the figure who is often seen as archetypally English, Sherlock Holmes. Doyle was well aware of the role of empire: he wrote in 1881 "The Gully of Bluemansdyke," a story set in Australia long before he visited it, and he dealt with native resistance to Belgian African imperialism in "J. Habbakuk Jephson's Statement" (1883). He also had Indian interests, and both colonizers and colonized could be criminal. In the 1887 story "The Mystery of Uncle Jeremy's Household," the half-Indian governess is involved with Thuggee and child sacrifice, but as Sidiqui notes, the story is "open-ended" without "orderly or conclusive closure."[6] Allotting guilt differently, in *The Mystery of Cloomber* (1889) a British officer returned from India eventually dies in a Scottish bog as punishment for long ago murdering a Buddhist holy man.

Wynne has argued that as a man of Irish family, born and raised in Edinburgh, Doyle was never entirely at one with English colonial policies.[7] He was consistently in favor of some moderate form of Home Rule and saw empire as a potential disruption of English order, not as violence-based appropriation. In *The Sign of Four* (1890), as in *The Moonstone*, treasure stolen from India generates local crisis – here a steamboat chase on the Thames, where poison blowpipe faces revolver and loses. The treasure is sunk in the river – empire brings no profit. But when Watson marries Miss Morstan, who through her family brought the puzzle to the detective, she may be a form of compensation for the wound that led him to leave military medical service on the frontier.

In the Holmes short stories, the bearers of threat are also at times men damaged by empire. Australian criminality is the cause of murder in "The Boscombe Valley Mystery" and of ultimate disgrace in "The Adventure of the 'Gloria Scott.'" In "The Crooked Man" the encounter of military empire and human passion creates modern dramas, while "The Adventure of the Blanched Soldier" dwells on the aftermath of Boer War action. Most strikingly, in "The Speckled Band" the heat of empire still excites the returned Dr. Roylott (essentially an anti-Watson), who sends a snake through a hole in his step-daughter's bedroom wall – that he wants her money acts as euphemization, but his death, with the snake around his head, is a modern classic of imperial impact at home. However, this effect is not a major part of Doyle's narrative imagination: it is primarily the fallibilities of the English bourgeoisie that fill his canvas.

Postcolonial Beginnings

Though it occasionally interrogated imperial values, early crime fiction remained broadly consistent in its structures and values with the imperial and colonial missions of the Euro-American communities where the form first emerged – like any admirable empire-builder, the detective is rational, individualistic, bravely adventurous, all-conquering, bringing through special enlightenment-linked skills a notionally productive peace to an environment troubled through what the narrator sees as its own weaknesses. Evidently aware of the implications of the disciplinary individualism at the core of detective fiction, postcolonial crime fiction will often disavow the simplicities of the all-solving detective and his single evidentiary sequence leading to an indisputable conclusion, and will vary the detective-linked patterns for what are felt to be more veridical, and less colonial, forms of the genre. Sometimes postcolonial writers look to the crime novel, the psychothriller, or the supernatural mystery, all part of the broad field of crime fiction outside the confines of disciplinary detection. This formal resistance can generate a marked richness of viewpoint, tone, and plotting, all evident in what appears to be the earliest substantial area of resistance to racial oppression in this genre, African American crime writing.

Transported by force from their homelands to labor for capitalist profit in the southern American imperial context, African Americans were classically victims of colonialism, though their struggles to gain real social and economic liberty were to climax in the mid- to late twentieth century, well after official liberation in most colonies. This process is highly visible in crime fiction, where African American crime writing establishes itself as a strong force, before other resistances emerged in the genre such as feminist detection and gay and lesbian crime writing.

Periodicals primarily for black American readers carried as early as 1901–2 Pauline Hopkins's *Hagar's Daughter*, developing through a murder and court scenes a melodrama of race prejudice, and in 1907–9 John Edward Bruce, a slave-born writer and historian, published *The Black Sleuth*, with an African-born detective and emphasizing both the richness of African civilization and the international nature of racism. Soitos comments that both writers "used the formulas of detective fiction to contrast this Afrocentric world-view with a racist Euro-American hegemony."[8] Such hegemony was not easily confronted: in the 1920s and 1930s the mainstream *Saturday Evening Post* published the "Florian Slappey" series, comic and basically belittling stories by the white Southerner Gustavus Roy Cohen, one of many appropriations that would appear around the world of a potentially resistant position from its racial opposite. The Harlem renaissance writer Rudolph Fisher took a new step in *The Conjure-Man Dies* (1932), which operates in a fully African-American environment; uses an ironic tone; and, as Cacioppo comments, though this is in a way a classic locked-room mystery, displaces the single authority of the disciplinary tradition through its four different detectives, from policeman to former African king.[9]

These sporadic early moves were followed by a sequence of powerful novels by Chester Himes – yet they too did not arrive easily. After serving a jail sentence for theft and working as a writer in Los Angeles, which he found very racist, Himes moved to France: his first Harlem crime novel, stimulated by a French crime publisher, was *For Love of Imabelle* (1957), retitled *A Rage in Harlem* (1965). The dual heroes are tough New York cops, whose activities Schmid calls "an exercise in mayhem,"[10] mixing what Soitos calls "absurd humour" with "a pessimistic world-view,"[11] as they respond in extreme ways to a drastic situation. Archetypal of the energy and the challenge of the novels is *Cotton Comes to Harlem* (1965): a bale of cotton in New York might potentially symbolize a form of freedom, but there are also nonwhites running a scam to extract money from poor Harlemers who believe in a return to Africa. Criticized by some African Americans as being overnegative, and often himself seeming less than liberal (notably in dealing with women and gay characters), Himes's vision is increasingly dark: the story moves into what Muller calls an "apocalyptic sphere of violence,"[12] as the detectives with their tracer bullets set on fire not only two criminals but also the church where they, like African Americans across time, have tried to hide. Difficult as he was for many to accept in his own period, critics and readers alike have since acknowledged

Himes's ability, as Schmid put it, "to reveal the extent of damage to the black psyche caused by racism."[13]

Probably because its sheer disruptive power eschewed calm consolatory endings, Himes's work did not start a school of writers. A major step toward mainstreaming Afro-American crime writing was taken by John Ball, a white author, with *In the Heat of the Night* (1965). This won prizes in the United States and the United Kingdom and was influentially filmed with a powerful performance by Sidney Poitier as Virgil Tibbs, who both solves a racial murder and faces down color-based hostility in a southern town. A strong contribution though this was, a comic recoil was still possible, and George Baxt produced the gay – and camp – Afro-American detective Pharoah (sic) Love in *A Queer Kind of Death* (1966) and, as if in reflex, Ernest Tidyman created in *Shaft* (1970), an Afro-wearing version of the swinging Bondesque private eye.

A positive and recurrent figure arrived in Walter Mosley's *Devil in a Blue Dress* (1990) with black Los Angeles private eye Easy Rawlins displacing the image of Sam Spade and Philip Marlowe. Easy is curious and cautious, solving problems by observing and taking advice – his is not a heroic viewpoint and he sometimes needs help from his friend Mouse, violent and distinctly Himesian. Easy finds his persistent way to success, and even a quasi-bourgeois lifestyle, but he is not appropriated to the white world: he is essentially a trickster. Gruesser has noted Mosley's use of Henry Louis Gates's ideas in creating a "signifyin'" detective, and Nash has linked to Easy's adventures the "double consciousness" of the Afro-American, consciously living in a world of "liminality."[14]

While the Easy Rawlins stories have gained wide liberal approval as a reshaping of the American private eye, Mosley produced from *Always Outnumbered, Always Outgunned* (1997) stories and then novels about a different and more difficult figure, Socrates Fortlow, who is indeed tough, but a man without a wise or flexible response to problems and threats or even specific crimes. The author's commitment to this figure's epic struggles, following the crime novel format, not the detective style, suggests how the classical intellectual/individual detective has limitations as a credible representative of resistance to colonialism of various kinds.

A rich response to the rise of the black detective in the United States has been among women writers. It has been suggested that the first of these authors, known as "Dolores Komo," was also produced by a white man, the ultraproductive and undoubtedly pseudonym-using Dean Koontz, but he has denied this. Perhaps suggestive of inauthenticity, in the first novel, *Clio Brown: Private Investigator* (1988), the central figure is less than a heroine of resistance, described by Munt as "fiftyish, fat and folksy."[15] A stronger female detective appeared with Nikki Baker's *In the Game* (1991), starring Ginny Keeley, a black lesbian detective, an amateur from the professional class, who as Reddy comments often confronts race and gender oppressions.[16] A very effective writer, producing rapidly a four-book series, Baker appears to have started a flow.

Eleanor Taylor Bland created Marti MacAlister, a Chicago police officer widowed with two children, in *Dead Time* (1992): the novel combines procedural detection with social issues, as does Valerie Wilson Wesley's *When Death Comes Stealing* (1994) with Tamara Hayle, a black single-mother private eye who left the police because of racism and tends to work inside the Afro-American community. Variety was provided by Charlotte Carter, from *Rhode Island Red* (1997), starring Nanette Hayes, a well-educated and sophisticated detective, but as Soitos notes,[17] the series moves toward issues of female identity rather than racial politics.

That is certainly not the case in the powerful novels by BarbaraNeely (she eschews the space between her names as part of her challenge to convention) about a black working woman called, with ironic assertiveness, Blanche White. In *Blanche on the Lam* (1992) to escape a fine for passing bad cheques she masquerades as a housemaid, easily enough through being large and very black. Soitos sees in her both a "signifyin'" trickster and "double consciousness,"[18] and the story of the novel shows how she can sympathize with downtrodden white people without yielding her stern view of racial oppression: Reitz comments she operates in "the contact zone of race, class and gender."[19] The second novel, *Blanche Among the Talented Tenth* (1994), takes her into the domain of the African American high achievers whom Du Bois felt would bring liberty to their race, but Neely exposes their position as one of incorporation, and essentially consent to the practices of oppression – they worry a lot about skin color. Strongly written and firmly focused on racial politics, Neely's novels have gone beyond the volatile suggestiveness of Mosley's stories to be the strongest and most direct of the African American resistance to continuing forms of once-colonial oppression.

Postcolonial World Crime Fiction

The American initiative was widely followed. Mike Phillips, a British writer of Caribbean origin, has, as Wells records,[20] commented how he chose crime fiction to present a black British figure who was, suitable to the context, not violent as in Himes and could transmit social as well as racial issues. In *Blood Rights* (1989), Sam Dean, a journalist and researcher from the West Indies, acts as an amateur private eye – not being in the police itself expresses something about the West Indian experience in London, but the impact is also general: Reddy notes that he challenges "the usually disguised centrality of whiteness."[21] Phillips has tended to deal with wider world issues in his later fiction, sometimes without Dean's presence, but less ambitious, and more firmly embedded in real crime and racial entanglements in Britain is Victor Headley's strong crime novel series starting with *Yardie* (1992): like a calmer version of Himes, it explores crimes within as well as against the black British community. But, just as in the United States, there have been dilutions: the prolific white crime writer Reginald Hill produced a series starting with *Blood Sympathy* (1993) featuring Joe Sixsmith, a lower-middle-class black detective whose adventures are more comic than racially resistant. Something of the same neocolonial quality is offered by Robert Barnard, another prestigious white writer, who in *Death and the Chaste Apprentice* (1989) started a series with a black police detective, but one who has little to do with race or indeed social tensions, and is belittlingly named Charlie Peace, after a famous nineteenth-century murderer.

Equally patronizing was the name Boney, short for Napoleon Bonaparte, chosen by Arthur Upfield for his detective in the long series starting with *The Barrakee Mystery* (1929). Boney is a calm half-Aboriginal man with a university degree (forty years before that actually happened). A roving police Inspector, he solves crimes among distantly rural white families with indigenous servants and neighbors, combining his knowledge of country with close attention to people. Donaldson said the figure "idealizes a contemporary world of real pastoral supremacy and subterfuge,"[22] and many commentators, including indigenous people, feel Upfield offers a fantasy of appropriation and incorporation disavowing the real crimes done in the process of land-taking and never reparated, and see the stories as classic settler crime fiction. Other commentators take a blandly positive approach, as in a recent Australian book of essays, which reprinted but did not respond to Donaldson's essay.[23] This approach is common in America. Browne wrote an essay entitled "The Frontier Heroism of Arthur W. Upfield," while Rye has, however incredibly, written that Boney is an "inspired creation" to "lessen the distress to mankind."[24]

Australian indigenes have responded with some effect. Mudrooroo Narogin started a short series of stories in 1990 with "Westralian Lead," featuring Detective Inspector Watson Holmes Jackamara of the Black Cockatoo Dreaming who, as well as having a challenging name, is a determined, self-aware indigenous man, sorting out confusions and crimes that result largely from incomer oppression. The initiative was pursued by Philip McLaren in 1995 with *Scream Black Murder*, a novel set in Sydney's Redfern with the first aboriginal police detectives in the state. They deal with a serial killer of black women, and with the broad racism found among the

public and still the police, and they confront their own difficulties of positioning. McLaren has continued with *Lightning Mine* (1999), a historical
account of antiindigenous brutalities from harassment to massacre, and
Murder in Utopia (2006 in French, 2009 in English), which introduces an
American doctor to central Australia and reveals oppressions social and
economic as well as racial.

White writers have turned to this theme with some impact. In Adrian
Hyland's *Diamond Dove* (2006) a young indigenous woman resolves crimes
back in her distant rural community, and she has continued in *Gunshot
Road* (2010). Less full, but of wider dissemination, are indigenous themes in
the work of Peter Temple: the prize-winning *The Broken Shore* (2005)
includes a plot line about the police shooting of young indigenous men in
rural Victoria: the police detective Joe Cashin both sympathizes with the men
and has part-indigenous relatives. An aboriginal detective plays a role in the
investigations and in the succeeding novel *Truth* (2009) he has moved to the
city, where indigenous issues are part of the web of tensions in this somberly
powerful novel.

Indigenous writers did not immediately pursue McLaren's initiative in the
crime fiction mode, though violence and government harassment of aboriginal people recurs through the work of major writers such as Kim Scott,
Alexis Wright, Tony Birch, and Helen Lucashenko, and an indigenous
terrorist plot is focal to Sam Watson's dark futurist thriller set in Queensland, *The Kadaitcha Sung* (1990). The genre was resumed by his daughter
Nicole Watson, a Brisbane lawyer, in *The Boundary* (2011), where Queensland's long-standing mistreatment of indigenes is the context for the murder
of three public servants, one indigenous. A young Aboriginal woman lawyer
is central; also engaged are elders long engaged in land rights resistance and
a "clever man" or tribal sage. The novel avoids simple liberal solutions: the
oppressions continue, penalties are doubtful, and the woman lawyer is
largely exhausted.

In other contexts the treatment of indigenes in crime-solving has been
reminiscent of the settler pattern of partnering a native and an incomer
detective. In New Zealand Laurie Mantell included a Maori policeman in
Murder and Chips (1980), while Gaylene Gordon from *Above Suspicion*
(1990) on produced a basically procedural series featuring Detective Sergeant Rangi Roberts, and Paul Thomas created vigorous and witty accounts
of what Sturm called the "renegade Maori detective Sergeant Tito Ihaka,"[25]
starting with *Old School Tie* (1994; in Britain, neutralized as *Dirty
Laundry*). None of these authors claimed Maori identity, though their indigenous creations had considerable strength. Indigenous New Zealand
writers have avoided the patterns of crime and detection, though Patricia

Grace's *Potiki* (1986) is a powerful statement about past and continuing racial pressures on the Maori people, and Alan Duff has produced an unsentimental crime novel about young Maori men, *One Night Out Stealing* (1995), as well as his very successful, and often crime-linked, consciously political examinations of the Maori position, beginning with *Once Were Warriors* (1994).

In Canada, Scott Young's *Murder in a Cold Climate* (1990) introduced Inspector Matteesie Kitiologita, an Inuit Mountie, who, the Macdonalds comment, while a rational officer, "does not reject the old beliefs of his people."[26] In *Everybody Knows This Is Nowhere* (2006) John McFetridge makes a native Canadian the leader among his Toronto police, but his ethnicity is as underplayed as his name, Armstrong. Far to the north, Stan Jones's series beginning with *White Sky Black Ice* (1999) features Nathan Active, a part-indigenous state trooper resolving crimes and his own identity in his mother's Inupiat territory, and M. J. (Melanie) McGrath's *White Heat* (2011) features Edie Kiglatik, a half-Inuit former polar bear trapper solving an apparent hunting accident far out on the ice. In these novels both the traditions of indigenous people and the austerity of their surroundings are realized in some tension with the interests of armchair tourism.

An early recognition in South Africa of indigeneity was the series written in Britain by South African journalist James McClure beginning with *The Steam Pig* (1971) and extending to *The Song Dog* (1991). Afrikaans Inspector Kramer and Zulu Sergeant Zondi combine to solve crimes in a mostly procedural way. Zondi does have native skills that can be useful, and a sly sense of destabilization. Schleh found the real friendship between the two "hopeful," but saw the process as "slow and evolutionary,"[27] while Winston found the stories "a reassuring and apparently hopeful vision of accommodation rather than one of meaningful though disturbing collective action."[28]

The French Caribbean has, as Herbeck has shown, produced several writers of clearly postcolonial crime fiction such as Raphaël Confiant's *Le Meutre du Samedi-Gloria* (1997, 'The Murder on Holy Saturday'), in which the Martinican Inspecteur Dorval pursues his inquiries among disrespectful slum-dwellers like a classic detective, but also uses antidisciplinary guess-work. Also set in Martinique, Patrick Chamoiseau's *Solibo magnifique* (1988) stands out as a classic postcolonial crime novel in its vigorously abrogating style and its challenge to what Wright sees in contrast as the "static, homogenous, death-like" technique of the rational imperial mystery.[29] An expert in Creole culture,[30] Chamoiseau makes the famous Creole story-teller Solibo die in the first scene, but through exploring his life and values the novel both memorializes the richness of Creole culture and demonstrates its capacity to survive in a present where France mediates to the region the hostile forces of international modernity.

In terms of numbers and profile, the most successful contribution to postcolonial crime fiction about a directly colonized native people has been the range of novels dealing with Native Americans: more than twenty white and more than ten native authors are recorded by the MacDonalds and Sheridan.[31] As with Afro-American and Latina crime fiction, the period of emergence was the late 1980s, and, like John Ball, a white writer was the apparent stimulus. Tony Hillerman, a war veteran and journalist brought up in the Navajo region, was the first to present crime's effect on Native American people, and also involve their concerns and values in its resolution, in *The Blessing Way* (1970): his third, *Dance Hall of the Dead* (1973), won the year's Mystery Writers of America award and was a major international success, reprinted in London's Pluto radical crime series. Joe Leaphorn, a Navajo police detective, is the focus for understanding the pressures native people face both from white intruders and from temptations to join mainstream American life – Hillerman also clarifies the rich variation among Native American cultures. In his fourth novel, *People of Darkness* (1980), he introduces Jim Chee, a younger, better-educated man with more experience of the extra-Navajo world, but for whom the native traditions have a stronger, even mystical, appeal. While events and knowledge are never clearly only supernatural, the force of the superrational is strong, and recognized by both detectives. While Hillerman retains a focal mystery and provides some narrative resolution, there remain areas of uncertainty about the explanations and a general lack of the mechanical closure of the traditional mystery novel.

Hillerman's impact was substantial. As Cawelti says, "Many Americans have probably gotten more insight into traditional Navajo culture from his detective stories than from any other recent books"[32] and he has stimulated writing by people with Native American identification. Linda Hogan, a poet and writer of Chickasaw extraction, produced *Mean Spirit* in 1990, a closely woven novel dating back to the Oklahoma oil finds and showing how fraud, intimidation, and murder gather around the new wealth of the native people. Crimes are investigated by a Native American federal agent, Stacey Red Hawk, in ways that, as Linton puts it, resist "the linear logic of clue added to clue," and challenge "normative Western conceptions of knowledge."[33]

A more folkloric approach was taken by Jean Hager, herself part Cherokee, who started a series with *The Grandfather Medicine* (1989), where an Americanized half-Cherokee police chief Mitch Bushyhead solves crimes with full-blood Cherokee help and also explores his own identity. A variation develops from *Ravenmocker* (1992) with the half-Cherokee

Molly Bearpaw as investigator, urban but also strongly aware of native culture. For both, visions can communicate knowledge, though they are often confirmed in a less antienlightenment mode.

Louis Owens, with Choctaw-Cherokee lineage, has some resemblance to Chamoiseau, being both a university professor and novelist. In *The Sharpest Sight* (1991) he employs a Mexican-American detective who both resolves the cause of a Native American's death and also comes to recognize his own part-indigenous origins, linked to the vision that starts the story. As with Chamoiseau, formal variations of the standard crime novel are themselves part of its challenge to the meaning and context of traditional crime fiction: the case is solved ten chapters before the end, but there is more for the detective to learn, including aspects of his identity. The novel deploys a set of multiple viewpoints and considerable stylistic variety, and later novels use the Choctaw brother of the murdered man as detective in what Browne calls an "intellectualized and angry series."[34]

Native American crime fiction has generated some surprises: Robert Westbrook has used the American private-eye, even "hard-boiled," tradition. From *Ghost Dancer* (1998) on, Howie Moon Deer, as a private investigator, encounters corrupt officials and exploited Native Americans in an atmosphere that combines folkloric awareness with a sense of his own version of Chandleresque deracination. Locationally unusual is the Alaska-set work of Dana Stabenow, herself part Aleut, starting with *A Cold Day for Murder* (1992). Kate Shugak, small, brave, and determined, returns to her Aleut roots and becomes involved in local investigations, which often deal with the situation of the native people. The unusual setting and well-structured plots have made Stabenow a major success, and as Kate has matured she has consciously inherited something of the "wise woman" role her grandmother played in the early novels.

Crime fiction produced by the slowly devolving colonized parts of Britain tends in Scotland and Wales to be primarily self-celebratory, if also at times both anxious and earnest as in Ian Rankin's very successful Edinburgh-based Rebus series starting with *Knots and Crosses* (1987), or like the Welsh Robert Lewis's *The Last Llanelli Train* (2005) where the tone approaches self-indulgence, as well as being drink-sodden. Scots crime writers Denise Mina and Christopher Brookmyre have been more postcolonially aware, described by Kim as investigating "cultural hybridity" and exploring "larger cultural myths of race and otherness."[35] In Northern Ireland the long conflict between the native and largely Catholic population and the implanted Protestant English has led to a very large amount of recent crime fiction – six hundred books by two hundred authors from the 1960s on was a recent estimate. Many of these, from both sides, were pulp "troubles thrillers" mixing blood and bigotry, but Colin Bateman offers a richer account in a series effectively beginning with *Cycle of Violence* (1995) where Dan Starkey, a Belfast journalist, explores the complexities of postimperial crime and vice: a local touch is recurrent humor – the novel was retitled *Cross Ma Heart* in 1999, referring the site of major recent troubles, Crossmaglen.

Ireland itself has recently generated a range of crime fiction which explores with an awareness of past empire both national identities and international threats. Writers tend, in a clearly postcolonial choice, to favor the American private eye, though Ken Bruen started writing London-based police stories before, in *The Guards* (1998), creating his alcoholic ex-cop private eye Jack Taylor. The range of criminographical self-realization has been wide: Declan Burke has in *Eight-Ball Boogie* (2003) started a series of distinctly American-style crime novels with Irish jokes, while Tana French from *In the Woods* (2007) began a more Europe-oriented psychothriller-like series, and the distinguished novelist John Banville has, as "Benjamin Black," produced forensically oriented mysteries among Dublin society.

Postcolonial Elements in World Crime Fiction

Many recent writers around the world have used the modes of crime fiction to juxtapose crime and investigation and explore abuses, corruption, and imbalances of power both past and present in their own countries, including leading authors such as Gabriel García Márquez in *Chronicle of a Death Foretold* (1981, 1983 in English), a Kafkaesque story where a village murder is both foreseen and explained in terms of communal failure, or Mario Vargas Llosa with *Death in the Andes* (1993, 1995 in English) in which a triple disappearance/murder is linked to brutal Maoist guerrillas, but the story also moves into uncovering the native cruelties, historic and contemporary, of the Peruvian nation. These authors work in the conscious context of imperialism, though it may be internal to a state or, if international, take the form of modern capitalist exploitation, and they all adapt and expand the single inquiry form of disciplinary crime fiction to tell a fuller and more complex story about threats and values. Similarly, Leonardo Sciascia, with his penetrating accounts of both Mafia corruption and the inherent inadequacy of the modern Italian state, starting with *Il giorno della civetta* (*The Day of the Owl*, 1961, 2003 in English), consciously uses a crime model to interrogate the abuses of the modern state. Similarly, Didier Daeninckx sees the crimes of the Parisian authorities, as in *Meutres pour mémoire* (*Murder in Memoriam*, 1984, 1991 in English) the assault on Algerian protestors in

1962, as the basis for searching inquiries into traditional French freedoms and their relative modern absence.

Paco Ignacio Taibo II has given a probing account of modern Mexico through the eyes of Hector Belascorián Shayne, a distinctly hybrid detective bearing a surname straight from American pulp fiction (as in Mike Shayne), and exploring the long years of recent corruption, beginning with *Dias de Combate* (*Days of Struggle*, 1976), where the detective confronts the military/state/criminal complex with an undisciplinary technique combining, as Nichols puts it, "curiosity" and "stubbornness."[36] Later novels, such as *Sombra de la Sombra* (*Shadow of a Shadow*, 1996), avoid a single inquirer and use a quartet of public observers to penetrate the range of dark complexities. Better known in the Anglophone world has been the series by Manuel Vásquez Montalbán starring Pepe Carvalho, wit, master chef, and ex-Communist, starting effectively with *Tatuaje* (*Tattoo*, 1974) and best represented by *Los mares del Sur* (*Southern Seas*, 1979, 2012 in English). Though setting and attitudes focus on Barcelona, the difficult, perhaps incomplete, post-Franco transition is the main topic: as Belenguer notes, Vásquez Montalbán's focal purpose is to create "a 'moral chronicle' of the Spanish transition to democracy."[37] The threats in these much-admired novels, like those of Taibo, are not so much postcolonial as neoimperial: Nichols comments that for both writers "greed continues to motivate criminals, but multinational capitalism and U.S. imperialist intentions magnify individual alienation."[38] A closer interest in the Catalan cause, though one without Vásquez Montalbán's broader critique, is found in women writers: as White and Godsland report,[39] Maria-Antònia Oliver starting from *Estudi en lila* (*A Study in Lilac*, with Doylean reference, 1985), and Isabel Olesti in *El marit invisible* (*The Invisible Husband*, 1999) have written in Catalan (Oliver, in fact, in Mallorquine) and developed plots that question the authority of central Spanish government as much as that of the patriarchy.

Some writers of these national-inquiry crime stories, however, come closer to the patterns and interests of postcolonial fiction, and it is hardly surprising that several of them are from the Indian subcontinent. After some years of popular, close to pulp, fiction in indigenous languages, relocating British models, usually Sherlock Holmes (with the well-known film director Sa Ray a significant producer), sophisticated English-language crime fiction has been produced. Amitav Ghosh's futuristic *The Calcutta Chromosome* (1995) multiplies mysteries, detection, and setting through space and time: merging into poststructuralism, the novel, as Lauder comments, "transcends the legacies of colonialism."[40] This is also the case with the frequently discussed *Anil's Ghost* (2000), by Michael Ondaatje, and set in his native Sri Lanka, in which he relocates the popular forensic thriller when a Sri Lankan specialist,

Anil Tissera, returns from the United States to be drawn into an apparent murder. Her confidence in disciplinary knowledge weakens among the elusive loyalties of people who have survived the civil war, and the outcomes in narrative and for people are both dangerous and obscure. Vikram Chandra created Sartaj Singh, a Sikh police detective – a rarity in Mumbai – who in a long short story and the powerful, and very long, *Sacred Games* (2006) works through a very complex series of inquiries and engagements, including minor local crime, police corruption, large-scale gangsterism, and high-level political crises involving both religious extremism and threatened terror. This novel markedly challenges traditional rational structures – as Chambers comments, in "physical form [it] is as deconstructed as psychological identity,"[41] and both charts in detail the complexity of the modern megalopolis and reaches out into the threats of modern world politics, with its conflicting forms of up-to-date imperialism.

Similarly moving beyond classic crime fiction into regional and world politics is the Kenyan Ngũgĩ wa Thiong'o with the powerful *Petals of Blood* (1977), a detective-free crime novel disruptive of the calm confidence of the genre through its multiple structures. Acting as what Carter calls a "major attack on neo-colonialism,"[42] it treats crimes that are the sequel to, not the aftermath of, empire, but also deals vigorously with the pressures of international capitalism as they have deformed Kenyan society after independence.

The themes of racial and exploitative oppression are central to texts which realize the pressures still, even increasingly, placed on ethnic groups who have found, usually by immigration, a place in the modern state. A striking instance is the German-set series published under the name Jakob Arjouni, starting with *Mehr Bier* (1991). A Turkish *gastarbeiter*, Kemel Kayankaya (who speaks no Turkish), is a private investigator of crimes that involve racism and forms of mercantile corruption, but above all "the criminality that German society projects onto its minority populations," as Teraokoa puts it.[43] An added complexity, and offence to some, emerged when the author was revealed as a native German, apparently named Jakob Bothe, well-educated and cultured, claiming to have grown up with Turks and clearly of a radical, as well as satiric, disposition.

A similar conflict is explored by Jean-Claude Izzo in *Total Khéops* (1995) where Fabio Mondale, a detective of Spanish-Italian origin based in Marseille, discovers the pressures placed on Algerian refugees in the city by the French right wing, some of whom were themselves imperial agents in North Africa: their actions mesh with what Maillot calls "the narrowness and dangerous overtones" of the growing French right.[44] Comparable are the Algerian-set French-language novels by Yasmina Khadra, later revealed as young liberal army officer Mohamed Mollessehoul. The series started with *Le dingue au bistori* (*The Madman with a Scalpel*, 1990) and expresses dissatisfaction with decay of long FLN rule, to be replaced by military takeover in 1992. Commissaire Llob, also a writer, is engaged with the repressions and state crimes of the period: the novels have faith only in the people themselves, and the humor of the first two is, as Burtscher-Bechter comments, "replaced by bitter comments and critical accusations against those responsible for this calamitous situation."[45]

A different mode of European ethnic and social conflict is explored by Swiss-German novelist Roger Graf, who in *Zurich bei Nacht* (1996) takes his detective Biondi back to trace crimes surrounding wealth, some of it going back to Nazi times, and the officially tolerant environment of the modern country is seen as permitting a range of corruptions through what Jones calls "the stereotypical Swiss desire for money and neutrality."[46] Austrian crime writing responded to the late 1980s when Kurt Waldheim's Nazi links were explored and in the following decade when Jörg Haider gained influence for the extreme right: Gerhard Roth's *Der See* (1995) links the country's Nazi past with modern crimes including arms smuggling to the Balkans, while Doron Rabinovici's *Suche nach M* (*Search for M*, 1997) focuses on the difficulties faced by Holocaust survivors in Vienna in the face of both the sheer impact of Nazi invasion and also continuing issues of Austrian national identity.

European tensions largely avoid crime fiction in the Low Countries. Vanacker reports both the Dutch and Flemish areas as having limited interest in crime fiction, preferring to source violence in Belgium, but she does note the intensity of some of the work by Flemish Jef Geeraerts, exploring parainternational tensions of religion and corruption in fact-linked crime novels such as *The Public Prosecutor* (2009). A less serious discourse of ethnicity is, unusually, developed in a Friesland setting by Janwillem Van de Wetering in *De Ratelrat* (*The Rattle-Rat*, 1984, 1985 in English), a novel she finds ultimately "unburdened by any dark hints of real oppression or racial hatred."[47]

National scrutiny through crime fiction in South Africa has developed from earlier colonial mysteries by writers such as Elspeth Huxley and M. M. Kaye, as outlined by Schleh.[48] One path has been combining the Afrikaans tradition of farm novels with detective fiction, as in Etienne Leroux's *Een vir Azazel* (*One for the Devil*, 1964), which meshes murder with superstition and mob rule, or in the works of Etienne van Herden, a scholar whose novel *Die swye van Mario Salviati* (*The Long Silence of Mario Salviati*, 2000, 2003 in English), where a Boer war crime becomes involved with modern rural mystery, offers an epitome of the country in what Ester calls "distorted social relations and a situation where almost everyone is the hostage of the other."[49] The Swaziland-born, now Australia-resident, screenwriter Malla Nunn has written a series of 1950s-set novels where an English-born detective uncovers racial tensions in village crime, beginning with *A Beautiful Place to Die* (2009). Urban analysis is offered in Wessel Ebersohn's novels, beginning with *A Lonely Place to Die* (1979) where a prison psychiatrist, Yudel Gordon, supported by a tough but liberal Afrikaans policeman, exposes official crimes against black people: *Closed Circle* (1990) is a strong account of extremists defending the crumbling system of apartheid. More internationally up to date in tone is the series by London-born but long-term African resident (including time in jail for resisting apartheid) Margie Orford, with a woman police profiler investigating, first in *Like Clockwork* (2007), serial killing and trafficking in women, both across the races. The indigenous writer Meshack Masondo, working in publishing, has had wide success with stories and novels in Zulu, where the ironic detective Themba Zando deals with the interface between Zulu tradition and modernity: one translation is in the anthology *Bad Company* (2009), and there are plans to publish his 1987 novel *Iphisi Nezinyoka* in English as *The Hunter and the Snake*.

Just as America led the way in social and ethnic resistance through crime fiction with the Afro-American writers, so it has made a major contribution to realizing both the difficulties and the status of other ethnic groups in the country. Rolando Hinojosa started a series in Spanish in 1973 and it has made an impact in English, from *Ask a Policeman* (1993), featuring Rafa Buenrostra, a small-town police chief in the far south, near the Rio Grande, dealing as much with racial interactions as with modern corruption. The poet and teacher Lucha Corpi created in *Eulogy for a Brown Angel* (1992) Gloria Damasco, a former activist Californian private investigator gifted with foresight as well as persistence. In Corpi personal crimes have both social and ethnic forces and the plots, as Libretto comments, can reveal "imperialist aggression toward Third World people globally."[50] Latina crime fiction has, as Knepper has shown, been a wide-ranging and popular form, which like other postcolonial narratives combines multiple viewpoints, the "double colonisation" of women through patriarchy and conquest, and a consistent hybridity in both the detective and the viewpoint, here seen as a *mestiza* phenomenon.[51]

Other American ethnicities have been both defended and celebrated in crime fiction, notably Jewishness in Harry Kemelman's popular and wrily searching series starting with *Friday the Rabbi Slept Late* (1965) and Faye Kellerman's series starting with *The Ritual Bath* (1986) about the nonobservant police detective Peter Decker, who is helped both in his cases and in recognizing his identity by Rina Lazarus, to become his wife – though, as Birkle argues, later texts make it clear she has American female vigor as well as Jewish fidelities.[52] Another strand has been Asian-American: after a banal comic start with Earl Derr Biggers' Charlie Chan and J. P. Marquand's Mr. Moto, other non-Asian writers were more serious with Howard Fast (as E. V. Cunningham) writing about Masao Masuto, a Beverly Hills detective, from *Samantha* (1967), and S. J. Rozan with Lydia Chin, a part-Chinese private eye, in *China Trade* (1994). Recently some limited impact has been made by Asian writers: Chang-rae Lee, a Princeton academic, created Henry Park, a Korean-American surveillance agent in the widely praised *Native Speaker* (1995), but has produced no more in the crime genre. Suki Kim has produced a single complex novel, *The Interpreter* (2003), about a Korean in New York whose inquiries into crime also reveal, as Kim comments, "the difficulty of culture interpretation in the age of globalization."[53] Dale Furutani introduced Ken Tanaka in *Death in Little Tokyo* (1996) but after one more United States-set novel, the hero and action moved to Tokyo.

The world-wide activities of postcolonial crime fiction are striking, but neocolonialism is also abroad. The Welsh suffer an American resident, under the name Rhys Bowen, writing low-level mysteries set in the Snowdonia mountains about a detective called Evans, the first trivializingly named *Evans Above* (2007). There are better known and better informed neocolonialists. William Marshall, with *Yellowthread Street* (1975), started a series of touristic police procedurals set in a somewhat imaginary Hong Kong (and followed up with a series set in Manila and another in New York). These are sometimes called "postcolonial," as are others of this neocolonial kind.[54] The India-set Inspector Ghote mysteries of H. R. F. Keating, starting with *The Perfect Murder* (1964), while knowledgeable about the country, also value it as, Chambers comments, "a more innocent place than post-imperial Britain."[55] The same patronizing approach has led to the remarkable success of Alexander McCall Smith's novels about the plump Botswanan private detective Precious Ramotswe, who, as Bettinger has noted,[56] investigates local misdemeanors in the atmosphere of folklore, gossip, and mild tricksterism, with no sign of the real pressures of Africa, present or past. A corrective is the novels of Unity Dow, who, as in *The Screaming of the Innocent* (2002), uses a brave young woman investigator to investigate a hideous local crime as well as the casual brutalities of the modern Botswanan authorities, a bold initiative by the first native woman to become a high court judge in the country.

Neocolonially curious authors, and readers, do not only visit formerly imperial zones. The delights of short-term travel to Italy appear to be behind the success of authenticity-claiming Italian crime fiction as produced by

Donna Leon and Michael Dibdin: presumably Simenon has spoiled the market for armchair criminal travel to France. The recent triumph of Swedish crime fiction by Henning Mankell and Stieg Larsson markets a cooler, even masochistic, form of national self-revelation; the success may also relate to the fact that for Western readers this material is both pleasingly, quasi-educationally, foreign and also essentially familiar in themes, not as challenging as a truly postcolonial crime fiction might be. Yet if in part touristic, this material is also seriously against corruption, sexism, and the rise of neofascism. A similar mix of the touristic and the politically critical is located elsewhere: Simon speaks of more than eight hundred crime novels in the last century from the United States and Britain, largely in spy-thriller mode, seeing the Middle East through confidently, if sometimes anxiously, Western eyes.[57] She shows that in the very late twentieth century a few expressed post-Gulf War doubts, but after 9/11 the output has both accelerated and grown ever more certain of the rectitude of neoimperialism.

Crime fiction has always juxtaposed the searching and the trivial – in the early nineteenth century, Godwin, Brockden Brown, and Hogg did so beside the bourgeois sadomasochism of *Blackwood's* "Tales of Terror"; post-World War II, the insightful Ross Macdonald against crass Mickey Spillane; for the Cold War spy fiction's sensational patriotism, from James Bond to the dismayed realism of Len Deighton and John le Carré. In the same multiple ways, postcolonial crime fiction offers some banalities, often by authors exploiting rather than exploring the form and its contexts. But it also provides substantial areas of illuminating achievement as in the work of writers who, like African Americans, indigenous Australians, French Caribbeans, Europeans attuned to migrant pressures, South and Central Americans and post-Franco Spaniards exploring their situations, and Indians and Africans exploring the crime-ridden aftermath of empire, have redeployed crime fiction's usual simple opposition of disruption and resolution to describe and resist the negative forces evident in the worlds of empire and colonialism, ancient and modern.

Notes

1 Caroline Reitz, *Detecting the Nation: Fictions of Detection and the Imperial Venture* (Columbus: Ohio State University Press, 2004), pp. xvi and xix.
2 See Allardyce Nicoll, *A History of Early Nineteenth Century Drama 1800–1850*, 2 vols. (Cambridge, Cambridge University Press, 1930). Vol. 2 contains a full list of plays mounted in the period in London.
3 Upamanyu Pablo Mukherjee, *Crime and Empire: The Colony in Nineteenth-Century Fictions of Crime* (Oxford: Oxford University Press, 2003), p. 185.

4 On the development of crime fiction see Stephen Knight, "'...some men come up': the Detective Appears," chap. 1 of *Form and Ideology in Crime Fiction* (London: Macmillan, 1980), and Heather Worthington, *The Rise of the Detective in Early Nineteenth-Century Popular Fiction* (London: Palgrave 2005).

5 Mukherjee, *Crime and Empire*, see pp. 177–9 for Ashish Roy's critique of *The Moonstone* and also pp. 181 and 185.

6 Yumna Siddiqui, *Anxieties of Empire and the Fiction of Intrigue* (New York: Columbia University Press, 2008), p. 61.

7 Catherine Wynne, *The Colonial Conan Doyle: British Imperialism, Irish Nationalism and the Gothic* (Westport, CT: Greenwood, 2002).

8 Stephen F. Soitos, *The Blues Detective: A Study of African-American Detective Fiction* (Amherst: University of Massachusetts Press, 1996), p. 221.

9 Marina Cacioppo, "Insider Knowledge versus Outside Perspective in Early Italian American and African American Detective Stories," in Dorothea Fischer-Hornung and Monika Mueller, eds., *Sleuthing Ethnicity: The Detective in Multiethnic Crime Fiction* (Madison, WI: Fairleigh Dickinson University Press, 2003), pp. 23–35, see pp. 28–32.

10 David Schmid, "Chester Himes and the Institutionalization of Multicultural Detective Fiction," in Adrienne Johnson Gosselin, ed., *Multicultural Detective Fiction: Murder from the 'Other' Side* (New York: Garland, 1999), pp. 283–302, p. 286.

11 Soitos, *Blues Detective*, p. 152.

12 Gilbert H. Muller, *Chester Himes* (New York: Twayne, 1989), p. 100.

13 Schmid, "Chester Himes," p. 291.

14 John Cullen Gruesser, "An Un-Easy Relationship: Walter Moseley's Signifyin(g) Detective and the Black Community," in Gosselin, *Multicultural Detective Fiction*, pp. 235–55, p. 235; William R. Nash, "'Maybe I killed My Own Blood': Doppelgängers and the Death of Double Consciousness in Walter Mosley's *A Little Yellow Dog*," in Gosselin, *Multicultural Detective Fiction*, pp. 303–24, p. 305.

15 Sally Munt, *Murder by the Book? Feminism and the Crime Novel* (London: Routledge, 1994), p. 111.

16 Maureen T. Reddy, *Traces, Codes and Clues: Reading Race in Crime Fiction* (New Brunswick, NJ: Rutgers University Press, 2003), pp. 68–72.

17 Soitos, *Blues Detective*, p. 223.

18 Ibid., pp. 35–6.

19 Caroline Reitz, "Do We Need Another Hero?," in Gosselin, *Multicultural Detective Fiction*, pp. 213–233, p. 221.

20 Claire Wells, "Writing Black: Crime Fiction's Other," in Kathleen Gregory Klein, ed., *Diversity and Detective Fiction* (Bowling Green, OH: Bowling Green State University Popular Press, 1999), pp. 205–223, p. 206.

21 Reddy, *Traces, Codes*, p. 114.

22 Tamsin Donaldson, "Australian Tales of Mystery and Miscegenation," *Meanjin* 50 (1991), pp. 341–52, p. 347.

23 Kees de Hoog and Carol Hetherington, eds., *Investigating Arthur Upfield: A Centenary Collection of Critical Essays* (Newcastle: Cambridge Scholars, 2012).

24 Ray B. Browne, "Arthur Upfield as Frontier Hero," *Clues* 7 (1986), pp. 127–45; Marilyn Rye, "Upfield's Napoleon Bonaparte: Postcolonial Detective Prototype

as Cultural Mediator," in Ed Christian, ed., *The Postcolonial Detective* (London: Palgrave, 2001), pp. 55–72, p. 72.

25 Terry Sturm, *The Oxford History of New Zealand Literature*, 2nd ed. (Auckland: Oxford University Press, 1998), p. 624.

26 Gina and Andrew Macdonald, *Shaman or Sherlock, The Native as American Detective* (Westport, CT: Greenwood, 2002), p. 235

27 Eugene Schleh, "Spotlight on South Africa: The Police Novels of James McClure," in Eugene Schleh, ed., *Mysteries of Africa* (Bowling Green, OH: Bowling Green University Press, 1991), pp. 106–12, p. 112.

28 Robert P. Winston, "Anatomizing the Other: The Novels of James McClure," in Robert P. Winston and Nancy C. Mellerski, eds., *The Public Eye: Ideology and the Police Procedural* (New York: St. Martin's, 1992), pp. 52–89, p. 89.

29 Greg Wright, "Out on Parole: Suspending Oral Culture's Death Sentence in Patrick Chamoiseau's *Solibo Magnifique*," in Nels Pearson and Marc Singer, eds., *Detective Fiction in a Postcolonial and Transnational World* (Aldershot: Ashgate, 2009), pp. 81–95, p. 93.

30 See Patrick Chamoiseau, Jean Bernabé, and Raphaël Confiant, *Éloge de la créolité* (*In Praise of the Creole*, Paris: Gallimard, 1989).

31 Andrew and Gina Macdonald and MaryAnn Sheridan, *Shapeshifting: Images of Native Americans in Recent Popular Fiction* (Westport, CT: Greenwood, 2000).

32 John G. Cawelti, *Mystery, Violence and Popular Culture* (Madison: University of Wisconsin Press, 2004), p. 281.

33 Patricia Linton, "The Detective Novel as a Resistant Text: Alter-Ideology in Linda Hogan's *Mean Spirit*," in Gosselin, *Multicultural Detective Fiction*, pp. 17–35

34 Ray B. Browne, *Murder on the Reservation: American Indian Crime Fiction: Aims and Achievements* (Madison: University of Wisconsin Press, 2004), p. 86.

35 Julie H. Kim, *Race and Religion in the Postcolonial British Detective Story* (Jefferson, NC: McFarland, 2005), pp. 211 and 236.

36 William J. Nichols, *Transatlantic Mysteries: Crime, Culture, and Capital in the "Noir Novels" of Paco Ignacio Taibo II and Manuel Vásquez Montalbán* (Lewisburg, PA: Bucknell University Press, 2011), p. 54.

37 Susana Bayó Belenguer, "Montalbán's Carvalho Series as Social Critique," in Anne Mullen and Emer O'Beirne, eds., *Crime Scenes: Detective Narratives in European Culture since 1945* (Amsterdam: Rodopi, 2000), pp. 300–11, p. 300.

38 Nichols, *Transatlantic Mysteries*, p. 140.

39 Anne M. White and Shelley Godsland, "Popular Genre and the Politics of the Periphery: Catalan Crime Fiction by Women," in Marieke Krajenbrink and Kate M. Quinn, eds., *Investigating Identities: Questions of Identity in Contemporary International Crime Fiction* (Amsterdam: Rodopi, 2009), pp. 43–55.

40 Maureen Lauder, "Postcolonial Epistemologies: Transcending Boundaries and Re-inscribing Difference in *The Calcutta Chromosome*," in Pearson and Singer, *Detective Fiction*, pp. 47–62, p. 48.

41 Claire Chambers, "Postcolonial Noir: Vikram Chandra's 'Kama,'" in Pearson and Singer, *Detective Fiction*, pp. 31–46, p. 41.

42 Steven R. Carter, "Decolonization and Detective Fiction: Ngugi wa Thiong'o's *Petals of Blood*," in Schleh, *Mysteries of Africa*, pp. 72–91, p. 73.

43 Arlene A. Teraokoa, "Detecting Ethnicity: Jakob Arjouni and the Case of the Missing German Detective Novel," in Krajenbrink and Quinn, *Investigating Identities*, pp. 113–29, p. 124.

44 Agnès Maillot, "Jean-Claude Izzo, *Total Khéops* and the Concept of Marseillais Identity," in Krajenbrink and Quinn, *Investigating Identities*, pp. 95–111, p. 102.

45 Beate Burtscher-Bechter, "Wanted: National Algerian Identity," in Krajenbrink and Quinn, *Investigating Identities*, pp. 183–98, p. 194.

46 Christopher Jones, "Cultural Identity in Swiss German Detective Fiction," in Krajenbrink and Quinn, *Investigating Identities*, pp. 229–42, p. 236.

47 Sabine Vanacker, "Double Dutch: Image and Identity in Dutch and Flemish Crime Fiction," in Krajenbrink and Quinn, *Investigating Identities*, pp. 215–28, p. 227.

48 Eugene Schleh, "Colonial Mysteries," in Schleh, *Mysteries of Africa*, pp. 5–8.

49 Hans Ester, "Perspectives on the Detective Novel in Afrikaans," in Krajenbrink and Quinn, *Investigating Identities*, pp. 171–82, p. 181.

50 Tim Libretti, "Lucha Corpi and the Politics of Detective Fiction," in Gosselin, *Multicultural Detective Fiction*, pp. 61–81, p. 63.

51 Wendy Knepper, "Hot on the Heels of Transnational America," in Pearson and Singer, *Detective Fiction*, pp. 157–79.

52 Carmen Birkle, "Of Sherlocks, Shylocks and the Shoah: Ethnicity in Jewish American Detective Fiction," in Fischer-Hornung and Mueller, *Sleuthing Ethnicity*, pp. 53–80, p. 65–6.

53 Soo Yeon Kim, "Lost in Translation: the Multicultural Interpreter as Metaphysical Detective in Suki Kim's *The Interpreter*," in Pearson and Singer, *Detective Fiction*, pp. 195–207, p. 206.

54 Ed Christian, editor of *The Postcolonial Detective*, includes Keating and Marshall among the authors analyzed, while Elfi Bettinger, in "Riddles in the Sands of the Kalahari: Detectives at Work in Botswana," in Christine Matzke and Susanne Mühleisen, *Postcolonial Postmortems: Crime Fiction from a Transcultural Perspective* (Amsterdam: Rodopi, 2006), pp. 161–79, explores at some length Smith's postcolonial qualifications, though is finally dissatisfied with them.

55 Chambers, "Postcolonial Noir," p. 34, note 2.

56 Bettinger, "Riddles in the Sands," pp. 161–79.

57 Reeva Spector Simon, *Spies and Holy Wars: the Middle East in 20th-Century Crime Fiction* (Austin: University of Texas Press, 2010), p. 2.

11

RASHMI VARMA
University of Warwick

The Gleam and the Darkness

Representations of the City in the Postcolonial Novel

> It's not that what is past casts its light on what is present, or what is present its light on the past; rather, image is that wherein what has been comes together in a flash with the now to form a constellation. In other words, image is dialectics at a standstill.
>
> Walter Benjamin, "Awakening," *Arcades*

Raymond Williams's path-breaking study *The Country and the City*, which chronicled the ways in which "the decisive transformations, in the relations between country and city" since the Industrial Revolution shaped English literature, provides a salient critical template for any consideration of the city in postcolonial literature as well.[1] But there is a significant question that lies submerged in Williams's work on the country and the city. That question concerns the city's emergence as a powerful signifier of relations of colonial rule, and of urbanism as key to the colonial project, such that the metropolitan city of the colonial world became the exemplary model of modernist urbanity everywhere. Such a modular view, however, ran counter to the real ways in which notions of center and periphery were scattered, twisted, and reconstituted by contestations with, and transformations of, the imperial project, and the centrality of the city within it. After all, we know from the historical record that modernity's norms crucially shaped the forms of cities in the colonized world, but equally that the peripheral modernity of the colonized city leaked into, if not flooded, Europe's metropoles. Thus rather than understanding the city in the postcolonial world as derivative of the modernist city, one could therefore read it in terms of an imperial genealogy that can also be placed within the project of resistance to imperialism.

In this chapter I argue that the relations between the country and the city, always mediated by colonialism, nationalism, and later by ideologies and projects of development and neoliberal globalization, have shaped the postcolonial novel in particular in substantive ways. Michael McKeon has noted that the postcolonial novel focalizes the question of narrative form by moving the issue of "formal coherence" from one of historical diachrony to that of historical synchrony. He writes of how "within this framework, the 'tradition' of the hinterlands is understood to be contemporaneous with the 'modernity' of the metropolitan centre, and 'modernization' is conceived as a means of getting not from 'then' to 'now' but from 'there' to 'here.'" There is thus a "foregrounding of spatial difference" that "throws into relief the existence of alternative periodizing conventions – not only 'traditional-modern-postmodern,' but also 'traditional-colonial-postcolonial' – which are roughly parallel but not for that reason homologous."[2] In his theorization of the postcolonial novel, therefore, McKeon draws attention not only to the troubled relationship between postmodern narrative and postcolonial literature that focalizes issues of style and generic convention and experimentation, but also to the formal contrast generated between the "far more consecutive and incremental" chronology of the first world as opposed to the "overlapping and foreshortened timing" in the third world, pointing to the uneven development that characterizes postcolonial societies. This unevenness of form, time, and space, I suggest, is indicative of key features of both the postcolonial city and the postcolonial novel.

Indeed, the city is central to understanding the postcolonial novel as a highly contested literary *space* that condenses issues of history, identity, ideology, and canonicity, among others.[3] The discourses of urbanism that the postcolonial novel inherited from modernist aesthetics (in which the city was the quintessential site for the experience of modernity) are re-cited as well as shattered and reconfigured in a range of novels written in the aftermath of decolonization and formal national independence. In my following readings of particular novels, I hope to elaborate how postcolonial novels not only transform the cultural representation of cities by engaging the "others" that modernity produces, but historicize the imperial (and neo-imperial) history of the production of urban space that is simultaneously local, national, and global.

A key theoretical problematic that the question of the city within the postcolonial novel highlights is that of imagining and grasping the postcolonial as both inside and outside the west simultaneously, in a way that does not merely replicate and reproduce the centrality of western modernity, or simply negate it. Sunil Khilnani writes of how in India

> the British Raj ... created a masquerade of the modern city, designed to flaunt the superior rationality and power of the Raj, but deficient in productive capacities. The modernity of the colonial city had a sedate grandeur to it, but it remained external to the life of the society – few bothered about it.[4]

Khilnani's analysis reflects a deep pessimism about postcolonial Indian cities that are for him above all embodiments of a failed idea, even as urbanization moved apace in postcolonial India. Partha Chatterjee expresses a similar view by arguing that Indian cities "had failed to make the transition to proper urban modernity." Chatterjee endorses the sense of postcolonial cities as anomalies, as out of sync with the time of capitalist development and modernity.[5] In the case of Africa, Frederick Cooper furthers this point by arguing that "the kind of society that emerged" in colonial Africa "was not a natural derivative of a social category known as urban."[6] Simon Gikandi extends the theme of colonial modernity (of which cities were seen as constitutive expressions) as an exclusionary and external project by posing the question: "why was the African theoretically excluded from modernity but politically forced into its institutional apparatus?"[7] Gikandi's point is useful in terms of underscoring how the colonial city was of course the perfect example of simultaneous exclusion and forced inclusion into the colonial project. I suggest that the postcolonial novel, in contradistinction with this theorizing, registers a far more complicated traffic between the *externality* of colonial urbanity (where it is a project of domination) and the *internality* of urban modernity (where it is a project of hegemony) as a condition of possibility for the narration of postcolonial citizenship.

Further, postcolonial novels provide a literary realm that does not simply duplicate Eurocentric presuppositions of culturally specific forms of literacy as universal or normative for democratic engagement. The constant traffic between native languages, English, and other high European languages, and the profusion of street languages, popular culture, oral narratives, local and regional languages such as *sheng* and *bambaiya*, and languages of the underground, the yards and the shantytowns, result in multiple, broken, regional, vernacular, subnational and transnational public spheres that coexist in the worldly and literary spaces of postcolonial novels. In terms of form, as well, postcolonial novels seem to occupy the full spectrum of the genre, from those reworking forms of realist novels to those engaging in experimentation with magical realism, postmodern narrative, and most recently with the graphic form.[8]

Imperial Legacies

Already in the novels of early twentieth century writers such as Jean Rhys, Virginia Woolf, and E. M. Forster, the colony is only the partially submerged alter-geography of the imperial metropolis. Virginia Woolf's 1925 novel *Mrs. Dalloway* is a useful case in point. In it, the novel's protagonist Clarissa Dalloway, a middle-aged, upper-class woman married to an important politician, prepares to take a walk in London. As she sets out to soak in the wonder and the glory of imperial London (albeit in the aftermath of

World War I), she is haunted by the specter of a time when London would be "a grass-grown path and all those hurrying along the pavement this Wednesday morning (would be) but bones."[9] Clarissa Dalloway's ruminations underscore the fact that the still-to-come postcolonial city marks the imperial city's internalized limit, and becomes its spectral, shadowy double. In her novel *Voyage in the Dark*, Jean Rhys deploys the black Atlantic as an imaginary double of metropolitan modernity, thus at least fictionally enabling the political imagining of the destruction of the colonial city. As the novel "cuts" between the Caribbean and London, Rhys frames her narrative in geospatial terms, situating its protagonist Anna Morgan, who has arrived from the Caribbean, and her movements in the city, within a global traffic in goods, cultural artifacts, performances, texts, and migrants that pours surplus value into the imperial capital of London. But as the novel self-consciously shifts the gaze from the hinterland in the direction of the metropolis itself, its wealth and grandeur only evoke a cold disgust and gray fear even as home (the Caribbean) is remembered as "white-paved and hot," a "fire-colour."[10]

Alongside Rhys's works that render the imperial metropoles of London and Paris off-center, one might place the work of the generations of writers to come from and of the colonial worlds who were to also present critical portraits of imperial cities such as London and Paris. Among such writers and works one could list Sam Selvon's *Lonely Londoners*, Buchi Emecheta's *Second Class Citizen*, Timothy Mo's *Sour Sweet*, Salman Rushdie's *The Satanic Verses*, Hanif Kureishi's *The Buddha of Suburbia*, Monica Ali's *Brick Lane*, Andrea Levy's *Small Island*, and Zadie Smith's *White Teeth* and *NW*. Rushdie's evocation of London in *The Satanic Verses* as "a city visible but unseen," irretrievably tropicalized by its former colonial subjects – the Bangladeshis, Jamaicans, Indians, and Africans who form the "unseen" figures in the first world city – is a critical variation on the postcolonial novel's evocation of the dialectical image of the city through metaphors of the gleam and the darkness that the title of this chapter references.

In Monica Ali's *Brick Lane*, the gleaming office blocks of transnational London's financial district, constructed out of concrete, steel, and glass, provide a telling contrast to the grimy and gritty atmosphere of the Tower Hamlet blocks where Bangladeshi immigrants live lives of increasing marginalization in the wake of growing religious fanaticism, racism, and poverty. In what could be read as a postcolonial riff of Woolf's Clarissa Dalloway's walk in high imperial London, Ali elaborately constructs a scene in which the protagonist Nazneen, a young lower middle-class Bangladeshi woman emerges from her public housing estate in the East End of London and confronts official, high capitalist London. This is how Ali describes Nazneen's first encounter with the city/City:

> Nazneen walked ... She sensed rather than saw, because she had taken care not to notice. But now she slowed down and looked around her. She looked up at a building as she passed. It was constructed almost entirely of glass, with a few thin rivets of steel holding it together. The entrance was like a glass fan, rotating slowly, sucking people in, wafting others out. Nazneen craned her head back and saw that the glass above became dark as a night pond. The building was without end. Above, somewhere, it crushed the clouds.[11]

In this classic evocation of the moment of the immigrant's arrival in the imperial city, Ali offers a stark instance of the ways in which global capitalism is figured in the shape, texture, and color of the building in the City. Hywel Williams attributes the imbuing of the City's capitalist machinery with fetishistic qualities to the 1980s deregulation of financial services that severed capitalism's connection to state and social control.[12] But London's hypercapitalist present is only a reiteration as much as it is a successor to the city's accumulating imperial past. Williams writes: "Britons nostalgic for the age of empire need only visit the City to find the heirs of Clive of India seeking the plunder and dividing the spoils. Here is the great mercenary army of our time, the most achingly modern and frighteningly efficient of Britain's imperial institutions."[13]

So it is in this context of global London that the novel tells us about *how* Nazneen *sees* the city:

> Every person who brushed past her on the pavement, every back she saw, was on a private, urgent mission to execute a precise and demanding plan: to get a promotion today, to be exactly on time for an appointment, to buy a newspaper with the right coins so that the exchange was swift and seamless, to walk without wasting a second and to reach the roadside just as the lights turned red. Nazneen, hobbling and halting, began to be aware of herself. Without a coat, without a suit, without a white face, without a destination ...
>
> But they were not aware of her. ... They knew that she existed ... but unless she did something, waved a gun, halted the traffic, they would not see her. (41)

In this remarkable scene that reverberates with echoes from Woolf, the novel presents the imbricated nature of cultural difference and neoliberal capitalism as ideologies that nestle together within the space of London as a global city. Capitalism's selective and uneven rendering of culture as another form of commodification is exposed in the ways in which Nazneen's cultural difference is rendered invisible ("they would not see her") precisely because it is superfluous to the calculus of commodity production, even as her awareness of difference is mediated by the geography of high capitalism.

"Zone of Occult Instability"

In an essay titled "Concerning Violence," Frantz Fanon, the Martinican/ Algerian revolutionary writer, describes the colonial world in the following terms:

> The colonial world is a world cut in two. .... The settlers' town is a strongly built town, all made of stone and steel. It is a brightly lit town; the streets are covered with asphalt, and the garbage cans swallow all the leavings, unseen, unknown and hardly thought about. .... The settlers' town is a well-fed town, an easy-going town; its belly is always full of good things.
>
> The town belonging to the colonized people, or at least the native town, the Negro village, the medina, the reservation, is a place of ill fame. .... The native town is a hungry town, starved of bread, of meat, of shoes, of coal, of light. The native town is a crouching village, a town on its knees, a town wallowing in the mire.[14]

Fanon's narrative of the emergence of postcolonial urban modernity represents the latter as fundamentally distorted by the colonial experience. It is this double-edgedness of colonial urbanity – as both a hellish place of exclusion and immiseration *and* a longed-for paradise – that undergirds the postcolonial city as a "zone of occult instability" in which desire and power collide and provide a heady cocktail of repression and revolution. Fanon's writings seek to wrench open the forbidden zone of the colonial city to show that the articulation of western values (urbanity, civility, order, and light) was only possible through dehumanizing the native and consigning her to darkness; the native is what allowed for the west to urbanize itself.

The colonial city as the city of light that Fanon describes is an image that has been voraciously re-cited and has had longstanding resonance in post-colonial novels, particularly when we recall Aye Kwei Armah's evocation of Accra in terms of a colonial gleam in *The Beautyful Ones Are Not Yet Born*, or Ngũgĩ wa Thiong'o's Nairobi as the city of glittering metal in *Petals of Blood*. Picking up on the representation of the city in Fanon's work, elaborated through images of darkness and light, Aye Kwei Armah's *The Beautyful Ones Are Not Yet Born* opens at the break of dawn, with the protagonist, known as the "man," making his way into the city on a rust-eaten bus to his office where he works as a railway clerk. Seen through the man's eyes, the city is littered with the detritus of everyday life in Ghana – overflowing trash bins, peeling paint, and excrement. But on the other side of this city of waste is Accra as the city of "the gleam" emanated by the Atlantic-Caprice, a tourist hotel whose patrons are the rich and the powerful. There the neoco-lonial elites adorn themselves in luxury furs and diamonds and drive around in swanky foreign cars, embodying the gleam of capital itself. The gleam contrasts sharply with images of the rotting wood bannister in the railway office and the rusty metal that holds the public buses together as they transport the city's impoverished residents between work and home. It is such a manifestation of the gleam – in desired and unattainable luxury goods – that blinds people to reality and blunts the difference between right and wrong. The gleam is the ultimate figure of hegemony in the novel. Neil Lazarus writes of it as an "ideological configuration" wherein the gleam imposes itself on the world as reality such that its social symptoms of corruption and illicit, garish success appear to be "natural."[15] Armah's novel offers a dark existentialist portrait of the postcolonial city in the immediate postindependence period, in which all hopes of social justice are extinguished by the neocolonial elites who have grabbed power from the white colonizers only to perpetuate and exacerbate inequality. The only hope rests in the dialectical image of the city that the novel finally offers in the sign sprawled across a rickety truck passing through the city, announcing that the "beautiful ones are not yet born," with the "yet" barely visible under the peeling paint.

In Ngũgĩ wa Thiong'o's *Petals of Blood* the city is central to the narrative of postcolonial disillusionment and disempowerment.[16] Nairobi is a city of "a thousand mirages" to which young men and women are drawn, seeking escape from the drought and the impoverishment of the village (110). But once in the city they confront the dizzyingly contrasting physical spaces – one of the tall buildings, the luxury cars, the fashionably dressed men and women, the posh residential areas such as Blue Hills; the other of the rubbish heaps that are "the slums" where the naked children play in the narrow streets (159).

In an important way, *Petals Of Blood* also injects the question of gender in its representation of the city. For it is in Nairobi that novel's female protagonist Wanja is raped and finds herself working as a bar girl catering to Kenya's corrupt politicians and businessmen and their Western clients. The proliferation of women in high heels in the city and its nesting of scorpion-like traders redefines gendered urban modernity and the city as a place where only the white man is at home. The city is the symbol of moral and cultural inauthenticity, of a "spiritual drought," a quintessentially modernist space contaminated by western ideas and values, and bereft of African tradition (195).

The idea of the city as the space both of neocolonial accumulation (the nation's "swollen centre") and of postcolonial resistance is worked out in the novel through the figure of the young revolutionary Karega. His education in the "university of the streets," as the novel puts it, imparts the disillusioning pedagogical lesson that the city brings no jobs or futures for men like him. All they can do is become road-boys and street vendors, part of the surplus labor force of neocolonial urbanization.

The novel underlines the idea that there is no lasting promise in the metal roads and urban high rises that pass for development in an impoverished nation. Urban form is articulated with money form, as both are governed by a logic and structure that is exploitative, illusory, and alien to African rationality. Thus, money is understood by the nation's poor as "glittering metal" imbued with evil power, while the call to the city is the veritable call of the devil, emanating from the city's tarmac roads and its electricity poles. The city's "metallic promises" are just that – mere illusions that mimic the form of reality. The critical challenge, as in Armah's novel, is to open up narrative space where distinctions can be made visible.

For Ngũgĩ, the form of the novel inscribes the people's struggles as a historical struggle over *space*. This is of course crucially complicated in that spatially, the novel's most meaningful action takes place *between* the city and the countryside. It is a between-ness that signals several things at once – literally, it is in the journey *between* the city and the country that the space for a renewed cultural and political struggle of the people is produced, even as a rapacious neocolonial regime produces a proliferation of other "in-between" or intermediary spaces such as the village transformed into the township of New Ilmorog, experientially blurring while materially reinforcing the distinction between the country and the city.

As Nyakunya, Wanja's grandmother who has lost her land to national development, puts it in the novel: "we must surround the city and demand back our share"; the novel rewrites the narrative of the city as one of a war between the city and country, between the landless poor and the wealthy elites ensconced in their luxury homes (116). It is only through maneuver and movement that any semblance of social justice is possible. The novel's commitment to a resolutely materialist understanding of urban space is what allows its characters to look forward to a revolution yet to come, whose protagonists will be the workers and the road boys in the city.

There is no such redemption in the dark urban trilogy of another Kenyan writer, Meja Mwangi. In his trilogy *Kill Me Quick*, *Down River Road*, and *The Cockroach Dance*, Mwangi emerges as a furious chronicler of the grimy underbelly of the postcolonial city in the era of national development. He uses fast-paced narration to depict the city's proletarian and subproletarian lives, but without the erudition and self-conscious commitment to social change of Ngũgĩ. *Kill Me Quick* narrates the experiences of two high school graduates who come to the city to seek a better future. But the city offers them no such chances, and they survive by resorting to petty crimes. *Down River Road* is set in the seedy bars and nightclubs of River Road in Nairobi and chronicles the lives of construction workers involved in building what is ironically named "Development House." *The Cockroach Dance* narrates the life of Dusman Gonzaga, who lives in a squalid old building crawling with cockroaches and riddled with filth. The building is inhabited by a mix of people – garbage collectors, conmen, vendors, and witch doctors – forming a community of social outliers to the world of the neo-colonial elites. The protagonist Dusman tries to mobilize the tenants to stop paying rent unless their rogue landlord addresses their problems, but that resistance is, however hopeful, ultimately localized and without the possibility of changing the deep structures of an inhospitable city.

Behind the Beautiful Forevers

The decade of the 1970s emerges as the period when disillusionment and despair in light of the hopes ignited by national independence in the post-colonial worlds of Africa, India, the Caribbean, and elsewhere give way to cynicism and social breakdown. This is the decade of major political and economic restructuring that was to pave the way for the IMF and World Bank-led structural adjustments of the 1980s and the global neoliberal revolution of the 1990s. In the work of postcolonial novels, the city became the concentrated site of narrating the trauma of the new structures, and of the attendant despair and desperation. It is where the arc of the painful repression of history – from slavery and colonialism to a neoliberal world disorder – is made visible in the literary struggles over urban form and politics.

Earl Lovelace's *The Dragon Can't Dance* is set in the slum of Calvary Hill in Port of Spain, Trinidad. The space of the slum is the veritable product of a violent colonial history and racial division between descendants of European rulers, Creole ex-slaves with origins in Africa, and the Indian-origin indentured laborers, as well as of new social tensions introduced by a globalizing oil economy. It is in Port of Spain's slums, its "pathetic and ridiculous looking shacks planted in this brown dirt and stone," that the novel's protagonist Aldrick Prospect pours his life energy into re-creating a dragon costume for the Carnival, an event of communal hope and healing that is based on increasingly remote memories of rebellion, "the guts of the people, their blood," that are now played out nostalgically in the strains of the Calypso. But already in the late 1970s, the Carnival is increasingly susceptible to commercialization as tourism comes to provide one of the few channels for economic prosperity in Jamaica.[17] As Calypso's radical urban rhythms are packaged into attractive-sounding world music, the social scene of the ghetto becomes a threat to the establishment and Prospect and his friends become "loiterers" whose rebellion against police crackdown is resoundingly defeated.

Michelle Cliff's *No Telephone to Heaven* also provides a bleak representation of the city in the context of structural adjustment in Jamaica. Tracing the life story and struggles of its central character Clare Savage to find her "true" identity as an antiimperial revolutionary of sorts, the novel moves between several geographical locations – from rural and urban Jamaica to the United States and England – and traverses the decades of the '60s, '70s, and '80s. While the city is not the central focus of the novel, it provides a crucial locale for Cliff to explore the savage legacy of colonial rule and the growing immiseration of Jamaica under structural adjustment policies introduced in the early 1980s. In this, the figure of the orphaned servant boy Christopher who goes on to become "de Watchman" of Kingston becomes emblematic of Jamaica's virulent history. After brutally hacking off his long-term employers with a machete, he becomes a mad prophet of sorts, and the subject of a reggae song recalling the depredations of colonial racism and capitalism. But as the novel's plot culminates toward an unraveling of hope, he too is commodified – co-opted as he is to play the role of a "wild native" in a new documentary being filmed to narrate the story of Jamaican independence. The novel's rather bleak ending underscores the idea that in a Jamaica reeling under privatization and growing indebtedness, any possibility of resistance is vanquished comprehensively.

Rohinton Mistry's novel *A Fine Balance* is set in the period of the Emergency in India that was promulgated by the then-Prime Minister Indira Gandhi in 1975, and its aftermath, leading up to her assassination in 1984.[18] Mistry narrates this period in Indian history through the experiences in the city of the novel's four main characters – two of them, Ishwar and Omprakash, refugees of caste violence in the village, a young student named Manek who is studying for a vocational degree, and a middle-class widowed woman called Dina – who all come together in the space of "the city by the sea" that is Bombay, finding unexpected points of solidarity and friendship across differences of caste, class, and gender. Mistry's choice of the city is quite pointed – the city in the novel is like the novel itself – a veritable "story factory," "a spinning mill" (383) out of which emerge stories of intertwined lives and unexpected encounters in a time of tremendous economic and social violence and precarity.

Bombay (renamed Mumbai by the right-wing Hindu party Shiv Sena in 1995) has historically been India's financial center and the symbol of national cosmopolitanism. As the site of a world-famous film industry, Bombay is widely imagined in both high and popular culture as the nation's city of dreams, as "the city of promise" where the poor and dispossessed, like Ishwar and Om in the novel, arrive with hopes of survival and progress (153). But as in Ngũgĩ's novel, instead of a euphoric arrival, entering the city for the dispossessed villager is nothing but a "nightmare of arrival." What they *see* is described in terms that re-cite the idea of the dialectical image of the city where the image encapsulates the whole of historical time:

> The pavements were covered with sleeping people. A thin yellow light from the streetlamps fell like tainted rain on the rag-wrapped bodies, and Omprakash shivered. "They look like corpses," he whispered. He gazed hard at them, searching for a sign of life. . . . But the lamplight was not sufficient for detecting minute movements.   (153)

The image of the living corpses underscores the ways in which urban experience involves the reduction of existence to bare life. The ideology of the Emergency was the perfect expression of a late postcolonial developmentalist state's last gasp, marking the end of paternalistic democracy. With massive unemployment within the nation and a global economic downturn, the Emergency was projected as an instrument to speed up the fading promises of social justice of the Nehruvian era. This entailed the exercising of brute biopolitical power to control the population physically and to discipline it toward efficiency and greater economic output. It is this drive to obtain the state's full control over the bodies of its citizens that propelled the family planning campaigns in which the young Omprakash is "sterilized," made incapable of reproducing life. And although the emasculated, the maimed, and the brutalized populations seem to mimic the living, life in the slums goes on, and the poor find ways to profit from their physical deformities, in acts of irrepressible affirmations.

But the Emergency also involved large-scale urban restructuring where the poor were forcibly displaced on to the city's margins, slums were under constant threat of being razed to the ground, and the city had to be made beautiful so that its functions could be streamlined for national growth. It is precisely this juncture in the historical development of the postcolonial city that Mistry's novel so pointedly and poignantly represents.

In a subsequent iteration of the interplay of light and darkness, the novel registers how:

> Splatches of pale moonlight revealed an endless stretch of patchwork shacks, the sordid quiltings of plastic and cardboard and paper and sackcloth, like scabs and blisters creeping in a dermatological nightmare across the rotting body of the metropolis. When the moon was blotted by clouds, the slum disappeared from sight. The stench continued to vouch for its presence.   (379)

This is a resounding critique of the Emergency's urban planning vision – the slum can be made invisible through the beautification drives of the state, but its stench perseveres and overtakes the metropolis. The decades of the 1970s and 1980s also witnessed other kinds of ruptures within the postcolonial polity, particularly those that tear apart the ethic of cosmopolitanism, cultural tolerance, and coexistence within the city. In particular, Salman Rushdie's trilogy of novels on Bombay – *Midnight's Children*, *The Moor's Last Sigh*, and *The Satanic Verses* – track the decline of Bombay from the period of effervescence and hope for social justice in the immediate aftermath of independence in *Midnight's Children* to the city's capitulation to fantasies of right wing power in *The Moor's Last Sigh* to the final breakdown of secular communities in *The Satanic Verses*. Vikram Chandra's *Love and Longing in Bombay*, a collection of five interconnected short stories of various characters negotiating their way in the city against the backdrop of communalism and neoliberalism, and Shashi Deshpande's *That Long Silence*, about a middle-class woman who records the shifting memories and experiences of the city in the wake of the 1980s' deindustrialization and religious conflict, similarly register moments of rupture in the city, materialized in a definitive break that is marked by both the fraying of secular community and the entry of neoliberal capitalism in the nation and the effects of those as visualized in the city. It is in these decades that the city became a key site for the writing of the postcolonial novel in India.

The New Wretched of the Earth

The post-1990s retreat of manufacturing industry in many postcolonial cities across the world paved way for the influx of financial and service industries, such that the postcolonial city begins to function as a "node of an inter-metropolitan and global network carrying out information processing and control functions."[19] The concentration of the call center and outsourcing business in ex-colonial cities is only one manifestation of the articulation of the postcolonial city with the new global financial economy and has been prolifically represented in popular culture, fiction and film, throughout the postcolonial world.[20] The whole apparatus of proficiency in metropolitan languages (erstwhile colonial languages), through "accent-neutralization programs" and English workshops that teach how to speak in the colonial tongue are meant to erase traces of the postcolonial as a complex polyglot and resistant cultural and political formation. Postcolonial cities today are seen as experiencing deep incursions of western capitalist urbanity (as opposed to colonial urbanity represented in the idiom of cultural order, hierarchy, and stability) via a representational assault of globalized images, signs, and commodities.

At the same time and in spite of ever increasing new expressions of a globalized urbanity, the new spatiality that the postcolonial city embodies is not so much virtual as material. After all, it is the new economy postcolonial city in which slums and shantytowns are cleared for office blocks and shopping malls, in which agricultural land is appropriated for ever-expanding urban conurbations, and where a new managerial and techno-cratic elite overlaps with older elites seeking to maintain control of the processes of material and cultural accumulation in the city. Underneath these new projects of accumulation lie older logics of colonial rule even as the postcolonial state and social movements seek to foreground the postcoloni-ality of these cities – colonial buildings, spaces, trade networks, social rules, and street names constitute the postcolonial city as a palimpsest of a messy colonial history and a postcolonial present in crisis.

Mike Davis writes of the

> cities of the future, rather than being made out of glass and steel as envisioned by earlier generations of urbanists, are instead largely constructed out of crude brick, straw, recycled plastic, cement blocks, and scrap wood. Instead of cities of light soaring toward heaven, much of the twenty-first-century urban world squats in squalor, surrounded by pollution, excrement, and decay.[21]

The majority of the inhabitants of the contemporary city are thus, according to Davis, the "*new* wretched of the earth," an "outcast proletariat" that is "not a socialized collectivity of labor" (emphasis in the original).[22] At the same time, Davis concedes that this "outcast proletariat" does possess "yet unmeasured powers of subverting urban order."[23] The simultaneity of the assault on collectivity under neo-liberalism, most sharply on the collectivity named as class, and the eruption of radical creativity among the new social movements and contingent urban communities makes the task of analyzing contemporary postcolonial urbanity especially challenging. After all, the self-help city of the urban poor is too often a product of the postcolonial state reneging on its contract with the destitute and the dispossessed in the service of global capital. The postcolonial city is thus precisely the site where the universality of global capitalist development comes up against the speci-ficities of colonial history and postcolonial politics.

Postcolonial cosmopolitanism in the new global set-up is understood as no longer elsewhere, or as situated in geographic London or New York, but in the here and the now and in the everywhere that capitalism traverses.[24] The multimedia images purveyed through consumer shopping channels, the Internet, popular cinema, malls, multiplexes, and cable television networks run through both urban and rural spaces, small towns and metropolises. In the process, they purportedly erase historical and local determinants, even as they produce the postcolonial city as "a place of new social disparities."[25] Social inequalities are no longer measurable solely through income and wealth indicators, or caste and religion; globalized commodity images provide sites for new desires and aspirations and encode a new calculus for success and happiness, for inclusion and exclusion. The global is now no longer the sole developmental fantasy of the urban elite imagination; it is always already in tension with nationalist and localized/regionalized moorings and class tensions.

These tensions are subjected to fictional pressure in Arvind Adiga's Booker Prize-winning novel, *The White Tiger*.[26] Written in the voice of a lower-caste man from "Darkness," the epithet given to his village in the backward Indian state of Bihar, the novel narrates the career of Balram Halwai who makes his way relentlessly toward metropolitan "Light" – first to Dhanbad, a provincial mining town, then into the national capital region finally ending up in the city of Bangalore, hailed as India's Silicon Valley. His movements are propelled by dint of the sheer capacity to survive and to absorb the social deformities of the neoliberal age. It is the story of a servant who uses cold-blooded calculation (that involves murdering his employer in Delhi) to become a successful entrepreneur in a new India. The servant-turned-entrepreneur talks in a tone that bristles with a raw sense of irony about the increasing economic, social, and political gap in the face of the new creed/greed of global capitalism: "our nation, though it has no drinking water, electricity, sewage system, public transportation, sense of hygiene, discipline, courtesy, or punctuality, does have entrepreneurs. Thousands and thousands of them ... we virtually run America now" (4).

The central events of the novel that plot the story of this low-caste man's move from his village to his employment as a driver in Delhi and its suburb Gurgaon are linked closely to the novel's evocation of the placelessness of the emerging postcolonial city. Adiga's novel, along with Bhagat's *One Night @ the Call Centre*, is among the first to be set in the vast new urban formation of New Delhi's National Capital Region (NCR). Balram's employer Ashok describes Gurgaon (a key part of NCR) as "the modernest suburb of Delhi. American Express, Microsoft, all the big American companies have their offices there. The main road is full of shopping malls – each mall has a cinema inside! So if Pinky Madam (Ashok's wife) missed America, this was the best place to bring her" (101).

Here, while his master and mistress live on the thirteenth floor of the Buckingham Towers B Block, Balram lives as part of a "warren of interconnected rooms where all the drivers, cooks, sweepers, maids and chefs of the apartment block can rest, sleep and wait." In a place of such extreme and brutalizing inequalities, class warfare has become an every day affair, rising from the literal subterranean depths of the servants' quarters. As the rich barricade themselves within the new gated communities where the only thing Indian is the address (to quote an advertisement for a housing development that hoped to attract Non-Resident Indians back to India), their paranoia of crimes associated with the dispossessed multiplies. For outside the barricaded housing complexes (and inside them, too) lawlessness, corruption, murder, and rape are unchecked.

In the form of a letter to the Chinese Premier Wen Jiabao about to arrive for a visit in Bangalore, Balram Halwai, the protagonist, begins (and Adiga begins his novel) with this: "Mr Premier, Sir. Neither you nor I speak English, but there are some things that can be said only in English" (3). This is both an ironic comment on the new imperialism of English that is perpetuated through the mechanisms of late capitalist globalization and an acknowledgment of today's global realities in which English has been deterritorialized once and for all. Thus although the book received the prestigious Booker Prize in 2008, several critics have questioned the novel's literary merit. Sanjay Subrahmanyam has criticized the novel for the inauthenticity of the voice given to Balram. Subrahmanyam is rankled by "the falsity of the expressions" as exemplified in Balram's staccato English. For Subrahmanyam, "this is a posh English-educated voice trying to talk dirty."[27] Subrahmanyam argues that although Adiga gets the world of the bourgeois right, especially in the scene in which Balram is mocked by his employers for pronouncing pizza as "piJJa," the novel overall fails to provide adequate representation to the voice of the underdog.

While there is something to be said about the limits of the new postcolonial novel in the age of neoliberalism to adequately represent the voices of the victims of the new order, we must also draw attention to the proliferation of new subjects in the city who do not fit the subaltern–elite binary. Through the figure of Balram, Adiga's novel portrays the amoral world of the city in which the subaltern is no longer the absolute figure of victimhood and the writer the privileged vanguardist promoter of his or her invisibility. The new postcolonial city throws up a range of characters such as Balram, antiheroes who are the true protagonists of a new world order, offering unprecedented challenges to the politics of the postcolonial novel.

Chris Abani's novel *Graceland* narrates the story of 16-year-old Elvis's coming of age in the slums of Maroko in Lagos, Nigeria.[28] The story of Elvis's arrival in the city, like that of so many rural migrants, is one of loss and dislocation. Tricked by the lure of political office in the city, Elvis's father loses his respectable teaching job in the village and brings his family to the city. The novel chronicles the everyday struggles for survival by the residents of Maroko, pitted as they are against huge odds unleashed by Nigeria's policies of neoliberal economic development that have made urban living for vast masses of people into a massive experience of underprivilege and disenfranchisement. However, in spite of the low level of expectations and possibilities for any kind of advancement or the absence of political hope, Abani depicts existence in Maroko, "half-slum, half-paradise," as robust, comic, and life-affirming.

One response to the question of the future of postcoloniality, typically centered on the city, has been the reiteration of politics as a struggle for survival that entails *local* appropriations of space such as that carried out in slums such as Maroko in Lagos, Dharavi in Bombay, Kibera in Nairobi, or Heliopolis in Sao Paulo. In the postcolonial novel, there is an attendant aestheticization of survival in the city that is nevertheless also represented as a political strategy. The hasty borrowing of elements, a hodgepodge of things that have been thrown together, a practice of making do, are seen to constitute the content and practice of daily life in the postcolonial city.

One symbol of the ethic and mode of survivalism in Abani's novel is the city's fleet of molue buses that recall the rust-eaten bus of Armah's novel. Built from the debris and waste of industries in a postindustrialization West, molues are held together as if by magic (as their name suggests), and succeed in transporting hundreds of the city's poor inhabitants from place to place. The idea of creating something useful and meaningful out of detritus in the city has been picked up by a range of African writers and artists. The 2005 "Africa Remix" exhibition of contemporary African art at the Hayward Gallery in London reinforced this notion. Cramped into five small gallery spaces inside a building flanked by high touristic London as exemplified by the South Bank, the theme common among the artists represented there was this idea of provisionality, ephemerality, and making do with the detritus, the remains of high modernity (steel, weapons, art), both in order to make sense of a senseless reality and in order to survive.

At a personal level, Elvis resignifies the work of survival into an art form by undertaking impersonation as a way of being. Elvis's chief mode of dealing with the harsh inequalities of life in the city is via the metaphorics of impersonation that challenge hegemonic notions of propriety and tradition. In taking on the identity of Elvis Presley, that most popular icon of American popular culture (and after whom his mother had named him), Elvis creates imaginative space for the reinvention of the self in the city. This involves a material makeover as well that includes making up his face, hair, and clothing as well as learning new bodily movements to entertain American tourists sunbathing on the beaches of the city. Elvis's potential as an entertainer is of course severely threatened by diminishing tourism as a result of Nigeria's expanding political and economic crises and the proliferation of high crime and attendant lawlessness. Thus Elvis has to eventually abandon his performances in favor of even more precarious and dangerous informal survivalism that borders on criminality. With help from his friend Redemption, an "area boy," who, like others like him, is part of street gangs involved in petty crime and extortion, Elvis's various jobs include laboring on a construction site, working as a gigolo, wrapping cocaine in condoms for export to the United States, and guarding kidnapped children for the international trade in organs.

AbdouMaliq Simone writes: "most African cities don't work, or at least their characterizations are conventionally replete with depictions ranging from the valiant, if mostly misguided, struggles of the poor to eke out some minimal livelihood to the more insidious descriptions of bodies engaged in near-constant liminality, decadence, or religious and ethnic conflicts."[29] On his view, images of incessant movement – of throbbing, migrating bodies, of lives lived on the edge – jostle with and reinforce the idea of the African city as a "stage too clogged with waste, history and disparate energy."[30]

In many ways, Abani's representation of Lagos reinforces Simone's analysis. For by the end of the novel the very existence of Maroko is threatened by "Operation Clean the Nation," a project that dubiously promises to transfer prime real estate of the slum district to elite developers and capitalists. On the day of the demolition, Maroko's residents barricade themselves, form a protest and challenge the power of the police, all the while singing to Bob Marley's revolutionary song "Get Up, Stand Up" (266). But in spite of this heroism, they lose the fight and the popular protest is crushed by the power of state and capital. Elvis now has no choice but to leave Maroko and to become part of the disposable population of immigrants on the global stage. In Edward Kamau Braithwaite's docu-poetic account of Kingston in the 1990s, *Trenchtown Rock*, Marley's song again provides an ironic subtext to Braithwaite's representation of Kingston as the City of Dis ruled by "Distress, Dispair & Disrespect."

Patrick Chamoiseau's novel *Texaco* (1998) condenses many of the threads in the long discussion that has been elaborated thus far.[31] Set in Fort-de-France, capital of Martinique (Fanon's native country), the novel culminates in Texaco (named after the multinational oil company), a collection of squatter districts clustered around Fort-de-France in the aftermath of deindustrialization. The novel narrates the making of the city from the perspective of global capitalism's disposable populations, its "illegal" citizens, the new wretched of the earth. Ashley Dawson uses the phrase "squatter citizen" to describe Chamoiseau's central protagonist, a figure that he argues is "central to the urban imaginary of the twenty-first century's global cities."[32] In chronicling the story of Marie-Sophie Laborieux, a remarkable squatter citizen, Chamoiseau deploys a range of genres, languages, linguistic registers, textual fragments, indigenous and borrowed accents, and literary traditions, making the text a highly hybrid entity. Such a textual entity then mirrors the form of the resistant city that the novel privileges, one that is able to challenge the hegemony of both colonial and neocolonial urbanism, understood as intimately connected with and dependent on historical forces. The extremely polarized geography that is the product of the colonial project of urban planning, of modernization as destruction, is condensed in the phrase "Urbanity is a violence" that is found in the Urban Planner's Notes (148).

The racialized and abjected others of Fanon's native city are transformed into neocolonial capitalism's slum dwellers who remain unsightly in the city but whose labor enables the accumulation of capital globally. Marie-Sophie arrives and exists in the city as one such disposable, unsightly citizen. Undaunted by the power of the state and of global capitalism, she decides to strike root in the city and build a home there. The ramshackle hut that she builds on a hillside, however, proves to be a threatening reminder of the symbolic power of the poor in the capitalist city. A local representative of the Texaco oil company reports her to the French police and invites them to evict Marie-Sophie and her comrades from their homes. The slum settlements are swiftly destroyed, but for Marie-Sophie that is an expected outcome that doesn't take away from her determination to build and build again. We see in this in the novel's celebration of the power of a squatter woman/citizen to mobilize other squatter women/citizens to take on the might of global capital, and, indeed, to defeat it.

The novel places the struggles of the residents of Texaco within the context of a larger history of slavery, colonialism, and neocolonialism: "to escape the night of slavery and colonialism, Martinique's black slaves and mulattoes will, one generation after another, abandon the plantations, the fields and the hills to throw themselves into the conquest of cities." This is akin to Nyaki-nyua's political vision of the displaced and marginalized residents surrounding the city in order to reclaim it in Ngũgĩ's novel. The urgent political task, the novel suggests, is to re-create the city as a "creole space of brand new solidarities" (320). The novel leaves hope alive as it figures the squatter citizen as one that is central to today's urban imaginary, even as she is extraneous to established notions of belonging and tradition. After all, the struggles of squatter citizens – over land, rights, housing, water, jobs, the environment, and life itself – will define this century that is still unfolding.

This chapter suggests that postcolonial novels have had to confront in a concentrated form issues of geographical and cultural location as tied to the

---

very genre they inhabit. The disjuncture between an inherited narrative form, the novel, and an authentic experience of colonization that cannot be neatly contained within the literary form of the novel, mirrors the disjuncture expressed by Frantz Fanon in the struggles over space between the colonizer and the colonized. These broken, mottled histories of contestation over urban space and form are expressed most vividly in fictions of the postcolonial city.

Notes

1 Raymond Williams, *The Country and the City* (New York: Oxford University Press, 1973).
2 Michael McKeon, "The Colonial and Postcolonial Novel," in McKeon, ed., *Theory of the Novel: A Historical Approach* (Baltimore, MD, and London: The Johns Hopkins Press, 2000), p. 851.
3 For a detailed exploration of the constitutive role of the city in the formation of the postcolonial novel, see my book *The Postcolonial City and its Subjects: London, Nairobi, Bombay* (New York and London: Routledge, 2011).
4 Sunil Khilnani, *The Idea of India* (New York: Farrar, Straus and Giroux, 1999), p. 110.
5 Partha Chatterjee, *The Politics of the Governed* (New Delhi: Permanent Black, 2004), p. 134; Nirmal Kumar Bose, "Calcutta: A Premature Metropolis," *Scientific American* 213.3 (1965), pp. 91–102.
6 Frederick Cooper, "Introduction," in Frederick Cooper, ed., *Struggle for the City: Migrant Labour, Capital, and the State in Urban Africa* (London: Sage Publications), pp. 7–8.
7 Simon Gikandi, "Reason, Modernity and the African Crisis," in Jan-Georg Deutsch, Peter Probst, and Heike Schmidt, eds., *African Modernities* (London: James Currey, 2002), pp. 135–57; p. 143.
8 The graphic novel on the contemporary Indian city is witnessing explosive popularity at the moment. Some examples include Sarnath Banerjee's *Corridor: A Graphic Novel* and Samit Basu's *Local Monsters* set in Delhi, and Rajesh Devraj and Meren Imchen's *Sudershan (Chimpanzee)* and Sourav Mohapatra and Vivek Shinde's *Mumbai Confidential* that are set in Mumbai.
9 Virginia Woolf, *Mrs. Dalloway* (New York: Harcourt Brace and Company, 1997), p. 16. First published 1925.
10 Jean Rhys, *Voyage in the Dark* (New York: W. W. Norton and Co., 1982), p. 26. First published 1934.
11 Monica Ali, *Brick Lane: A Novel* (Scribner, 2003), p. 39.
12 Hywel Williams, "Britain's ruling elites now exercise power with a shameless rapacity," *The Guardian* (Tuesday, April 11, 2006), 25.
13 Hywel Williams, "Britain's ruling elites."
14 Frantz Fanon, *The Wretched of the Earth*, trans. Constance Farrington (New York: Grove Press, 1963); pp. 52–3.
15 Neil Lazarus, *Resistance in Postcolonial African Fiction* (New Haven, CT: Yale University Press, 1990).

16 Ngũgĩ wa Thiong'o, *Petals of Blood* (New York: Penguin, 1991). All page numbers appear in the main text.

17 Earl Lovelace, *The Dragon Can't Dance* (London: Faber, 1998), p. 131. First published 1979.

18 Rohinton Mistry, *A Fine Balance* (London: Faber and Faber, 1996). All page numbers appear in the main text.

19 Partha Chatterjee, *The Politics of the Governed* (New York: Columbia University Press, 2006), p. 143.

20 The best-known example in film is Danny Boyle's blockbuster *Slumdog Millionaire* (2008) and the best-selling novel *One Night @ the Call Centre* (2005) by Chetan Bhagat.

21 Davis, *Planet of Slums* (London: Verso, 2006); p. 19.

22 Mike Davis, "The Urbanization of Empire: Megacities and the Laws of Chaos," *Social Text* 81, 22. 4 (2004), p. 11.

23 Davis, "The Urbanization of Empire," p. 12.

24 To this end we can refer to Anthony King's argument that in a sense all cities are world cities now, subject to the vagaries of global capitalism, its tense negotiations with nation states and local cultures. See his *Urbanism, Colonialism, and the World Economy* (London: Routledge, 1990), p. 82.

25 Chatterjee, *The Politics of the Governed*, p. 144.

26 Aravind Adiga, *The White Tiger* (London: Atlantic Books, 2009). All page references to be provided in the main text.

27 Sanjay Subrahmanyam, "Diary: Another Booker Flop," *London Review of Books* 30.21, (2008), pp. 42–3.

28 Chris Abani, *Graceland* (New York: Picador, 2004). All page references to be provided in the main text.

29 See AbdouMaliq Simone, *For the City Yet to Come: Changing African Life in Four Cities* (Durham, NC: Duke University Press, 2004), p. 1.

30 Simone, *For the City*, p. 1.

31 Patrick Chamoiseau, *Texaco: A Novel* (Vintage, 1998). All page references to be provided in the main text.

32 Ashley Dawson, "Squatters, Space, and Belonging in the Underdeveloped City," *Social Text* 81, 22.4 (2004), p. 19.

12

ROBERT ZACHARIAS
University of Waterloo

Space and the Postcolonial Novel

> Is it conceivable that the exercise of hegemony might leave space
> untouched?
>
> Henri Lefebvre[1]

Much has been made about a broad-based "spatial turn" that is said to have
reoriented the Humanities and Social Sciences over the past several decades,
but scholars of postcolonialism have long argued that the geographic, linguistic, and cultural displacements that characterize the colonial experience
mean that their field has always already been about space. In a new collection dedicated to unpacking what they deem "the inherent spatiality of
postcolonial studies," for example, Andrew Teverson and Sara Upstone
insist "space in all its forms" is "integral to the postcolonial experience."[2]
Edward Said begins his foundational study *Culture and Imperialism* by
insisting that no one is ever "outside or beyond geography," nor are they
ever free of "the struggle over geography,"[3] while Bill Ashcroft, Gareth
Griffiths, and Helen Tiffin name "place and displacement" as the primary
concerns through which "the special post-colonial crisis of identity comes
into being."[4] And yet while it is true that the sweeping geographies and
myriad displacements of colonial history mean that postcolonialism is
unavoidably concerned with space, scholars have only recently begun to
consider the underlying assumptions and broader implications of spatiality
in the postcolonial context, especially where it is crossed with concerns
about space in literary texts.

This chapter draws on work from the broader spatial turn to consider the
form and function of space in postcolonial theory and fiction. What are the
assumptions that have underpinned the "inherent spatiality" of postcolonial
studies to date? What does it mean to speak about space in a field that,
indebted as it is to anticolonial nationalism, long assumed the nation-state to
be the natural scale of critique? How is contemporary postcolonialism
responding to the shifting borders of the broader critical discourse, which
continue to bend toward the trans- or postnational? How do time and space
interact in the postcolonial context, and what are the politics driving a

renewed emphasis on space? And how might a consideration of the field's spatiality help us to better understand postcolonial novels?

Paris, Algeria, and the Epoch of Space

One place to begin a conversation about postcolonial space is in Paris, in March of 1967, where Michel Foucault presented an enigmatic but influential lecture entitled "Of Other Spaces." Arguing that history had been the "great obsession of the nineteenth century," Foucault announced that the "present epoch" is "above all the epoch of space."[5] Anticipating the work of Henri Lefebvre, he suggested "we do not live in a kind of void, in which we could place individuals and things," but rather in "a set of relations that delineates sites which are irreducible to one another."[6] In a gesture typical of his genealogical approach, Foucault insisted that the "space which today appears to form the horizon of our concerns . . . itself has a history,"[7] which he briefly traced from the Middle Ages through Galileo to Bachelard. He then turned his attention to "heterotopias," or those places that, being both real and mythic, "are something like counter-sites" in which "all the other real sites . . . are simultaneously represented, contested, and inverted."[8]

Foucault's famous lecture, however, has a history of its own. Left unpublished until after his death in 1984, "Of Other Spaces" has been much cited as a progenitor of the broader spatial turn. But it is also a useful case study for the positioning of colonialism within that turn. In the essay's little-discussed conclusion, Foucault briefly addresses colonies as a "general organization of territorial space." Some colonies, he suggests, can be understood as "heterotopias," in that they "create a space that is other, another real space, as perfect, as meticulous, as well arranged as ours is messy, ill-constructed, and jumbled."[9] In describing colonies as soothing outposts of order, Foucault is, of course, addressing the role that the idea of the colony plays in the colonizers' imagination. And yet nowhere does he explicitly acknowledge how thoroughly this portrait of colonial space is structured by a singular geopolitical perspective, or how the conceptualization of the colonies as an "other" space effectively positions the colonizer's space as normative.

At the time of Foucault's lecture, in 1967, France was just five years removed from having lost a brutal decolonization war in Algeria that some describe as the "very archetype of the mid-twentieth-century struggle to end Western colonialism."[10] It was in the midst of this very war, in fact, that Frantz Fanon published *The Wretched of the Earth,* anticipating Foucault's spatial emphasis by setting himself the task of "penetrating [the] geographical configuration" of colonialism.[11] Describing the colonized sector as "a world with no space," Fanon argued passionately for the need to "blow the colonial world to smithereens."[12] At the same time, Foucault's fellow Frenchman Jean-Paul Sartre addressed the Algerian battle at length, writing extensively about its implications for France. "This is the age of the boomerang," Sartre warned.[13] "Terror has left Africa to settle here."[14]

Gayatri Chakravorty Spivak has rightfully noted that the questions raised by the decolonization of Algeria would be impossible for the French to ignore even decades later,[15] yet Foucault managed to do just that working in its immediate shadow. As Robert Young writes, "Foucault had a lot to say about power, but he was curiously circumspect about the ways in which it has operated in the arenas of race and colonialism."[16] Indeed, when set alongside Fanon and Sartre's contemporaneous descriptions of colonial space, the absence of Algeria in Foucault's lecture can be seen as reflecting what Fanon called the larger "geographical configuration" of colonial thought. It was the underlying politics of such configurations that would lead Said to contrast Fanon and Foucault and conclude that the latter was not merely guilty of "ignoring the imperial context of his own theories," but that his thought had come to "represent an irresistible colonizing movement."[17] In a parallel argument, Spivak suggests that "Foucault is a brilliant thinker of power-in-spacing, but the awareness of the topographical reinscription of imperialism does not inform his presuppositions." As such, she continues, his work "produces a miniature version of the imperial project."[18] Such damning critiques of Foucault's broader oeuvre appear particularly pointed when returning to his 1967 lecture: looking for examples of colonial space, Foucault turned not to France's disastrous and still-smoldering escapades in North Africa but to the Puritan colonies of British North America and the Jesuit colonies of Spanish South America, several centuries earlier. The former, he wrote, were "absolutely perfect other places"; the latter, "marvellous, absolutely regulated colonies in which human perfection was effectively achieved."[19] Of Algeria, he wrote nothing at all.

What does all this tell us about space in the postcolonial novel? My point here is not simply that Foucault's work, so central to postcolonial literary critics, can be read as complicit with a certain colonial logic, although this is true. Rather, I mean to stress that unpacking the spatiality of postcolonial fiction requires a close attention to the ways in which colonial space is conceptualized not only in the novels themselves, but also in the critical genealogy upon which we draw as engaged readers. What is more, I want to suggest that the shifting conceptions of colonial space in the earlier discussion is indicative of much of the broader field of postcolonial studies. With Ella Shohat, I recognize that the growth of postcolonial scholarship has produced a "disorientating [... and] dubious spatiality," encompassing an impossibly broad range of geopolitical locations and histories and effacing a host of "critical differences" in the process[20] – differences that make, say, the Jesuit colonies in Spanish South America of the seventeenth century fundamentally different from the French colonies in North Africa of the twentieth. And yet as necessary as it is to consider the differences not only between given colonial locations but also between types of colonialism (including administrative arrangements, settler colonialism, post-plantation economies, and so on[21]), the "dubious spatiality" of postcolonial studies is not simply or solely a matter of historical specificity. That is, among the reasons why Foucault and Fanon turn their sights to such different colonial spaces is, surely, that they are engaging space itself in fundamentally different ways. As such, we need to attend more closely not only to the specific locations of colonial history, but also to the broader spatial assumptions underlying our work, to better understand what it is that we are talking about when we are talking about colonial space.

Postcolonial Space: Real or Imagined

A second place one could begin a consideration of colonial space is on an English estate in Northampton in the early nineteenth century, where a young woman named Fanny Price has come to live with her wealthy relatives, the Bertrams. As Edward Said has pointed out in his influential reading of Jane Austen's *Mansfield Park*, the wealth and glamour of the Bertrams' estate, which dominates the text, can be traced back to slave labor on the family's plantation in Antigua. The novel's direct references to the plantation are limited to a handful of offhand remarks, but it is precisely in such passing references, Said insists, that such texts "include, even as they repress" the reality of colonialism.[22] Bertram's English estate, in this sense, is built on Caribbean soil.

Said's influential contrapuntal approach reads canonical colonial texts to understand what he called the "social space" that facilitated the broader colonial project, beneath which could be located "the actual geographical underpinnings" of colonialism.[23] Even as Said was criticized for what some saw as his overestimation of the role of culture and literary fiction in colonial history, then, his understanding of colonialism as consisting of "actual contests over land and the land's people" suggests that his ultimate concern was, as he put it, a "geographical inquiry into historical experience."[24] Indeed, in his contrasting of "actual geographi[es]" and "actual contests" against their ideological representations, Said's work arguably relies on a geography that is understood to be outside of, or at least prior to, imagined space.[25]

While Said focused on exposing the colonial underpinnings of canonical texts, many postcolonial novelists undertook a parallel project of writing the colonial experience back into those same imperial narratives. Some of the best-known postcolonial novels are nationalizing narratives that respond directly to colonial narratives, through which the Empire can be understood as writing back to the center.[26] Jean Rhys's *Wide Sargasso Sea*, for example, quite literally inscribes the Caribbean experience into British cultural history by writing the story of Antoinette, the creole woman denigrated as Bertha in Charlotte Brontë's *Jane Eyre* (a rewriting canonized in postcolonial literary criticism by Spivak through her influential essay "Three Women's Texts and a Critique of Imperialism"). Similarly, J. M. Coetzee's *Foe* inserts a new character into the plot of Daniel Defoe's *Robinson Crusoe* to highlight the limitations of the original novel's representation of colonial power, while Chinua Achebe's decision to name his account of colonial encounter *Things Fall Apart* repurposes Yeats's canonical poem into a critique of British colonialism. Such novels are but the most overt examples of postcolonial counterdiscourse, texts that, as Stephen Slemon writes, "'read' and contest the social 'text' of colonialism," and seek to "contest and subvert colonialist appropriation."[27]

Indeed, while Said was set on identifying the "actual" colonial world that sat repressed beneath Jane Austen's *Mansfield Park*, one could just as easily begin a consideration of postcolonial space in the fictional "bastard world" of V. S. Naipaul's novel *The Mimic Men*.[28] Naipaul's novel is set in Isabella, an imagined Caribbean island moving through the various stages of decolonization. Midway through the novel, the young Ralph Singh drives through the foothills outside the city, passing racially and ethnically segregated villages resulting from the island's colonial history, including the "Negro areas," the "Indian areas," the "mulatto villages," and so on; "the Caribs," meanwhile, "had been absorbed and had simply ceased to be." "[I]t was like being in an area of legend," Singh explains, where "the rise and fall and extinction of peoples, a concept so big and alarming, was concrete and close."[29] Uninterested in the specifics of "actual" history but deeply invested in the past, Naipaul's account of an imagined colonialized island displays the postcolonial spatialization of history, in which the various stages of Caribbean colonialism – of conquest, genocide, slavery, indenture, hybridization, and independence – are manifested in the "little bastard world" that is Isabella.[30]

Ultimately, however, Naipaul is more interested in the contours of colonial subjectivity than he is in colonial landscapes. *The Mimic Men* explores how colonial subjects, alienated from their own culture and landscape, come to internalize the colonial power structure. It is Naipaul's exploration of colonialism as a condition of subjectivity, for example, that draws Homi Bhabha to the novel as part of his analysis of colonial mimicry. Describing the imperial dream of replicating a single culture across the globe in representational terms as a "flawed colonial mimesis,"[31] Bhabha argues that the result is instead a type of colonial mimicry. Rather than accurately replicating the colonizer, this mimicry produces a subject "that is almost the same, but not quite," a threatening "comedic turn from the high ideals of the colonial imagination" that ultimately destabilizes the colonial discourse by revealing its underlying ambivalence.[32] Indeed, Naipaul's narrator is self-consciously but unflaggingly colonial, affecting the mannerisms and habits of the British even as he is moving the country toward formal independence. Throughout, however, he believes both the island and his own life to be but pale imitations of the "reality" that is the imperial center. "We pretended to be real," Singh explains, "to be learning, to be preparing ourselves for life, we mimic men of the New World."[33]

In my reading, the cynicism of Naipaul's portrait of Singh ultimately undermines Bhabha's brief use of the novel as an example of the destabilizing force of mimicry. In fact, while Singh does come to recognize the artificiality of the colonial center, his political career strikes me as an uncanny portrait of what Fanon called the "national bourgeoisie" of postcolonial countries, that administrative class of colonial politicians which "mimics the Western bourgeoisie in its negative and decadent aspects,"[34] which "never stops calling for the nationalization of the economy,"[35] but which ultimately "turns its country virtually into a bordello for Europe."[36] Nonetheless, Bhabha's reading of Naipaul's complex portrait of Ralph Singh exemplifies a broader critical shift in postcolonial studies away from direct considerations of concrete geographic space. Colonial subjectivity outlives the legal structure of the colonial project, and for Bhabha – as for many others – subjectivity itself has become the central "space" of the postcolonial novel.

I have briefly contrasted Austen's and Naipaul's novels to demonstrate two approaches to (post)colonial space, but in fact it is Said's and Bhabha's reading practices that better exemplify a broad division in the spatial assumptions of postcolonial studies. In Edward Soja's account of the field, for example, this division consists of work that "tends to sublimate its overtly spatial emphasis, eschews metaphorical flair, and strives for solid materialist exposition of real politics and oppression," and work that "thrives on spatial metaphors like mapping, location, cartography, and landscape, and excels at literate textual analysis."[37] In a parallel argument,

Graham Huggan suggests that an unacknowledged split between conceptual and concrete understandings of colonial space has resulted in a general confusion of postcolonial spatiality, with those advocating historical projects of recuperation speaking past those searching for new ways of conceptualizing hybrid postcolonial identities.[38] Although the extent of the field's binary division is easy to overstate,[39] it is true that postcolonial scholars have rarely engaged the underlying spatiality of their arguments with sufficient intentionality to prevent an implicit conceptual/material split from undermining the field.

In his seminal study *The Production of Space*, Henri Lefebvre describes a similar confusion across the humanities. Lamenting philosophers' incessant but careless invocations of spatial metaphors, tropes, and concerns, Lefebvre notes readers are now "confronted by an indefinite multitude of spaces, each one piled upon, or perhaps contained within, the next: geographical, economic, demographic, sociological, ecological, political, commercial, national, continental [... along with] nature's (physical) space, the space of (energy) flows, and so on."[40] Seeking a "unitary" understanding of spatiality, Lefebvre insists that "(social) space is a (social) product,"[41] a fact concealed, he suggests, by two common and reciprocal illusions: the "illusion of opacity," which holds that space is fully knowable in its materiality, as nature itself; and the "illusion of transparency," which holds that space is a mental construct, and therefore fully knowable "through the mental eye which illuminates whatever it contemplates."[42] Clearly anticipating postcolonialism's division into "concrete" and "conceptual" engagements with space, Lefebvre insists space is neither a concrete, preexisting reality, nor a simple projection of the mind, but rather a *"product* to be used, to be consumed, [as well as] a *means of production."*[43] Lefebvre was principally concerned with the production of space in modern capitalism, and his theorization of space is notoriously inconsistent – even Soja, a deep admirer of Lefebvre, calls *The Production of Space* "a bewildering book, filled with ... perplexing inconsistencies and apparent self-contradictions."[44] Nonetheless, his primary call to attend to the agency and complexity of space as a lived, social product remains a central insight in the modern spatial turn, and one which has only recently been intentionally brought to bear on postcolonial studies. As Alexander Moore argues, the "neat divide between 'real space' and 'social space'" has meant "postcolonial theory by and large ignores the complex *production* of space."[45]

Before moving on to consider the production of postcolonial space, its relationship to colonial time, and the field's tendency to rely on the nation for both its temporal and spatial trajectories, however, it is important to note the space of the postcolonial novel is further complicated by an ongoing debate about the spatial and temporal *formal* aspects of novels and narrative themselves. Several prominent thinkers on narrative, for example, including Paul Ricoeur and Peter Brooks, have argued that narratives are fundamentally temporal in their structure: for Ricoeur, this temporality is founded on narrative's function in linking events through time; Brooks expands this to consider how readers spend time with a text. Hayden White, Homi Bhabha, and Benedict Anderson, meanwhile, have examined the ideological politics of narrative's temporality, the latter two drawing on Walter Benjamin to emphasize the narrative production of "homogeneous empty time" to imagine a coherent community out of the state's diverse population. Even Joseph Frank's well-known discussion of spatiality in modern literature begins with the assumption that literature, as a narrative form, is "naturally temporal" or "a time-art."[46] While Frank goes on to suggest that the abstraction common in modern literature reaches toward spatiality (in its attempt to reveal everything at once), others have read narrative as being fundamentally spatial. Unsurprisingly, perhaps, Said has insisted that narrative is "principally" a spatial rather than temporal notion, in that only in narrative is there "the possibility of producing a territorial object, if you like, or a territorial location."[47] Similarly, Michel de Certeau argues that "narrative structures have the status of spatial syntaxes," for they "regulate changes in space ... made by stories in the form of places put in linear or interlaced series."[48]

My point in this too-brief survey is not to reach toward anything like a definitive claim on the formal spatiality of narrative or the novel, of course, or even to fully take narrative spatiality into account for the purposes of this essay. Rather, I simply mean to flag the formal elements of fiction as yet another concern, to note that the debate around the nature of postcolonial space – whether it is concrete, conceptual, or something else altogether – is further complicated by the debate that continues to swirl around the spatiality of novels and of narrative itself.

Imperial Time and Colonial Space

Yet another place one could begin a conversation about postcolonial space is in the unnamed outpost at the edge of an unnamed empire in J. M. Coetzee's novel *Waiting for the Barbarians*, where an unnamed magistrate considers his complicity in the horrors of imperialism. Shaken by the arrival of a colonel from the capital who has tortured prisoners held in the outpost's granary, the magistrate's thoughts turn to the ruins he has had excavated from a set of nearby dunes. Admitting he once dreamt of receiving some omen of their former use – Might this ruin be built on the ruins of yet another fort from a former empire, he wondered, so that deep beneath him lies "the head of a magistrate like [him]self"?[49] – the magistrate now declares himself cured of such embarrassing romanticism:

> The space about us here is merely space, no meaner or grander than the space above the shacks and tenements and temples and offices of the capital. Space is space, life is life, everywhere the same. But as for me, sustained by the toil of others, lacking civilized vices with which to fill my leisure, I pamper my melancholy and try to find in the vacuousness of the desert a special historical poignancy. Vain, idle, misguided! How fortunate that no one sees me![50]

Coetzee has been criticized for refusing to locate the novel in a recognizable colonial context, and, as a consequence, losing what one reviewer calls the "urgency that a specified historical place and time may provide."[51] Part of this urgency returns through the critical conversation that surrounds the text, which has speculated on historical analogues for Coetzee's outpost. But surely much of this immediacy is being sacrificed intentionally, by an author who aims to explore a less concrete model of colonial space than is available when engaging a specific "place and time" – to consider, that is, whether the magistrate is right to be embarrassed of his efforts to contemplate the place on which the outpost sits, or if it is true that "space is space ... everywhere the same."

The magistrate's dismissal of colonial space as unworthy of his concern does not suggest, of course, that his Empire no longer interested in controlling the territory. To the contrary, it is precisely through the rejection of the specificity of the outpost that the magistrate works to justify the Empire's efforts to reassert its control. After all, it is only *after* the colonel tortures and maims the magistrate's prisoners, forcing the magistrate to concede the full extent of his complicity in the imperial project, that he gives up on his attempt to excavate the ruins. Coetzee reveals his narrator's sudden disinterest in spatial matters as central to the operation of empire, which rationalizes its geographic expansion in temporal terms. "Empire has created the time of history," the magistrate concludes near the end of the novel. "Empire has located its existence ... in the jagged time of rise and fall, of beginning and end, of catastrophe."[52] As David Attwell writes, Coetzee undertakes an "objectification and demystification of History" – note the capital H – showing it to be "a structure of ideas ... in the hands of Empire."[53] In the novel's final pages, as the magistrate attempts to justify his role in the brutal subjugation of the region, he once again turns to temporality. "I wanted to live outside the history that Empire imposes on its subjects, even its lost subjects," he writes. "I never wished it for the barbarians that they should have the history of Empire laid upon them."[54]

Although there is a sense in which it is obviously true to say that colonialism is always "about space," Coetzee's novel is a useful reminder that it is a mistake to assume that colonial projects can understood in exclusively in spatial terms. As Sara Upstone writes, "it is not a coincidence that the time in which history comes to overshadow space – the nineteenth century – is also the height of empire and spatial violence."[55] This, in fact, is the grounding assumption of Foucault's "Of Other Spaces," which begins by taking it for granted that the "great obsession of the nineteenth century was, as we know, history."[56] In the privileging of time over space that dominated the colonial period, geography itself was understood through the lens of a teleological temporality that worked to justify the expansion of empire as the forward march of civilization. Contrary to the magistrate's declaration that "space is space," then, as Anne McClintock insists,

> in colonial discourse, *space is time*, and history is shaped around two, neces-
> sary movements: the "progress" forward of humanity from slouching depriv-
> ation to erect, enlightened reason. The other movement presents the reverse:
> regression backwards from (white, male) adulthood to a primordial, black
> "degeneracy" usually incarnated in women.[57]

In this understanding of the colonial imagination, the spread of empire is not focused on the expansion of territory and wealth at all, but rather about those "savage wars of peace" that Kipling christened the "White Man's Burden": noble efforts to drag the "new-caught, sullen peoples, / Half devil and half child" reluctantly "to the light."[58] This is the logic through which entire continents get temporalized as "New" and "Old," and through which the spatial binaries of colonialism – center/periphery, metropole/colony, north/south, First World/Third World, and so on – are naturalized by their emplotment along a linear narrative of progress, geographies crushed into colonies by having "the history of Empire laid upon them."

In its refusal of the specificity of a recognizable geopolitical referent but insistence on the geographic particularity of mimetic realism, Coetzee's novel explores colonial space as a concept, considering, we might say, space *as* place, investigating the former with a care usually reserved for the latter. In fact, one way of understanding the colonial temporalization of space is to consider the distinction between these two related concepts, wherein *place* is understood as a specific, meaningful location, imbued with history, and *space* is understood as abstract, empty, and set outside of history.[59] In the colonial imagination, this understanding of space is most vividly represented in the colonial-era maps with empty spaces, or phrases such as "here be monsters" inscribed where Europeans had yet to venture, in contrast with the heavily detailed "places" of the colonial center. It is precisely this concept of empty space that Marlow describes in Conrad's *Heart of Darkness* as part of his youthful "passion for maps": of all the "blank spaces on the earth,"

Marlow declares, none was more inviting than the Congo, "the biggest, the most blank" space of them all. While explicitly spatial, the notion of "blank spaces" plots space onto a historical timeline via the trope of "emptiness" that is at once the product of the colonial imagination and its precursor, priming the location for the colonial encounter. Marlow's description of the Congo as the "most" blank signals the way that even emptiness itself is structured along colonial lines: rather than simple reflections of the limits of geographic knowledge, these "empty spaces" are better understood to be rendering those lands as *terra nullius* – that is, lands-to-be colonized – and thus brought into the realm of history proper.[60] Far from it being true that "space is space, everywhere the same," as the magistrate insists, the conceptualization of abstract space is itself complicit in a colonial project that requires the fiction of empty sameness for its operation.

It is against the aggressive temporalizing of imperial history that the postcolonial emphasis on space is routinely imagined as constituting a necessary response. An emphasis on space was pressing, this argument runs, as a corrective to the longstanding effacement of spatial concerns in favor of the grand narratives of time and history, in which, as Robert Tally Jr. writes, "space appeared to matter only as the location where historical events unfolded."[61] And yet even as postcolonial critics invested in the spatial turn routinely set space against time, McClintock's insistence that "space is time" in colonial discourse offers a welcome warning against overemphasizing the spatial elements of the field at the cost of the temporal. Indeed, to the extent that the *post* in *post*colonial is to be understood in historical terms, the field is arguably just as invested in a temporal frame as it is a spatial one. As McClintock goes on to insist, "the extent that the field has set itself up against this imperial idea of linear time" is the extent to which it will be "haunted by the very figure of linear 'development' that it sets out to dismantle."[62] While this has been reason enough for some critics to set the postcolonial aside altogether,[63] there is no need to understand postcolonialism's temporality solely in such tautological terms. Indeed, as even my brief reading of Coetzee's novel demonstrates, a fuller consideration of the post-colonial must consider the ways in which the temporal and spatial are mutually implicated in each other, and insist upon a geographic simultaneity that fractures the monologic foundations of imperial history and recuperates the various "othered" spaces that have been set, conceptually and literally, outside of the narrative of progress.

If the "bastard world" of *The Mimic Men* demonstrates the spatialization of postcolonial history, *Waiting for the Barbarians* demonstrates the aggressive temporalization of colonial space. Just as Coetzee promises in his novel's title, the violent management of the local population in the unnamed outpost shows the expansion of empire to be a spatial project masquerading as a temporal process. Far from the heart of the empire but tethered to its myopic vision, the imperialists project their fears and desires alike onto the lives and landscapes of others, clinging to "the time of history" that produces, rather than reveals, a deeply colonial space and the various barbarians that occupy it.

The Nation and/as Postcolonial Space

A fifth place that one could begin an investigation of postcolonial space is on the west coast of India, at the stroke of midnight on August 15, 1947. "I was born in Bombay ... once upon a time," begins Salman Rushdie's *Midnight's Children*, briefly setting aside time before conceding its importance. "No, that won't do, there's no getting away from the date," it continues. "At the precise instant of India's arrival at independence, I tumbled forth into the world ... I had been mysteriously handcuffed to history, my destinies indissolubly chained to those of my country."[64] Where Coetzee's novel engages colonial space in the abstract and Naipaul's novel is set on a fictional island, Rushdie's seminal novel – like Ngũgĩ wa Thiong'o's *Grain of Wheat*, M. G. Vassanji's *In-Between World of Vikram Lall*, and innumerable other postcolonial novels – takes its ironic-yet-earnest focus on the birth of a newly independent postcolonial nation-state. Where some such texts are relatively straightforward in their celebration of a nation's independence, *Midnight's Children* is exemplary of the broader field's complex engagement with the nation-state. Saleem Sinai's mystical ability to telepathically communicate with the one thousand and one other children born at the strike of India's independence shows utopian possibilities initially projected onto the nation, but this celebration is deeply undermined as the novel progresses. Not only does India's independence begin with its partition from Pakistan, Rushdie emphasizes the violence and injustices that attend the construction of the state – including the declaration of a state of Emergency and the clearing of the slums – and the children scatter and fight, their idealized community fracturing and their telepathic powers dissipating. And yet the novel's celebration of India remains: as Neil Ten Kortenaar writes, *Midnight's Children* "explodes the notion of the nation having a stable identity and a single history," but nonetheless "invites a skeptical, provisional faith in the nation that it has exploded."[65]

Although I am late in this essay in coming to the nation-state, the "nationalist writing" of the decolonizing post-1945 world is so central to the field that, according to Elleke Boehmer, it "is usually considered paradigmatic of the postcolonial" itself.[66] Early in the field, colonialism was widely recognized as operating at both the political and the cultural level, and literature produced in newly independent nations was explicitly understood as a "front for nationalist mobilization," in the belief that "a people's identity, though long suppressed, lay embedded in its cultural origins and was recoverable intact, unadulterated by the depredations of colonialism."[67] Recovering an "unadulterated" pre-colonial identity through literature was complicated, however, by the fact that many of these nations were themselves the bureaucratic constructs of colonial projects, but also by the fact that the ostensibly "decolonizing" texts were often written in the colonizer's language. Postcolonial scholarship has been famously split over the question of language: Chinua Achebe argued it was not only possible but also necessary to write an authentically "African" novel in English, for example, but Ngũgĩ wa Thiong'o countered that rejection of English itself was part of the decolonization process, as was the recuperation of native languages in literary form.[68] Writing of the intersection of race and gender in postcolonial studies, Audre Lorde extended this argument by insisting that "the master's tools will never dismantle the master's house," and suggesting that "when the tools of a racist patriarchy are used to examine the fruits of that same patriarchy ... only the most narrow perimeters of change are possible."[69]

The field's emphasis shifted in the early 1990s, however, when Homi Bhabha drew on Benedict Anderson to theorize nations as "imagined communities" that sought to suppress cultural differences in the construction of oppressively homogenizing narratives, rather than as the natural culmination of decolonization movements. In this context, the mixing of colonial and native culture was no longer understood as a betrayal of an "authentic" precolonial identity, but rather an unavoidable and powerful extension of the processes of hybridization that always constitute the construction of culture. And yet even where scholars drawing on Bhabha's theories of hybridity and the "third space" worked to interrupt what he called the "narration of the nation," the field largely continued to emphasize the nation-state as the natural scale for the postcolonial – now simply as its object of critique, or allegorical engagement.[70] To the extent that much of the field remains, as Ato Quayson has suggested, "in the thrall to extant forms of methodological nationalism," the "space" of postcolonial literary studies remains the nation-state.[71]

Unsurprisingly, this enduring emphasis on the nation has lead some to question postcolonialism's relevance in a rapidly globalizing world. As early as 2000, Michael Hardt and Antonio Negri warned that postcolonial scholars are "pushing against an empty door," unwitting accomplices of the neoliberal project restructuring the globe though their offering of anti-nationalist critiques that are parallel to, rather than in conflict with, the new cultural dominant of postnational capital.[72] And indeed, even as a great deal of postcolonial fiction is celebrated as – and thus recuperated into the service of – national literary traditions, much of it seems to demand trans- or postnational approaches. Literature of the Black Atlantic, to take a single but key example, routinely inscribes the full transatlantic history of the slave trade within its narratives, whether tracing that route in their entirety (such as in Lawrence Hill's *Book of Negroes*), or remaining rooted in the colonial metropoles while actively reflecting the consequences of their broader imperial geography (such as in Zadie Smith's *White Teeth*). Accordingly, postcolonial scholarship has sought to move beyond the nation by working at different registers of space, most often at scales that are larger than the nation (including the transnational, diasporic, cosmopolitan, hemispheric, global, Black Atlantic), but also at scales that emphasize the local (including the regional, the urban, the glocal, border studies)[73] – and, increasingly, indigenous and First Nations.[74] At the same time, however, the nation remains stubbornly relevant despite scholars' postnational predictions. Whether as a valued model for resisting broader sovereignty claims or as a key regulatory scale in the ascension of transnational capital, whether as a reinvigorated bulwark in a time of heightened economic and security concerns or as an imagined retreat from the increasingly multicultural West, the nation endures, to the point that it has become "practically axiomatic that obituaries of the nation are premature."[75] In this expanded context, postcolonialism's longstanding engagement with the nation may ultimately prove less a harbinger of the field's obsolescence than a key aspect of its ongoing relevance.

Whatever the scale at which postcolonialism operates, the majority of work in the field has engaged space either through the ideological representations of concrete histories of oppression, or as a means of understanding the psychological impact of colonialism and conceptualizing alternative models of identity. The most recent work in the field, however, is interested in overcoming the field's concrete/conceptual spatial divide to consider how postcolonial space – of whatever kind – is produced in the first place.

Real-and-Imaginary Spaces

Another place we could begin a consideration of postcolonial space is in the Evil Forest of Chinua Achebe's *Things Fall Apart*. Much of the novel examines the lives and cultures that preceded colonial contact, and, like much of Achebe's work, it has been "popularly received for [its] representation of an early African nationalist tradition that repudiates imperialist and colonialist ideology."[76] Rather than simply accepting *Things Fall Apart* as a straightforward mimetic assertion of African nationalism, however, we might pause to consider the contest over colonial space that occurs midway through the novel. When newly arrived Christian missionaries request land to build a church in the village of Mbanta, the local leaders happily offer the growing religious community "as much of the Evil Forest as they cared to take." Each clan had its Evil Forest, the narrator explains, a place that was "alive with sinister forces and powers of darkness," and the leaders had offered this land as a "battlefield" to test the missionaries' "boast about victory over death." To their surprise, however, the missionaries not only accept the land, but go on to build their church in the forest without suffering any retribution from the forces of darkness, a lack of punishment that is interpreted as evidence of missionaries' "unbelievable power."[77]

How are we to understand this space? On the one hand, what is at stake here is clearly a specific, concrete location, a literal *place* that is the beginning for a process that will culminate in the wider area's colonization. On the other hand, what makes it possible for the missionaries to build on that particular site, and what subsequently imbues that building with the power that will facilitate the colonial project, are competing conceptualizations of that space. To emphasize either the concrete or the imaginary aspects of this space at the expense of the other is to fall into what Lefebvre identified as the illusions of opacity or transparency, and to miss the social production of the space itself. Building on Lefebvre's work, Soja names the overemphasis on the "material world" as a "Firstspace perspective," and the overemphasis on interpreting the "imagined" representations of material reality as a "Secondspace perspective." What is urgently needed, he argues, is a "Thirdspace perspective," one that attends simultaneously to the "real-and-imagined" nature of lived social space.[78]

In Soja's terms, the missionaries of Achebe's novel transgress the taboos surrounding the Evil Forest with impunity because they hold to an entirely different understanding of the lived social space itself. The point, emphatically, is not that missionaries are proved "right" in their demystification of the Evil Forest; after all, they promptly re-sacralize the location, constructing a Christian church on the site. Nor is it particularly important that the competing social visions of the forest are routed through religion. (This is Foucault's error in "Of Other Spaces," where he assumes that the declaration of some spaces as "sacred" is what *others* them from the secular spaces that can be understood as natural, or normative.) Much as scholars have recognized the political assumptions behind the argument that the widespread de-sacralization of temporality in the eighteenth century resulted in a universal, homogeneous, and empty time,[79] the de-sacralization of space does not result in an abstract empty space that is experienced equally around the globe. "Abstract space *is not* homogenous," as Lefebvre insists; "it simply *has* homogeneity as its goal."[80]

The key point, rather, is that while the missionaries in Achebe's text accept the offer to build in the Evil Forest because they reject the Igbo's sacralization of it and see it as "merely" natural space, even this very idea of "natural" is produced as part of the missionary/colonial project. As Soja reminds us, the space of "nature" is socially produced, an idea "filled with politics and ideology, with relations of production, and with the possibility of being significantly transformed."[81] Indeed, the missionary's understanding of the Evil Forest as being merely natural is deeply ideological, signifying the form of precolonial "emptiness" or "blankness" that we have already located in Conrad and Coetzee: space, that is, which actively anticipates the colonial encounter. In this context, it makes little sense to argue whether the Evil Forest of Achebe's novel is ultimately a "real" space or an "imagined" one – it is both *real and imagined*, and for this reason, its implications stretch well beyond the churchyard. Fittingly, the novel's final words reveal that the new District Commissioner has plans to write a history of the area with a deeply political name that will inscribe it onto both the colonial map and the linear narrative of historical progress: *The Pacification of the Primitive Tribes of the Lower Niger.*

If Foucault was looking to understand colonial spaces as heterotopias, which are "simultaneously represented, contested, and inverted,"[82] places which are "outside of all places, even though it may be possible to indicate their location in reality," which, like mirrors, show a reality that is "at once absolutely real ... and absolutely unreal,"[83] it is to places such as these that he could have turned. The Evil Forest, and the host of similar places that can be found across postcolonial fiction, are the "counter-sites" of postcolonialism, places where the spatial multiplicities of colonialism are most pressing and conflicted, and thus laid open toward the future.[84]

Conclusion

From the unnamed outpost in Coetzee's novel to the Algeria absent from Foucault's Paris lecture, from the partition of India in *Midnight's Children* to the birth of Isabella in *The Mimic Men*, from the Antiguan plantation in *Mansfield Park* to the Evil Forest of *Things Fall Apart*, I have tried to suggest something of the wide breadth of space in the postcolonial novel. If it is true that postcolonialism is a fundamentally spatial field of study, it is also true that it has more often been *of* space than *about* it. The conflation of the various aspects of space, place, and other related concepts has not only muddied the critical project of unpacking the legacies of colonialism, but has also arguably reflected the power dynamics of colonialism itself. That is because, for all its ostensible investment in order and compartmentalization, colonialism itself relied on the collapsing of spatial categories for its function. As Daniel Coleman writes in a related argument about "national-racial-ethnic terms" and literary studies, a certain sense of "genealogical sloppiness" is not a hindrance to the function of colonial space, but is "central to [its] operation."[85]

The proper response to such a generative sloppiness, I have argued, is to work to disaggregate its various forms and concerns without losing sight of the ways in which they operate together. While turning to literature further complicates this discussion by introducing questions about the spatiality of plot and narrative, the centrality of culture and the arts in the lived experience of social space has led many to see postcolonial literature as an invaluable site for the investigation of colonial space, as well as offering "transformative potential in producing alternative images of space and identity."[86] Importantly, the move from concrete and conceptual understandings of space in this essay through to the national, temporal, and ultimately social aspects is not meant to indicate a progression in the evolution of an argument, nor a climb up a hierarchical ladder of critical sophistication. Rather, my attempt to begin anew throughout is meant to model the broader simultaneity of spatial concerns that cannot be fully disaggregated, even as they should not be collapsed into each other.

In much the same way that McClintock rightly took the proliferation of *posts* in the theory in the 1980s as indicative of a "widespread, epochal crisis in the idea of linear, historical 'progress,'"[87] the proliferation of explicitly spatial critical paradigms that have arrived in contemporary theory in part as a consequence of this crisis of temporality – including diaspora, hemispheric, New South, the black Atlantic, transnational, glocal, rooted cosmopolitanism, and Third Space, as well as the spatial turn itself – can be said to reflect a widespread epochal crisis in the idea of space as a stable, empty container for history. The range of discourse about space *within* postcolonial criticism can be read as further reflecting this crisis, even as it indicates competing assumptions about the proper aims or methodology of the field.[88] "The challenge" today, as Quayson writes, is "how to assemble reading practices that allow us to read the rhetorical, the historical, and the spatial all at once."[89] Rather than strain toward a pure ground for postcolonial space, I hope to have suggested a more productive approach, which is to read these competing understandings of space not as reified locations of a reality that transcends their contradictory theorizations, but as active participants in a more complex spatiality that emerges through and across their intersections.

Acknowledgments

I gratefully acknowledge that this research was undertaken with the support of a Banting Postdoctoral Fellowship, held in the Department of English Language and Literature at the University of Waterloo, and in the productive offices of the Centre for Diaspora and Transnational Studies at the University of Toronto, where I am a Visiting Scholar. I would like to thank Dr. Ato Quayson for the invitation to write this chapter, and for valuable direction and feedback on early drafts.

Notes

1 Henri Lefebvre, *The Production of Space*, trans. Donald Nicholson-Smith (Malden, MA: Blackwell, 2012), p. 11.
2 Andrew Teverson and Sara Upstone, *Postcolonial Geographies: The Politics of Place in Contemporary Culture* (New York: Palgrave Macmillan, 2011), p. 6, 1.
3 Edward Said, *Culture and Imperialism* (New York: Vintage Books, 1994), p. 7.
4 Bill Ashcroft, Gareth Griffiths, and Helen Tiffin, *The Empire Writes Back: Theory and Practice in Postcolonial Literatures*, 2nd ed. (London: Routledge, 2002), p. 8.
5 Michel Foucault, "Of Other Spaces: Utopias and Heterotopias," in Neil Leach ed., *Rethinking Architecture: A Reader in Cultural Theory* (New York: Routledge) p. 330.
6 Ibid., p. 332.
7 Ibid., p. 330.
8 Ibid., p. 332.
9 Ibid., p. 337.
10 Todd Shepard, *The Invention of Decolonization: The Algerian War and the Remaking of France* (Ithaca, NY: Cornell University Press, 2006), p. 1.
11 Frantz Fanon, *The Wretched of the Earth*, trans. Richard Philcox (New York: Grove Press, 2004), p. 3. First published 1961.
12 Ibid., pp. 4, 6.
13 Jean-Paul Sartre, "Preface," trans. Richard Philcox, in Frantz Fanon, *The Wretched of the Earth* (New York: Grove Press, 2004), p. liv.
14 Ibid., pp. 1, lxi.
15 Gayatri Chakravorty Spivak, "Can the Subaltern Speak?," in Patrick Williams and Laura Chrisman eds., *Colonial Discourse and Post-Colonial Theory: A Reader* (New York: Columbia University Press, 1994), p. 84.
16 Robert J.C. Young, "Foucault on Race and Colonialism," *New Formations* (1995), p. 57. Stephen Legg is more direct, writing that Foucault's "silence on the colonial construction of European modernity and the mutual constitution of the 'metropole' and 'periphery' is astounding." Stephen Legg, "Beyond the European Province: Foucault and Postcolonialism," in Jeremy W. Crampton and Stuart Elden eds., *Space, Knowledge and Power: Foucault and Geography* (Burlington, VT: Ashgate, 2007), p. 265.
17 Said, *Culture and Imperialism* (London: Vintage), p. 278.
18 Spivak, pp. 85, 86.

19 Foucault, p. 8.
20 Ella Shohat, "Notes on the 'Post-Colonial,'" *Social Text* 31/32 (1992), pp. 103, 102.
21 Here I am drawing on Ato Quayson's essay "Periods versus Concepts: Space Making and the Question of Postcolonial Literary Inquiry," *PMLA* 127.2 (2012), p. 344.
22 Said, *Culture*, p. 93.
23 Ibid., p. 78.
24 Ibid., p. 7.
25 See Alexander Moore, "Postcolonial 'Textual Space': Towards an Approach," *SOAS Literary Review* 3 (2001), pp. 10–15. Edward Soja, however, considers Said's emphasis on "imaginative geographies" as an important precursor of his own work, suggesting that Said "enters Thirdspace through a side door." See Soja, *Thirdspace: Journeys to Los Angeles and Other Real-and-Imagined Places* (Malden, MA: Blackwell, 1996), p. 137.
26 I am gesturing, of course, to the Ashcroft, Griffiths, and Tiffin study.
27 Stephen Slemon, "Monuments of Empire: Allegory/Counter-Discourse/Post-Colonial Writing," *Kunapipi* 9.3 (1987), p. 11. See also Helen Tiffin, "Postcolonial Literatures and Counter-discourse," *Kunapipi* 9.3 (1987).
28 V.S. Naipaul, *The Mimic Men* (1967; New York: Vintage, 2001), p. 146.
29 Ibid.
30 Ibid.
31 Homi Bhabha, *The Location of Culture* (New York: Routledge, 2004), p. 125.
32 Ibid., p. 122.
33 Ibid., p. 175.
34 Fanon, *Wretched*, p. 101.
35 Ibid., p. 100.
36 Ibid., p. 102.
37 Edward Soja, "Foreword," in Andrew Teverson and Sara Upstone eds., *Postcolonial Geographies* (New York: Palgrave Macmillan, 2011), p. x.
38 Graham Huggan, *Interdisciplinary Measures: Literature and the Future of Postcolonial Studies* (Liverpool: Liverpool University Press, 2008).
39 Bhabha's "third space," Mary Louise Pratt's "contact zone," and Said's emphasis of the reciprocity of culture and imperialism are just three of the best-known examples of postcolonial scholarship that has, at very least, intentionally aimed to move beyond such reductive thinking.
40 Lefebvre, *Production*, p. 8.
41 Ibid., p. 26.
42 Ibid., p. 28.
43 Ibid., p. 85.
44 Soja, *Thirdspace*, p. 8.
45 Moore, "Postcolonial 'Textual Space,'" p. 4. Moore's use of "social space" here picks up on Said's use of the term, but should not be confused with Lefebvre's use of the same term.
46 Joseph Frank, "Spatial Form in Modern Literature: An Essay in Two Parts," *The Swanee Review* (1945), pp. 651, 649.
47 Edward Said, interviewed by W.J.T. Mitchell, "The Panic of the Visual: A Conversation with Edward W. Said," *Boundary 2* 25.2 (1998), pp. 42–50.

48 Michel de Certeau, *The Practice of Everyday Life*, trans. Steven F. Rendell (Los Angeles: University of California Press, 1988), p. 115.

49 J.M. Coetzee, *Waiting for the Barbarians* (London: Random House, 2004), p. 16.

50 Ibid., pp. 17–18.

51 Irving Howe, "Stark Political Fable of South Africa," The *New York Times* 18 April 1982.

52 Coetzee, *Waiting for the Barbarians*, p. 146.

53 David Attwell, *J.M. Coetzee: South Africa and the Politics of Writing* (Los Angeles: University of California Press, 1993), p. 72.

54 Ibid., p. 169.

55 Sara Upstone, *Spatial Politics in the Postcolonial Novel* (Burlington, VT: Ashgate, 2009), p. 4.

56 Foucault, "Of Other Spaces," p. 330.

57 Anne McClintock, "The Angel of Progress: Pitfalls of the Term 'Post-colonialism,'" in Williams and Chrisman, *Colonial Discourse*, p. 292. My emphasis.

58 Rudyard Kipling, "White Man's Burden," *The Collected Poems of Rudyard Kipling* (Ware, Hertfordshire: Wordsworth Editions, 2001), pp. 334–5. First published 1899.

59 Paul Carter concisely marks this distinction by defining "place" as "a space with a history" in *The Road to Botany Bay: An Exploration of Landscape and History* (Minneapolis: University of Minnesota Press, 2010), p. xxiv.

60 I'm thinking here specifically of the "agriculturalist argument," in which, as David Armitage writes in the context of British justifications for the colonization of America, "dominion fell to those best able to cultivate the land to its fullest capacity." *Foundations of Modern International Thought* (New York: Cambridge University Press, 2013), p. 111.

61 Robert T. Tally Jr., *Spatiality* (New York: Routledge, 2013), p. 30.

62 McClintock, "The Angel of Progress," p. 292.

63 The Cherokee critic and novelist Thomas King, for example, rejects postcolonialism as a concept partially on account of its temporal assumptions. Noting that the term "assumes that the starting point ... is the advent of Europeans in North America" as well as a narrative of "progress and improvement," King concludes that "the full complement of terms – pre-colonial, colonial, and post-colonial – reeks of unabashed ethnocentrism and well-meaning dismissal." See Thomas King, "Godzilla vs. Postcolonial," in Cynthia Sugars ed., *Unhomely States: Theorizing English-Canadian Postcolonialism* (Peterborough, ON: Broadview, 2004), p. 185, 184.

64 Salman Rushdie, *Midnight's Children* (1981; Toronto: Random House, 1997), p. 9.

65 Neil Ten Kortenaar, "'Midnight's Children' and the Allegory of History," *Ariel: A Review of International English Literature* 26.2 (1995), pp. 41–42.

66 Elleke Boehmer, *Colonial and Postcolonial Literature*, 2nd ed. (Toronto: Oxford, 2005), 177.

67 Ibid., 98.

68 Chinua Achebe, "The African Writer and the English Language," *Morning Yet on Creation Day* (New York: Anchor Press, 1975); Ngũgĩ wa Thiong'o's "The Language of African Literature," *Decolonizing the Mind: The Politics of Language in African Literature* (James Currey: London, 1986).

69 Audre Lorde, "The Master's Tools Will Never Dismantle the Master's House," in Reina Lewis and Sara Mills, eds., *Feminist Postcolonial Theory: A Reader* (New York: Routledge, 2004), p. 25.

70 Among the notable exceptions is Stuart Hall's "Cultural Identity and Diaspora" (in Williams and Chrisman, *Colonial Discourse*), which explicitly rejected the notion of "pure" ethnic identities and embraced the transnational hybridization of identity in diaspora. For competing visions of the role of allegory in postcolonial literature, see Slemon, "Monuments," and Fredric Jameson's "Third World Literature in the Era of Multinational Capital," *Social Text* 15 (1986). For a trenchant response to Jameson, see Aijaz Ahmad, "Jameson's Rhetoric of Otherness and the 'National Allegory,'" *Social Text* 17 (1987).

71 Ato Quayson, "Postcolonialism and the Diasporic Imaginary," in Ato Quayson and Girish Daswani, eds., *A Companion to Diaspora and Transnationalism* (Malden, MA: Blackwell, 2013), p. 151.

72 Michael Hardt and Antonio Negri, *Empire* (Cambridge: Harvard University Press, 2000), p. 138.

73 A widespread effort to conceptualize these various registers through postcolonial theory has been underway for some time, with Arjun Appadurai's exploration of the interlocking scales of contemporary experience among the most influential (see "Disjuncture and Difference in the Global Cultural Economy," in Williams and Chrisman, *Colonial Discourse*). The host of other examples include David Chariandy, "Postcolonial Diasporas," *Postcolonial Text* 2.1 (2006); Diana Brydon, "Global Designs, Postcolonial Critiques: Rethinking Canada in Dialogue with Diaspora," *Ilha do Desterro: A Journal of Language and Literature* 40 (2001); and Robert Spencer, *Cosmopolitan Criticism and Postcolonial Literature* (New York: Palgrave Macmillan, 2011). Similarly, Claudia Sadowski-Smith and Caire F. Fox describe hemispheric America studies as a field "largely rooted in postcolonial theory"; "Theorizing the hemisphere: Inter-Americas work at the intersection of American, Canadian, and Latin American studies," *Comparative American Studies* 2.1 (2004), p. 8, while the special issue of *Postcolonial Text* on "Glocal Imaginaries" begins with the declaration that it aims to "join attempts to move beyond the limits and exclusions of nationalism, reified notions of the local and facile celebrations of globalization, testing, as it does so, the continued potential and limitations of a postcolonial rubric" ("Special Issue: *Glocal Imaginaries*, Preface," *Postcolonial Text* 6.2 (2011)).

74 Work that considers First Nations literature alongside postcolonialism is most active in settler–invader colonies, including Canada. See Helen Hoy's *How Should I Read These? Native Women Writers in Canada* (Toronto: University of Toronto Press, 2001), the essays compiled under "Teaching/Reading Native Writing" in Cynthia Sugars's collection *Home-Work: Postcolonialism, Pedagogy and Canadian Literature*, (Ottawa: University of Ottawa Press, 2004), and, along with King's "Godzilla vs. Postcolonial," the essays compiled under "First Nations Subjects" in Cynthia Sugars's *Unhomely States*, especially Lee Maracle's "The Post-colonial Imagination" and Marie Battiste's "Unfolding the Lessons of Colonization." See also Daniel Heath Justice and Anne Brewster, "Indigenous Writing in Canada, Australia, and New Zealand," in Ato Quayson, ed., *The Cambridge History of Postcolonial Literature*, Vol. 1 (Cambridge: Cambridge University Press, 2012).

75 Antoinette Burton, "Introduction: On the Inadequacy and the Indispensability of the Nation," *After the Imperial Turn: Thinking With and Through the Nation* (Durham, NC: Duke University Press, 2003), p. 1.

76 Kwadwo Osei-Nyame, "Chinua Achebe Writing Culture: Representations of Gender and Tradition in *Things Fall Apart*," *Research in African Literature* 30.2 (1999), p. 148.

77 Chinua Achebe, *Things Fall Apart* (1958; Toronto: Random House, 2009), p. 149.

78 See Soja, *Thirdspace*, p. 6. Although there are overlaps between Bhabha's "Third Space" and Soja's "Thirdspace," the two are not equivalent. Perhaps most relevant, in this context, is Soja's critique of Bhabha's "Third Space" as "occasionally teasingly on the edge of being a spatially ungrounded literary trope," part of what he sees as the implicit "privileging of temporality over spatiality" in Bhabha's work (see Soja, *Thirdspace*, pp. 141–2).

79 On this point, see Partha Chatterjee's consideration of the colonial implications of Anderson's account of "homogenous, empty time," in "Anderson's Utopia" *Diacritics* 29.4 (1999).

80 Lefebvre, *Production*, 287.

81 Edward Soja, *Postmodern Geographies: The Reassertion of Space in Critical Social Theory* (London: Verso, 1989), 121.

82 Foucault, "Of Other Spaces," p. 3.

83 Ibid., p. 4.

84 The "history house" of Arundhati Roy's *The God of Small Things*, for example, occupies just such a real-and-imagined space: the decaying colonial plantation, refurbished as a tourist destination, is a manifestation of India's colonial history and neocolonial nostalgia, but it is also the space of a transgressive cross-caste affair, the failure of a socialist response to the legacy of colonial hierarchies, and so on. Given the textual cues Roy applies to the house – the children call it the "Heart of Darkness," for example – a full account of its spatiality would need to attend to its position in British literary history. In other postcolonial novels, the real-and-imagined spatiality exceeds any given location, and is manifested as a broader competition of semiotic codes. For an exemplary case of this, see Michael Ondaatje's *The English Patient*.

85 Daniel Coleman, "From Contented Civility to Contending Civilities: Alternatives to Canadian White Civility," *International Journal of Canadian Studies* 38 (2008), p. 225.

86 Stanka Radović, *Locating the Destitute: Space and Identity in Caribbean Fiction* (Charlottesville: University of Virginia Press, 2014), p. 9.

87 McClintock, "The Angel of Progress," p. 292.

88 For a survey of the question of postcolonialism's proper end, see Vijay Mishra and Bob Hodge's "What Was Postcolonialism?," *New Literary History* 36.3 (2005), pp. 375–402.

89 Ato Quayson, "Periods versus Concepts," p. 347.

13

ATO QUAYSON
University of Toronto

Tragedy and the Postcolonial Novel

Much that is reported as sad and tragic in today's news media from the postcolonial world gives pause for concern: wars and rumors of war, failing states, civil conflicts, the rape and abuse of women, religious intolerance and the concomitant violence that comes with of it, and so on. And yet as sad and tragic as these news items are, from literary perspective the term "tragedy" and its cognates are not coterminous with the understandings to be found in the news media. As a literary concept tragedy takes its roots from fifth-century Athenian theater. The original Greek meaning has been progressively transformed through the mediations of various other traditions such that today to speak of tragedy in the literary sense is at once to pay homage to the Greek example and to invoke the many iterations of the concept that have appeared in various epochs and cultures. Thus Jacobean and Elizabethan England saw the invigoration of tragedy from different standpoints, and without necessarily replicating the Greek example. The Senecan formulas of violent murders were coupled to madness, rape, retributive justice, and sometimes even cannibalism and became central to the Jacobean revenge tragedies of Thomas Kyd, John Marston, Thomas Middleton, and others, while Shakespeare produced multidimensional tragedies that sometimes incorporated comedic interludes (such as in *Macbeth* and *Hamlet*) as well as subplots that served to expand the range of the action as a whole (as in *King Lear* and *Antony and Cleopatra*). By the late nineteenth and into the early twentieth century new expressions of tragedy emerged that took on a more existentialist tincture. Chekov, Ibsen, Strindberg, Eliot, and Yeats are some of the playwrights who expressed this new orientation while also mixing the form with references to a fresh set of cultural mythologies. Despite George Steiner's widely debated view that the modern world cannot produce tragedy because of the demise of a universe populated by gods and epic heroes, the tide of tragedy appears not to have been stemmed, with subsequent generations producing good examples of tragedy from a variety of genres and directions, including, as we shall see in this chapter, several

230

from the postcolonial world.[1] Given that all the key conceptions of tragedy start from the standpoint of theater, this chapter will proceed from post-colonial theater adaptations of Greek tragedy before shifting from a view of tragedy as tied to dramatic theater to a conception of tragedy as a philo-sophical discourse and thus evidently applicable to the postcolonial novel. However, in this shift we will revisit the central terms laid out in Aristotle's *Poetics*. Given the scarcity of available criticism on tragedy from a postco-lonial perspective, the focus on Aristotle's key terms proves to be a handy expedient for establishing a working framework by which to understand what is tragic in postcolonial writing and the ways in which this provides fresh inflections to established ideas of tragedy.[2] Central to the concept of postcolonialism that forms the backdrop to this chapter are complex ideas of transition between individualism and community, between tradition and modernity, between nation and narration, and between homelands and diasporas in a world thoroughly shaped by the afterlives of colonialism and the resistance to it.[3]

Postcolonial Adaptations

Reception and adaptation theories have been the main terms within which postcolonial tragedy has so far been discussed. And in these debates even though everywhere adaptations of Shakespeare can be found, it is African adaptations of the classics that seem to loom large. Thus twelve of the nineteen pieces in Hardwick and Gillespie's *Classics in Post-Colonial Worlds* center on African examples.[4] The most well-known of such African adaptations include Ola Rotimi's *The Gods are Not to Blame* (*Oedipus Rex*), Wole Soyinka's *The Bacchae of Euripides* (*The Bacchae*), and Femi Osofisan's *Tegonni* (*Antigone*). As Aktina Stathaki also shows in her study of South African adaptations of Greek tragedies, the country has since the fall of apartheid in 1994 seen adaptations of *The Oresteia, Antigone, Medea*, and *The Trojan Women* in performances that highlight multicul-tural choruses and the themes of truth and reconciliation that have them-selves become central to the discourses of nation building in that country. The apartheid era itself saw some adaptations, the most well-known of which was Athol Fugard's *The Island* in which he telescoped the events of Antigone into a play-within-the-play set in the then-infamous prison of Robben Island. Notwithstanding the accounts in Hardwick and Gillespie and in Stathaki, adaptations of the Greeks has not been exclusive to African examples, with Sophocles' *Antigone* being by far the most popular of those to have been adapted in the postcolonial world. Kamau Brathwaite's *Odale's Choice*, Felix Morisseau-Leroy's *Antigone in Haiti*, and a Tamil language *Antigone* are only a handful of examples that might be highlighted from beyond the continent. Greek tragedies have continually been adapted because they establish relations of equivalence, comparison, and commensurablity between the classical world and our own in a post-colonial setting. As the Indian playwright Suresh Awasthi points out, adaptations go to the heart of claims of authority: "The very claim of authority and the attempt for its realization in doing classics, foreign or our own, is a self-defeating objective. It negates the very purpose of doing a classic, which by its nature lends [itself] to different kinds of interpretation and approaches in accordance with contemporary tastes and values of theatre practice."[5]

There is a dimension of intertextuality inherent to the adaptation of previous models of tragedy, whether from the Greeks, Shakespeare, or elsewhere, that provides a particular modulation to postcolonial tragedy. In *The Island* Athol Fugard not only telescopes *Antigone* and sets it in the context of the infamous prison of Robben Island during apartheid, but he also draws great parallels with Samuel Beckett.[6] The similarity of John and Winston to Beckett's Estragon and Vladimir in *Waiting for Godot* falls into this mould, with the main difference between the two sets of characters being that unlike in Beckett, John and Winston are constantly imagining scenarios and creating roles that they enact, thus effectively rehearsing the adoption of different characters as central to their existential condition. The two cell-mates regularly rehearse different roles to play, including make-believe scenes from movies for their mutual entertainment, an imagined telephone conversation with their friends on the mainland, and a long drawn-out scene about the things that will take place when John finally returns home when the cellmates discover that he has been offered early release from his prison sentence, and that he will be returning home after three months. Contras-tively, even though they imagine different situations Estragon and Vladimir do not alter their essential personalities to match these situations. They are not characters rehearsing the identities of other characters in different scen-arios. The situations that they invoke flow directly from their (vaguely) remembered pasts and the future they anticipate in waiting for Godot. In Fugard's play John and Winston imagine many different scenarios and the positions that they might take in anticipation of their interlocutors. This makes the play a medium of heterogeneous mediations of the self, since the effect of the proliferation of scenarios and the continual rehearsals of these scenarios serves to (a) multiply interlocutory others and (b) engender new modes of address in relation to such interlocutory others. Fugard thus constructs his play as a medium of heterogeneities within which the tele-scoped Antigone as a model for translating the Greek example into a multilayered example of the antinomies of political identities under the oppressive and totalitarian regimes.

The intertextuality of tragic references in the postcolonial novel is so ubiquitous as to require its own independent exploration. Even though Harold Bloom does not consider *Things Fall Apart* as conforming to the mold of Greek tragedy, he insists that Okonkwo is similar to Shakespeare's Coriolanus: "If *Coriolanus* is a tragedy, then so also is *Things Fall Apart*. Okonkwo, like the Roman hero, is essentially a solitary, and at heart a perpetual child. His tragedy stands apart from the condition of his people, even though it is generated by their pragmatic refusal of heroic death."[7] In this particular instance, the intertextuality is being inserted as a hermeneutic from the viewpoint of the critic, in this case Bloom, but we might wish to qualify his assertion that Okonkwo does not fulfill the terms of a Greek tragic hero. There are many instances however where the intertextuality is not an imposition that is elicited from the reader but is foundational to the postcolonial text itself. In examples as varied as Tayeb Salih's *Season of Migration to the North* (Othello and Desdemona, Kurtz, and Marlow), Jean Rhys's *Wide Sargasso Sea* (Jane Erye), Yvonne Vera's *Without a Name* (Medea), and Mohsin Hamid's *The Reluctant Fundamentalist* (Hamlet, Ophelia, Genghis Khan, and Gatsby), the intertextual references are designed to elicit immediate and automatic comparison to other texts and also to import the sense of seriousness that attends all tragedies.

Returning to the question of adaptation, we should note that all adaptations of *Antigone* share the philosophical tradition of reinterpreting the play that can be traced at least to Hegel. In his own account Hegel notes that the essential form of a tragedy depends on certain inescapable collisions, but that these collisions are not necessarily the collisions of directly opposed ethical conceptions but rather conceptions that essentially participate with one another. Thus, writing about the mutual entanglement of the familial and political principles in Greek tragedy, he suggests that "the opposition . . . is that of the *body politic*, the opposition, that is, between *ethical life in its social universality* and the family as *the natural ground of moral relations*."[8] The dialectical interplay that Hegel stipulates is between a form of social universality, essentially an abstraction, and a natural ground of moral relations that must perforce be rendered concrete within the microcosm of interpersonal relations (i.e., the family). We must qualify Hegel's terms slightly in order to account for a different kind of dialectical pairing, particularly so as the ethics of a social universality in a place such as then apartheid South Africa or today's Palestine are seriously called into question because of the uneven political domain within which such a universality might be articulated. In other words, social universality cannot be taken for granted under conditions of oppression; the social universal itself becomes the grounds for contestation and struggle. And since the domain of interpersonal relationships both offers the grounds for working through morality and is itself produced by the essential logic that dominates any system, that domain then takes on a coloration from the problematic social universal that is being shaped under the impress of unfreedom.

Postcolonial/Tragedy

Once we shift from a notion of tragedy as being the consummate condensation of theater traditions and move instead to view tragedy as a philosophical discourse, other dimensions make themselves manifest that seem best exemplified in the postcolonial novel. The intriguing views on the tragedy expressed by Obi Okonkwo in Chinua Achebe's *No Longer at Ease* provide productive points for a preliminary discussion of the postcolonial tragic novel. Consider his views:

> Real tragedy is never resolved. It goes on hopelessly forever. Conventional tragedy is too easy. The hero dies and we feel a purging of the emotions. A real tragedy takes place in a corner, in an untidy spot, to quote W. H. Auden. The rest of the world is unaware of it. Like that man in *A Handful of Dust* who reads Dickens to Mr. Todd. There is no release for him. When the story ends he is still reading. There is no purging of the emotions for us because *we are not there*. (Emphasis added; Chinua Achebe, *No Longer at Ease*)[9]

The trigger for Obi's views is the fate of Scobie, the central character of Graham Greene's *The Heart of the Matter*, who commits suicide at the end of that novel, which is itself set in colonial Sierra Leone. To Obi Scobie's suicide is a too-easy resolution to what seems to him like a straightforward Aristotelian tragedy. On closer inspection we find Obi's interpretation of what constitutes *catharsis*, and by implication the Aristotelian tragic formula that produces it, to be not entirely accurate, as we shall see later. And yet his views are no less significant for that matter. For by invoking Auden's "Musée des Beaux Arts" Obi invokes a contrast that is significant for conceptualizing of tragedy. In Auden's poem the Old Masters understood the "human position" of suffering, the way an event of tragic proportions might be taking place alongside human actions of mundane or even indifferent import, such as "eating, or opening a window, or just walking dully along." In a painting of the crucifixion, for example, a torturer's horse "scratches its innocent behind on a tree" while the messy divine event takes place, further establishing the contrasting scales between tragic suffering and the relief of a sentient irritation unconnected either to the scene that is unfolding or indeed to anything else other than its immediate and time-bound necessity. At issue in Auden, however, is something more than just the contrast between suffering and the quotidian, for his poem also implies the idea of spectatorship and thus, by implication, of witnessing. Spectatorship or indeed its opposite is evident in the description of ekphrasitic depiction of Brueghel's *Icarus* that Auden produces at the end of the poem, where the people on the "expensive, delicate ship" and the ploughman on the shore both see something amazing, a boy falling out of the blue sky, and yet still turn away to mind their own business. Despite the Icarus myth having inspired themes of the unbridled human quest for knowledge captured in works as varied as Christoper Marlowe's *Dr. Faustus*, Mary Shelley's *Frankenstein*, Stephen Spielberg's *Jurassic Park*, and Pepetela's *Return of the Water Spirit*, the spectators to this amazing fall consider it "not an important failure" and so return to their own more mundane concerns. The dialectic between spectatorship and its possible opposite is manifested between scene (of a tragic unfolding) and seeing (of the persons seeing/not seeing, witnessing/not witnessing that scene). Given the fact that the entire poem simulates the poet's reverie-like stroll through a museum of fine arts, another layer of seeing is reproduced within the poem that converts us, its readers, into surrogates of the poetic persona. It is this layered structure of spectatorship that Obi Okonkwo appears to be invoking in his comment at the end of the passage when he refers to our *not being there*.

When Obi references Evelyn Waugh's Tony endlessly reading Dickens to the demented Mr Todd he is also indirectly raising the question of the link between malaise and stasis, and of stasis as a form of imprisonment. Achebe has through his mouthpiece essentially given us two types of tragic closure that he considers not adequately tragic: the first pertains to suicide and the inception of a too-easy catharsis and the second to an endless stasis which also fails as a form of tragic closure because we are not necessarily present at its inception and unfolding. But what is this "there" before which we are presumed to be not present? Does this speak to a problematic of empathy and identification, and thus of witnessing? Where does effective tragic closure inhere? Is it at the scene of unrelieved emotional suffering without end, or, as we might propose, at the moment of the *anagnorisis* of the protagonist? *Anagnorisis* is another key Aristotelian term that finds expression in much of the postcolonial tragic novel. It is not a problem that is rendered as necessarily exclusive to the cognitive processes of the tragic protagonist him- or herself. While it is not always that the protagonist's tragic recognition is made explicit at the moment of tragic reversal or death (think of Ibsen's Hedda Gabler and Díaz's Oscar Wao in contrast to Shakespeare's Othello and Chinua Achebe's Okonkwo, for example).

To complicate the question of tragic recognition even further we often find in the postcolonial novel male and female protagonists that are "afflicted by second thoughts," to quote the description of the disabled Paul Rayment in Coetzee's *Slow Man*. This affliction is no ordinary affliction. For it frequently implies an ineluctable demand to recognize one's predicament as tied to a wider set of significances beyond oneself. The moment of recognition is not univocal or set completely within a specific event but is a lengthy and complex process of negotiating the dialectic between individualism and community, defined not merely as a structure of social relations marked by specific agglutinative rituals but more in terms of real and idealized affiliations marked by race, gender, and sexual orientation. Thus a person's community may not exclusively derive from among the people with whom he or she resides but may also embrace others of a similar orientation across space and historical epochs. In the postcolonial novel recognition is often not rendered in the form of the teleological sequence implicit in Aristotle's disquisition on complex plots, but rather as a messy set of competing cognitions that elude coherent ordering yet are tied to a sense of community or communal consciousness. This is what we find in examples such as Chinua Achebe's *Arrow of God*, Tayib Salih's *Season of Migration to the North*, Arundhati Roy's *God of Small Things*, and Bapsi Sidhwa's *Cracking India*, among others. Contrastively, the affliction of second thoughts may also be the means by which the tragic protagonist comes to gaze upon him- or herself as the object of painful self-reflection, thus effectively being converted into a self-witness. It is not for nothing that I take the phrase "affliction of second thoughts" from Coetzee, because his protagonists are exemplary in this regard. Whether with already mentioned *Slow Man*, *Waiting for the Barbarians*, *Foe*, or even *Disgrace*, the essential structure of self-perception is the same. And in Michael Ondaatje's *The English Patient*, Anne Michaels's *Fugitive Pieces*, Yvonne Vera's *Without a Name*, Keri Hulme's *The Bone People*, and Jean Rhys's *Wide Sargasso Sea* the contours of this self-witnessing are tied to different kinds of trauma.[10] This second, trauma-related fracture and attendant affliction of second thoughts, can be distinguished from the ways individualism is tied to the cognition of communal consciousness that we see in Achebe, Salih, Roy, and Sidhwa. Both types are fraught forms of tragic recognition that may also be read as coterminous or overlapping in various postcolonial novels. The point is to determine the central emphasis of such tragic recognition – instigated by specific traumatic events or linked to a lengthy process of back-and-forth reflections; tied to individual self-spectatorship or yoked to community – before embarking on the process of reading them together.

In many respects, however, the two types of tragic recognition, rendered not as discrete and separable entities but as mutually reinforcing elements, is best encapsulated not in postclonial writing but in the work of the cultural and social theorist Frantz Fanon. Fanon is correctly taken in postcolonial studies as an exemplary theoretician of the decolonization struggle. The key principles that he put forward regarding colonial violence, the complicities of the postcolonial elites, and the overall nature of colonized identities under erasure remain pertinent to the field to this day.[11] Though Fanon's work is not conventionally read for its literary features, I would like to suggest that the two types of anguished spectatorship we have just noted are nowhere better expressed than in his essay "The Fact of Blackness," to be found in *Black Skin, White Masks*.[12] At a point in his reflections in that chapter Fanon proffers a fascinating self-reflexive insight: "[I]n one sense, if I were asked for a definition of myself, I would say that I am one who waits; I investigate my surroundings, I interpret everything in terms of what I discover, I become sensitive."[13] This statement is paradigmatic of the discursive maneuvers that underpin *Black Skin, White Masks* in general. In this one statement Fanon imputes the role of an interlocutor in eliciting a definition of the self ("if I were asked"), the eternal vigilance that he brings to bear on that enterprise ("I am one who waits"/"I become sensitive"), and, above all, the degree to which all that he discovers depends ultimately on a fervent interpretation of his surroundings, both historical and cultural. As Sekyi-Otu has adroitly pointed out in *Fanon's Dialectic of Experience*, Fanon's discourse is a mixture of propositions and almost immediate self-revisions, much like the second thoughts that we noted as pertaining to postcolonial tragic novels earlier.[14] He identifies Fanon's rehearsal of certain linguistic acts within which there lie many subtle and surrogate dramaturgical devices: "stage directions, signals of imminent plot twists and complications, markers of incipient ironies and reversals, choric commentaries and points of strategic complicity or critical difference between protagonal utterance and authorial stance" (1997: 8). While Sekyi-Otu proceeds to insert Fanon into the dialectical heritage marked by Hegel and Sartre, both of whom Fanon is clearly indebted to, it is also possible to take the discursive dramaturgical structure that he identifies as signs of the elaboration of a psychoexistential complex whose form of articulation is the conversion of the self into a spectator–witness not of others but of one's own self.

At the heart of this psychoexistential complex is also the device of positing the self as representative of a much larger category, be it an immediate community, the entire race, or a form of the universal. While Fanon feels a sense of anguish regarding his experience of colonial race relations he also projects his individual condition as representative of the colonized or black man's psychoexistential complex in general. But where might this dialectic of individualism and representativeness be traced to? What is its genealogy or grounds of articulation? Homi Bhabha has already laid bare the nature of colonial anxiety of the colonizer. In essays such as "Of Mimicry and Man" and "Signs Taken for Wonders" (1994) Bhabha traces how the colonizer retains a consistent state of anxiety regarding the possibility, first, of not knowing the colonized (as in the form of systematized bodies of knowledge), and, second, of being confronted by an uncanny reflection of the colonizer's own assumed unassailability via colonized's mimicry: "white but not quite," as he memorably put it.[15] To understand the Fanonian dialectic of identity, however, we are obliged to grasp it in the first instance as an aspect of the condition of imagining an alternative universal deriving from the experience of colonialism. This dialectic of experience is by necessity also part of a semiotic–discursive form that is itself as the direct product of the systematic delirium of colonialism. For the colonialized Other (in colonial discourse described variously as black, dirty, lying, childlike, incapable of self-regulation, uncivilized, barbarian, effeminate, over-sexed, etc.) is primarily a location within a structure of determinations. This structure writes itself in history within the series of cross-cultural encounters in which colonialized Otherness is assigned a particular quality of impoverishment and evolution-ary backwardness as its indelible signatures. No idle semiotic, this structure of determinations spawns both material and psychoexistential effects. Fanon puts the matter succinctly: "I am given no chance. I am overdetermined from without. I am the slave not of the 'idea' that others have of me but of my own appearance."[16] In a quite real sense all changes to the knowledge–economy nexus within which the colonized are denominated, for example in the course of the decolonization or at independence, have to go through their own genre chains in which knowledge is aligned with new forms of manage-ment (in the economic, political, and also discursive sense) as well as with power. However, these genre chains are only partially situated within the domain of localized self-conceptions. The attempt to contest, write back, or otherwise challenge the colonial structure of denominations involves either overloading the referent ("Get used to me, I am not getting used to anyone," "Fact of Blackness," 131; or the "I am Black and Proud" slogan of the 1970s), or, as we also see in Fanon, oscillating between individualism and representativeness as a means of eliciting identification with an alternative form of universal. When in Wretched of the Earth Fanon calls for violence it is partly also to proffer a charged value to the Other that converts it into an alternative universal to transcend the colonial structure of denominations. This is seen as a necessary move to force the structure of colonial denomin-ations to confront, in its starkness, that which had been designated negative in the first place. Some might see the new genre chains as entailing a mere inversion, yet the difference between an inversion of binary terms and the obverse denomination to be seen at work in Fanon is that the colonizer is not cast straightforwardly as negative.[17] Rather, we might note with David Scott (2005) in his discussion of the difference between histories of decolonization grounded in romance and those deriving from tragedy that the process of acquiring freedom entails for the colonized a rapid oscillation between attraction and rejection of the colonizer. Figures such as Toussaint L'Ouverture, one of the key protagonists of Haiti's revolution (1791–1804), and for C. L. R. James, whose *The Black Jacobins* reconstructs the revolution as a form of romance, the attraction to the discourse of Western Enlightenment of which freedom and self-determination are a central part is countered by the extreme shock and disillusionment at the West's failure to uphold its own values.[18] This is what leads the colonized to become "conscripts of modernity," in the felicitous phrase of Scott's title.

Chi versus *Fukú*: The Postcolonial Tragic Novel and the Question of History

At the heart of postcolonial studies is the question of history, its colonial and postcolonial temporalities, who claims the right to interpret it, the pastness of the past and its relationship to the present, and what might arise from (mis)understanding the past in its consequences for the present. The question has been formulated in the postcolonial tragic novel in a number of ways, some of which couple history to the categories of determinism and contingency to be found in other tragic traditions. What is normally understood from Greek tragedy as fate or the will of the gods is posited in the postcolonial tragic novels we are going to look at as an aspect of specific metaphysical categories that themselves imply a view of history. We see different forms of such implication arising from the *chi* of Achebe's *Things Fall Apart*, the *fukú* of Junot Díaz's *Brief Wondrous Life of Oscar Wao*, and in the entire magical realist apparatus to be found in Salman Rushdie's *Midnight's Children*, Gabriel García Márquez's *One Hundred Years of Solitude*, Isabel Allende's *House of Spirits*, and Ben Okri's *The Famished Road*, among others.

The concept of *chi* in *Things Fall Apart* points to the belief in a personal god, personal fate if you will, but in such a way as to defy easy explanation even to the people of the fictional Umuofia.[19] The Umoufians believe that when a man says "yes" strongly enough his *chi* is bound to agree. But when Okonkwo's gun goes off at Ogbuefi Ezeudu's funeral and kills the dead man's son to trigger his exile from the clan it looks like his chi has begun to say no to his self-affirming yes. Since the *chi* is not a material entity it cannot be understood except via a range of sociocultural relations as laid out in the novel: the relations of gender exchange and reciprocity that are manifest at different material and symbolic levels of the clan, the relation between a proverbial language of cultural interpretation and a rapidly changing world, the economy of exclusions that peripheralize certain constituencies within the culture despite the essentially meritocratic impulses upon which the culture has been constructed (*osus*, twins, "effeminate" men, etc.). In other words, Achebe suggests that the *chi* must not be understood exclusively as pertaining to personal choice or action but must be grasped instead through a form of embedding that takes the whole range of possible and potential sociocultural relations into account.

And yet on closer examination the concept of *chi* in the novel also serves to raise a question about the ultimate elusiveness of history. This places the *chi* at a certain remove from the Greek gods, contradictory and capricious as they sometimes appear. The inherent elusiveness of the *chi* (its belated "no" to Okonkwo's self-affirming "yes") parallels to an uncanny degree the problematic status of the historical processes that affect the culture and lead things to fall apart. When the white man first comes to Umuofia in the form of the early missionaries he is perceived as easily explicable through the conceptual schemes available within the culture. What are these but a bunch of "clucking hens" as Okonwko derisively asserts? They are nothing but *efulefu*, effeminate men who can do no harm and who should either be chased away immediately or just tolerated as a nuisance that would hopefully vanish in time without trace. The Umuofians, of course, turn out to be tragically wrong. The significance of their misinterpretation is not their failure to recognize history when it walked into their midst in the form of Christianity, but that this potential for misrecognition inheres in any human encounter with world-historical processes as such. For such world historical processes appear deceptively innocent until after they have successfully gained a society's acquiescence through the defeat of the alternatives that are set up against it. (We see this process worked out fully in *Arrow of God*, the second in Achebe's planned trilogy but which is published third, after *No Longer at Ease*.) The world-historical process that is colonialism posits a new universal, in which, as we saw in our discussion of Fanon, the African is presumed inferior. The process of grounding this flawed universal is far from straightforward, and many colonial societies often involved forms of violence. But in *Things Fall Apart* colonial universal is depicted as that much insidious because it conscripted already-existing cultural schisms to achieve its dominance. Twins (taken as the signs of an anomaly in nature), untitled men (the *efulefu* of Okonkwo's derision), and *osus* (considered sacred and thus not allowed to mix or intermarry with the freeborn) are the first to join the ranks of the Christians.[20] It is these hitherto peripheralized constituencies that lead to social splits within the clan, things fall apart because the center cannot hold, as we find in the epigraph to the novel from Yeats's "The Second Coming."

When Okonkwo beheads the district commissioner's messenger in the penultimate chapter of the novel the salience of this momentous event is not so much in the evidence it provides of Okonkwo's final severance from his society as in the peculiar contrast suggested in his "knowing" that the tribe will not go to war that is set against their bewildered question: "Why did he do it?" (*Things Fall Apart*, p. 145). For the contrast amounts to the difference between a profound Aristotelian *anagnorisis* (recognition) and an insuperable epistemological impasse that might be codified as the ultimate severance of the hero from his chi. But the event also serves to focalize the historical moment when the community of Umoufia reveals its ambiguity with regard to its own past. In the past conveyed in the novel the messenger's decapitation could have meant only one thing, namely, a call to arms against the disrespectful invading culture of the colonizer. Yet now, the military heroic ethic for which Okonkwo has been rewarded throughout the narrative and which had allowed him to rise to become a lord of the clan is subject to doubt if not disavowal. It is to Achebe's credit that he bifurcates the response to the decapitation, thus making it impossible even for us readers to settle on an easy conclusion. The attitudes of the Umoufians to their own heroic past is suddenly and without apparent preparation riddled with ambiguities, the consequence of which is that Okonkwo is left to belatedly recognize that he is no longer of the clan. This is also the work of the *chi*, but the *chi* not as the clan imagined it, but as an articulation of subtle yet inexorable historical processes. There is a certain homology in the discursive conceptual structure of *Things Fall Apart* that is only discernible when the *chi* is seen as the parallel of the elusive face of a tragic history. And the face of this tragic history is encapsulated in the *chi*'s unanticipated "no" to the hero's insistent "yes" that is revealed first as an accident (the shooting of Ogbuefi Ezeudu's son) and then as an irritating historical wrinkle (the arrival of the Christians). One might venture even to argue further that the *chi* is itself a historicizing concept that the culture deploys to explain personal fortune and culpability but whose ramifications in fact encompass much wider details of historical process. The *chi* concept and history, then, might be thought to raise identical epistemological questions, the first articulated at the level of the personal, the other at the level of historical unfolding, yet both remaining inextricably interconnected.

In Junot Díaz's *Brief Wondrous Life of Oscar Wao*, on the other hand, *fukú* seems to play the role of historical determinism and a magical curse, as well as pure bad luck.[21] Even though the novel opens in its first pages with an elaborate description of the *fukú americanus*, the curse of the Antilles (read Caribbean) through the Black Atlantic, it doesn't take long for *fukú* to also be linked to the mindless political violence of the Domincan Republic's Rafael Trujillo , who ruled the country with an iron fist from 1930 to 1961. All the descriptions of the violence his regime suggest that Trujillo himself is the lord of *fukú*, since he establishes a frightening network of surveillance that invades the privacy of every individual and exposes them to the certainty of dire and immediate consequences if they do not agree with him. And yet when Trujillo himself dies under a hail of bullets later on in the novel the *fukú* seems to have turned against him. To compound the status of *fukú* even further, the entire family line of the Cabral-Leons seems to be afflicted by some kind curse, much like the House of Atreus in Aeschylus's *Oresteia*: "There are still many, on and off the island, who offer Beli's near fatal beating as irrefutable proof that the House of Cabral was indeed the victim of some high level *fukú*, the local version of the House of Atreus" (152). Is Beli's miraculous rescue from the grips of child slavery and her subsequent tumultuous existence in the Dominican diasporas of New Jersey (breast cancer, mastectomy, loss of hair, incessant fights with her daughter Lola) not a sign of the reign of *fukú* within the family saga? And what do we make of Oscar Wao himself? That, unlike other male Domincanos in the diaspora he seems to the only one who doesn't manage to "get laid," and who when he does fall in love and get laid he has to be first beaten to an inch of his life by the henchmen of the police officer whose girlfriend he happens to have fallen in love with, and then, at the very end, that he has to die under a hail of bullets for his trespasses. (*Fukú* again?) It is when Díaz comes to detail the rise and fall of Abelard Luis Cabral, the famous doctor and Oscar and Lola's grandfather, that the speculation on what might be *fukú* gets even more confusing. Abelard gets into serious trouble for hiding one of his beautiful daughters from the rapacious Trujillo, the systematic sexual predator. In what appears to be a setup, Abelard is accused in a moment of drunken camaraderie of saying that Trujillo may have put a dead body in the boot of his car. He is promptly arrested, submitted to a series of humiliations, and thrown into jail, to reemerge as imbecile, with the "proud flame of his intellect extinguished" (251). Despite the lengthy description that is provided of the cause of his incarceration being linked to his attempt to protect his daughter's chastity, Díaz later dismisses this as a generic commonplace and instead adds a further speculation that Abelard may have got himself into trouble because was writing a supernatural history of the Trujillo regime to expose uncomfortable secrets he happened to know about El Jefe. It was this, we are now told, that got him into trouble and not his attempts at protecting his daughter. Which was the cause of his troubles, then we ask: beauty or the beast? Through his mouthpiece Yunior, narrator of the novel, Díaz provides a lengthy speculative digression on the confusing relation between contingency, agency, and culpability:

> There would always be speculation. At the most basic level, did he say it, did he not? (Which is another way of asking: Did he have a hand in his own destruction?). Even the family was divided. . . .
>
> Most of the folks you speak to prefer the story with a supernatural twist. They believe that not only did Trujillo want Abelard's daughter, but when he couldn't catch her, out of spite he put a fukú on the family's ass. Which is why all the terrible shit that happened.
>
> So which is it? You ask. An accident, a conspiracy, or fukú? The only answer I can give you is the least satisfying: you'll have to decide for yourself. What's certain is that nothing is certain. We are trawling in silences here. Trujillo and Company didn't leave a paper trail – they didn't share their German contemporaries' lust for documentation. And it's not like the fukú itself would leave a memoir or anything. The remaining Cabrals ain't much help, either; on all matters related to Abelard's imprisonment and to the subsequent destruction of the clan there is within the family a silence that stands monument to the generations, that sphinxes all attempts at narrative reconstruction. A whisper here and there but nothing more.
>
> Which is to say if you're looking for a full story, I don't have it.   (242–243)

We cannot miss the fact that with the phrase "sphinxes all attempts at narrative reconstruction," Díaz is slyly introducing a reference to Sophocles' *Oedipus Rex*, and thus importing an entire debate about determinism and the inscrutability of fate into his novel. Like Achebe's *chi* concept, *fukú* seems to be a way of explaining the lack of fit between causality and consequence. Everything seems to be contingent upon a variety of factors, some profound, but others seemingly quite banal and elusive in their immediate significance. Their significance comes to be known much later, *after* the tragic consequences have taken place. Some events have multiple causalities that confound our capacity for ordering them. However, the fact that they have been generated from multiple causes does not mean that their tragic effects are any less damaging or indeed intriguing. They elicit interpretation while simultaneously confounding the capacity for interpretation. There is thus a form of incommensurablity between tragic effect and the (multiple) causes that might be taken to have produced it. For the Cabral-Leons, the real tragedy is not that of laboring under a curse but the fact of being human, and thus, in the words of Donne, being "slave to fate, chance, kings, and desperate men."

If concepts such as *chi* and *fukú* indicate the link between metaphysical categories and the question of history, then postcolonial magical realism also establishes a firm connection between the metaphysical, violence, and history. Unlike the traditional historical novel, it is the unsuccessful assimilation of historical data that is foregrounded in magical realism. As Linda Hutcheon points out with respect to the historiographic metafiction of which she considers magical realism a part, in such writing details are not referred to in order to produce a patina of verifiability; rather they are there to show how difficult it is to verify history in the first place.[22] Magical realism embraces the various processes and contradictions by which the historical is established, producing what, to echo Raymond Williams, is a structure of (absurdist) feeling with respect to history. It is then possible to extract philosophies of history that form constitutive dimensions of the magical realist text.

Díaz's novel deploys certain key magical realist devices in the metaphysical mongoose and the man without a face that appear in turns when both Beli and much later her son Oscar are taken to the cane fields to be tortured, and, in the minds of their torturers, hopefully disposed of permanently. But the magical realist devices in Díaz's novel are context-specific and do not transfer their significance to the overall conduct of the narrative as would be expected from fully magical realist texts.[23] In postcolonial magical realism violence relates to a wider political domain, sometimes rendered parodically, as in *One Hundred Years of Solitude*, or as an apparently transcendental signified that is only partially assimilated to the magical causalities of the narration. In such cases its nonassimilation puts violence in stark relief to the magical as mechanisms for explaining historical causality. There are at least two distinct ways in which violence is represented as eluding assimilation. First is when the systemic disorder engendered by political violence is not routed through the consciousness of any individual character but retains the essential features of the blind motor of history itself. Such is the case in Allende's *The House of Spirits* in particular. In this novel the represented political domain institutes historical causality but there is no direct correlation between the political domain and that of the magical real. It is as if the magical realist discourse transcends the ability of the political to become a motivational explanation for it. It poses an explanatory challenge to the political domain, much like what we see in *One Hundred Years of Solitude* when an alternative account of the United Fruit Company's banana plantation massacre that took place in the town of Ciénaga in northern Colombia on 6 December 1928 is routed through the eyes of José Arcadio Segundo, who later becomes an apprentice to the by then invisible gypsy Melquíades. Contrastively, in Ben Okri's *The Famished Road* and Salman Rushdie's

Midnight's Children political violence is so firmly assimilated to magical realist explanatory mechanisms and routed through the consciousness of the characters themselves that the systemic disorder produced by political violence appears to be a direct consequence of the magical realist itself. Thus in *Midnight's Children* when the magical realist narrator Saleem Sinai pauses to note that he has reported Gandhi's assassination on the wrong date he refuses to correct it, suggesting that Gandhi's death was "untimely" anyway, and being untimely cannot be assigned to the correct date. We see this as completely normal within the terms set up by the text, even if a bit funny.

Each of the magical realist texts we have seen so far ends up with various disasters: partition, rape, assassination, genocidal massacres, the destruction of families, solitude, and even a final apocalyptic resolution of a mysterious strong wind and a plague of ants. And yet in each of these instances, and in the other tragedies that we have looked at, the tragedy of loss and dissolution does not retain the last word. To take a lead from Wole Soyinka writing about African thought, we might conclude that the postcolonial understanding of tragedy is marked by "an acceptance of the elastic nature of knowledge as its own reality, as signifying no more than a reflection of the original coming-into-being of a manifest complex reality."[24] Hence the appearance in the postcolonial novel of the *chi, fukú*, the dynamics of obverse denominations as a grounding of new forms of the universal, and magical realism as key templates for understanding what is tragedy today.

Notes

1 George Steiner, *The Death of Tragedy* (New Haven, CT: Yale University Press, 1996).

2 Reflections on the tragic status of certain postcolonial protagonists is not uncommon, but the sustained analysis of the relationship between tragedy and postcolonial representations is really only to be found in Timothy J. Reiss's *Against Autonomy: Global Dialectics of Cultural Exchange* (Stanford, CT: Stanford University Press, 2002), and David Scott's *Conscripts of Modernity: The Tragedy of Colonial Enlightenment* (Durham, NC: Duke University Press, 2005). At the same time both Reiss and Scott are interested mainly in outlining a philosophy of postcolonial history so that their remarks on tragedy, though insightful, do not focus predominantly on literary examples.

3 On current revisions to the term postcolonialism, see especially Ato Quayson, "Introduction: Postcolonial Literature in a Changing Historical Frame," in *The Cambridge History of Postcolonial Literature*, Vol. 1, ed. Ato Quayson, (Cambridge: Cambridge University Press, 2012), pp. 3–29, and Graham Huggan, "Introduction: Postcolonialism and Revolution," in *The Oxford Handbook of Postcolonial Studies*, ed. Graham Huggan (Oxford: Oxford University Press, 2013), pp. 1–28.

4 Lorna Hardwick and Carol Gillespie, eds., *Classics in Post-Colonial Worlds* (Oxford: Oxford University Press, 2007).

5 Sudesh Aswati, quoted in Helene Foley, "Modern Performance and Adaptation of Greek Tragedy," *Transactions of the American Philological Association*, 129 (1999), p. 4.

6 See, for example, Werner Huber, "The Transformations of Samuel Beckett: The Case of Athol Fugard," *Liberator* 10.3 (1989), pp. 48–54, and Edward S. Brinkley, "Proustian Time and Modern Drama: Beckett, Brecht, Fugard," *Comparative Literature Studies* 25.4 (1988), pp. 352–66. The Brinkley piece was winner of the first annual A. Owen Aldrige Prize in Comparative Literature and well worth attention.

7 Harold Bloom, "Introduction," *Modern Critical Interpretations of* Things Fall Apart (Philadelphia: Chelsea House Publishers, 2009).

8 G.W.F. Hegel, "Tragedy as a Dramatic Art," in *Tragedy*, ed. John Drakakis and Naomi Conn Liebler (London: Longman, 1998), p. 39.

9 Chinua Achebe, *No Longer at Ease* (London: Heinemann, 1964), p. 33.

10 Even though it falls beyond the purview of this chapter, there are good grounds for including Toni Morrison's *Beloved* in this list of postcolonial texts. The key justification for adding this book would be the diasporic emphasis on Black Atlantic traumas that are invoked in the character of Beloved. But Sethe's affliction of second thoughts and self-witnessing are also comparable to the postcolonial novels we have just described.

11 For a fine comparison of Fanon with other decolonization critics, see Anjali Prabhu, "Fanon, Mmmi, Glissant and Postcolonial Writing," in *The Cambridge History of Postcolonial Literature*, Vol. 2, ed. Ato Quayson (Cambridge: Cambridge University Press, 2012), pp. 1068–99.

12 Frantz Fanon, "The Fact of Blackness," in *White Skin, Black Masks*, trans. Charles Lam Markmann (New York: Grove, 1967), pp. 109–140.

13 Fanon, *Black Skin, White Masks*, p. 120

14 Ato Sekyi-Otu, *Fanon's Dialectic of Experience* (Cambridge, MA: Harvard University Press, 1997).

15 Homi K. Bhabha, "Of Mimicry and Man," *The Location of Culture* (London: Routledge, 1994), p. 85–92.

16 Fanon, *Black Skin, White Masks*, p. 116.

17 The notion of a structure of denominations was first inspired by a response that I was invited to write to Achille Mbembe's "Modes of African Self-Writing," *Public Culture* 14.1 (2002), pp. 239–273. See Quayson, "Obverse Denominations: Africa?," *Public Culture* 14.3 (2002), pp. 585–8.

18 C.L.R. James, *The Black Jacobins: Toussaint L'Ouveture and the San Domingo Revolution* (New York: Random House, 1963).

19 Chinua Achebe, *Things Fall Apart* (London: Heinemann, 1958). All references to be provided in main text.

20 On the *osus* as a residual sign of slavery in precolonial and colonial Igbo society, see Taiwo Adentunji Osinubi, "Abolition, Law, and the Osu Marriage Novel," *Cambridge Journal of Postcolonial Literary Inquiry* 2.1 (2015), pp. 53–72.

21 Junot Díaz, *The Brief Wondrous Life of Oscar Wao* (New York: Riverhead, 2007). All references to be provided in main text.

22 Linda Hutcheon, "Historiographic Metafiction: Parody and the Intertexts of History," in *Intertextuality and Contemporary American Fiction*,

eds. P. O'Donnell and Robert Con Davis (Baltimore, MD: Johns Hopkins University Press, 1989), pp. 3–32.

23 The genre of magical realism, see especially Chris Warnes, *Magical Realism and the Postcolonial Novel: Between Faith and Irreverence* (London: Palgrave Macmillan, 2009), Mariano Siskind, "Magical Realism," in Quayson, *The Cambridge History of Postcolonial Literature*, Vol. 2, pp. 833–68; and *Magical Realism: Theory, History, Community*, eds. Lois Parkinson Zamora and Wendy B. Faris (Durham, NC: Duke University Press, 1995). The connection between magical realism, violence, and history is more fully elaborated in Ato Quayson's "Fecundities of the Unexpected: Magical Realism, Narrative, History," in *The Novel*, Vol. 1: *History, Geography, and Culture*, ed. Franco Moretti (Princeton, NJ: Princeton University Press, 2006), pp. 726–56.

24 Wole Soyinka, *Myth, Literature, and the African World* (Cambridge: Cambridge University Press, 1976), p. 53.

RECOMMENDED READING

Achebe, Chinua. *Home and Exile*, Oxford: Oxford University Press, 2000.
"An image of Africa: Racism in Conrad's Heart of Darkness," in *Joseph Conrad: Heart of Darkness*, New York: W. W. Norton, 2006, pp. 336–49.
Adéèkó, Adéléké. *Proverbs, Textuality, and Nativism in African Literature*, Gainesville: University Press of Florida, 1998.
Anderson, Benedict. *Imagined Communities: Reflections on the Spread and Origins of Nationalism*, London and New York: Verso, 1983.
Appadurai, Arjun. *Modernity at Large*, Minneapolis: Minnesota University Press, 1996.
Ahmad, Aijaz. *In Theory: Classes, Nations, Literatures*, London: Verso, 1992.
Alloula, Malek. *The Colonial Harem*, Minneapolis: Minnesota University Press, 1986.
Ashcroft, Bill, Gareth Griffiths, and Helen Tiffin. *The Empire Writes Back: Theory and Practice in Post-Colonial Literatures*, London: Routledge, 1989.
Attridge, Derek. *The Work of Literature*, Oxford: Oxford University Press, 2015.
Attridge, Derek, and Marjorie Howes (eds.). *Semicolonial Joyce*, Cambridge: Cambridge University Press, 2000.
Attwell, David, and Derek Attridge. *The Cambridge History of South African Literature*, Cambridge: Cambridge University Press, 2012.
Bakhtin, Mikhail. *The Dialogic Imagination*, trans. C. Emerson and M. Holquist, ed. M. Holquist, Austin: University of Texas Press, 1981.
Baucom, Ian. "History 4°: Postcolonial method and anthropocene time," *The Cambridge Journal of Postcolonial Literary Inquiry* 1.1 (2014), pp. 107–122.
Bhabha, Homi K. *The Location of Culture*, London: Routledge, 1994.
Boehmer, Elleke. *Colonial and Postcolonial Literature: Migrant Metaphors*, Oxford University Press, 1995.
Bourdieu, Pierre. *Language and Symbolic Power*, trans. and ed. Gino Raymond and Matthew Adamson, Cambridge: Polity Press, 1991.
Brah, Avtar. *Cartographies of Diaspora: Contesting Identities*, London: Routledge, 1996.
Brantlinger, Patrick. *Rule of Darkness: British Literature and Imperialism, 1830–1914*, Ithaca, NY: Cornell University Press, 1988.
Brennan, Timothy. *Salman Rushdie and the Third World*, London: Macmillan, 1989.
Butler, Judith. *Undoing Gender*, New York: Routledge, 2004.

Giving an Account of Oneself, New York: Fordham, 2005.

Casanova, Pascale. *The World Republic of Letters*, trans. M.B. DeBevoise, Cambridge, MA: Harvard University Press, 2004.

Chakrabarty, Dipesh. *Provincializing Europe: Postcolonial Thought and Historical Difference*, Princeton, NJ: Princeton University Press, 2000.

Childs, Peter. *Post-Colonial Theory and English Literature: A Reader*, Edinburgh: Edinburgh University Press, 1999.

Chow, Rey. *Writing Diaspora: Tactics of Intervention in Contemporary Cultural Studies*, Bloomington: Indiana University Press, 1993.

Christian, Ed (ed.). *The Post-Colonial Detective*, London: Palgrave, 2001.

Clayton, Jay, and Eric Rothstein. "Figures in the corpus: Theories of influence and intertextuality," in *Influence and Intertextuality in Literary History*, Jay Clayton and Eric Rothstein (eds.), Madison: University of Wisconsin Press, 1991, pp. 3–36.

Cleary, Joseph. *Literature, Partition and the Nation-State: Culture and Conflict in Ireland, Israel and Palestine*, Cambridge: Cambridge University Press, 2002.

Clifford, James. *Routes: Travel and Translation in the Late Twentieth Century*, Cambridge, MA: Harvard University Press, 1997.

Clifford, James, and George E. Marcus. *Writing Culture: The Poetics and Politics of Ethnography*, Berkeley: California University Press, 1986.

Cohen, Robin. *Diasporas: An Introduction*, London: Routledge, 1996.

Cohn, Dorrit. *Transparent Minds: Narrative Models for Presenting Consciousness in Fiction*, Princeton, NJ: Princeton University Press, 1978.

Damrosch, David. *What is World Literature?*, Princeton, NJ: Princeton University Press, 2003.

DeLoughrey, Elizabeth, Renée K. Gosson, and George B. Handley (eds.). *Caribbean Literature and the Environment: Between Nature and Culture*, Charlottesville: University of Virginia Press, 2005.

DeLoughrey, Elizabeth, Jill Didur, and Anthony Carrigan (eds.). *Global Ecologies and the Environmental Humanities*, London: Routledge, 2015.

Dirlik, Arif. "The postcolonial aura: Third World criticism in the age of global capitalism," *Critical Inquiry* 20 (1994), pp. 328–56.

Donnell, Alison. *Twentieth-Century Caribbean Literature*, London: Routledge, 2006.

Donnell, Alison, and Sarah Lawson Welsh (eds.). *The Routledge Reader in Caribbean Literature*, New York: Routledge, 1996.

During, Simon. "Postcolonialism and globalisation: a dialectical relation after all?," *Postcolonial Studies* 1 (1998), pp. 31–47.

Edwards, Brent Hayes. *The Practice of Diaspora: Literature, Translation and the Rise of Black Internationalism*, Cambridge, MA: Harvard University Press: 2003.

Fabian, Johannes. *Time and the Other: How Anthropology Makes Its Object*, New York: Columbia University Press, 1983.

Fanon, Frantz. *The Wretched of the Earth*, trans. Constance Farrington, New York: Grove Press, (1961) 1963.

Black Skin, White Masks, trans. Charles Lam Markmann, New York: Grove Press, (1952) 1967.

Faris, Wendy B. *Ordinary Enchantments: Magical Realism and the Remystification of Narrative*, Nashville, TN: Vanderbilt University Press, 2004.

Fernández Retamar, Roberto. *Caliban and Other Essays*, Minneapolis: University of Minnesota Press, 1989.

Fischer-Hornung, Dorothea, and Monika Mueller (eds.). *Sleuthing Ethnicity: The Detective in Multiethnic Crime Fiction*, Madison, WI: Fairleigh Dickinson University Press, 2003.

Fraser, Robert. *Lifting the Sentence: The Poetics of Postcolonial Fiction*, Manchester: Manchester University Press, 2000.

Friedman, Susan Stanford. *Mappings: Feminism and the Cultural Geographies of Encounter*, Princeton, NJ: Princeton University Press, 1998.

Frow, John. *Marxism and Literary History*. Oxford: Basil Blackwell, 1986.

Gates, Henry Louis, Jr. *"Race," Writing and Difference*, Chicago, IL: University of Chicago Press, 1986.

Genette, Gérard. *Narrative Discourse: An Essay in Method*, trans. J.E. Lewin, Ithaca, NY: Cornell University Press, 1980.

Gikandi, Simon. *Reading Chinua Achebe: Language and Ideology in Fiction*, London and Nairobi: Heinemann, 1999.

Slavery and the Culture of Taste, Princeton, NJ: Princeton University Press, 2011.

Gilroy, Paul. *The Black Atlantic: Modernity and Double Consciousness*, Cambridge, MA: Harvard University Press, 1993.

Gosselin, Adrienne Johnson (ed.). *Multicultural Detective Fiction: Murder from the "Other" Side*, New York: Garland, 1999.

Grewal, Inderpal. *Home and Harem: Nation, Gender, Empire and the Cultures of Travel*, Durham, NC: Duke University Press, 1996.

Grove, Richard H. *Green Imperialism: Colonial Expansion, Tropical Island Edens and the Origins of Environmentalism, 1600–1860*, Cambridge University Press, 1995.

Guha, Ranjit. "The prose of counterinsurgency," in *Subaltern Studies II: Writings on South Asian History and Society*, Ranjit Guha (ed.), Oxford: Oxford University Press, 1983, 1–42.

Guillory, John. *Cultural Capital: The Problem of Literary Canon Formation*, Chicago, IL: University of Chicago Press, 1993.

Halbwachs, Maurice. *On Collective Memory*, trans. and ed. with an introduction by Lewis A. Coser, Chicago, IL: University of Chicago Press, 1992.

Hall, Catherine. *Civilising Subjects: Metropole and Colony in the English Imagination, 1830–1867*, Chicago, IL: University of Chicago Press, 2002.

Hall, Stuart. "New Ethnicities," in *Critical Dialogues in Cultural Studies*, David Morley and Kuan-Hsing Chen (eds.), London: Routledge, 1996, pp. 441–449.

Hofmeyr, Isabel. *The Portable Bunyan: A Transnational History of the Pilgrim's Progress*, Princeton, NJ: Princeton University Press, 2004.

Holden, Philip. *Autobiography and Decolonization: Modernity, Masculinity, and the Nation State*, Madison: University of Wisconsin Press, 2008.

Huggan, Graham. *Australian Literature: Postcolonialism, Racism, Transnationalism*, Oxford: Oxford University Press, 2007.

The Oxford Handbook of Postcolonialism. Oxford: Oxford University Press, 2013.

Hulme, Peter. *Colonial Encounters: Europe and the Native Caribbean, 1492–1797*, London: Methuen, 1986.

Hulme, Peter, and Neil L. Whitehead (eds.). *Wild Majesty: Encounters with Caribs from Columbus to the Present Day*, Oxford: Clarendon Press, 1992.

Hulme, Peter, and Tim Youngs (eds.). *The Cambridge Companion to Travel Writing*, Cambridge: Cambridge University Press, 2002.

Hutcheon, Linda, and Mario Valdes (eds.). *Rethinking Literary History: A Dialogue on Theory*, Oxford: Oxford University Press, 2002.

Innes, Lynn. *The Cambridge Introduction to Postcolonial Literatures in English*, Cambridge: Cambridge University Press, 2007.

A History of Black and South Asian Writing in Britain, Cambridge: Cambridge University Press, 2008.

Irele, Abiola. *The African Imagination: Literature in Africa and the Black Diaspora*, Oxford: Oxford University Press, 2001.

Irele, Abiola, and Simon Gikandi (eds.). *The Cambridge History of African and Caribbean Literature*, 2 vols., Cambridge: Cambridge University Press, 2004.

Jameson, Frederic. "Third World literature in the era of multinational capitalism," *Social Text* 15 (Autumn 1986), pp. 65–88.

JanMohamed, Abdul R. *Manichean Aesthetics: The Politics of Literature in Colonial Africa*, Amherst: University of Massachusetts Press.

JanMohamed, Abdul R., and David Lloyd. *The Nature and Context of Minority Discourse*, New York: Oxford University Press, 1990.

Jeyifo, Biodun. "The nature of things: Arrested decolonization and critical theory," *Research in African Literatures* 21.1, pp. 33–48.

Joshi, Priya. *In Another Country: Colonialism, Culture, and the English Novel in India*, New York: Columbia University Press, 2002.

Julien, Eileen. *African Novels and the Question of Orality*, Bloomington: Indiana University Press, 1992.

Kabir, Ananya. *Territory of Desire: Representing the Valley of Kashmir*. Minneapolis: Minnesota University Press, 2009.

Kamboureli, Smaro. *Scandalous Bodies: Diasporic Literature in English Canada*, Toronto: Oxford University Press, 2000.

Kelleher, Margaret, and Philip O'Leary. *The Cambridge History of Irish Literature*, 2 vols., Cambridge: Cambridge University Press, 2006.

Klein, Kathleen Gregory (ed.). *Diversity and Detective Fiction*, Bowling Green, OH: Bowling Green State University Popular Press, 1999.

Krajenbrink, Marieke, and Kate M. Quinn (eds.). *Investigating Identities: Questions of Identity in Contemporary International Crime Fiction*, Amsterdam: Rodopi, 2009.

Krishnaswamy, N., and S. Archana. *Burde, The Politics of Indians' English: Linguistic Colonialism and the Expanding English Empire*. Delhi: Oxford University Press, 1998.

Lazarus, Neil (ed.). *The Cambridge Companion to Postcolonial Literary Studies*, Cambridge: Cambridge University Press, 2004.

Li, Victor. *The Neo-Primitivist Turn: Critical Reflections on Alterity, Culture, and Modernity*, Toronto: University of Toronto Press, 2006.

Lionnet, Françoise. *Autobiographical Voices: Race, Gender, Self-Portraiture*, Ithaca, NY: Cornell University Press, 1989.

Loomba, Ania. *Colonialism/Postcolonialism*, London: Routledge, 2005.

Macdonald, Andrew, Gina Macdonald, and MaryAnn Sheridan (eds.). *Shapeshifting: Images of Native Americans in Recent Popular Fiction*, Westport, CT: Greenwood Press, 2000.

Matzke, Christine, and Susanne Mühleisen (eds.). *Postcolonial Postmortems: Crime Fiction from a Transcultural Perspective*, Amsterdam: Rodopi, 2006.

Mbembe, Achille. *On the Postcolony*, Berkeley: University of California Press, 2001.

McClintock, Ann. "The angel of progress: pitfalls of the term 'post-colonialism,'" *Social Text* 31.32 (1992), 84–98.

McLeod, John. *Postcolonial London: Rewriting the Metropolis*, London and New York: Routledge, 2004.

Mingolo, Walter. *Local Histories/Global Designs: Essays on the Coloniality of Power, Subaltern Knowledges, and Border Thinking*, Princeton, NJ: Princeton University Press, 2000.

Mishra, Vijay, and Bob Hodge. "What is post(-)colonialism?," *Textual Practice* 5.3 (1991), pp. 399–414.

Mohanty, Chandra Talpade. "Under Western eyes: Feminist scholarship and colonial discourses," *Boundary 2*, 12.3 (1986), pp. 333–58.

Moore-Gilbert, Bart. *Postcolonial Theory: Contexts, Practices, Politics*, London: Verso, 1997.

Moretti, Franco. *Distant Reading*, London: Verso, 2013.

Mukherjee, Ankhi. *What is a Classic?: Postcolonial Rewriting and Invention of the Canon*, Stanford, CA: Stanford University Press, 2013.

Mukherjee, Upamanyu Pablo. *Crime and Empire: The Colony in Nineteenth-Century Fictions of Crime*, Oxford: Oxford University Press, 2003.

Mullen, Anne, and Emer O'Beirne (eds.). *Crime Scenes: Detective Narratives in European Culture since 1945*, Amsterdam: Rodopi, 2000.

Nandy, Ashis. *The Intimate Enemy: Loss and Recovery of Self Under Colonialism*, New Delhi: Oxford University Press, 1983.

Ndebele, Njabulo. *South African Literature and Culture: Rediscovery of the Ordinary*, Manchester: Manchester University Press, 1994.

Ngũgĩ, wa Thiong'o. *Decolonising the Mind: The Politics of Language in African Literature*, London: Heinemann, 1986.

Nixon, Rob. *Slow Violence and the Environmentalism of the Poor*, Cambridge, MA: Harvard University Press, 2011.

Norridge, Zoe. *Perceiving Pain in African Literature*, London: Palgrave Macmillan, 2012.

Okpewho, Isidore. *The Epic in Africa: Toward a Poetics of Oral Performance*, New York: Columbia University Press, 1979.

Olaniyan, Tejumola, and Ato Quayson. *African Literature: An Anthology of Criticism and Theory*, New York: Blackwell, 2007.

Orsini, Francesca. *The Hindi Public Sphere 1920–1940: Language and Literature in the Age of Nationalism*, New York: Oxford University Press, 2002.

Park, You-me, and Rajeswari Sunder Rajan (eds.). *The Postcolonial Jane Austen*, New York and London: Routledge, 2000.

Parry, Benita. *Postcolonial Studies: A Materialist Critique*, London: Routledge, 2004.

Pearson, Nels, and Marc Singer (eds.) *Detective Fiction in a Postcolonial and Transnational World*, Aldershot: Ashgate, 2009.

Phillipson, Robert. *Linguistic Imperialism*, Oxford: Oxford University Press, 1992.

Pollock, Sheldon (ed.). *Literary Cultures in History: Reconstructions from South Asia*, Berkeley: University of California Press, 2003.

Prabhu, Anjali. *Hybridity: Limits, Transformations, Prospects*, New York: SUNY Press, 2007.

Pratt, Mary Louise. *Imperial Eyes: Travel Writing and Transculturation*, London: Routledge, 1992.

Prince, Gerald. "On a postcolonial narratology," in *A Companion to Narrative Theory*, James Phelan and Peter Rabinowitz (eds.), London: Blackwell, 2005, pp. 372–81.

Quayson, Ato. "Fecundities of the unexpected: Magical realism, narrative, and history," in *The Novel, Vol. 1: History, Geography, and Culture*, Franco Moretti (ed.), Princeton, NJ: Princeton University Press, 2006, pp. 726–756.

Aesthetic Nervousness: Disability and the Crisis of Representation, New York: Columbia University Press, 2007.

The Cambridge History of Postcolonial Literature, 2 vols., Cambridge: Cambridge University Press, 2012.

Quayson, Ato, and Girish Daswani. *Companion to Diaspora and Transnationalism*, New York: Blackwell, 2013.

Reddy, Maureen T. *Traces, Codes and Clues: Reading Race in Crime Fiction*, New Brunswick, NJ: Rutgers University Press, 2003.

Richardson, Brian. *Unnatural Voices: Extreme Narration in Modern and Postmodern Contemporary Fiction*, Columbus: Ohio State University Press, 2006.

Robertson, Roland. *Globalization: Social Theory and Global Culture*, London: Sage, 1992.

Rushdie, Salman. *Imaginary Homelands: Essays and Criticism 1981–1991*, London: Granta, 1991.

Said, Edward W. *Orientalism*, London: Routledge & Kegan Paul, 1978.

Culture and Imperialism, New York: Knopf, 1993.

Scott, David. *Conscripts of Modernity: The Tragedy of Colonial Enlightenment*, Durham, NC: Duke University Press, 2004.

Sekyi-Otu, Ato. *Fanon's Dialectic of Experience*, Cambridge, MA: Harvard University Press, 1996.

Soitos, Stephen J. *The Blues Detective: A Study of African-American Detective Fiction*, Amherst: University of Massachusetts Press, 1996.

Soyinka, Wole. *Myth, Literature and the African World*, Cambridge: Cambridge University Press, 1976.

Spivak, Gayatri Chakravorty. "Three women's texts and a critique of imperialism," *Critical Inquiry* 12.1 (1985), pp. 243–61.

"Can the subaltern speak? Speculations on widow sacrifice," *Wedge* 7.8 (1985), pp. 120–30; repr. in *Marxism and the Interpretation of Culture*, Cary Nelson and Lawrence Grossberg (eds.), Champaign: University of Illinois Press, 1988, pp. 271–313.

Death of a Discipline, New York: Columbia University Press, 2005.

Stiker, Henri-Jacques. *A History of Disability*, trans. William Sayers, Ann Arbor: University of Michigan Press, 1999.

Stoler, Ann Laura. *Race and the Education of Desire: Foucault's History of Sexuality and the Colonial Order of Things*, Durham, NC: Duke University Press, 1995.

Suleri, Sara. *The Rhetoric of English India*, Chicago, IL: Chicago University Press, 1992.

Teverson, Andrew, and Sara Upstone. *Postcolonial Geographies: The Politics of Place in Contemporary Culture*, New York: Palgrave Macmillan, 2011.

Valdés, Mario J. "Rethinking the history of literary history," in *Rethinking Literary History: A Dialogue on Theory*, Oxford University Press, 2002, pp. 63–115.

Vergès, Françoise. *Monsters and Revolutionaries: Colonial Family Romance and Métissage*, Durham, NC: Duke University Press, 1999.

Wallerstein, Immanuel. *The Modern World-System: Capitalist Agriculture and the Origins of the European World-Economy in the Sixteenth Century*, New York: Academic Press, 1974.

Warnes, Christopher. *Magical Realism and the Postcolonial Novel: Between Faith and Irreverence*, London and New York: Palgrave Macmillan, 2009.

Watson, Tim. "Is the 'post' in postcolonial the US in American studies? The US beginnings of Commonwealth studies," *ARIEL* 31.1–2 (2000), pp. 51–72.

Caribbean Culture and British Fiction in the Atlantic World, 1780–1870, Cambridge: Cambridge University Press, 2008.

Webby, Elizabeth. *The Cambridge Companion to Australian Literature*, Cambridge: Cambridge University Press, 2000.

Wenzel, Jennifer. "The pastoral promise and the political imperative: The *plaasroman* tradition in an era of land reform," *MFS: Modern Fiction Studies* 46 (2000), pp. 90–113.

Williams, Raymond. *The Country and the City*, London: Hogarth Press, 1993.

Wynne, Catherine. *The Colonial Conan Doyle: British Imperialism, Irish Nationalism and the Gothic*, Westport, CT: Greenwood, 2002.

Young, Robert J. C. *White Mythologies*, London: Routledge, 1990; 2nd ed. 2004.

Postcolonialism: An Historical Introduction, Oxford: Blackwell, 2001.

Zamora, Lois Parkinson, and Wendy B. Faris (eds.). *Magical Realism: Theory, History, Community*, Durham, NC: Duke University Press, 1995.

INDEX

INDEX

Tiffin, Helen 4, 97 n18, 208, 225 n4, 226 n26, 226 n27
Time 11, colonial time 214
Tinsley, Omise'eke Natasha 128 n3, 128 n4, 131 n32
Tocqueville, Alexis *Democracy in America* 26
Toronto 175
Totalitarianism 233
Tourism 81, 89, 90, 175, 196
Tragedy 230, Greek tragedy 231, 239, Greek tragic hero 233, postcolonial novel 236, South African adaptations of Greek tragedies 231, tragic closure 235
Tragicomic poetics 47, 51
Transgender 126
Transsexuality 116, 124
Trauma 52, 104, 107, 109, 122, historical 78, Roger Luckhurst 80 n21
Travel 20, 90, intra-Caribbean travels 22
Trinidad 22, 24, 196, exile 24, 31
Trinidadian writers 120, 124
The Trojan Women 231
Trumpener, Katie: 17, 18, 19, *Bardic Nationalism* 16, 33 n4, 33 n6
Tunisia 144
Tutuola, Amos *The Palm Wine Drinkard* 77

Union Carbide 92
United Nations 38, 137
United States 7, 17, 23, 32, 45, 46, 67, 91, 99, 101, 112, 142, 171, 173, 197, postcolonialism 23, Chinese diaspora 143, 144, Filipino diaspora 145, Korean diaspora 144, 147
Updike, John 35, 37, 38, 57 n1
Upfield, Arthur 185 n23, *The Barrakee Mystery* 173
Upstone, Sara 208, 217, 227 n55
Urbanism 83, 93, 188, 199, urbanization 10, 81, 89, 189, neocolonial urbanization 195
Urry, John 82, 96 n6

Valdés, Mario J. 3, 13 n6
Valens, Keja 128 n3, 128 n4, 131 n32
van de Wetering, Janwillem *De Ratelrat (The Rattle-Rat)* 181
van Herden, Etienne *Die swye van Mario Salviati (The Long Silence of Mario Salviati)* 181
Vanacker, Sabine 181, 187 n47
Vanita, Ruth 129 n6, 130 n22

Vassanji, M. G *In-Between World of Vikram Lall*. 219
Vera, Yvonne 125, *The Stone Virgins* 70, 107, 108, 113, 115 n27, 122, *Without A Name* 122, 236, *Without A Name* and tragedy 233
Victorian fiction 25, Victorian ideology 118
Victorian novels 24
Vidocq, Eugène-François *Mémoires of Vidocq* 167
Vienna 181
Vietnam 38
Violence 7, 9, 19, 21, 27, 35, 37, 43, 44, 52, 67, 68, 70, 90, 100, 104, 106, 110, 159, 192, 244, disability 105, 107, environmental violence 85, political violence 244, religious violence 230, spatial violence 217
Virilio, Paul 58 n25
Viswanathan, Gauri 25, 33 n2, 34 n18
Volpi, Jorge 39

Walcott, Derek 5, "Air", "The Castaway", "The Sea is History" 165 n17
Wales 177
Walkowitz, Rebecca (modernism) 58 7n
War 106
Warner, Michael 122, 131 n26
Warnes, Chris 72, 75, 76, 80 n24, 80 n30, 80 n35, 247 n23, Salman Rushdie 75, Wales 16
Watson, Nicole *The Boundary* 174
Watson, Tim 174, *The Kadaitcha Sung* 174
Watt, Ian *The Rise of the Novel* 17, 33 n5
Watts, Michael ("liberation ecologies") 87, 97 n25
Waugh, Evelyn 3
Weixlmann, Joe 131 n29
Wells, Claire 185 n20
Wendell, Susan 114 n4
Werbner, Pnina "impossibility of arrival" 135, 137, 150 n15
Wesley, Valerie Wilson *When Death Comes Stealing* 172
West Indies 18, 20, 31, 172, West Indian Creole 19
Westbrook, Robert *Ghost Dancer* 177
White 23, white hierarchy 22, 172, white society 26, white superiority 21, 24, whiteness 173, whiteness and hegemonic identity 101, white women 118, white subjectivity 161
White, Anne M. 179, 186 n39

272

Printed in Great Britain
by Amazon